FOOTPRINTS IN THE SAND

Jamaica has struggled with issues common to many small island states – high debt, low growth, limited fiscal space, and economic vulnerability arising from climate change and global economic shocks. *Footprints in the Sand* details how Jamaica, through disciplined and deliberate policymaking, confronted these and other issues and emerged resilient in this time defined by polycrisis. Nigel's well-organised book holds valuable lessons for countries big and small!

Mia Mottley, Prime Minister of Barbados

Jamaica's macro-economic indicators are the best they have been in nearly fifty years. If you want to understand the thought processes behind the economic policies that led to this achievement and that institutionalised economic stability, increased economic resilience, guided and realised economic recovery from historic economic crises and that created opportunity for Jamaicans, while pioneering ground-breaking transactions, then this book is definitely for you. Nigel's data driven analytic approach, clear-thinking pragmatism and courageous implementation have left *Footprints in the Sand*, that are worthy of emulation.

Horace Chang, Deputy Prime Minister of Jamaica

Nigel's footprints in the sand are very large indeed! Under his leadership, Jamaica moved from serial failure of IMF programmes to being the institution's crown jewel of macroeconomic management. If you want to know what countries, large and small, can learn from the journey, Nigel's book is a must read.

Peter Blair Henry, Senior Fellow, Hoover Institution,
and author of *TURNAROUND: Third World*
Lessons for First World Growth

Footprints in the Sand stands as a major contribution to the practice of fiscal reform and grounded economic transformation. Through his unique, insider's perspective, Nigel Clarke chronicles one nation's journey in successful crisis management strategies, and illuminates more general pathways toward sustainable economic independence. His account of Jamaica's transformation from debt-ridden instability to a model of macro-economic stability reveals the high-stakes challenges and bold policies that shaped this Caribbean success story. It is essential reading for policymakers, economists, and specialists in emerging economies. And for the general reader interested in the story of one nation's triumph against economic odds, *Footprints in the Sand* provides both inspiration and invaluable insights.

Orlando Patterson,
John Cowles Professor of Sociology, Harvard University and author of
The Confounding Island: Jamaica and the Postcolonial Predicament

Footprints in the Sand

The Jamaican Economic Policymaking Experience 2016–2024

Nigel Clarke

FOREWORD BY
Christine Lagarde
President of the European Central Bank

IAN RANDLE PUBLISHERS
Kingston • Miami

First published in Jamaica, 2024 by
Ian Randle Publishers
16 Herb McKenley Drive
Box 686
Kingston 6
www.ianrandlepublishers.com

National Library of Jamaica Cataloguing-In-Publication Data
Name: Clarke, Nigel, author.
Title: Footprints in the sand : the Jamaican Economic
Policymaking Experience 2016–2024 / Nigel Clarke.
Description: Kingston, Jamaica : Ian Randle Publishers, 2024. |
    Includes bibliographical references and index.
Identifier: ISBN 9789768339249 (hbk). 9789768339423 (pbk)
Subjects: LCSH: Macroeconomics. | Economic policy. | Finance,
    Public – Jamaica. | Economic stabilisation – Jamaica. | Jamaica –
    Economic conditions. | Jamaica – Social conditions.
Classification: DDC 339.5 -- dc23.

Cover design by Ian Randle Publishers
Book design by Sandra M. Roberts

Printed in United States of America

**Nigel Clarke prepared this book before his appointment,
effective October 31, 2024, as a Deputy Managing Director of
the International Monetary Fund. The views in this book are his
own and do not reflect the views of the International Monetary
Fund, its Executive Board, Management, or staff.**

DEDICATION

To my parents, Neville and Mary Clarke, who raised me with an unshakable belief in the promise and potential of Jamaica, and to all the people of Jamaica

CONTENTS

FOREWORD

Christine Lagarde
President of the European Central Bank

The story of Jamaica in recent years has been one of economic transformation.

Today, the Jamaican economy has established a solid foundation for future growth. But for much of its history since independence, the country has struggled with economic instability.

A string of shocks over the decades – including oil crises, a domestic banking crisis, and the global financial crisis – combined with suboptimal fiscal policies to result in a legacy of high inflation, elevated unemployment, and unsustainable levels of public debt.

By the time I had become Managing Director of the International Monetary Fund (IMF) in July 2011, Jamaica had reached what appeared to be an impossible juncture.

The country's debt-to-GDP ratio stood at over 140% – making it one of the most indebted nations in the world. Its Stand-By Arrangement (SBA) with the IMF, agreed the previous year, had gone off track. And the country had no access to international capital markets.

The gap between Jamaica's potential and its reality was enormous. Above all else, Jamaican citizens yearned for stability in their lives.

The country's impressive turnaround began in 2013. As part of a multi-layered reform agenda outlined in a new Extended Fund Facility (EFF) with the IMF that year, the Government of Jamaica demonstrated an unprecedented degree of resolve. It embarked on an ambitious fiscal consolidation and implemented difficult structural reforms aimed at boosting growth and employment.

It was during the years that followed that Nigel and I would get to know each other well. After the national elections of 2016, Nigel served as Ambassador at Large for Economic Affairs and was a vital interlocutor between the Government of Jamaica and the IMF at a delicate moment of transition between governments. I saw first-hand how this cooperation only strengthened when he later became Minister of Finance and the Public Service.

Thanks to Nigel's astute guidance, Jamaica swiftly transitioned to a three-year Precautionary SBA, which replaced the EFF that would soon expire. In the subsequent years, his strategic vision and oversight ensured Jamaica's exemplary performance, meeting all structural benchmarks and quantitative criteria set forth by the programme.

Citizens could start to feel the economic benefits of the country's success. The level of public debt fell substantially. Unemployment began to decline. And from the start of 2015 to late 2019, the Jamaican economy experienced a sustained spurt of economic growth – the longest stretch of quarterly economic growth on record since Jamaica started measuring growth quarterly in 1997.

Keep in mind that all this happened in the 2010s – an exceptionally difficult decade for many nations still reeling from the lingering effects of the global financial crisis. So, what was Jamaica's secret? What were the ingredients behind the country's economic transformation at a time when other countries struggled to enact change?

In my mind, three stand out.

The first was commitment. During this time, the Government of Jamaica made enormous sacrifices to undo the economic damage of past policies. That created a degree of trust with the IMF, which would slowly build as Jamaica passed each review scheduled under the EFF and the Precautionary SBA that followed.

Over time, this commitment blossomed into a sense of partnership, and more importantly ownership.

An organisation of stakeholder representatives emerged – the Economic Programme Oversight Committee (EPOC), which included civil society. The EPOC monitored the government's progress in implementing the IMF agreement, reporting back regularly to the Jamaican people and boosting transparency. As Nigel writes, 'The "IMF Programme" became "Jamaica's Programme"' in the minds of citizens.

The second ingredient was continuity. Jamaica benefited from a smooth transition between governments in 2016, and the Precautionary SBA was a decisive signal by the new administration that it would support continuity. This agreement was instrumental in increasing confidence in the Jamaican economy at a moment of uncertainty.

And the third ingredient? In a word, courage.

Certainly, Jamaica's economic transformation can be credited to the resilience of the Jamaican people to endure short-term sacrifices to enact real change in the long term. That required no small amount of courage and endurance in the face of adversity.

But it also requires policymakers with courage – something that Nigel has in spades. At moments of crisis and transition, old truths are replaced by new uncertainties. It takes a steady pair of hands to help steer the economy through uncharted waters. And Nigel's boldness and resolve is evident throughout the speeches, interviews and articles that can be found in these pages.

Jamaica is indeed "a small country with big lessons", as Nigel observes. Those lessons have never been more important than today as nations around the world grapple with rising levels of public debt and increasingly polarised political spheres.

The story of Jamaica in recent years demonstrates that countries can embrace agency in determining their own future. The country has shown that nothing is inevitable, and that everything is possible.

Frankfurt am Main, October 2024

PREFACE

Every book has its own origin story, just as every person does and every nation. Although I did not know it at the time, this book began long ago, even prior to my taking on the role of Minister of Finance and the Public Service of Jamaica. In October 2016, I served as Ambassador of Economic Affairs, appointed to the role, six months earlier, by Prime Minister Andrew Holness. The government was seven months old, and we were about to unveil a new IMF programme to build upon the previous administration's successes – and to continue to make good on the many sacrifices Jamaican citizens endured in pursuit of economic stability.

For the announcement of the new programme, I had prepared draft remarks for the prime minister to deliver. He reviewed the four pages I handed to him and returned the first two to me. 'You speak at the function and deliver these remarks as your own,' he said. The prime minister's intentional move was a defining moment for me. I was comfortable assisting behind the scenes. Now he challenged me to publicly own my role in this chapter of Jamaica's story.

In the years since, I have sought to pull back the curtain on the economic policymaking process by publicly sharing my written thoughts on policy through articles, opinion pieces, and letters. I thought this important, as such a view is what I would have wanted for myself as a private citizen.

Naturally, political and public life generate a lot of words, so the task of deciding which of countless selections to include in a book, and how to present them, proved far from simple. I will let this volume's introduction speak to the value of the pieces that made the cut and the story they tell of Jamaica's perseverance, but suffice to say, the selection process occasionally felt as challenging as steering the macro-economy of a developing nation. In the end, what mattered most was that the pieces capture my thoughts on some of the major policy issues and significant predicaments faced during my eight and a half years as Ambassador of Economic Affairs and Minister of Finance and the Public Service.

In terms of arrangement, I chose to group the works thematically, and within that structure to present a respectful (if not strict) chronology, so that I could convey a sense of the integrated yet dynamic nature of policymaking, without losing the sense that it is always a journey. Collation by themes allowed the pieces to be presented within the context of, or in contrast to, the relevant slice of Jamaica's economic history, the effect of which is to shine further light on the purpose of policies pursued.

Occasionally, discussion of important policy matters – across many years and in different fora – creates an overlap in content. (Politicians and public officials also repeat themselves!) To eliminate excessive duplication, I have opted to present excerpts of speeches and have otherwise condensed previously published material. Selections have also been lightly edited to create greater ease or clarity of reading across the pieces, as well as for uniformity of typographic style and deference to publishing guidelines. While taking these steps to provide what I hope will be a more seamless reading experience, I also endeavoured to remain as faithful as possible to the original content, as a matter of record. Care has been taken to preserve my meaning, tone, and point of view as I expressed myself at the time, within my various roles. I should also be clear that all views expressed are my own and any mistakes are mine as author.

Grateful acknowledgment is made in the back of the book to the publications and venues that gave me a platform for sharing important matters of economic policy, and further documentation is provided in the notes and bibliography for those who wish to read more. However, upfront, I must thank the Daily *Gleaner*, the *Daily Observer, the Sunday Observer,* and the *Sunday Gleaner* for permission to reproduce some of my Op Eds, letters, and articles published over many years. I am also grateful to the *Financial Times, Foreign Policy, the IMF Country Focus,* and *Linacre News* for allowing me to share some important transferable lessons from Jamaica's economic turnaround with their global audiences, and for their permission to include pieces in this book.

Every book takes a village to produce. I am indebted to my editor, Allison Parker, for the thoroughness of her advice. This book benefited from her energy, experience, and insights. I am grateful to my publisher, Ian Randle, who supported this project from the beginning, and to the editorial and production teams at Ian Randle Publishers who turned my desire to create a book into the tangible reality you hold in your hands. They did so with professionalism and efficiency.

But there would be no story to tell about Jamaica's inspiring macro-economic transformation were it not for the scores of public-sector, union, business, and civil-society leaders; the hundreds of ministry and agency staff; the Members of Parliament, regardless of party – all of whom worked, debated, compromised, and persevered together to achieve these results. I am deeply grateful to my Cabinet colleagues for the many axes of collaboration, for their support, and for the unity of purpose we share, and I am equally grateful for Jamaica's broader social cohesion, which has been, and remains, an incredibly powerful source of strength with which much more can be built.

This acknowledgment necessarily takes on a different shape given that by the time this book goes to press, I will officially have moved on from my public service role in Jamaica. This is bittersweet. I should state emphatically here that I am most grateful to Prime Minister Andrew Holness, who entrusted me with great responsibilities of state and who provided unwavering support, even in the most difficult times. It has been a special honour to serve my country, and I thank Prime Minister Holness for providing both the encouragement and the opportunity for me to do so.

Of course, there would also be no book of this nature without policy successes. And there would be no policy successes without the contribution of teams. In that regard, I thank the team at the Ministry of Finance and the Public Service, including Ministers who served over various periods: Fayval Williams, Marsha Smith, and Xavier

Mayne. In particular, I must specially recognise and sincerely thank the Financial Secretary Darlene Morrison and Deputy Financial Secretaries Lorris Jarrett, Dian Black, Wayne Jones, Pamella Wade-Fearon, Hope Blake, Carlene Smith, the late Carlene O'Connor, and her successor, Alisha Bish, as well as their staff. I also express gratitude to Trevor Anderson, Principal Director in the Fiscal Management Branch, who maintained the models that guided our approach to fiscal policy. The head of the Transformation and Implementation Unit, Maria Thompson-Walters – supported by Financial Secretary Morrison and Deputy Financial Secretary Jones – carried a heavy load during this period of public-sector transformation. I am therefore most grateful to Maria Thompson-Walters and her staff. The Accountant General's Department performs an indispensable function in the execution of policy and I am therefore grateful to the Accountant General Anya Jones and her team. I express gratitude to the boards, leadership, and staff of the agencies within the Ministry of Finance and the Public Service. I thank Wayne Henry, Chairman and Director General of the Planning Institute of Jamaica (PIOJ), his board, and his team of Barbara Scott, James Stewart, Easton Williams, Rochelle Whyte, Claire Bernard, and others. I relied on the PIOJ for coordination of external cooperation, economic data, and analysis.

I thank the Commissioner General of Tax Administration Jamaica (TAJ), Ainsley Powell, and Deputy Commissioners General Marlene Parker, Dave Jeffery, Judith Smith-Richards, and Hank Williams, as well as senior leaders Bevon Sinclair and Vaughn Thomas and their teams for the faithful execution of revenue policy. I thank the Advisory Board of the TAJ led by Paul Lalor, and previously Gina Phillips Black, for supporting strategic objectives.

The Jamaica Customs Agency was also critical to our policy successes and I thank the Commissioner of Customs, Velma Ricketts-Walker, for her steely resolve and Deputy CEOs Selina Clarke-Graham, Marlon Lowe, Senior Director – Legal Affairs Hazel Edwards, other senior directors, and their teams.

I relied heavily on reports and data from the Statistical Institute of Jamaica (STATIN) in the formulation of policy and I thank the Board of STATIN led by Robert Stennett and previously David Tennant, outgoing Director General, Carol Coy, Deputy Director General, Leesha Delatie-Budair, and their teams.

We were able to implement meaningful changes at the Student Loan Bureau (SLB). Thanks to Nicholas Scott who chaired the board of the SLB, his directors, and Executive Director Nickeisha Walsh.

Thanks to Keron Burell who took on a huge task at the Financial Services Commission, to his management team and to his predecessor Everton McFarlane and, very importantly, to the board led by Richard Byles and his predecessor, Jackie Stewart-Lechler. Thanks, too, to Clovis Metclafe, along with his board, and Vitus Evans and team at the Betting Gaming and Lotteries Commission.

Additionally, I express sincere appreciation to the Governor of the Bank of Jamaica, Richard Byles, and his team for their faithful embrace of independence, their dedication to the BOJ's mandate, and for the collaborative working relationship. I also thank the previous Governor of the BOJ, Brian Wynter, with whom I also worked closely. The transitions required in our exchange rate and monetary arrangements, prior to full independence, were challenging and Governor Wynter was a dependable partner.

For the Finance and Public Service ministry, legislation is critical to the implementation of policy – more so than at most other ministries. I thank the hardworking team at the Attorney General's Chambers, the Attorney General, and the Solicitor General, as well as the Minister of Legal Affairs, the Minister of Justice, the Legal Reform Unit, the Chief Parliamentary Counsel, and their staff for assistance in pushing through legislation, often within compressed time schedules.

The Jamaican economic transformation benefited from domestic ownership and oversight of which the Economic Policy Oversight Committee (EPOC) was a central expression. I am grateful to Keith Duncan, who chaired EPOC since 2016, and to other members of EPOC, for their commitment to constructively discharging their oversight role while helping to keep Jamaicans informed about economic and budgetary outcomes and policy developments.

Success in significantly improving Jamaica's AML-CFT framework represented teamwork at its finest. I am grateful to Maurene Simms, Celeste McCalla, and the entire National Anti-Money Laundering Committee (NAMLC) for their commitment and support. The Prime Contact Secretariat, established by and hosted at the Bank of Jamaica, was key to successful coordination. I am again grateful to the Governor of the Bank for the collaboration.

Importantly, I am grateful to the Jamaica Labour Party for approving me as a candidate for electoral office, and for supporting me along the way. In our system, one cannot be Minister of Finance without first being elected to the House of Representatives. I therefore thank the constituents of St Andrew Northwestern for embracing me and for twice electing me to serve. I also could not have served in that role without the support of Councillors Vernon McLeod, Duane Smith, and Andrew Harris who deputised for me when duties at the Ministry of Finance and the Public Service presented a scheduling conflict.

My achievements at the Ministry of Finance and the Public Service depended on support from, and collaboration with, the IMF, the World Bank and the Inter-American Development Bank in addition to our bilateral partners and Jamaica is most grateful.

I also depended on ministerial and parliamentary offices staffed with energetic professionals. Among them I thank Stephanie Abrahams and Novelette Howell, who often went beyond the call of duty, as well as Karelle Samuda, Keenan Falconer, Viralee Latibeaudiere, and Hillary Robertson, who in addition to secretaries Serena Connolly and Vanessa Moving, over various periods, supported me in my work. I am grateful to Kimerlin Fuller, Dorothy Foster, the St Andrew Northwestern Executive team, and the late Sabrena Smith for support at the constituency level. I must also express thanks to my close protection officers the late Sergeant Marlon Smith, Corporal Jhavanne Hutchinson, Constable Kerron Edwards, and Constable Buckley, in addition to Dave Davis, and Joycelyn Smith.

To the many friends who supported my journey. You know yourselves. Thank you.

Finally, but in no way last, I thank my wife, Professor Rupika Delgoda, for selflessly supporting me in public life. None of this could have been possible without her steadfast and dependable backing from the very beginning.

It really does take a village.

Nigel Clarke
October 2024

ABBREVIATIONS

BOJ	Bank of Jamaica
CARICOM	Caribbean Community (comprising twenty-one countries)
CDF	Capital Development Fund
CFATF	Caribbean Financial Action Task Force
CFT	Countering the Financing of Terrorism
DTI	Deposit-Taking Institution
EFF	Extended Fund Facility of the IMF
EGC	Economic Growth Council
EPOC	Economic Programme Oversight Committee
FATF	Financial Action Task Force
FRF	Fiscal Responsibility Framework
FRL	Fiscal Responsibility Law
FSC	Financial Services Commission
GCT	General Consumption Tax
GOJ	Government of Jamaica
IDB	Inter-American Development Bank
IMF	International Monetary Fund
MOFPS	Ministry of Finance and the Public Service
MSME/SME	Micro, Small, and Medium-sized Enterprises
NHT	National Housing Trust

NIF	National Insurance Fund
NIS	National Insurance Scheme
PBSA/SBA	Precautionary Stand-By Arrangement of the IMF
PIMS	Public Investment Management System
PIOJ	Planning Institute of Jamaica
PLL	Precautionary and Liquidity Line of the IMF
PPP	Public-Private Partnership
RSF	Resilience and Sustainability Facility of the IMF
SLB	Student Loan Bureau
STATIN	Statistical Institute of Jamaica

INTRODUCTION

We were not supposed to get this far. If you asked any observer of Jamaica's history in the past century to describe the country's prospects, they might well have cited the title of the late Michael Manley's book, which summarised the structural nature of our economic challenge as going *Up the Down Escalator*.[1] But in the sixty-plus years since Independence – a significant milestone of which every Jamaican can be proud – the Jamaican people have defied the odds and have survived, flourished, and influenced the world.

Jamaica has given birth to a globally celebrated culture. Jamaican music is played and imitated in all corners of the world. Jamaica's contribution to humanity includes a globally recognised philosophical outlook and religion based on unity, peace, tolerance, and love. Our cuisine is enjoyed across all continents; the international achievements of our sportsmen and sportswomen defy our small size.

As we often say, 'Wi likkle but wi tallawah!'

Most importantly, Jamaica has shown the capacity for self-healing, partnership, innovation, and growth in the transformation of our electoral system from one that was violently corrupt and unreliable to one that reveals our nation as a dependable beacon of freedom in the world. This must not be taken for granted.

As if to underscore the point of our determination, relative to its dire situation just a short decade ago, Jamaica may now fairly be seen to have beaten all odds and expectations in terms of its economic position. We have once again proven ourselves exceptional, this time using a combination of sustained fiscal discipline and coalition-based oversight to reduce our national debt by a dramatic three-fourths of GDP (gross domestic product), even despite the COVID-19 pandemic, and by implementing additional reforms to stabilise our hitherto downward spiralling economy. In the process, we have become a model for other emerging markets, developing countries, and even economically advanced nations, particularly in the current global environment of increasing debt and political polarisation.[2] Jamaica's macroeconomic restoration – which has occurred without debt write-offs, fiscal support from 'friends,' or internal strife – is just the latest example of our capacity for national, internally driven, transformation.

As any interested observer of Jamaica's macroeconomic history and our reliance on institutions such as the International Monetary Fund (IMF) will know – certainly anyone of my generation – this success story indeed runs contrary to repeated experience.

I was born towards the end of the first decade of political independence and grew up with the promise of a Jamaica that would forge corridors of opportunity for its people and consistently improve standards of living. Instead, during much of my life, Jamaica bounced from crisis to crisis, often requiring life support from the outside world. This macroeconomic roller coaster began in the second decade of Independence. While Jamaica experienced a rapid and sustained economic expansion in the 1960s (critics will note that the benefits were unequally distributed), whatever economic gains had been achieved largely evaporated in the decade that followed.

Despite much-appreciated social change and other important legislative achievements, real GDP per capita in Jamaica (or average income, in real terms) plummeted by 40 per cent between 1972 and 1980 within the context of significantly large recurrent expenditure increases[3] that led to an unstable fiscal trajectory.[4] Jamaica's debt-to-GDP ratio climbed from 28 per cent in 1972 to 97 per cent in 1981, as the government ran large, double-digit fiscal deficits[5] and financed them with a combination of central bank borrowing (i.e., printing of money) and foreign loans.[6]

A focussed reduction of unsustainable expenditure in the 1980s, along with a sharp devaluation of the Jamaican currency, briefly helped to eventually reduce fiscal deficits,[7] improve foreign exchange dynamics, and create a platform for a return to growth, and eventual economic recovery, which was only temporarily interrupted by the impact of an alumina price shock in the mid-1980s. There was therefore a pronounced rise in real GDP per person by the end of that decade.[8] However, earlier devaluation and increased external borrowing (from just under US$1.9 billion in 1980 to just over US$4.1 billion by 1990) impacted Jamaica's debt-to-GDP ratio which rose acutely,[9] settling at just under 140 per cent by 1990. Fiscal surpluses, real GDP growth and the hyperinflationary environment of the early 1990s[10] had the effect of reducing Jamaica's debt burden, and debt-to-GDP declined to 74 per cent by 1997,[11] but the accompanying harsh monetary conditions and the prior liberalisation of the financial sector without a strong regulatory and supervisory framework, among other factors, including financial sector malfeasance,[12] contributed to the onset of a monumental financial-sector crisis. The government led a debt-financed intervention that cost 40 per cent of GDP, and debt-to-GDP again soared to unsustainable levels. Our debt climbed further over the decade and a half that followed, surpassing 145 per cent of GDP in 2013.

All told, over the period between 1973 and 2013, fiscal unsustainability, price instability, and an insufficiency of foreign exchange reserves largely characterised Jamaica's economic history. Jamaica ran fiscal deficits for thirty-four of the forty years in that period[13] and had negative net foreign exchange reserves and double-digit inflation for almost half the time, while thirteen IMF programmes ended in failure.[14]

In addition, structural factors such as small size, an undiversified economic base, geographical location, and an unhealthy dependence on imported energy commodities have made Jamaica especially vulnerable to economic shocks. Adverse events, such as the oil-price shocks of 1973–74 and 1979, aggravated and further destabilised the already unsustainable economic trajectories, resulting in the Jamaican experience of continuous debt, foreign-exchange, and financial-sector crises.

These crises have been enormously costly and damaging. One sobering assessment of the cumulative effect, published by the International Monetary Fund (IMF) in February 2022 as part of its Article IV Consultation on Jamaica (a kind of economic health check-up), states: '[Real] GDP Per Capita is lower today than it was in 1970, partly the result of repeated fiscal, balance of payments or banking crises.'[15] Jamaica's history of economic instability and crisis has choked opportunity and stifled the economic independence of Jamaica and its people.

I learned that political independence does not necessarily translate into economic independence. I also learned that an absence of the latter can compromise the former. The goal of current and future generations must therefore be to secure Jamaica's economic independence, where Jamaica creates the policy space to address its opportunities and challenges, without over-reliance on others, in a manner that preserves and entrenches that independence.

Economic independence requires that Jamaica maintains sufficient foreign exchange reserves that enable households, businesses, and the government to sustainably pay their external obligations as they come due, under a variety of benign and adverse scenarios. It requires stable prices that allow economic agents to confidently maintain a long-term perspective without fearing the need for continuous tax increases. It requires low debt that preserves the ability of the government to engage in counter-cyclical policies in response to economic shocks, leading to quicker recoveries. And economic independence requires a stable financial sector that provides the financial intermediation required to facilitate growth.

The Footprints of Policy

In my work as Minister of Finance and the Public Service, and before that as Ambassador at Large for Economic Affairs, I have sought to bring economic policy discussions into the public sphere, making the government's purpose and positions known not only through my annual budget presentations but also through broadcast and social media, and with articles written for our national newspapers and for international publications. The collection presented in this book, extensive as it may seem, is by no means a complete representation of this administration's efforts or Jamaica's economic improvements. However, I am guided by the idea that future capacity requires broad internalisation of our progress to date, and by the notion that the best way to capture and understand that progress is by laying bare the thought process and principles behind a virtuous cycle of disciplined economic policymaking.

In that spirit, I have arranged content into five main parts: 'Beginnings,' 'Intention,' 'Stability,' 'Crises,' and 'Opportunity.' This organisational structure conveys my belief that to obtain lasting beneficial results, first you must position yourself in history and recognise the origins of the situation you are called upon to manage. In 'Beginnings,' I present three pieces, one previously unpublished, that describe the background against which our most remarkable ten-year economic reversal has taken place: from Jamaica's crashing out of its 2010 Stand-By Arrangement with the IMF, to the test of successive administrations and ongoing public sacrifices, to arriving at a time when we can share the lessons of discipline, continuity, and productive partnerships (among government, unions, and the private sector, and between Jamaica and multilateral institutions).

Only once you understand where you have come from can you chart a course for the future. Doing this requires that you have 'Intention' – that you clearly define where you want to go and what policies you will use to get there, and then signal those intentions to stakeholders in advance. This section begins, intentionally, towards the start of Prime Minister Andrew Holness's second administration when I served as Ambassador at Large for Economic Affairs and we announced, in October 2016, a new programme with the IMF that would replace, ahead of schedule, the not-yet-expired Extended Fund Facility. Orchestrating this new programme's timing, signalling the new government's intent to continue the prior administration's fiscal policies and progress, was nothing if not intentional. Other readings, from March 2018 and later, broadcast the intentions of the Ministry of Finance under my leadership to pursue economic independence by building resilience and strengthening buffers to allow the country to absorb economic shocks.

Of course, knowing your destination is not enough to get you there if the road you are attempting to travel keeps shifting underfoot. In the case of a nation's economic fortunes, nothing of lasting value will come without a stable foundation. Macro-stability is the critical underpinning of a prosperous society, and it is what allows for successful navigation of, and quicker recovery from, the inevitable crises. The extensive readings in 'Stability' provide a deeper dive into policies that form the guardrails of economic stability, in three critical areas: price stability and Central Bank independence; fiscal responsibility; and aspects of financial sector stability. The introduction to this section also provides a sober look at the costs of instability in our history.

In March of 2020, the entire world experienced an unprecedented level of disruption arising from the public health crisis of the COVID-19 pandemic. This event underscored the duty of government to prioritise those principles of stability that allow an economy the flexibility to accommodate an appropriate, compassionate response to crises when they occur – without jeopardising that stability. From the suspension of Jamaica's fiscal rules (and their timely readoption) to the design of targeted interventions such as the CARE Programme, the selections in 'Crises' that relate to the pandemic show how transparent, principled, and rules-based use of resources in response to a crisis unfolding in real time allowed Jamaica to make a recovery that outpaced other countries.

And as an island nation with high climate exposure, maintaining an appropriate disaster risk financing strategy is of course imperative, given the increased frequency and intensity of natural disasters and the capacity of these to imperil fiscal dynamics and compromise economic independence. 'Crises' also therefore includes pieces that discuss Jamaica's multi-layered disaster risk financing framework, now regarded as the most advanced in the Caribbean region and which could arguably provide a template that other climate-vulnerable countries could replicate.

Finally, the ultimate goal of national policymaking should be to create greater opportunity for the population as a whole. The Jamaican project stalls without sustainable economic growth to provide the revenues with which development can be pursued. Policymaking must therefore create an environment favourable to the sustainable expansion of economic activity. The section on 'Opportunity' includes measures undertaken to eliminate distortionary taxes in favour of this objective and to expand opportunity for individuals and businesses. Later in this section I describe our policy of broadening the ownership base of the economy by divesting government assets by way of initial public offerings on the Jamaica Stock Exchange with a 'bottom up' allocation of shares.

Creating a platform that is conducive to business serves the government's interest in multiple ways. In addition to generating revenue and jobs, such an environment also allows the government to share the risk of projects with the private sector through long-term structured transactions such as public-private partnerships. In 'Opportunity,' I highlight how we can leverage relationships with multilaterals to assist in the development of these projects.

The ongoing pursuit of stable policies will result in increased fiscal space over time. It is critical that this is used to finance the public investment required to improve quality of life and opportunity for all Jamaicans. Increased public investment in hospitals, schools, court houses, police stations, buses, garbage and fire trucks, water, sewerage, technology systems, bridges, roads, and highways will be both feasible and necessary. A robust and efficient public investment management system will support the pursuit of value for money as well as safeguard project implementation success.

The public sector is indispensable to the opportunity economy, and its governance is of macro-critical significance. I therefore present two pieces on the reform to the governance of public bodies, a policy that consumed considerable political capital. Governed properly, the public sector can accomplish marvellous objectives if it has the ability to attract and retain the technical talent it needs. 'Opportunity' therefore also includes multiple pieces on the complex policy that concurrently restructured compensation across all of government.

In the end, all policy must serve the people's interest. The goal of improving individual citizens' circumstances must be situated at the centre of policy considerations. Of course, the axes on which we measure improvement are multidimensional. However, improvements lts that are foundational across all dimensions flow from enabling greater opportunity for social mobility through easier access to tertiary education and by strengthening the social safety net.

Readers will therefore encounter within 'Opportunity,' policies that improved access to the financing of tertiary education, as well as pieces that portray my focus on fortifying the social safety net, in collaboration with colleagues, in a hopefully enlightened approach to economic sustainability. Through development of the social pension, advancement of unemployment insurance, and fortification of the National Insurance Fund, I endeavoured to demonstrate our values that true, long-term sustainability is only achieved when people have sustainable lives. By this time, however, I had also long internalised the economic lessons of Jamaica's past: people cannot have sustainable lives without a stable economy.

Jamaica, a Work in Progress

Jamaica has always been exceptional, and an enduring message of the last decade is that we can create the future we want. Guided by intentional and internally consistent policymaking, Jamaica can climb the ladder of prosperity, steadily improving standards of living for all. Clearly, macroeconomic stability cannot automatically, by itself, create the education, health, and social outcomes we also desire. But our history shows that we will not consistently achieve these either, as an independent country, without the prerequisites of economic sustainability and stability.

Now that we have achieved macroeconomic stability with sustainable fiscal and monetary dynamics, we must studiously avoid a mindset where it is believed that initial conditions determine outcomes. Initial conditions are important, but they do not create an inevitable path. Our economic history has not been inevitable.

Similarly, our future has not been fully determined by our progress to date. We create our history every day with the policy choices we make. While I am proud of the critical fiscal, monetary, governance, and disaster-risk-financing architecture we have built together; proud of the economic recovery we have attained, and the substantial improvements we have achieved with respect to our macroeconomic variables, it is important to maintain the mindset that our Jamaican project remains a work in progress.

As such, the most important lesson is that, in all we do, we should never, ever sacrifice policy sustainability, economic resilience, or macroeconomic stability. If lost, these take decades to restore. Also, this cannot be the burden of any sitting government or minister of finance only. This must be a shared national awareness and a shared responsibility across all institutions, all segments of the population, across public and private sectors, and across party lines. As a society we have to avoid myopic policymaking that pursues short-term gain at the expense of painful long-term adjustment. Policy choices must weigh the pros and cons of today, but also of tomorrow.

Without vigilance – without our continued commitment to intentional policymaking, macroeconomic stability, opportunity, and the partnerships that drive all these – the crises that marred our past and dampened our prospects can still occur and set our country back for generations. It is paramount, therefore, to absorb the lessons of our economic history, just as it is important that as a nation, we take pride in our economic accomplishments and do so with the confidence that we have agency and can determine the future we want.

Ultimately, it is my hope that in providing the background, policy articulation, and rationale for at least some of what has been accomplished during my time in the Jamaican public service, I will have done my part to guide others who will write the next chapters, leaving as it were, my footprints in the sand.

PART ONE

BEGINNINGS

In The Beginning

The Kings Pawn Opening. That is the game Andrew Holness played early one October morning in 2011. Waiting in a hotel lobby in Washington, DC, we took advantage of a lonely chess board atop an ornate table. My response stopped his pawn advancing, even as he projected a serene calm, alert to the surroundings, with great presence of mind.

I was in a different zone. I had agreed to accompany my friend and minister, Andrew, into unfamiliar territory, and the gravity of our task that morning weighed heavily on me. This showed in my game, which Prime Minister Bruce Golding's arrival in the lobby quickly cut short. We followed as the Secret Service escorted PM Golding into a waiting vehicle, and we got into the back seats. Sirens blaring, we made our way to a series of four back-to-back meetings.

Just weeks prior, Prime Minister Golding had indicated that he would step down and 'make way for new leadership to continue the programmes of economic recovery.'[1] His successor was thereafter quickly selected by his peers, and within days Andrew Holness would make history, becoming the ninth and youngest Prime Minister of Jamaica at age thirty-nine.

The outgoing prime minister planned for a smooth transition. To achieve this, he decided to take the incoming prime minister, plus one, to meet the presidents of the Inter-American Development Bank and the World Bank, the managing director of the International Monetary Fund (IMF), and officials from the US Treasury, given the grave economic circumstances in Jamaica that required immediate attention.

Back then, I occupied a full-time job in the private sector, building businesses in the Caribbean and Central America. However, I worked closely with Andrew, who was Minister of Education at the time and had appointed me Chairman of the HEART Trust, the leading vocational education institute in Jamaica and a significant public body in his ministry. Given our professional proximity, my commercial and finance experience, and our friendship, I was his plus one for that day in Washington.

Our meeting at the IMF was extremely sobering. Managing Director Madame Christine Lagarde was only three months into her job, the Global Financial Crisis was raging, the Eurozone was in trouble, and she now had tough news to deliver to us visiting Jamaicans. Flanked by senior Western Hemisphere IMF staff, she received us graciously. However, her colleagues never smiled for the duration of the meeting. And we knew why.

Months before, Jamaica had spectacularly crashed out of its 2010 Stand-By Arrangement as its fiscal trajectory veered off track, resulting in the noncompletion of scheduled reviews (the fourth and fifth reviews, for end-December 2010 and end-March 2011). Arguably, this was the worst kind of crash – a crash in slow motion, with rescheduled reviews by the Fund and a veil of hopeful denial put up by the Government of Jamaica (GOJ), through which many could nevertheless see the unfolding drama.

In fact, Prime Minister Golding's administration had embarked on an ambitious and courageous path, which started well, and the respect accorded to the prime minister by the IMF was obvious. Achieving prior actions required to secure the 2010 arrangement, the Golding government, with Audley Shaw as Finance Minister, demonstrated considerable resolve and called for tremendous sacrifices by the people. In a declining economy, the GOJ had imposed a heavy tax package of 2 per cent of GDP in December 2009. They launched and completed a debt-exchange programme on locally issued debt that generated interest savings of 3.5 per cent of GDP, and they reached an agreement to divest Air Jamaica, the national airline, which was reported to have lost US$1 billion over a ten-year period[2] – equivalent to 8 per cent of 2010 GDP. Furthermore, the first, second, and third scheduled reviews (in March, June, and September 2010) had been successful, with quantitative performance and structural benchmarks met. A fiscal responsibility framework was embedded in the Financial Administration and Audit Act, which included fiscal rules; a time-bound plan to establish a central treasury-management system was completed; and a two-year (2010–12) public-sector wage freeze had been achieved.

Nevertheless, with the remaining five reviews uncompleted, the programme went completely off the rails, and the working relationship between the IMF and Jamaica had broken down.

I remained silent for the entirety of the meeting. This was between principals. It was my job to listen quietly and observe closely, with the aim of parsing, deconstructing, and advising later. However, there was little to parse as the point was abundantly clear: the ball was in Jamaica's court. Without successful reviews, the Fund had suspended Jamaica's ability to draw down under the Stand-By Arrangement, and their stamp of approval, which provides a strong signal to markets, would remain absent. Meeting medium-term targets would require closure of the fiscal gap through significant revenue-raising measures and/or expenditure rationalisations. Resumption of reviews would require a clear path to that end, supported by concrete action.

Lest anyone wonder why we needed the 2010 Stand-By Arrangement in the first place, and what exactly was at stake, the fact is that Jamaica's economic prospects at the time depended on external assistance – and accountability – to get back on track. In 2010, the world economy was still reeling from the 2007–08 Global Financial Crisis and the Great Recession, which the IMF called 'the most dangerous of the post–World War II era' due to its 'pervasive reach' and 'threat to global prosperity not experienced in 70 years.'[3]

But long before this crisis, Jamaica's finances were wholly unsustainable. For example, by 2005–06 and 2006–07, just two categories of expenditure – interest costs and public-sector salaries – together comprised 22 per cent of GDP, against tax revenues of 23 per cent of GDP![4] With such constraints, there was no space to fund social-safety-net or other programmes, nor room for capital expenditure without borrowing, further increasing interest costs and increasing debt, which was already at 120 per cent of GDP. Jamaica was in a vicious cycle.

The Global Financial Crisis only deepened existing troubles. By 2009, interest and salary costs peaked at just under 29 per cent of GDP, bauxite earnings collapsed, remittances fell, and pressures intensified throughout the economy as the current account deficit ballooned to an unsustainable 10 per cent of GDP.[5] Not only was Jamaica experiencing a chronic fiscal emergency; we were in a dangerous balance-of-payments catastrophe, too. The US$1.3 billion lifeline from the IMF was necessary assistance in a crisis, but now it was in jeopardy.

Making a serious economic correction, involving painful reform measures, with a new prime minister stepping in more than four years into a five-year parliamentary term, seemed daunting to say the least, and we were unlikely to achieve these goals without a renewed electoral mandate, which was not forthcoming.

Towards a New Agreement

During the December 2011 general election debates, Portia Simpson-Miller – who was then the Opposition Leader, and who would very soon replace Andrew Holness in her second tour as prime minister – famously implied, in response to a question from the moderator, that she would secure an IMF agreement within two weeks of forming a new government.[6] She was off by a mere sixteen and a half months.

Meanwhile, Jamaica's finances continued to deteriorate. Fiscal pressures accumulated as 2012–13 ended with another large budget deficit, and the debt-to-GDP ratio climbed to just over 145 per cent.[7] Jamaica was in a debt spiral. While it had taken forty-six years, from 1962 to 2008, for Jamaica's debt to reach $1 trillion, it would take only seven additional years to accumulate the next trillion.[8] The country's net foreign exchange reserves headed in the opposite direction: between January 2012 and April 2013, they plummeted from US$1.9 billion to US$866 million.[9]

The difficulty in securing a new IMF agreement had much to do with the size of the fiscal adjustment required, the unpalatable options for closing it, and the depletion of Jamaica's credibility. This burden fell on the shoulders of Jamaica's then Minister of Finance and Planning, Peter Phillips. The collapse of the 2010 Stand-By Arrangement had punctured trust in Jamaica's ability to honour its commitments. Nevertheless, after an anxious and intensely difficult period, the GOJ made progress on an agreement 'on which our very survival as a country rested,'[10] and in May 2013, the IMF Executive Board approved an Extended Fund Facility (EFF) agreement of US$932 million for Jamaica.

But trust deficits have their costs. With the experience of the derailed arrangement still fresh in the minds of the Fund, this new programme would require even more front-loading of structural reforms. Funding drawdowns would also be more cautiously staggered. Whereas the 2010 arrangement disbursed just over 50 per cent of funding upon approval of the programme, the 2013 EFF only disbursed 18 per cent of programme resources up front. The remainder would come in tranches over four years, based on successful implementation.

And while the original Stand-By Arrangement had envisaged a debt-to-GDP ratio of 100 per cent by 2016, the GOJ signed on to new medium-term projections that pushed this goal farther into the future and now targeted achieving it by 2020. This would require an excess of revenues over non-interest expenditure, otherwise known as a primary surplus, of 7.5 per cent of GDP.[11] It was a monstrous requirement, unheard of anywhere in the world. The outcome of bad economic management and unsustainable policy choices – in place over decades and across administrations – meant that Jamaica had to endure an economic adjustment of unprecedented scale to regain stability. During the best year of the 2010 arrangement, Jamaica only managed a primary surplus of 4.6 per cent of GDP. Now it needed to substantially better that effort.

Furthermore, prior actions would again be required: a three-year freeze of public sector wages and another debt exchange that would reduce debt-to-GDP by 8.6 percentage points, among other initiatives. This was devastating. It was as if the sacrifices three years earlier were for nought. If a trust gap had opened up between Jamaica and the IMF, the trust deficit between the Government of Jamaica and its people was even wider.

It is always a shame when governments call on individuals, households, and businesses to make advance sacrifices related to policies agreed as prior actions under IMF-supported programmes, only to have the programme collapse later. The people have the unfortunate experience of hurting at least twice – during the initial sacrifices, then again through the inevitable economic dislocation and deterioration that accompanies programme implosion. The derailment of the 2010 arrangement hurt everyone.

Now, financial institutions and their clients, who bore the brunt of the debt exchange, and public-sector labour unions, whose members endured the wage freeze, demanded assurances that this time their sacrifices would not be in vain.

The government, to their enduring credit, responded to this need. In a nationally televised broadcast in February 2013,[12] Prime Minister Portia Simpson-Miller and the Minister of Finance and Planning, Peter Phillips, together announced the need for another debt exchange, pleaded for understanding, and pledged to take 'an unprecedented step of public accountability and transparency.' The Minister of Finance and Planning would institute an 'implementation and coordination unit' to operate within government and ensure programme targets were met, and professionals from outside the public sector would supplement this unit.

Furthermore, for the first time anywhere in the world, Jamaica would create an Economic Programme Oversight Committee (EPOC) comprised of stakeholder representatives from the public and private sectors, the central bank, trade unions, and civil society, empowered to 'monitor the compliance and progress of the ministries, departments, and agencies with regard to the implementation of the IMF agreement'[13] and report to the Jamaican people. This was monumental. EPOC met monthly with senior government technocrats, who provided progress updates measured against programme targets. Monthly, EPOC held press conferences and published bulletins reporting on the GOJ's fiscal, legislative, and policy achievements versus targets. The media joined the effort and amplified EPOC's communiques.

This transparency boosted confidence in the intentions of the government to implement the programme and created support for programme policies, which in turn provided needed political space. This was unprecedented for Jamaica.

The legislative demands emanating from commitments under the EFF were challenging. One of the first tasks after the programme's approval was to address the stock of tax arrears, most of which was uncollectible. Large uncollectible tax-arrears balances lead to overestimation of projected revenue and are therefore a potential source of fiscal underperformance. The system was unreliable; it was better to start anew.

In November 2013, the Opposition Leader appointed me to the Upper House of Parliament, where I led the Opposition's response to finance bills, most of which were associated with EFF commitments. The Senate met deep into the Christmas holidays to accommodate passage of some bills, and the intensity continued into 2014.

Legislation tabled by the Minister of Finance around this time, which was debated and passed by the House of Representatives and the Senate, overhauled the fiscal waiver regime with the Charities Act, virtually eliminating discretionary waivers, and revamped the incentive regime with the Omnibus Tax Incentive Act. The GOJ, through the legislature, also strengthened fiscal rules and amended the Revenue Administration Act and the Tax Collection Act to enhance revenue collection. The General Consumption Tax (Amendment) Act, passed in 2014, removed many exemptions, abolished the zero-rating of supplies to government and overhauled the interest and penalty regime, all in a successful effort to boost domestic revenue mobilisation. The contours of a Public Investment Management System (PIMS) were set forth. Working together, members in the Houses of Parliament established a centralised collateral registry and introduced a regulatory framework for collective investment schemes. The Banking Act was amended to strengthen regulations, and the Bank of Jamaica Act was updated to remove the minister's power to give directions in supervisory matters.

In June, September, and December of 2013, Jamaica passed the first three reviews out of fifteen scheduled for the EFF, and Jamaicans began to take note. *We have been here before; will this continue?* The government then passed the fourth, fifth, sixth, and seventh reviews in 2014. The cheering gallery grew louder. *Jamaica can do this!* With high-level political commitment, and dedicated public-sector technocrats, the implementation unit and oversight innovations were working. Enter 2015, and programme success continued: the eighth, ninth, and tenth reviews were passed.

Jamaica had entered a new era, and the political calculus had shifted. The Portia Simpson-Miller administration, with Peter Phillips as Finance Minister, normalised the passing of IMF reviews. Such became the confidence in the programme's execution, that Jamaican stakeholders began to suggest inclusion of favoured policies to ensure their implementation. The 'IMF Programme' became 'Jamaica's Programme.' We owned it.

Continuity

The February 2016 general election brought Andrew Holness back to power with a historically thin parliamentary majority of a single seat. To some, this appeared to be an unstable foundation on which to build a government, and elements within the private sector and civil-society leadership, desirous of policy continuity, questioned the incoming government's ability to sustain the hard-won progress.

There was an additional problem. The incoming government's signature tax proposal, to multiply the income-tax threshold by a factor of 2.5, although electorally successful, was unfunded and therefore fundamentally incompatible with the contours of Jamaica's domestically owned IMF programme. Within corridors of influence, anxiety about continuity quickly mushroomed into fears of policy reversal.

But momentum was on our side. By March 2016, Jamaica had experienced noteworthy improvements in the macro environment: as measured against 2013, the debt-to-GDP ratio declined by approximately thirty percentage points; unemployment dropped three percentage points; poverty declined seven and a half percentage points; and foreign exchange reserves doubled.

Upon winning the general election, the prime minister tasked me to engage with the IMF as his special envoy, to ensure a smooth policy transition. Within days I met with an IMF team from Washington who visited for that purpose. Across the weeks that followed, I worked with them mostly on options for resolving discontinuities and unsustainable elements of the new government's flagship tax-reform proposal. Meanwhile, the prime minister formalised this arrangement by appointing me to a newly created post: Ambassador at Large for Economic Affairs.

My early collaboration with the Fund culminated in an unprecedented presentation by the IMF to the Cabinet. With respect to the tax-reform policy, the rest is history. The GOJ embarked on a revenue-neutral shift from direct to indirect taxation, later described by the Fund as 'bold.'[14] In this reform, the income tax threshold was multiplied as intended, which increased disposal income for hundreds of thousands of Jamaicans – as promised in the election campaign – and improved the incentive to work. The reform also increased economic efficiency while doubling allocations to the social safety net.

This was a major victory for the Government of Jamaica and the IMF. The IMF's flexibility, within the boundaries of a necessarily rigid macro-fiscal framework, and the GOJ's intentionality, within the context of a demonstrated commitment to medium-term fiscal targets, provided the foundation for a strong relationship between the Fund and the incoming administration.

Success begat success, and, building on all that came before, we were keen for the increasing confidence in the Jamaican economy, and the reform programme that was delivering positive results, to continue. Three successful reviews under the EFF (the eleventh, twelfth, and thirteenth) followed the change of government, but this was not enough. Soon, we knew, anxiety would creep in about what would follow the EFF, which was set to expire in March 2017. With the prime minister's approval, and supported by key technocrats, I therefore began negotiations with the IMF on a successor programme, and, in October 2016, in a positive surprise, we announced the early termination of the US$932 million EFF and its replacement with a three-year US$1.6 billion Precautionary Stand-By Arrangement.

This arrangement was 'precautionary' as Jamaica did not anticipate a need to drawdown on financing from the Fund, which represented progress. However, macroeconomic stability had not yet been achieved, given debt and foreign exchange reserve levels, and the economy remained highly vulnerable. So, we needed the IMF's line of credit, as well as continued policy and legislative reform, along with the assurances and signals that these all provided.

We have come a long way from the early days of facing what looked like the end. Back in 2013, no one would have believed that Jamaica could have made its way through the gauntlet of fifteen reviews scheduled under the EFF, let alone achieve the 2020 debt target. Among the doubters was myself, and even as I worked towards programme goals in the Senate, I expressed this doubt in public commentary published by the *Gleaner* in 2014 (see page 11), where I called for entrenchment of the fiscal rule in our Constitution as a safeguard against political waywardness and reform fatigue.

But fatigue was not an option. Jamaica has now registered seven positive fiscal balances over the past eleven years since 2013, including every year since 2017-18, only excluding 2020–21, the year of the COVID-19 pandemic.[15] Our debt-to-GDP ratio, which was 145 per cent, is on track for 68 per cent, or lower, this fiscal year, the lowest level in nearly fifty years. Unemployment, at 4.2 per cent, is at its lowest since independence sixty-two years ago, and stands in dynamic contrast to, at least, four decades of high double-digit unemployment rates. The business cycle has been elongated with the absence of quarterly economic contraction for a decade to date, i.e., since 2015, outside of the impact of the COVID-19 pandemic and a Category 5 hurricane and foreign exchange reserves at US$5.7 billion have never been higher, having increased six-fold from April 2013, our recent economic nadir. If there can be said to have been an endgame in all the strategies and struggles that came along with our engagements with the IMF, we might call it a path to economic independence. Jamaica can now claim successful completion, in November 2019, of the Precautionary Stand-By Arrangement, but also of two more programmes – a Resilience and Sustainability Facility and a Precautionary and Liquidity Line (PLL), both of which we successfully completed in August 2024. All tallied, across four Fund programmes between 2013 and 2024, all structural benchmarks and all quantitative criteria have been met. Furthermore, Jamaica's macroeconomic transformation was loudly telegraphed by our ability, in 2023, to access the PLL which requires 'sound economic fundamentals.'[16]

The results of our efforts, our principled decision-making, our newly successful partnership with the IMF, and our stunning economic turnaround, exist for the world to see. Jamaica is now a small country with 'big lessons' to impart, as detailed in the last writing in this section on 'Beginnings' (see page 9). But as I stated there, even with our accomplishments, 'the Jamaican project remains a work in progress, with much more to be achieved.' So even as we celebrate the conclusion of more than a decade of IMF programmes that have helped us reach a previously elusive stability, when it comes to our economic independence and generating an even brighter future, we are only now getting started.

Entrench the Fiscal Rule

Published Commentary, January 2014

At the bottom of the business cycle, of which we missed the top, Jamaica finds itself with staggering unemployment, weak consumer demand, and a sagging economy, which conspire to engulf us. Meanwhile, the Government, hamstrung by suffocating levels of debt, has limited fiscal options for a convincing and effective rescue.

While high levels of debt exist, the economy remains in jeopardy. Sanctioned by the International Monetary Fund (IMF), the Government, having been forced to extend the projection horizon, forecasts that public-sector debt will be equivalent to annual output in 2020, seven fiscal years away, counting the present, and three years beyond the end of the IMF [Extended Fund Facility] programme.

Achieving this crucial, but by no means secure, target requires extreme, punishing, and unrelenting fiscal consolidation. This must be maintained over the seven-year horizon, across one, possibly two election cycles and for half of the period without the watchful eyes of the IMF.

After all of the disciplined restraint and collective sacrifice forecasted to last at least one-third of a generation, we will remain highly vulnerable in 2020, with a public-sector debt-to-GDP ratio of 100 per cent, and even this assumes growth at the top end of our recent experience for most of the seven-year horizon.

The elephant in the room is that this is an extraordinarily risky, fragile, and improbable path that defies our collective experience. Point forecasts and estimates are silent on the probability distribution of outcomes and on the variability of supporting assumptions. Even with the best of intentions, many developments could derail the process.

The possibility, therefore, of meandering through thickets of pain, only to end up in the same bush where we are now confined, is

---

An earlier version of this article appeared in the *Jamaica Gleaner*, January 20, 2014.

real. Maintaining debt-reduction focus and execution across election cycles and into a post-IMF future is at odds with the historical experience of the last twenty-five years.

As such, despite the elevated prospect of near-term target attainment, there is a dangerous yet widespread view, here and overseas, that clouds of inevitable implosion hover. While that view exists, economic agents remain tentative, looking for ways of escape – or avoiding Jamaica altogether.

This gulf of confidence in the long-term viability of Jamaica's public finances must be addressed decisively. The government, propelled by the IMF, has signalled its intention to adopt a fiscal rule, enshrined in law, that commits this and future governments to a path of fiscal prudence and towards stable and sensible debt levels.

The rule would include a cocktail of corrective and automatic fiscal adjustments that would be triggered by deviations from the path, with appropriate escape clauses to allow for temporary responses to exogenous shocks.

However, it would be exceptionally naive and a grand waste of time if this rule were constructed in a manner that admitted the possibility of change, or even abandonment, with the support of a simple majority of Parliament. The existential threat posed by the precariousness of Jamaica's public finances, and the generational time frame required for rehabilitation, demand that the fiscal rule be irreversible. One way of achieving this would be for amendment thereof to only be permissible with the affirmative vote of a two-thirds majority of both Houses of Parliament.

Sound public finances are at the core of a strong and growing economy, while weak fiscal accounts imperil the soundest investments. Capital will, therefore, not commit itself for the long term where there is doubt. With the passage of an entrenched and well-thought-out fiscal rule, Jamaica would certify that it is on a continuous path of de-risking the economy and consolidating fiscal gains from this, prior, and future periods.

This would buoy assessment of our prospects and significantly improve the long-term outlook on Jamaica. The disposition of capital would change, and the defensive freeze of local businesses would thaw. Rather than wait until 2020, and beyond, for risk to subside, an immutable rule brings forward the benefits of full-programme and post-IMF execution to today.

There is no better way to enhance confidence that we can do what we have never done, than by making its undoing unthinkable.

13

Big Lessons from a Small Country – Jamaica's Economic Transformation, a Work in Progress
Feature Story, September 2023

Jamaica is known internationally for sports, music, culture, and the pristine quality of our beaches. However, recently Jamaica has attracted attention for its economic transformation.

Jamaica has successfully cut public debt by the equivalent of two-thirds of its gross domestic product (GDP) in a relatively short time frame without handouts, debt relief, or bilateral debt support from 'friends.'[17] Precedent achievements of similar scale are very scarce. Furthermore, Jamaica is among a small group of countries where public debt and unemployment levels are lower today than prior to the COVID-19 crisis and where quarterly economic output has surpassed the corresponding pre-COVID-19 threshold.

What exactly is the Jamaican economic experience? Does this experience contain lessons of potential value for other countries? What factors explain its recent economic rehabilitation?

The Jamaican economy grew rapidly in the 1960s with real per capita GDP increasing by 50 per cent over the period 1962–72. However, this metric plummeted by 40 per cent between 1972 and 1980,[18] even as the government significantly expanded social programmes. Fiscal deficits widened, compounded by external shocks, including the 1973–74 and 1979 oil shocks. The fiscal deficit averaged 14 per cent of GDP between 1976 and 1983. Despite social progress, this was an economically devastating period and, by 1980, when the government changed, foreign exchange reserves were negative US$453 million.

Structural adjustment in the early 1980s brought some stabilization. However, this involved currency devaluation and, as much of Jamaica's debt was foreign denominated, debt-to-GDP climbed. Real per capita GDP bottomed out in 1986 at 20 per cent

---

An earlier version of this article appeared in *Linacre News, the Magazine of Linacre College, Oxford* (2023), based on my lecture at Rhodes House, Oxford, on April 27, 2023.

lower than 1963 levels, after a bauxite/alumina price slump. From this nadir, real per capita GDP grew by 90 per cent between 1987 and 1995 on the strength of a period of very high growth (1987 to 1990), followed by continued but lower growth (1991 to 1994). However, even then, real per capita GDP was still below 1972 levels.

During the 1990s, liberalisation of the financial sector without a strengthened regulatory and supervisory framework, among other factors, contributed to a catastrophic financial-sector crisis. A deep recession ensued. The government's intervention cost 40 per cent of GDP, added to the national debt which continued to grow (By comparison, the cost of US government intervention in the 2007–09 Global Financial Crisis was approximately 10 per cent of US GDP).[19]

Jamaica entered the period of the Global Financial Crisis with chronic structural imbalances and unsustainable levels of debt, leading to an economic unravelling. Interest expenses peaked at 17 per cent of GDP. Additionally, balance-of-payment pressures intensified as bauxite earnings again collapsed, and remittances fell dramatically. Jamaica, once again, sought the assistance of the IMF in 2010.

Up to that point Jamaica had entered thirteen IMF programmes since Independence in 1962, and none was successfully completed. Even with successful local debt restructuring and the divestment of major loss-making state-owned enterprises, this fourteenth IMF programme failed as well.

The collapse of the 2010 IMF agreement coincided with the resignation of the prime minister, for unrelated reasons, and the appointment of thirty-nine-year-old Andrew Holness as Jamaica's youngest prime minister in October 2011. While in the private sector, I worked closely with the then-incoming prime minister, in his capacity as Minister of Education. Given my proximity and background, I became an advisor in this unexpected transition.

Jamaica was in economic turmoil, with yet another failed IMF agreement and a new prime minister. Intent on resurrecting the IMF programme and finishing the job, he told the electorate, in innocent and refreshing honesty, that 'Bitter Medicine' was to come. This proved pivotal. Within two months he lost power in a landslide election, having presided over the shortest-serving administration in Jamaica's history.

However, the political conditions in the aftermath of the 2011 general elections created space for the implementation of tough reforms. By 2012, the then-outgoing government, which now formed the Opposition, would have, in effect, campaigned on the inescapable necessity for austerity, and lost, while the incoming government had no choice but to implement it. Jamaica never had a better chance. To the credit of the 2012–16 government, they leveraged that chance, and our economic reform programme gathered new, unprecedented momentum.

Another decisive factor was that, for the first time, civil society demanded oversight of the reforms if they would again be called upon to make sacrifices. With a framework for oversight in place, unions, academia, media, business, and the political opposition supported the reforms. Building on a preexisting foundation of social partnership, an economic programme oversight committee (EPOC) was formed with stakeholders to closely monitor targets and communicate to Jamaicans. This became 'Jamaica's programme' with IMF support.

By March 2016, positive results were evident. The debt-to-GDP ratio declined from 145 per cent to 115 per cent; unemployment declined from 16.3 per cent to 13.3 per cent; the incidence of poverty declined from 24.6 per cent to 17.1 per cent; and foreign exchange reserves more than doubled.

The government changed again in 2016, with Andrew Holness returning as prime minister. There was some concern that Jamaica's economic gains could be reversed. The prime minister appointed me as Ambassador of Economic Affairs, responsible for Jamaica's engagement with multilateral financial institutions including the IMF, and then as Minister of Finance and the Public Service. Against expectation, we extended the arrangement with the IMF with a new three-year programme that reflected the new government's priorities but kept the broad quantitative macro contours intact. A third factor, therefore, was broad continuity across administrations on the scaffolding of macroeconomic policy.

By March 2020, Jamaica achieved seven consecutive years of primary surpluses above 7 per cent of GDP[20] and implemented legislative reforms covering tax and monetary policy, the financial sector, and the public sector, including public pension reform. These reforms restored government finances and entrenched macroeconomic stability. Debt fell to 94 per cent of GDP prior to COVID-19, which was the lowest level in nearly two decades; unemployment almost halved to 7 per cent, the then-lowest in Jamaica's history. The poverty rate sank to 11 per cent.

And then the COVID-19 tsunami arrived.

The Caribbean experienced the world's most severe economic contraction from the COVID-19 pandemic, as measured by GDP decline, which was as high as 16 to 20 per cent in some countries.[21] The global measures required to contain the spread of the virus decimated tourism, the main economic engine of many Caribbean economies. Jamaica's annual economic output declined by 10 per cent in 2020. Revenues caved in while expenses rose. Approximately 10 per cent of the workforce lost their jobs as unemployment nearly doubled to 13 per cent.

These developments threatened to derail Jamaica's achievements. By June 2020, however, the broad-based COVID-19 Economic Recovery Task Force, which the prime minister appointed me to chair, tabled a 133-page policy strategy document outlining the government's response. Importantly, it provided the principles that would govern economic intervention. The composition of the task force allowed us to achieve 'social consensus around a coherent policy agenda,' so that, despite the crisis, Jamaica could continue to 'embrace reform with ambition.'[22]

We triggered the escape clause in our fiscal rules, pushed back medium-term debt targets, and accessed fiscal, monetary, and natural-disaster risk buffers built in pre-pandemic years, inclusive of resources from privatisations concluded in the fiscal year prior to COVID-19. In addition, the IMF's Rapid Financing Instrument and allocation of the Fund's special drawing rights supplemented our foreign exchange reserves.

We implemented a programme of digitally accessible fiscal transfers to cushion the impact of the pandemic on the most vulnerable. And while COVID-19 provided an excuse to delay or renege on policy commitments, we did the opposite. We accelerated institutional reform.

In September 2020, I piloted legislation through Parliament to establish the Independent Fiscal Commission, as the arbiter of Jamaica's fiscal rules, bolstering accountability and fortifying fiscal transparency. In December 2020, I piloted legislation through Parliament that made our central bank independent, with an explicit price-stability mandate, while strengthening its governance and deepening monetary policy transparency. In 2021, with the assistance of the World Bank, Jamaica became the first small country in the world to independently sponsor a catastrophe bond which formed the final layer in our institutional, multi-layered strategy for the management of the fiscal risk posed by natural disasters. In 2021, we also passed legislation that provides for a transparent process for the nomination, selection, and appointment of directors to public-body boards.

A fourth factor of success to date has been the focus on building institutions.

Jamaica also differentiated itself with the return to our fiscal rules in the 2021 fiscal year, while continuing to support the vulnerable. Together with our institutional building during a time of crisis, these collective developments bolstered confidence in Jamaica's trajectory.

When the global inflation crisis arrived, we implemented a temporary and targeted policy response. We allowed prices to pass through but provided targeted support to the bottom 50 per cent of the population, measured by energy consumption.[23]

Results have been encouraging. By 2023, Jamaica's unemployment rate attained a historic, previously inconceivable low of 4.5 per cent. Debt-to-GDP is forecasted to be 74 per cent at the end of the 2023 fiscal year,[24] the lowest since the financial sector crisis approximately thirty years ago, and foreign exchange reserves have almost doubled since 2016.

The Jamaican project remains a work in progress, with much more to be achieved. However, the lessons thus far are clear. High debt exacerbates economic shocks and creates second-order crises that complicate and prolong economic recoveries. Jamaica's previous experiences were of economic recoveries measured on generational timescales. We have now defied this historical norm. Through high-level political consensus and continuity on the contours of macroeconomic policy, civil-society participation, ownership and oversight, the enactment of laws, and the building of institutions, Jamaica has managed to transform its economic prospects. But even these are not enough. One never knows the nature, timing, or duration of economic challenges that may emerge. As such, principled decision-making, which may not always yield popular reception but always delivers results, is the most important factor and the biggest lesson of all.

PART TWO
INTENTION

Victimhood is among the interwoven threads that comprise the tapestry of the national conversation. When convenient, we believe that our fortunes disproportionately evolve from the actions of others. Things are the way they are because 'a just suh di ting set.' We have little or no agency. We reason that sub-optimal outcomes are the result of the proverbial 'big man' working against us, always holding us back.

Of course, this line of thought exists in direct tension with Jamaica's otherwise strong identity and unmistakable projection of national self-confidence. We are, as Professor Orlando Patterson puts it, a country of contradictions.[1]

Perhaps it is unreasonable to expect that victimhood would have no place for a people who have persevered through a legacy of violent enslavement, colonialism, and imperialism. However, embracing a culture of victimhood underestimates our power and diminishes belief in our capacity to shape our future.

If this applies to the way we live our lives as individuals, it is no less relevant – indeed it is more so, given the impact on generations – for the way we approach Jamaica's economy, which requires our intentional action.

Intentional policymaking outrightly rejects the victimhood bias. It is unburdened by history. Instead, it embraces history and affirms the Malcolm X view that history is the *most important* subject.[2] Indeed, history is the springboard from which intentional policymaking emerges.

This approach asserts that we have agency over our circumstances. Through disciplined policy choices, we can master history and create the future we want. It ascribes values and priorities to policies based on their calculated or forecasted effects and not their optics. Politics is the indispensable tool used to address gaps between effect and optics, but the true goal of the intentional policymaker is to sustainably improve the standards of living of the Jamaican people – and politics must serve this purpose.

Intentional policymaking is bold yet transparent, broadcasting its goals and expectations, publicly, in advance, deliberately innovating and constructing policies to address identified problems, knowing this also means absorbing the adverse impact of the inevitable trade-offs.

There are few things as powerful as when purpose achieves its aims. So, the political calculus of intentionality is built on its regenerative capacity with respect to any political capital it may consume. It relies on the demonstration effect: the results, and impact on people's lives, will speak for themselves. But in a competitive political space this is incomplete without strident advocacy, clear articulation, and creative communication.

Intentionality, a Core Principle

Adhering to the core principle of intentionality, I am proud that we have been explicitly intentional in economic policymaking, with publicly articulated goals and a conviction that we can create the Jamaica we want.

The pages you are about to read demonstrate the economic policy intentions set by the government under Prime Minister Andrew Holness's second administration, which began in February 2016. They are purposefully arranged to begin with a pivotal point in time: the announcement – in October 2016, when I still served as Ambassador at Large for Economic Affairs – of Jamaica's Precautionary Stand-By Arrangement with the International Monetary Fund (IMF). This announcement, and indeed the new IMF programme itself, made manifest this administration's intention of policy continuity, coming as it did in advance of the expiration of the prior IMF programme, the Extended Fund Facility, and that I was careful to articulate. We were keen to continue the early successes of Jamaica's economic reform, which had progressed under the prior administration, and to allay any concerns about the transition. We knew stakes were high, and we were intentional about the value of maintaining and eventually increasing confidence in the Jamaican economy.

In fact, this new programme with the IMF, and the messaging surrounding it, represented a deliberate if subtle shift in tone and emphasis. At this time, the government's vocabulary of primary surpluses and fiscal targets began to be replaced by a narrative on growth and job creation. Public utterances about the requirement of primary surpluses to reduce debt were replaced by the economic truism that stability is necessary for growth and employment.

With intention as our guide, we made a choice to lead by vocalising the goals of policy, not simply the inputs. We articulated our intentions – growth, employment, resilience, economic independence, and increased public investments that improve quality of life – and narrated the connection between these and our actions. In doing so, it became all the clearer that people can work with intentions that are aligned with their interests, as long as these are being demonstrably fulfilled.

In 2017, I articulated the central organising principles of the government as economic growth and job creation, from which everything else by proximity derives value, and in the pages of the *Gleaner*, I described this era as representing the 'best chance in a generation.' In an interview with the IMF, also in 2017, I unambiguously set out the economic-stability intentions of the government and the intent to pursue policies that support lowering the unemployment rate, then at 12.7 per cent.[3]

On assuming the position of Minister of Finance and the Public Service in March 2018, I broadcast our intention to pursue economic independence by building resilience and strengthening buffers to provide the resources and flexibility required to absorb and recover from economic shocks.

We were deliberate and calculated, too, in our further engagement with the IMF, when we accessed the Rapid Financing Facility resources at the onset of COVID-19 pandemic; when we partially pre-financed sizable maturing obligations with the proceeds of the attractively packaged Resilience and Sustainability Trust; and when we obtained the security blanket of the Fund's Precautionary and Liquidity Line. This section also captures the rationale for these choices as expounded at the time.

As part of my public advocacy for our bill that made the Central Bank independent, legislated inflation-targeting, and strengthened governance, I publicly declared that with successful passage and implementation, we would float a Jamaican currency bond in international capital markets by 2024. I had been intentional about the policy dividend that would accrue from the reform measure and specified a time frame of five years to accomplish this. We achieved this goal in 2023, with a year to spare.

Intentionality has been a core value that has permeated economic policymaking over this critical stretch of Jamaica's story, as we have turned our fortunes around and advanced towards economic independence. It is therefore a very good place to start exploring what more mature economic policy looks like, understanding that this – not victimhood – can be our destiny.

Entering a New Precautionary Stand-By Arrangement with the IMF

Press Statement by Ambassador Clarke, October 13, 2016

Ladies and Gentlemen, thank you for your attendance today to this joint press conference by the Government of Jamaica and the IMF.[4]

Let me begin by welcoming: Alejandro Werner, Director of the IMF's Western Hemisphere Department; Dr Uma Ramakrishnan, IMF Mission Chief of Jamaica; and Dr Constant Lonkeng [Ngouana], IMF Resident Representative for Jamaica.

Dr Ramakrishnan led a mission to Jamaica during the last two weeks of September, which was successfully concluded.

We are fortunate to have a very productive and positive working relationship with the International Monetary Fund. Due to the broad commitment and programme ownership by successive Jamaican governments, the public sector, the private sector, unions, the Opposition, and civil society, Jamaica has successfully passed thirteen IMF reviews under the Extended Fund Facility arrangement. Jamaica has exhibited good governance, strong policy coordination, and effective implementation.

Jamaica is now an example to the Caribbean and, I indeed say, Mr Werner, to the Western Hemisphere.

As the minister and governor will tell you, fiscal and monetary management have been strengthened, public debt has been significantly reduced, and macroeconomic stability is being entrenched as evidenced by low inflation, the build-up of foreign currency reserves, and a decline in the current account deficit. However, economic growth has lagged.

Despite this progress, or perhaps because of it, there has been an understandable level of uncertainty and even anxiety on the part of stakeholders on what will follow the Extended Fund Facility.

Economic and policy uncertainty are inimical to investment and economic growth. In this context, the ultimate display of maturity and acceptance of our responsibility as stewards is to put an end to any speculation regarding the Government of Jamaica's commitment to maintaining policy credibility and macroeconomic stability following the completion of the Extended Fund Facility arrangement.

As such, the Prime Minister of Jamaica the Most Honourable Andrew Holness has an announcement to make[5] (regarding early termination of the Extended Fund Facility and the entry into a new Precautionary Stand-By Arrangement with the IMF).

The Best Chance in a Generation

Published Commentary, March 2017

Every administration and every government, has, whether explicitly expressed or implicitly assumed, a core set of organising principles from which everything else by proximity derives value. For this government (the GOJ), a central organising principle, as articulated by the prime minister, is the focussed pursuit of economic growth and job creation.

Expansion of economic opportunity is a necessary standard around which to organise and prioritise, especially now. After two-and-a-half decades of stagnation in the real average income of Jamaicans, as measured by real per capita GDP, and the stifling of options for social mobility, factors that favour economic expansion must inform priorities, contextualise choices, and frame decision-making.

The first manifestation of such an outlook is the acknowledgment and recognition that the organising principle of shared economic expansion is best served by a disposition towards building on the collective achievements of preceding periods, even while charting new directions.

In this context, given the primordial relationship of necessity, though not sufficiency, between stability and growth, maintenance of the former in pursuit of the latter has been, and remains, a priority. As such, of the choices available, the decision was made to pre-empt potential speculation and uncertainty about the medium term, through an early negotiated arrangement with the IMF, ahead of the expiration of the then-existing facility. This affirmation of the GOJ's commitment to policy credibility and stability, within an enlarged insurance envelope of US$1.6 billion, was framed by reference to the imperative of shared economic expansion.

An earlier version of this article appeared in the *Jamaica Gleaner*, March 2, 2017

Business and consumer confidence are at all-time highs, a cumulative development no doubt. Economic expansion has continued for seven consecutive quarters, the longest period of growth in a decade, and the Statistical Institute of Jamaica (STATIN) reports that the economy added approximately thirty-five thousand jobs between October 2015 and October 2016.[6] Furthermore, absolute employment is at record levels. The size of the employed labour force has never been as large as the levels reached in 2016.

Partnerships have been renewed, deepened, and broadened in a triumvirate of public-private monitoring bodies – the Economic Growth Council (EGC), the Economic Programme Oversight Committee (EPOC), and the Public Sector Transformation Oversight Committee (PSTOC), with differentiated focus – and the social umbrella Partnership for a Prosperous Jamaica. Wide EGC consultation has led to public adoption, by the government, of policies that bring reinvigorated focus to the task of reducing supply-side bottlenecks such as limited access to finance, a densely bureaucratic business environment, and lack of citizen security.

Meaningful progress has been made in the process of rebalancing revenues from direct to indirect sources, enhancing efficiency while providing greater incentive to work. Conditional cash transfers, school feeding, and other forms of poverty relief will receive increases in allocation larger than the cumulative increases of the last five years combined. In addition, policy to improve financial inclusion, by bringing financial services and access to the un-banked, is being implemented.

National Housing Trust (NHT) housing starts, over the next two years, are anticipated to almost triple as compared against any consecutive two-year period since the turn of the century, perhaps longer, adding construction momentum to growth and job creation prospects. Planning and construction of privately and publicly financed business-process outsourcing facilities now exceeds any previous period. As a result, job opportunities should materially scale, given the buoyant tenancy forecasts.

Meanwhile, the engine of growth is being shifted from the public to the private sector. Investments in productive capacity made by the local and regional private sectors are of a pace and nature not seen in decades. The availability of credit support for small- and medium-sized businesses through the Development Bank has increased. Pursuit of growth-enhancing efficiencies in the public sector – through a process that shares services where there are replications, merges entities where duplications exist, and divests where there is potential for greater utilisation – has gathered impetus.

Greater utilisation of assets that galvanises investment, catalyses expansion, and creates jobs has found expression in the completion of the divestments of the Kingston Container Terminal and Caymanas Track Limited; the restart of the divestment process for the Norman Manley International Airport; and the announced sale of the government's remaining shares in the Jamaica Public Service Company to the Jamaican public. It is expected that this policy direction will gather momentum.

Transformative, strategic investments that have a multiplier effect on competitiveness continue. The largest power-plant facility ever constructed in Jamaica is expected to break ground on the South Coast this year. Energy diversification is a reality with last summer's launch of commercial operations for Jamaica's first utility-scale solar plant and the commissioning of the largest private wind farm, along with the October commencement of previously illusive LNG (liquefied natural gas) supply. This trend is set to continue as Jamaica's largest solar plant is expected to be operational next year.

Production at the Alpart bauxite facilities is anticipated to return to levels not attained in nearly ten years with the commencement of mining operations in the short term, while confirmed resort and hospitality investments are expected to add at least seven thousand hotel rooms over the medium term.

Increased demand, higher levels of employment, greater incentives for work, record levels of business and consumer confidence, large investments across multiple sectors, SME (Small and Medium-sized Enterprise) vibrancy, and the gradual removal of supply-side constraints conspire to create the most favourable atmosphere for sustained expansion of the economy in a quarter-century.

Risks remain and vulnerabilities exist. However, all things considered, this represents the best chance in a generation.

Jamaica's Economic Reform and Growth
Interview, May 2017

Since 2013, Jamaica has made significant strides in restoring economic stability: inflation is low, the current account deficit has been cut in half, and business and consumer confidence are high. But economic growth – an important barometer of prosperity – remains low, and unemployment and poverty rates remain high. Public debt, which is on a downward trajectory, is still at 120 per cent of GDP, adding to those challenges.

To support reforms, the government requested a new IMF loan in November 2016 – a Stand-By Arrangement (SBA), which it is treating as an insurance against unforeseen external economic shocks.

In [this interview with *IMF News*], Nigel Clarke, Jamaica's Ambassador of Economic Affairs and Deputy Chair of the Economic Growth Council, talks about his country's priorities and new initiatives, the role of multilateral institutions in supporting economic reforms, and policies underway to raise growth, create jobs, and achieve better social outcomes.

IMF News: What are your main economic priorities as Ambassador of Economic Affairs for Jamaica?

NC: Our key economic priorities are maintaining stability and supporting growth. It is important for Jamaica to continue implementation of the structural reforms required to entrench macroeconomic stability and fiscal sustainability while, at the same time, ensuring that economic expansion is given all possible support.

IMF News: While growth and employment are steadily improving, the unemployment rate is still high – at 12.9 per cent. What more can Jamaica do to support job creation?

NC: As we pursue economic growth, it is crucial that job creation be a part of that effort. In fact, the prime minister, who is also Minister of Economic Growth, deliberately named his ministry the Ministry of Economic Growth and Job Creation, recognising the need to ensure that jobs come with growth.

In Jamaica, the industries currently poised to absorb the most jobs are agriculture and business-process outsourcing. In the agricultural sector, the two key impediments are access to reliable water and a lack of strong linkages with the tourism sector. To ensure that agriculture can grow sustainably, employing more Jamaicans, we will need to invest in water storage and distribution systems, and irrigation. But the government doesn't have the capacity to do this on its own and will need to partner with the private sector.

Business-process outsourcing has an enormous capacity to employ more people. The forecasts indicate that this sector can employ an additional 20,000 to 30,000 people over the medium term. But to make that happen, we'll need to invest in training to ensure that interested persons have the right skills.

IMF News: What are the planned reforms of the public sector? How will they help stimulate growth?

NC: Public sector transformation is about simplification; transparent systems for hiring, promotions, and exits; unification of practises; merging entities with overlapping functions; sharing services where feasible; divesting public entities that can perform better in private hands; and ensuring more efficient and effective service delivery.

A big part of public sector reform is also public pension reform. The new Public Pension Act recently passed by the lower House of Parliament replaces, with a single law, thirty separate pieces of legislation that dealt with the award of public sector pensions. That's simplification. In addition, the retirement age has been raised, accrual rates have been changed, and pension contributions are required from all public sector employees.

Another strategy has been implementing mechanisms that promote greater utilisation of government assets through sales and privatisations, which spurs economic efficiency and momentum.

We believe that the transformation of the public sector will further ignite economic expansion as those additional public resources generated by streamlining are absorbed by the broader economy. As public entities move into private hands, resource allocation becomes more efficient.

IMF News: Tell us about the Economic Growth Council and its role in supporting growth.

NC: The Economic Growth Council was appointed by the Prime Minister to advise the government on a set of initiatives that can help stimulate economic growth. The idea is that the government then agrees on the initiatives that it can support, as well as on specific policy recommendations that fall under each initiative.

The process began with a long consultative period where the Council met with various groups in Jamaica, including labour unions, academia, civil society, private sector groups, ministries, departments and agencies, multilateral institutions, and diplomatic missions. Those consultations helped create consensus on a priority set of initiatives that have been well received by the public and are informing our approach towards economic growth.

Some of these policy recommendations have also been incorporated into the [SBA]. The Council has the mandate to follow up on the implementation of these policy commitments and report to the Jamaican public on a quarterly basis.

IMF News: Jamaica is committed to a primary surplus of 7 per cent of GDP over the medium term. Can this surplus be sustained? How will the government achieve this?

NC: It will be challenging, but the short answer is yes we can. The primary surplus that we have decided to pursue is not arbitrary;

it is designed to achieve a larger objective, which is the reduction in Jamaica's debt to levels that are sustainable. I would remind you that Jamaica achieved a primary surplus target of 7.5 per cent for a few years, though not without difficulty.

Maintaining a primary surplus of 7 per cent requires sustained growth in government revenues and the judicious management of expenditure. These, in turn, will necessitate continued expansion of the economy, increases in tax efficiency, and the prioritisation of critical spending along with the achievement of efficiency gains. We spoke briefly about growth earlier. With respect to increasing tax efficiency, the strategy has been centred on the move from a system of direct to indirect taxation.

The policy shift towards a greater reliance on indirect taxation has the advantage of broadening the tax base, simplifying collection while increasing the assurance of revenue. We've already seen the benefit of this switch. Tax revenues over-performed expectations in the last financial year, which is largely outside of the recent historical experience of Jamaica.

But [...] the 7 per cent primary surplus target is merely an intermediate goal. It is a means to an end. The substantive goal is the achievement of real economic independence, where Jamaica has the policy space to address its opportunities and challenges, without reliance on the multilateral community, in a manner that sustains and even enhances that independence.

IMF News: How will the new budget ensure that the most vulnerable groups are protected?

NC: Our numbers confirm that the absolute dollar increases in allocation for social-protection spending between this budget and the previous one are larger in absolute terms than the collective increases in budgetary allocation for social protection over the past four years combined. So, there has been a substantial increase in the provisions for social protection.

But we won't rest there. It's not only about the level; it's about the targeting and the delivery. Over the medium term, we expect to completely overhaul the system of social protection to ensure that the targeting is improved so that more categories of persons fall within the umbrella.

But, in the short term, the allocation has been increased dramatically, largely through two existing programmes: a school feeding programme that ensures that children who are going to school have adequate nutrition; and monthly stipends to cover the basic needs of the most vulnerable people.

IMF News: What is being done to improve the investment climate?

NC: To improve the investment climate [...] we need to reduce or remove some of the supply-side bottlenecks. The government is making it easier for businesses to procure licenses, comply with regulations, and to obtain permits. The government is also taking steps to ensure that small- and medium-sized entities have access to finance at reasonable rates and terms. Importantly, the government is also engaged in structural, legislative, and operational reforms to improve citizen security and public safety, thereby improving the productivity of labour and capital as well as enhancing general well-being.

IMF News: What roles do international institutions, such as the IMF, have in helping countries implement sound policies?

NC: Multilateral entities like the IMF have an abundance of experience gathered by working with diverse countries over long periods of time. So, they bring to the table the results of the world laboratory – the technical knowledge, skills, and advice – for what has worked and what hasn't worked so well. Multilaterals like the IMF have financial resources, which are always an important part of the mix.

Engagement with the multilateral community can therefore help keep countries on the right path, with these institutions acting as a collective policy bank and policy reservoir.

Given what is usually at stake, performing that role well requires an inclination to listen, to be aware of local nuances, local context, and local history. Although we sometimes disagree, on balance, our experience has been that the multilateral community and entities like the IMF are, ultimately, forces for good in the world.

Time for Economic Independence
Published Commentary, April 2018

In our programme engagements with the IMF in the 1970s, the 1980s, and the 1990s, our exits turned out to be short-lived. We exited those programmes only to return the following decade. This period of engagement, however, stands out as distinct.

Jamaica has gained significantly from the steadfast implementation of fiscal, monetary, and structural policy reforms across two consecutive administrations. It must be our ambition, therefore, that when we conclude with the IMF this time, we avoid reversal and instead manage our affairs in a thoughtful and disciplined way, so that our exit is sustained over time, with no need to return. This must be our goal even as Jamaica, a member institution of the IMF, always retains the option to access the wealth of the IMF's technical advice capacity over time.

As we consider the journey ahead, what ought to guide economic policymaking? After all, a variety of interests with sometimes-conflicting agendas seek to influence policy – sectoral interests, labour interests, capital interests, and even generational interests. This is normal. Policymaking, therefore, requires balancing these interests. But there has to be an overarching vision that frames decision-making.

We cherish the ideals of an open society and a competitive democracy, but as a young country, we do not see these as excluding the possibility of a shared national vision of who we are together and where we are going. Even as we pursue individual dreams, the national project must gain a fresh momentum around the goal of economic independence. Every good institution, whether in government, academia, business, or civil society, has a vision that provides the framework for establishing priorities, making decisions, and contextualising choices.

An earlier version of this article appeared in the *Jamaica Gleaner*, April 13, 2018.

For the Ministry of Finance, in an Andrew Holness administration, the organising principles are the pursuit of economic independence, the expansion of economic opportunity for all, and the protection of the vulnerable. These priorities are sometimes in conflict with each other. Pursuing one can work against the other. As a result, the policy options to support economic expansion have to be balanced by the mandate to secure our economic independence, even as the urgency of economic independence has to be moderated by the need to protect the vulnerable.

Responsibly Managing Our Financial Affairs

What is economic independence? As we all know, independence, in a political sense, is the exercise of sovereignty over a territory by a people who also exercise self-governance over that territory. The people of Jamaica earned political independence in 1962, and since that time, we, the Jamaican people, have chosen our own governments without external consultation. Political independence, however, does not automatically mean economic independence. And an absence of economic independence ultimately threatens political freedoms.

When a country remains economically dependent for a long time, it loses the space to adequately address its social problems (e.g., squatting, crime, low education outcomes), and, over time, these together threaten the ability for free political expression for many people.

The more responsibly we manage our financial affairs, the more we will have the ability to put a computer lab at Pembroke Hall Primary and improve the library at Maverley Primary and Junior High. Achieving economic independence requires, among other things, that successive Jamaican governments manage the affairs of Jamaica so as to maintain a sustainable and credible economic path for future generations. This does not imply that we do not borrow; it means we should be mindful of the long-term sustainability of public debt.

The following Jamaican proverb sums it up: 'A nuh one day monkey waan wife,' which means – our decisions today determine what we can have tomorrow. As has been our experience, high levels of national debt compromise our economic independence, threatening our ability to sustain ourselves without external assistance, leading to an overdependence on creditors, and in the process, we lose flexibility and space in the setting of economic priorities. This has been the primary economic lesson for Jamaica since Independence.

One of the guiding principles in economic policy-setting and decision-making, therefore, will be an evaluation of the degree to which a policy choice enhances or detracts from our pursuit of, and prospects for, economic independence.

Rationalisation and Independence

Jamaica finds itself today with a very large number of public bodies – approximately 190 in total, with 190 CEOs and 190 boards of directors, which have to meet. The complexity this introduces is simply unmanageable for a country of our size and resources. Each of these 190 public bodies produces an annual report that finds its way through ministries, to Cabinet, and eventually to Parliament. Let us be honest with ourselves: the sheer number of public bodies compromises the ability for effective parliamentary oversight, reflection, and review required for good governance.

Furthermore, to the extent that with thought and imagination we could do with fewer public bodies, it means we are absorbing resources in time and money that could be deployed elsewhere making our economy more efficient.

Just for sake of comparison, Singapore, with an economy twenty times the size as Jamaica's, has approximately one-third the number of public bodies or statutory boards. They have sixty-four. In each decade, we have created dozens of additional public bodies. According to data published by the IMF in the first staff review of the Precautionary Stand-By Arrangement: in the 1950s, we created eleven public bodies; in the 1960s, we created twenty-one public bodies; in the 1970s, another thirty-two; in the 1980s, twenty-six; in the 1990s, thirty-one; and after 2000, we created yet another thirty-one public bodies.[7]

There was good reason for all of these at that time. The challenge is that as time passes, technologies, opportunities, threats, and priorities change. New laws are needed, and new institutions required. But it is not economically viable to continuously add public bodies without the certain means to fund them sustainably. That compromises our economic independence.

To be in a position to add public bodies when necessary, we must rationalise where the possibilities exist. To put it another way, to be assured that the Jamaican government can innovate to provide the services required in the future, we have to ensure that we create space by efficient allocation today.

Lessons from Jamaica for Small Countries with Big Debts

Published Commentary, February 2019

Jamaica, a small island better known for its white sand beaches, reggae music, and sprinters, holds some lessons for the world at a time of growing concerns about rising debt and increased political polarisation. It is one of only a few countries that have successfully cut public debt by the equivalent of half its gross domestic product in a short time frame without handouts, debt relief, or bilateral debt support from 'friends.'

My country has a robust, and competitive, liberal democratic tradition. Not only are we ranked sixth in the world for press freedoms, we have been able to continue transforming our economy through competing political administrations and electoral cycles.

This maturity is relatively new. Jamaica has spent thirty-two of its fifty-seven independent years in successive IMF 'adjustment programmes' that were mostly unsuccessful. Over much of this period, policy implementation was poor, with results to match. Tribal politics and policy inconsistency helped drive economic uncertainty.

In the past six years, Jamaica has changed its course, defying expectations and providing an example for other emerging-market countries that find themselves heavily in debt.

How did we get here? A catastrophic banking crisis in the mid-1990s, coupled with the failure of several large state-owned enterprises and lax policy choices, plunged Jamaica into a debt spiral. By March 2009, debt was 124 per cent of GDP and interest costs consumed 50.2 per cent of tax revenues. The global financial crisis compounded an already impossible economic situation. Bauxite earnings evaporated, tourism earnings nose-dived, and 9 per cent of private sector jobs were lost.

In 2010, Jamaica again turned to the IMF. However, despite a local debt exchange, fiscal restraint could not be delivered and the agreement with the fund collapsed.

By 2013, Jamaica's debt had reached approximately 147 per cent of GDP, making Jamaica one of the most indebted countries in the world. Another IMF agreement was brokered. However, there was deep scepticism of Jamaica's commitment to the programme goals, so other international partners would provide only limited financing. Jamaica was virtually on its own.

This was a wake-up call. Our adjustment would have to be funded internally, which meant another local debt exchange, and we had to rewrite our budget to produce a primary surplus of 7.5 per cent of GDP, the highest in the world.

With most of the debt held by investors rather than governments or multilateral organisations, and any outright default deemed unconstitutional, once again, only local debt held by local entities could be restructured. Waning public trust was replaced with anger. Enough was enough. Civil society demanded fidelity to the reform programme in return for enduring new sacrifices.

Government, business, unions, media, academia, and the political opposition embraced the reforms. Building on a pre-existing social partnership foundation, an economic programme oversight committee (EPOC) was formed with all stakeholders – a first in the world – to closely monitor every target and communicate progress to the broader public. What began as an 'IMF programme' became 'Jamaica's programme' with IMF support.

The programme has now spanned two opposing political administrations and delivered strong results. We have had six consecutive years of primary surpluses in excess of 7 per cent. Reforms of tax and monetary policy, the financial sector, and the public sector, across administrations, have restored government finances and entrenched macroeconomic stability.

Debt is projected to fall to 96 per cent of GDP by March 2019 for the first time in nearly two decades. Inflation has been low and stable for four years. Unemployment has fallen from 16 per cent in 2013 to 8.4 per cent in 2018, the lowest ever in Jamaica's history. The incidence of poverty has declined by 19 per cent.

Reallocation of spending has allowed social spending to increase by 50 per cent and for capital expenditure to double. In addition, Central Bank reserves have never been higher.

We are not out of the woods. Economic growth has been lower than expected. While the 2 per cent GDP growth for the first half of 2018–19 is four times the average annual growth for the past twenty years, it is less than the 2.5 per cent originally forecasted. Structural reforms that will sustainably raise growth are required. Reducing the cost of doing business, combating crime and corruption, and boosting domestic industries that add value require more work.

As for debt, we are proud to be on track to achieve our target of 60 per cent of GDP by March 2026.

A bill currently before Parliament will make inflation targeting the cornerstone of monetary policy. We continue to strive for greater public-sector efficiency and improved disaster resilience.

Amid a period of profound uncertainty, Jamaica's experience offers an example to other small countries. Our unprecedented fiscal discipline, maintained through strong bipartisan leadership, citizen ownership of reforms, and close civil society scrutiny of the commitments, is an example worth sharing with others looking to transform their economies.

Jamaica's Matured Economic Policymaking is No Accident

Published Commentary, July 2019

I was amused to read the *Gleaner* editorial of Monday, July 22, 2019, which 'notes with satisfaction' the announcement by the International Monetary Fund (IMF) Resident Representative in Jamaica, Mr Constant Lonkeng, that the IMF will maintain its local office two years after the Precautionary Stand-By Arrangement (PSBA) is concluded in November.

While the *Gleaner* notes this development with 'satisfaction,' a May 27 release from the Ministry of Finance said, 'The Government has agreed with the IMF that the Fund will keep their office and staff in Jamaica, inclusive of the IMF resident representative, for two years after the end of the stand-by arrangement.' Furthermore, I was quoted as saying that this development is 'symbolic of our commitment to maintaining a credible and sustainable fiscal path long into the future that provides the foundation of economic opportunity for the current and future generations.'

By omitting a report on this when I originally announced it – and highlighting the development only after it has been disclosed by the IMF – the *Gleaner* incorrectly suggests Jamaica has no agency in these matters, and the IMF simply made this decision on its own. This could not be further from the truth.

In addition, the *Gleaner* proffers the opinion that Jamaica should enter an IMF staff-monitored programme when the PSBA expires.

As I stated in my very first speech as Minister of Finance, and repeated in my budget presentation, the end of the PSBA will usher in a new era of economic independence where we as a country are empowered to chart our own economic destiny, to set well-thought-out economic priorities, and to provide the framework, rules, and environment that will allow citizens to freely pursue economic activities in a way that promotes growth and well-being for all.

An earlier version of this article appeared in the *Jamaica Gleaner*, July 25, 2019.

Jamaica is well prepared for this period, as the PSBA has been characterised by Jamaican policy initiatives with IMF technical support. This was never the IMF's programme. This has been Jamaica's economic reform programme supported by the IMF.

Within this context, the Jamaican people should therefore know that the Government of Jamaica (GOJ) has been, and will remain, fully committed to our fiscal targets in accordance with our fiscal responsibility law, which anchors Jamaica's economic reform programme.

As for the IMF, once the PSBA expires, it will switch to a surveillance mode under which an annual Article IV Consultation will be conducted and published, as happens with all 189 member countries of the IMF. The IMF is also committed to help build capacity in Jamaica.

Jamaica's matured economic policymaking over the last six years is not an accident. It is deliberate action by policymakers across at least two administrations, combined with the many sacrifices of the Jamaican people and the participation of civil society (including the media), that have afforded us these outcomes.

This was recognised in Wednesday's (July 24, 2019) opinion piece by the IMF's Jamaica Mission Chief, Uma Ramakrishnan, and has been recognised by our other multilateral and bilateral partners in other fora.

However, much work remains to be done. The GOJ has been, and will remain, faithful to continued reforms and policy discipline.

Domestic institutions to safeguard this policy discipline are being put in place, and we will continue to count on the Jamaican people – to whom the GOJ is ultimately accountable – to help us implement these reforms and continue on our path of economic independence.

Monitoring Government Performance Beyond the IMF Programme

Press Release, August 22, 2019

The Government of Jamaica today signed a Memorandum of Understanding (MOU) with the Economic Programme Oversight Committee (EPOC) extending domestic monitoring of Jamaica's economic reform programme beyond the end of the Precautionary Stand-By Arrangement with the IMF.

The Government is far advanced in enacting legislation to modernise the Bank of Jamaica, inclusive of institutionalising independence in the implementation of monetary policy. We are also working to table legislation, by April 2020, to implement a Fiscal Council that will strengthen Jamaica's fiscal responsibility framework and be an independent arbiter of Jamaica's fiscal rules. Today we commit to empowering EPOC to continue in a monitoring role until our Central Bank and Fiscal Council policy commitments are operationalised.

Jamaica is set to successfully complete the Precautionary Stand-By Arrangement with the IMF in November 2019, having brought the prior Extended Fund Facility arrangement with the IMF to a successful early termination in November 2016. This will conclude approximately six and a half years of successful programme engagement with the IMF.

Over this period Jamaica's debt has been significantly reduced, macroeconomic stability has become entrenched, economic growth has returned, and there has been substantial growth in employment.

Given where we are coming from, the macroeconomic gains that Jamaica has enjoyed over these six and a half years are a Jamaican success story, recognised around the world. This success is wholly attributable to the effort and sacrifice of the Jamaican people, and we owe it to the Jamaican people to preserve and build on these gains even as we work to address the other important challenges.

This MOU extension with EPOC follows on the government's agreement with the IMF to keep its office in Jamaica for two years following the end of the Precautionary Stand-By Arrangement in November. These decisions are a demonstration of our commitment to maintaining a credible and sustainable macroeconomic path, including a fiscal trajectory that is consistent with our fiscal responsibility law, long into the future that provides the foundation of economic opportunity for the current and future generations.

Moving in the Right Direction
Budget Speech Excerpt, March 2020

Mr Speaker, Jamaica is among a small handful of countries in the world that can proudly boast of having a continuous, unbroken, liberal democratic tradition for more than seventy-five years – eighteen pre-Independence and fifty-seven post-Independence. Importantly, our democracy is not simply 'ballot box democracy.' Many countries in the world practise an illiberal form of democracy, which only works on election day. Our democracy is deep, and it is enshrined in liberal traditions and institutions (To be clear, I am using the word liberal in the sense of classical liberalism as opposed to liberal in the modern American political context).

Freedom of the press in Jamaica has ranked in the top ten in the world for decades. Think about that, Mr Speaker. Those in this chamber are acutely aware of how free the press is in Jamaica.

We enjoy genuine separation of powers, with different and co-equal branches of government that are independent of each other: the legislature, the executive, and the judiciary. And we have enjoyed this separation for more than seventy-five years.

We operate under the rule of law, and we are an open society where the rights of private property are enshrined, and citizens enjoy protection of their human rights, their civil rights, and their political freedoms. Freedom of speech is deeply embedded in our way of life. A few years ago, we enshrined these rights by way of an amendment that inserted the Charter of Rights and Freedoms into the Constitution.

Mr Speaker, for the past seventy-five years, Jamaica has enjoyed universal adult suffrage where every adult has had the right to vote. This is a longer period than, for example, Australia, Canada, Chile, Portugal, South Korea, South Africa, and many other far wealthier nations than ours, for whom segments of their populations have been

---

Adapted from the opening budget presentation delivered in Parliament March 10, 2020.

voting in general elections for a far shorter period. The world knows of few examples, if any, of countries that have climbed the ladder of economic success, all the way from developing to developed, with a purely liberal democratic model. Virtually all developed and advanced countries today experienced institutional illiberalism of one form or another. Virtually all, on their path to advanced status, have excluded or even subjugated segments of their populations, in some cases restricting freedom itself. Others, on the path to economic success, have had periods characterised by restrictions on political and/or civil rights, restriction on freedom of the press, freedom of speech, and other freedoms.

Jamaica is firmly and immutably entrenched on the path of freedom, rooted in seventy-five years of liberal democratic thinking and culture. The point is not to question that. The point, is that we need to be aware of the fact that we are attempting to do that which has not yet been done – to grow and develop as a nation, from developing to developed, within a liberal democratic model, a path for which no (or little) precedent of success exists. Our understanding of ourselves would be a lot healthier, Mr Speaker, and our interactions more productive, if we operated with consciousness of this simple fact. Instead of engaging in endless self-flagellation as a people, we would exude greater depth of pride, fully cognizant of the greatness of our ambition as a people even as we strive to implement and improve.

Liberal democracy, as you will no doubt agree, even if it requires some reflection, is an expensive form of government. The private and public institutions that provide, express, safeguard, and guarantee our political and economic freedoms require significant human and financial resources to operate effectively.

As a matter of historical fact, for many advanced countries, their political model evolved in step with their economic capacity to sustain that model. They became more and more liberal, more and more democratic, more and more free as they grew in wealth as nations.

It is the audacious disposition and eternal optimism of the Jamaican spirit that explains our path, which differs. Our founders, who agitated for universal adult suffrage seventy-five years ago and in whose footsteps we walk, were unequivocal that Jamaica views freedom, in all its forms, as a value in itself and essential for all other values to flourish.

It is for this reason that, for our model to be sustained over generations, it must be evident, through experience, that our political and liberal traditions consistently deliver – and deliver handsomely – for the Jamaican people.

As I said earlier, political freedom is of supreme value by itself. However, people cannot eat 'political freedom.' It is therefore necessary that the dividends of our political freedoms provide the capital with which our economic prosperity and our economic independence are built. Our political freedoms must translate into economic freedom and material benefit, improved well-being, and improved public service for all. Political competition, which is central to our liberal democratic model, must, ultimately, be in service of the sustainable, material progress of our people.

However, until recently, our economic history over much of the last fifty years has not delivered that. It has largely been characterised by systemic economic instability, with cycles of economic progress followed by economic reversal. As a result, the material condition of our people stagnated. Per capita GDP, one measure of material attainment, remained constant for two decades while many of our neighbours surged ahead.

To deliver for the people of Jamaica requires us to consistently move forward. The steps may be large at times and other times small. But they must always move us in the right direction.

In recent times, Jamaica has made significant progress, but vulnerabilities exist and much remains to be done. We still have a long way to go. For our model to be sustained, the people must know, from their own experiences, that we are committed to moving forward in the right direction, and, moreover, that as we make progress, they, too, are sharing in the gains. This is of critical importance. These gains, are best shared with all by investing in public services, improving conditions for business and employment to flourish, strengthening the social safety net, and preserving and increasing individual spending power.

This reflection is always necessary. We must be deliberate and strategic in what we do, ever conscious of the context in which we operate, because to paraphrase Marcus Garvey, 'Chance has never satisfied the hope of a suffering people.'[8]

Today, Mr Speaker, I will present a budget that is strategically focussed on moving forward, in the right direction, consistently, and where the fruits of our collective effort are shared. A budget, Mr Speaker, that demonstrates that our political model is working, and that our political freedoms and our liberal democratic traditions are ultimately in service of the sustainable increase in the material well-being of the Jamaican people.

Jamaica Requests Access to IMF's Rapid Financing Instrument

Press Statement, April 16, 2020

Last year Jamaica and the IMF came to an agreement for the IMF to continue to maintain an office in Kingston for two years. This has facilitated a close and open working relationship with frequent exchange of views and information. In particular, I have been in regular communication with the Fund over the past few months as the COVID-19 pandemic has grown in intensity.

Yesterday, on behalf of the Government of Jamaica, and in my capacity of Minister of Finance and the Public Service, I requested access to the IMF's Rapid Financing Instrument.

The Rapid Financing Instrument (RFI) provides rapid financing to IMF member countries with balance of payment needs but without the requirement of having a full-fledged IMF programme, ongoing reviews, and conditionality.

Last week, on April 6, the IMF substantially increased the amounts that member countries could access under the RFI window.

Jamaica enjoys a reasonable stock of foreign reserves, and we have contingency financing options that arise from (a) the availability of cash resources programmed for accelerated debt repayment, (b) the availability of domestic sources of financing, and (c) untapped capacity available from other multilateral institutions such as the Caribbean Development Bank, the Inter-American Development Bank, and the World Bank, including by redirecting existing projects.

Despite these mitigating factors, which provide the ability for Jamaica to absorb economic shocks, the duration of the 'global lockdown' is highly uncertain. The open-ended nature of the pandemic and its economic spillovers therefore pose intolerable balance-of-payments risks to Jamaica that threaten the economic gains of our seven-year reform effort.

For these reasons we believe it is prudent to access and have these resources available. The RFI, as the name suggests, should result in a quick disbursement, in a matter of weeks.

In the interest of transparency around our RFI request, I have taken the decision to release the letter to the IMF Managing Director now, at the time of the request.

Jamaica, like many other countries around the world, will experience a sharp decline in economic activity as a result of the COVID-19 pandemic. However, we have a number of options, including the RFI, which will assist Jamaica to endure this period, and emerge stronger, while preserving the macroeconomic stability that all Jamaicans have worked and sacrificed to achieve.

An Engagement of Choice: Entering New Agreements with the IMF

Public Statement, December 2022

Jamaica is experiencing a robust economic recovery from the COVID-19 pandemic. After growth of 8.2 per cent last fiscal year and a projection of 4.5 per cent for this fiscal year, economic output is expected to attain pre-COVID levels by 2023. Unemployment is lower today than it was prior to the pandemic. And our debt-to-GDP ratio is also lower than prior to the pandemic. With the possible exception of Guyana no other country in this hemisphere can claim a similar experience.

Despite this encouraging recovery, however, global uncertainties loom on multiple fronts. The war in Ukraine continues to have a global impact with no sign of ending. Europe is forecasted to experience an economic recession next year, and some analysts say that there is an appreciable risk that the United States may also experience an economic recession. In addition, global inflationary pressures are likely to remain for some time. Furthermore, international financial conditions are tightening as central banks around the world raise interests to battle inflation.

From our historical experience we know that building resilience and creating policy buffers in advance are important strategies for successful navigation of, and recovery from, economic shocks should they materialise.

Looking across the horizon, therefore, it is important that we act, in advance, and ahead of time in always seeking to increase fiscal space, broaden our options, and make Jamaica stronger.

Over the next two fiscal years – in 2023–24 and 2024–25 – Jamaica has over US$1 billion of external debt maturing that needs to be refinanced at what could possibly be interest rates that are higher than today.

This statement, adapted for print, was delivered by video uploaded to Twitter/X on December 15, 2022.

Earlier this year, the International Monetary Fund (IMF) launched a new product, the Resilience and Sustainability Facility (RSF) that would allow Jamaica to access up to US$763 million at an interest rate of approximately 3.8 per cent and a repayment period of twenty years, with no principal repayment for the first ten years.

This is a compelling instrument that, if we access, would not only support our climate resilience building strategy but also potentially save Jamaica nearly US$35 million per year over twenty years in interest costs as against accessing financing in capital markets, using our current average blended-market borrowing costs as a comparison, even before we consider that market interest rates may rise further. This combination of building resilience while also achieving fiscal savings would come at a critical time. It would allow us to invest in job-creating and resilient infrastructure, enhance our transition to renewable energy, reducing our energy vulnerability even as we continue to prioritise human capital development. Jamaica must take advantage of this opportunity.

At the same time, though we have over US$4.3 billion of gross foreign exchange reserves, in order to ensure that we are not overly exposed to external developments that could derail annual foreign exchange inflows, we will access the Precautionary Liquidity Line (PLL) where approximately US$1 billion would become available to us should we need it.

The PLL is an instrument of the IMF for countries with strong economic fundamentals, and Jamaica's qualification for this credit line is a signal of our economic strength and stability.

These arrangements will not interfere with our already planned programmes and activities. It is and will be business as usual, with the additional ability to access financing if the global outlook worsens.

My fellow Jamaicans, we are in a different era of our economic development, one where we anticipate events and provide for them. We have put in place a natural-disaster financing strategy, capitalised a national disaster fund, and launched the world's first catastrophe bond independently sponsored by a small country. These financing arrangements are designed to protect us from natural disaster shock.

Similarly, today we reached a Staff Level Agreement with the IMF for the Resilience and Sustainability Facility and a Precautionary

Liquidity Line to ensure that our development can proceed and continue, even in the event of possible external shock.

This is an engagement of choice. These are not arrangements that we *have* to make but rather financings we are *choosing* to take advantage of to keep us strong, build our economic and climate resilience, create buffers, expand our fiscal space, broaden our options, and help us prepare for any adverse external developments that may arise.

My fellow Jamaicans, with God's continued guidance we are taking charge of our economic future, and even in time of great economic recovery, expansion, and job creation, we are making preparations for possible shocks, just as strong and empowered countries do.

First International Issue of
a Local Currency Bond

Budget Speech Excerpt, March 2024

Madam Speaker, all countries need to borrow internationally to finance their operations.

However, when countries like Germany or Japan borrow, they don't need to borrow in US dollars or in any currency other than their own. Germany borrows internationally in Euros and Japan borrows internationally in Japanese Yen. This means that Germany and Japan have little or no foreign exchange exposure on their international debt. In other words, foreign exchange risk is effectively eliminated. This helps make them economically stronger and more resilient.

And international investors lending to Germany and Japan are content lending in Euros and Yen because they have trust in the stability of the economic environment in Germany and Japan – as well as in their institutional mechanisms, such as independent central banks that guarantee price stability.

For a developing country like Jamaica, the picture is quite different.

Developing countries also need to borrow internationally – there are not enough resources domestically to finance government without crowding out the private sector. Countries also need to diversify sources of funding beyond domestic so as not to exacerbate sovereign-financial vulnerabilities. But when developing countries choose to borrow internationally, they are compelled to do so in currencies other than their own. International investors want the comfort and safety of the US dollar or a similarly strong developed-world currency when lending to developing countries.

This has the effect of adding a source of risk to the economies of developing countries, because borrowing internationally in a

---

Adapted from the opening budget presentation delivered in Parliament March 12, 2024.

foreign currency like the US dollar introduces foreign exchange risk vulnerability.

In 2019, while advocating for central bank independence, inclusive of inflation targeting, I publicly stated that, with the implementation of this policy, Jamaica would launch its first local-currency bond internationally within five years. The *Gleaner* captured my commitment as follows: 'Clarke to take Jamaica to the world stage; Aims to borrow from the international markets in JMD within five years.'

I am particularly pleased that in November 2023, prior to the expiry date of that commitment, the Government of Jamaica (GOJ) issued its first ever Jamaican-dollar denominated debt instrument on international capital markets.

Promise made, promise kept.

That is, Madam Speaker, international investors from London, Zurich, Frankfurt, New York, Boston, and Los Angeles took local Jamaican-dollar exposure in lending to the Jamaican Government in an amount equivalent to $46.6 billion Jamaican dollars. International bond investors investing in a Jamaican-dollar-linked bond, and accepting Jamaican-dollar currency risk, would have been unimaginable five years ago. This is an extremely significant transaction that opens new frontiers for Jamaica.

The development represents a substantial policy dividend emanating from: Jamaica's substantially improved macroeconomic fundamentals; institutionalisation of fiscal responsibility through fiscal rules and an independent fiscal commission; deepening of monetary policy transparency; and the pursuit of low, stable, and predictable inflation as the objective of monetary policy through the law that established central bank independence. Through institutional reform, investors have the confidence that price stability and fiscal and external sustainability will be maintained long into the future.

The GOJ's new ability to tap international investors for local-currency-linked debt broadens, deepens, and diversifies the GOJ's funding sources while providing the opportunity, over time, of altering the currency mix of the national debt. This makes Jamaica more robust.

In addition, the more our national debt is denominated in, or linked to, Jamaican dollars the stronger and more resilient Jamaica will be. This transaction, therefore, enhances Jamaica's resilience and paves the way for similar international issues in the future.

Today, Jamaica's foreign debt is 62 per cent of our overall debt. We aim to improve Jamaica's resilience and economic strength by reducing this proportion to below 50 per cent within a reasonable time frame. We are proud of our commitment and successful efforts to launch a historic Jamaican-currency-linked international bond, and to reduce Jamaica's foreign-currency-denominated debt in the best interest of the people of Jamaica.

First Securitisation Transaction in International Capital Markets

Commentary, October 2024

The Norman Manley International Airport (NMIA) serves Jamaica's capital city and many of the parishes to the south and east of the island. Post 2013, as part of a set of reforms geared at optimising the use of capital, the Government of Jamaica (GOJ) decided to privatise the operations of NMIA using the modality of a public-private partnership. This had the benefit of, among other things, transferring the obligation for the required multi-billion (Jamaican dollars) capital expansion to the private operator.

Five entities were shortlisted and participated in the Public-Private Partnership (PPP) process. However, at 4:00 p.m. on December 31, 2015, when the bidding period closed, the GOJ received no bids.

This was a problem.

Upon change of government, the incoming administration was warned of the previous failure but dared to try again with the benefit of lessons learned from the prior effort. Feedback was solicited from the five shortlisted entities who participated in the earlier process but declined to bid. One of the main dissuasive factors from their perspective was the requirement of a concession fee, which consisted of two elements: an upfront payment, as well as a percentage of gross revenues over the life of the concession agreement.

The second privatisation attempt factored in this feedback. The GOJ expressed confidence in the future of the airport, the economy, and the country by eliminating the requirement for a hefty upfront payment. The new PPP bid process would require a concession fee that consisted of a percentage of gross revenues of the airport, but only a de minimis amount upfront. In our minds this was not a big concession to make. Though there was no precedent, we felt confident that we could securitise the future cash-flows and receive

---

Adapted from responses to questions in Parliament on October 8, 2024, and a presentation to Parliament on October 15, 2024.

an upfront payment by other means, which could then be used to help finance infrastructure development, and this was our intent.

At the end of the new bid period, on July 20, 2018, the GOJ received three high-quality bids, which included firms that had participated but declined to bid in the 2015 process. Jamaica granted the rights to operate NMIA for twenty-five years to the winning bidder, who took effective operating control of NMIA in October of 2019. Of course, the COVID-19 pandemic interrupted the GOJ's and the operator's plans considerably, and this led to an amendment of key terms in the concession agreement. By the end of 2023, however, NMIA passenger traffic volumes had recovered to 2018–19 levels. In 2024, therefore, the GOJ was able to embark on a transaction to raise revenue by securitising the variable concession-fee income of 52.33 per cent of the airport's revenues, paid over by the NMIA concessionaire.

A Cayman Islands special-purpose vehicle (SPV) known as Kingston Airport Revenue Finance Ltd (KingAir) was established with its shares held in trust by a global law firm specialising in these kinds of transactions. By construction, KingAir's actions are limited to the issuing of the debt (discussed below) and the exchange of these proceeds with the GOJ in return for the GOJ's rights to 52.33 per cent of the revenue generated by the Norman Manley International Airport.

The airport is Jamaica's long-term strategic asset, and NMIA's passenger traffic is predominantly diaspora related, complemented by business travellers to the capital city. NMIA's revenues are primarily in US dollars, derived from various fees charged to airlines, and this income is supplemented by smaller amounts of parking, rental, and other Jamaican-dollar income.

After an investor road show on both sides of the Atlantic, the Ministry of Finance and the Public Service proudly issued a press release on October 7, 2024, which included the following details:

> The [KingAir] bond issuance was highly successful, with applications totalling US$2.3 billion, representing an oversubscription of more than five times the US$440 million initially sought. The offer was upsized to US$480 million in response to this robust demand. The notes will bear a fixed

coupon of 6.75 per cent for twelve years and are rated BB and Ba1 by Standard & Poor's Global Ratings and Moody's Rating Agency respectively, one notch above each agency's sovereign rating for Jamaica. Additionally, the notes are the sole obligation of the issuer, Kingston Airport Revenue Finance Ltd, and there is no recourse to the Government of Jamaica. In other words, the notes do not represent debt obligations of the Government of Jamaica or any of its agencies.

Kingston Airport Revenue Finance Ltd will also annually distribute to the Government of Jamaica any surplus it achieves above established benchmarks. Once the bond is repaid, the full amount of the [53.22 per cent of the airport's revenue] will return to the Government of Jamaica.

The Government of Jamaica is pleased with the appetite demonstrated by the investor community in investing in Jamaican assets. The GOJ looks forward to now being able to accelerate critical investments in domestic infrastructure, while at the same time reducing the national debt burden – even in the context of the adverse travel advisory and hurricane-induced growth shock and the anticipated flat growth this year – for the benefit of all Jamaicans.

Beyond the details of the press release, it is significant that the KingAir bond offer was taken up by asset managers, insurance companies, private banks, and other investors in the United States, Europe, Asia, and Latin America, and the transaction brought new international investors to Jamaica. (Investors were compensated for taking on exposure to airport credit risk.)

This was ground-breaking for Jamaica – the first registered GOJ-sponsored securitisation transaction in international capital markets. Through this transaction, the GOJ monetised inflows that allowed Jamaica to, among other things, finance infrastructure development and reduce sovereign debt.

The transaction also represented an extremely efficient use of government revenues. At the time of the transaction, the GOJ's share of revenues from NMIA approximated US$40 million per year, so the GOJ effectively received US$12 of capital for every US$1 of revenue. By way of comparison, the GOJ's sovereign borrowings are approximately two times the GOJ's revenue. Through a structured transaction where these airport revenues were transferred to an SPV, with capped expenses of US$250 thousand per year, and where the SPV's revenues are therefore essentially equivalent to the SPV's earnings before interest, the GOJ was able to raise substantially more capital than would otherwise have been possible.

To be clear, prior to the privatisation of NMIA by way of PPP, the free cash flows generated by the airport that would have been available to the GOJ were substantially less than what became available post-PPP and post-COVID-19. For instance, in the 2018–19 fiscal year, the last full year under the GOJ's operational control, NMIA made a net profit of US$10 million and distributed US$0.5 million to the GOJ's coffers. As such, the PPP transaction represented a securitisation of revenue flows that were, for all practical purposes, new to the GOJ.

Of course, the GOJ has given up those annual flows until the SPV's bond is repaid. This trade-off of non-debt capital up front for a stream of flows in the future made sense because of the efficiency achieved (that is, obtaining twelve times the initial annual flow), and because of the present value of capital in the context of ongoing fiscal consolidation.

Sustaining fiscal consolidation over the long term requires tangible demonstration that, all things considered, the policy ultimately works in the people's interest. This means that we must leverage the dividends of the stability that consolidation brings and use these dividends to pursue meaningful quality of life improvements. In this regard, time is precious.

The NMIA securitisation transaction allowed the GOJ to bring the gains of stability forward. Rather than pursue needed infrastructure developments annually over the twelve-year life of the bond, we now have the opportunity to bring those flows from the future into the present time, without incurring sovereign debt – on the contrary, while reducing debt – and using proceeds for infrastructure development today.

For example, the condition of secondary roads has consistently ranked among the top three complaints of the Jamaican people. In response, the GOJ has embarked on a 'Shared Prosperity through Accelerated Improvement to our Road Network' programme (known by its acronym, SPARK). The planned investment for this two-year road improvement programme is, on an annualised basis, four to five times larger than the normal allocation to secondary roads.

The securitisation transaction makes **SPARK** and other infrastructure programmes possible, even in the context of Hurricane Beryl and the shocks (both growth and fiscal) that it delivered, while also staying on track to achieve a reduction in the debt-to-GDP ratio in the 2024–25 fiscal year, from 73 per cent to a projected 68 per cent or lower, by March 2025.

We are therefore harnessing the dividends of economic stability to deliver economic resilience, develop the country, and further entrench stability.

PART THREE

STABILITY

Iwas born in 1971 and have spent most of my life in Jamaica. For most of my lifetime, the Jamaican economy has been characterised by recurring episodes of sky-high interest rates, steep currency devaluations, runaway prices, double-digit-high unemployment, rising public debt, and excessive economic volatility accompanied by frequent declines in the nation's GDP. As a consequence of such instability, lives have been destroyed, opportunities have been squashed, and much human potential has remained unrealised.

On a national level, macro-instability has, in the past, compromised the economic sovereignty that is the goal and prime motivation for intentional policymaking, as the previous readings have shown. Macro-instability is therefore inconsistent with the Jamaican identity. The economically unstable country becomes overly dependent on the outside world for financial support and, for survival, locks itself into unfavourable economic and commercial arrangements.

Myopic policymaking with expectations of short-term gains – whether electoral victory or addressing some immediate problem – often creates long-term economic problems that later become harder to uproot. Thus, unsustainable policy choices ultimately lead to economic instability. Fiscal policy is unsustainable if the fiscal resources available for essential priorities are repeatedly applied towards non-productive spending, with little accountability or transparency, resulting in the dwindling of such resources.

Monetary policy is unsustainable if its pursuit leads to a depletion of foreign exchange reserves and a weakening of the country's external position, or if it severely compromises the viability of the financial sector.

The Jamaican experience illustrates these truths. However, if an entire generation is unacquainted with, and has never experienced, the benefits of sustainable policy choices, they are less likely to make the decisions required to achieve lasting stability. They will likely undervalue the opportunity costs associated with short-term views.

Both revenue and expenditure policy have the capacity to contribute to fiscal unsustainability. Within expenditure policy, specific sectoral policies can have unsustainable features if sectoral distortions are supported or aggravated. Similarly, revenue policy can be unsustainable if measures introduced create gaps in available resources that, if they persist, can only be financed by borrowing more and more, increasing debt, or through misuse or abuse of fiscal savings.

To be clear, instability can arise from mismanagement of public policy across many sectors – be it monetary, fiscal, the financial sector, or the energy sector – as well as from lack of planning for climate change and natural disasters. State-owned enterprise losses can also contribute to economic instability. Moreover, public policy mismanagement across sectors can quickly compound the problem given interdependencies.

Unsustainable policies can, of course, be corrected. Often, however, the political consequences of correction are such that governments choose to double down rather than address the source of the unsustainability through disciplined action. That is, the government responds to the depletion of resources created by unsustainable choices by printing money, accumulating debt, or raiding a source of national treasure. These strategies, if pursued long enough, create imbalances that compound instability. Eventually, sometimes with only a small economic shock, a crisis erupts.

The Cost of Instability, a Tragic Example

I want to illustrate the last point above – about raiding a source of national treasure – by sharing the story of our nation's Capital Development Fund (CDF). This fund was set up in 1973 to receive bauxite-levy inflows, sourced from the considerable proceeds of the commercial exploitation of Jamaica's bauxite, a non-renewable natural resource. The bauxite levy is a tax on all 'bauxite or laterite extracted or won in Jamaica on or after the 1st January, 1974.'[1] In the first decade of the bauxite levy, annual inflows into the Capital Development Fund regularly represented between 25 per cent and 35 per cent of tax revenues or between 4 per cent and 5 per cent of GDP.[2] Furthermore, between fiscal years 1974–75 and 2015–16, more than US$2.5 billion in bauxite levy was paid over by bauxite/alumina companies. Yet, by March 2016, only US$10 million remained in the CDF.[3]

How could this have happened? Juxtapose this depletion of national wealth against the achievement of other countries with natural-resource wealth – for example the hydrocarbon-rich Saudis, Emirates, and Norwegians, who have built substantial sovereign wealth funds from the accumulation of similar proceeds – and Jamaicans of current and future generations will ask, *What happened to our funds?* The considerable capital generated by the bauxite levy ought to have belonged to successive generations of Jamaicans in perpetuity through steady accumulation and prudent investments. Each generation could then consume the income derived from this national wealth, in their time, without compromising the accumulated capital. From today's vantage point it seems clear that it is profoundly unwise for the proceeds of *non-renewable* natural resources to be virtually consumed by, at most, two generations, as occurred in Jamaica.

When established, many Jamaicans saw the CDF as representing a major success against the 'international, exploitative, capitalist system.' With the benefit of hindsight, the irony is chilling. To the Jamaican born today, it would seem as if successive governments exploited future generations of Jamaicans by continuously raiding the CDF, until it was virtually emptied. What happened? In a few words: unsustainable policy choices and macro-economic instability.

The truth is that the relative evaporation of bauxite levy proceeds between the years of 1974 and 2016 represents one of the starkest examples of the staggering costs of Jamaica's history with macroeconomic instability arising from well intentioned, but unsustainable policy decisions, and repeated attempts to plug the financing or resource gaps they caused.[4]

Over most of the forty-two years, between the first budgetary drawdown from the CDF in 1974–75 and the last to date, in budget year 2015–16, Jamaica experienced chronic, debilitating macroeconomic instability. This fact is central to understanding the disastrous dissipation of this national treasure.

Sadly for Jamaica, each decade since the 1970s has been punctuated by one or more fiscal, monetary, inflation, natural-disaster, and/or financial-sector crises. Across the forty-two-year span between first and last CDF drawdowns to date: Jamaica's debt-to-GDP ratio was above 100 per cent for twenty-eight of those years; Jamaica had negative net international reserves in its central bank every year between 1976 and 1993,[5] and grossly insufficient foreign exchange reserves for the remaining years, some of it wasted on misguided exchange-rate policies that were incompatible with Jamaica's fiscal profile; inflation occupied double-digit territory for twenty-five of those years; the unemployment rate was in the double-digit realm for forty-one of those years, and exceeded 20 per cent for every year between 1973 and 1987 and exceeded 15 per cent for every year between 1988 and 2002;[6] and Jamaica endured one of most devastating financial-sector crises in the 1990s – one that cost 40 per cent of GDP and led to a debt mountain that took thirty years to unwind.

In addition to man-made catastrophes, Hurricane Gilbert devasted Jamaica in 1988, with damage estimated at 26 per cent of GDP, while Hurricanes Ivan in 2004 and Dean in 2007, among others, inflicted damage estimated at 5.7 per cent and 2.7 per cent of GDP respectively.[7] These adversely affected public finances.

The fossils of Jamaica's multi-generational instability are imprinted in the annual national budgets over the period. As a response to this instability – and to the fiscal unsustainability, which was both cause and effect – successive Jamaican governments turned to the CDF as a source of budgetary revenues (above and beyond the modest annual funding that goes directly to the Jamaica Bauxite Institute, bypassing the national coffers, and that is provided for in the legislation that established the CDF). In fact, over the period 1974–75 to 2015–16, for every year except one, the GOJ used that year's bauxite levy, and/or withdrew from the accumulated balance in the CDF, to finance that year's budgetary expenditure.[8]

Economic shocks also compound macroeconomic instability and therefore prolong recovery. The shocks of the 1970s – including the oil-price shocks, domestic social turmoil, and supply shocks

– deepened a fiscal crisis born of unsustainable policies. Within the first decade of the bauxite levy (1974–75 to 1983–84), the government transferred an equivalent of over US$1 billion of bauxite levy proceeds, or 34 per cent of 1984 GDP, to support budgetary revenues. Even with that influx of resources, however, the fiscal deficit over that same ten-year period still averaged a savagely unsustainable level of 12.4 per cent of GDP per annum. And the GOJ continued to use the CDF as a source of budgetary revenues throughout the remainder of the 1980s in an aggregate amount that exceeded US$350 million. Even with this influx of resources, the fiscal deficit, though improved, averaged a large 4.1 per cent of GDP.

For the decade after Jamaica's banking crisis (1995–96 to 2004–05), an equivalent of over US$550 million flowed from the CDF into the national budget as revenue. Even after this extraordinary support, the GOJ averaged a substantial fiscal deficit over this period of 4.7 per cent of GDP per year. By 2004–05, Jamaica's interest bill reached approximately 17 per cent of GDP, taking away precious resources from productive spending simply to pay for the borrowed money.

And for the three-year period that spanned the Global Financial Crisis (between 2007 and 2010), the equivalent of over US$120 million in bauxite-levy proceeds were redirected from the CDF to the GOJ's budgetary coffers to supplement revenues and support expenditures. After this support, however, the GOJ still registered untenable fiscal deficits averaging 7.4 per cent of GDP per annum. By 2011, Jamaica's debt-to-GDP ratio breached 140 per cent.

These examples highlight the trend. From the 1970s, and for each decade that followed, the GOJ racked up gaping budget deficits, even after incorporating proceeds from the transfer of the annual bauxite levy to budgetary coffers and/or from the raiding of the CDF. This depletion of Jamaica's bauxite-levy resources is just one glaring symptom of Jamaica's multi-decade struggle with unsustainable policy choices and macroeconomic instability.

Imagine, for a moment, an alternate economic history. Had the GOJ instead intentionally pursued sustainable policy choices that entrenched macroeconomic stability – which would itself have provided the policy flexibility required to respond in times of crisis – and had the GOJ invested the stream of bauxite-levy income and compounded these inflows at 5 per cent per annum over the forty-two-year period 1974–75 to 2015–16, instead of raiding the bauxite-levy flows, the CDF would have appreciated to approximately US$11 billion in value by March 2016 or 80 per cent of 2016 GDP.

Notwithstanding the enormous progress made in restoring economic stability over the last decade and a half, Jamaica's contemporary economic prospects would have been materially better had we optimised on our earlier opportunities. It is sad to contemplate the difference between a CDF valued at, or close to, US$11 billion versus our actual valuation of US$10 million, as at March 2016 – a 1,100-fold differential.

Having paid such a steep price in terms of lost opportunity, we are compelled to learn from this experience. Macroeconomic instability isn't free. It extracts a massive cost on society, destroying national wealth and creating intergenerational inequities and inequalities. Unsustainable policies eat through all available resources until there are no more. Unsustainable policies catalyse economic instability, while sustainable policy choices form the guardrails of economic stability.

Institutionalising Stability

Economic stability – the ability of the macroeconomy to weather economic shocks without excessive fluctuations and system-wide failures – is necessary to the goal of improving the well-being of the Jamaican population in good times and bad. The fact that stability is insufficient for achieving this aim is not an argument against it. Economic stability preserves intergenerational equity, while economic instability results in particular generations gobbling up and using more than their fair share of national resources. Economic stability is therefore so vital that it cannot be left to individuals alone. We need laws, but laws too are inadequate; we require institutions that become the guardians of stability long into the future.

Across my years as Minister of Finance and the Public Service, I have been an advocate of the pursuit and maintenance of macroeconomic stability and the building of institutions, and the following pages comprise a representation of some of this advocacy. I have tried to communicate to the Jamaican people the importance of sound policy and the development of strong institutions that preserve the future of Jamaica.

The articles and excerpts presented in this section follow a system of organisation designed to emphasise the preconditions of economic stability: price stability, in the form of low and predictable inflation; fiscal stability, including debt sustainability; external stability through the adequacy of foreign-exchange reserves; and financial-sector stability. These areas of policy are essential for macroeconomic stability and constitute the foundation upon which other reforms to generate faster growth should be pursued.

The articles included in 'Price Stability' were written as Jamaica transitioned to inflation targeting and as, with bipartisan support, we strengthened the governance of a newly independent central bank, whose mandate is to pursue low and stable inflation. Additionally, central bank directors are now appointed for ten-year terms on a staggered basis, providing continuity across administrations.

'Fiscal Responsibility' makes the case for an independent fiscal institution and advances the cause of fiscal and debt sustainability. Jamaica first instituted fiscal rules in 2010. These were considerably strengthened in 2014 and amended again in 2020 to legislate the emergence of the Fiscal Commission. The rules were amended yet again in 2024 to further institutionalise disaster-risk financing by mandating annual savings towards this purpose.

Finally, 'Financial Sector Stability' briefly catalogues Jamaica's experience with 'grey listing' by the Financial Action Task Force and the measures taken to graduate from that designation and highlights the importance of appropriate regulation in the financial sector to preserve our nation's overall and hard-won economic stability.

Price Stability and Central Bank Independence

Modernisation and Independence of the Bank of Jamaica
Policy Address, July 2018

She was a professional who started at the bottom. She didn't have a car for many years, took two buses to get to work – on time, I might add – put in a solid day's work to head home. Balancing work with children was tough, not to mention affording school fees and books. But she worked hard and progressed at the Ministry, retiring in a senior administrative position. Her boss held a wonderful send-off for her. She had made it.

Her problem, however, was that she retired in March 1993. Inflation in those days was sky high, 40 per cent per annum. Within five years, her pension was worth one third of its value; by March 2003, that is within ten years, it was less than one fifth of its original value. She died in 2007, dead broke.

There are many such stories: nurses, police officers, teachers, ancillary staff, janitors, and even parliamentarians and former ministers. The story would be similar, but less pronounced for those retiring in 2005. By 2010 pensions would be worth half of their value instead of one third.

I see the files every day at the Ministry of Finance, where there are many persons applying for compassionate consideration because, though they did their part, worked hard, and played by the rules, elevated historical inflation of yesterday defeated them.

Those, however, are just the ones who are visible to formal society. There is the larger category of the permanently seasonally employed, unemployed, and under-employed for whom inflation in Jamaica has dealt a harsh hand.

High, pervasive inflation has ruined tens, maybe hundreds of thousands of lives in Jamaica, and the primary and second-order effects have devastated thousands of businesses.

Adapted from address delivered to stakeholders (a gathering of private and public sector leaders, unions leaders, and academics), July 26, 2018, at the Pegasus Hotel, Kingston, Jamaica.

We have lived it. We know it. High inflation is synonymous with instability; it works against investment, it is not conducive to long term thinking, it retards or reverses development, leads to dysfunctional behaviour, and impoverishes people.

High inflation is the enemy of the poor, those without assets and those on fixed incomes. Meanwhile, those with large pools of unleveraged real assets are largely insulated from high inflation. In that sense, high inflation sows the seeds of inequity and breeds social injustice. Anyone who cares about economic dynamism or about social equity must be concerned with the pursuit of low, stable, and predictable inflation.

Inflation and Price Stability

What is Inflation? We know it when we experience it, but how do we define it? How do we measure it? Thirty years ago, in 1988, the Statistical Institute of Jamaica (STATIN) started the Consumer Price Index, which measures the movement in prices experienced by Jamaicans. The goal of policy should be to keep prices stable, and we measure price stability or instability by tracking the Consumer Price Index, changes in which give us inflation.

So whose job is it to ensure price stability? Firstly, monetary policy is used to influence the level of inflation in an economy. And by monetary policy, we mean movements in the level of interest rates as well as in the levels of the money supply, or the total money in circulation in an economy, both of which are in the purview of the central bank. If we want to maintain low and stable inflation, we have to make sure that the governance and institutional foundations of our central bank are suited to the purpose.

Economic Independence and Central Bank Modernisation

Achieving the objective of economic independence requires the development of strong public sector institutions, long-term thinking, and consensus-building processes. A few weeks ago, I announced that Cabinet had approved one of the key pillars of the vision of economic independence: the establishment in Jamaica of an independent fiscal institution.

Now, Cabinet has given its approval to detailed proposals for the modernisation of the central bank [the second key institutional pillar in our pursuit of Jamaica's economic independence], through amendment of governing legislation. The proposals would amend the Bank of Jamaica Act, the Banking Services Act, and the Public Bodies Management and Accountability Act (PBMA), and enable the issuance of new governance regulations for Bank of Jamaica (BOJ). These legislative changes would follow others in recent years in keeping with international best practises.

Revising the Central Bank Mandate

The reforms to be tabled in 2018 include a revision of the BOJ's mandate, which was expanded in 2015 to include responsibility for the maintenance of overall financial-system stability. This new revision establishes a clear and prioritised mandate of price stability as the goal of monetary policy. Today, the mandate of the central bank consists of multiple goals, which are sometimes in conflict. As a result, market participants and investors suffer from a lack of clarity around the BOJ's intent and actions. This has a cost.

Going forward, the principal monetary policy goal of the central bank will be to achieve an inflation target; all other tools and indicators will be subordinated to this aim. The lens through which the central bank will view other variables is the lens of the impact on inflation. By institutional design, therefore, Jamaican monetary authorities will pursue low, stable, and predictable inflation as the exclusive monetary policy goal.

Independence of the Central Bank

As Ben Bernanke observed, 'consensus has emerged among policymakers, academics, and informed observers around the world that the goals of monetary policy should be set by political authorities while the conduct of monetary policy in pursuit of those goals should be free from political control.'[9] The reasons for this have to do with the length of time it takes for monetary policy decisions to work their way through the economy and have their full effect on inflation.

Monetary policy decisions today may be expected to impact inflation outcomes in twelve to eighteen months, possibly even twenty-four months, so monetary policy practitioners need to have a long-term perspective. For this reason, the policy interest-rate setting is based on the BOJ's judgment of where inflation is likely to be in the future, not on what it is today.

Politicians, however, are notorious for our short-term perspective, so there is natural tension. If monetary policy is subject to political influence, monetary authorities can be pressured into pursuing expansionary policies for the short-term impact, which may be electorally convenient while having disastrous longer-term consequences on price stability.

A central bank under the control or influence of the political directorate can be pressured to sell and squander precious, hard-earned reserves to artificially fix the level of the currency in response to anxiety, even if this undermines inflation objectives and even if such interventions have no real lasting effect, simply because it may be politically advantageous for that to happen.

A central bank under the control or influence of the political directorate can also be pressured into helping finance the government, relieving it from the consequences of bad fiscal choices and policy, while imposing significant adverse consequences on the country over the medium term.

These concerns, in the Jamaican context, are far from theoretical. Jamaica is emerging from a long period of fiscal dominance from the early 1990s up until the last five years where, for much of the period arguably, monetary policy essentially propped up government finances. While not explicit, the path of interest rates had less to do with inflation objectives and more to do with ensuring that the government of the day could finance itself.

For this reason, the focus of this reform is to strengthen the central bank's independence in order to ensure that there can be no undue political influence on monetary policy decision-making. Given the long lead time for monetary policy to take effect, independence also allows for monetary policy continuity across political cycles.

As a single measure, this package represents one of the most consequential reforms of the last five years. Other features designed to strengthen independence include measures to ensure that the tenure of board members is long enough to provide for (a) individual independence, and (b) development of sufficient experience and capability to discharge the functions of accountability successfully.

Appointments will also be staggered so that, while board vacancies are certain to arise during each political administration, no single administration (i.e., within a single term), can change the entire board.

All this is with the aim of allowing the BOJ the operational space and independence required to pursue the monetary-policy objective of low, stable, and predictable inflation, delinking it from political pressures in this process.

Central Bank Accountability

For reasons of responsibility and democratic legitimacy, an independent central bank must be accountable – especially to the public – for its actions. As a result, an important feature of the reform will be to ensure that strong systems of accountability exist. The reform will therefore require the central bank governor to submit to Parliament and publish, at least every six months or more if directed by Parliament, or as determined by the governor, policy statements on the central bank's performance with respect to monetary policy, its achievements in relation to the inflation target, and a monetary policy update. In addition, the governor will be required to appear before Parliament at scheduled intervals to present updates and answer questions.

The central bank's governance structure will be enhanced with clear demarcation and assignment of roles and responsibilities for policy decision-making, proper internal oversight and day-to-day management. Decision-making will be collective in nature, with external participation, rather than concentrated in an individual, allowing a range of input. New statutory committees will be established, and existing ones will be strengthened. Specifically, the Monetary Policy Committee (MPC) will include outside members to bring broader perspectives to bear on monetary policy decisions.

Decisions of the MPC will be accompanied by a concurrent explanatory note, followed by disclosure of the minutes of MPC meetings on a lagged basis. In this way, investors, consumers, and businesses will have insight into the thinking of MPC members and what motivates their decisions. This transparency and enhanced accountability should allow for greater understanding of monetary policy action, and it should facilitate more informed economic and investment decision-making while reducing risk premia.

Prerequisites

Full-fledged inflation-targeting regimes are being used by an increasing number of countries, including developing countries, to achieve and maintain low inflation. With changes in the 1970s to Federal Reserve legislation in the US Congress that increased monetary policy independence – and the subsequent taming inflation that followed – the policy of central bank independence gained in credibility.

New Zealand in 1989, the UK in 1997, and the European Union in 1998, similarly made their central banks operationally independent, as have Canada and Australia and many developing countries such as Colombia, Mexico, Ghana, Uganda, and to varying degrees, Kenya and Tanzania, among others. Small countries like Iceland, too. The link between central bank independence, inflation targeting, and low inflation has been firmly established.

Characteristics of these types of regimes include increased transparency and accountability; the singular commitment of the central bank to the achievement of a time-bound, publicly announced inflation target; and policy actions that are based on a comprehensive set of inflation data, including the inflation forecast. We believe that this is the most effective monetary policy framework to deliver our objective of low, stable, and predictable inflation in Jamaica.

In this context, the modernisation of BOJ will see the institutionalisation of this inflation-focussed monetary policy regime, which should inspire market confidence and facilitate strengthening of financial markets while fostering sustainable growth and job creation.

There is consensus that certain key conditions should be in place for a country to adopt an effective inflation-targeting policy framework. These include:

1. formal, explicit adoption of an inflation target as the primary goal of the central bank;

2. absence of fiscal dominance;

3. Central Bank independence;

4. a flexible-exchange-rate regime;

5. sufficiently developed financial markets;

6. a stable financial system; and

7. a central bank with the capacity to formulate and implement monetary policy with an effective and transparent communication structure.

Jamaica has made significant advances in a number of these areas.

As mentioned above, a flexible exchange rate is a pre-requisite of a country's ability to have an effective inflation-fighting regime. Jamaica has had a flexible exchange rate for several years, and the mechanics of this have been strengthened over time.

Jamaica's flexible, or floating, exchange rate, allows us to pursue an independent monetary policy that is best suited to our economic circumstances at a given point in time and is focussed on achieving our inflation target. For example, it is because we have a flexible exchange rate, and therefore an independent monetary policy, that the Bank of Jamaica (BOJ) could reduce the policy interest rate eight times since October 2016, in response to our realities, even while monetary authorities in the United States have increased the US policy interest rate seven times over the same period. Without an independent monetary policy underpinned by a flexible exchange rate, our monetary authorities would be constrained to increasing interest rates even while domestic demand remains fragile.

The BOJ has been implementing many reforms towards a credible inflation-targeting framework, including the introduction of competitive, market-based, multiple-price auctions to buy and sell foreign currency, which reduces the Bank's footprint in this area and improves market information and price discovery.

The Central Bank also has responsibility for the management of Jamaica's foreign exchange reserves. The size of our reserves in relation to the value of our imports determines whether we can sustain ourselves without external assistance. That is, it determines our prospects for economic independence.

In 2013, Jamaica found itself in a position where we could not sustain ourselves and finance our imports without the financial assistance of the IMF. For Jamaica to sustain itself in the future, without the support of the IMF, it will need to have sufficient reserves for protection in the event of a rainy day.

Sufficient reserves are indispensable, for example, if oil prices rise significantly. If Jamaica does not have a sufficient buffer in those circumstances, we will be unable to sustain ourselves without external assistance – that is, our economic independence would be compromised. If there is a natural disaster and domestic production comes to a halt and we have to import every single thing, without sufficient reserves our economic independence would be compromised. If there is a deep recession in the United States that causes tourism receipts and remittance flows to tank, reducing foreign-exchange earnings, without sufficient reserves our economic independence would be compromised.

The buffer of adequate reserves makes sure Jamaica remains externally sustainable and can finance itself in all circumstances without external assistance. Time and time again, countries have gone to the IMF because their reserves have reached dangerously low levels. Jamaica knows this well. Economic independence is advanced by decoupling the implementation and management of monetary policy from the political directorate, and that is aim of this reform.

Expected Dividends from BOJ Modernisation

The best contribution that monetary policy can make to the economy is to provide an environment that preserves the value of money, i.e., maintaining low, stable, and predictable inflation. Where there is a credible expectation of low and stable inflation, interest rates – the cost of capital – can confidently be factored into long-term investment decisions with a low probability of adverse surprises, and the exchange rate, which we have all learned to focus on as a barometer of the state of the economy, can be allowed to retreat to the back of the stage as access to a well-developed foreign-exchange market removes anxiety from the inevitable exchange-rate fluctuations that are bound to occur in a competitive free market.

Within the paradigm of low, stable, and predictable inflation, wage negotiations will take on a different dynamic. In the Eastern Caribbean, where low inflation has been a persistent feature of life, wage agreements are routinely and successively five years in duration. This gives more time to focus on deeper structural issues, which means greater progress over time as compared with our historical experience within a context of high, unpredictable inflation.

Only 15 per cent of Jamaican employees have pensions. In an environment of high inflation expectations, pensions and savings generally are unattractive. However, in an environment where the political directorate signals its commitment to low inflation through the operational independence of the central bank, savings and products such as pensions become more attractive with the benefits of increased social security.

Those involved in pricing long-term assets and liabilities will have confidence that, over the life cycle of the product they are pricing, the only factors affecting monetary policy decisions will be economic. This will reduce risk premia and, all else equal, bring long-term real interest rates down across the credit spectrum. Jamaicans will be able to take a long view which will add vitality and strength to our economy.

I am confident that a strong institutional framework that delivers on a strict and narrowly defined mandate of price stability, with strong provisions for oversight and accountability and arrangements for embedding the best global practises for collective decision-making, is a necessary pillar in building the kind of future of which we can all be proud, and for which generations to come will thank us.

Inflation: The Most Important Price in the Economy

Published Commentary, August 2018

It was recently announced that with twelve-month inflation to June of 2.8 per cent, the Bank of Jamaica (BOJ) missed the government's inflation target range of 4–6 per cent. The 2.8 per cent result also meant that the BOJ missed the slightly wider June 2018 inflation target of 3.5–6.5 per cent established under the monetary-policy consultation clause of Jamaica's Precautionary Stand-By Arrangement with the International Monetary Fund (IMF). This latter missed target requires the BOJ to consult with the IMF Executive Board.

This has caused confusion as inflation was actually lower than the target, and conventional wisdom suggests that such an outcome is good. Others have questioned the level of the target, and some question what inflation actually measures. There has also been speculation as to what the corrective measures to raise inflation to the target range may be, and whether exchange-rate depreciation features among them.

Commitment to Transparency in Monetary Policy

I recently gave a policy address on the Government of Jamaica's (GOJ's) plan to modernise the BOJ inclusive of specifying its monetary-policy mandate as: maintaining domestic price stability, increasing central bank accountability, improving governance, recapitalising the BOJ's balance sheet, and removing the Minister of Finance's power to give directions on monetary policy.

As we approach this reform, and as the GOJ formally adopts inflation targeting as a policy objective, our interim accountability framework requires the BOJ to account to the Minister of Finance for the missed inflation target inclusive of corrective measures.

An earlier version of this article appeared in the *Jamaica Gleaner*, August 10, 2018.

I commit to making this correspondence (including my response) public.

As such, I hope that this openness with respect to official communication on corrective measures will completely dispel, refute, and rebut any speculation that exchange-rate depreciation is among such measures. I believe that transparency strengthens market efficiency and will not wait for passage of BOJ reform legislation for that to be incorporated into GOJ policy (Under our modernisation proposals, the central bank accountability relationship will pivot to be with the House of Parliament).

Inflation Is a Broad, Average, and Important Measure

The Statistical Institute of Jamaica (STATIN) started the Consumer Price Index (CPI) several decades ago, and in accordance with international best practises, it measures the movement in consumer prices experienced by Jamaicans. The CPI is obtained by comparing, through time, the cost of a fixed basket of goods and services purchased by Jamaican consumers. Every month, scores of officers from STATIN visit thousands of providers of goods and services and record current prices, which are used to update the CPI.

The basket consists of approximately five hundred items across the entire range of goods and services consumed by Jamaicans. Almost every regular good or service you can imagine is included. The weighting of a particular good or service in the basket is determined by dividing the amount Jamaicans spend on that good or service by the total consumption of all Jamaicans on all goods and services.

Items consumed by relatively few Jamaican households will tend to be weighted much less than items consumed by many Jamaican households. Within the category of spirits, therefore, white overproof rum has a weighting more than thirty times that of vodka, and in the transportation category, bus fares have a weight more than one hundred times that of airfares. This is so as Jamaicans spend far more on rum than on vodka, and many more Jamaicans take the bus than the plane for non-business purposes.

The inflation rate is therefore an average measure of broad price movements and is not intended to, nor does it, represent the measure for any particular individual. Similarly, per capita income is a useful average measure not intended to represent the income of any one individual.

However, these average measures are extremely useful and can be shown in theory and practise to have specific relationships with other variables and economic outcomes. Once expectations become firmly anchored for what the inflation rate will be, the individual decisions of hundreds of thousands of consumers and tens of thousands of businesses adapt and respond, and inflation will become the most important price in the economy.

How Monetary Policy Targets Inflation

One of the important relationships that I referenced above is that the inflation rate (i.e., the average measure of the movement of a broad set of prices) can be successfully targeted by monetary policy. Adjusting the levels of interest rates and liquidity conditions impacts consumer and business demand, which in turn leads to movement in prices. However, the time for monetary policy decisions to impact inflation can be long (e.g., twelve to eighteen months).

Lowering interest rates stimulates increased borrowing, by businesses for investment and by consumers for various purchases. This increases domestic demand and economic activity, which in turn increases economic growth, boosts job growth, and pushes prices upwards. The converse is also true. Increasing interest rates curbs borrowing, which decreases demand and dampens inflation.

Setting an Inflation Target That is Conducive to Jobs and Growth

Therefore, within the spectrum of 'acceptable' inflation rates, the pursuit of a higher (but still reasonably and historically low) target is broadly consistent with, but does not necessarily predict, loosening of monetary policy (i.e., lowering of interest rates), while the pursuit of a lower target is more consistent with, but does not necessarily predict, the opposite.

The GOJ, in setting the inflation target range some time ago, was and remains biased towards the imperatives of economic and employment growth within the reality of debt reduction. With those objectives, factors that favoured a loosening of monetary policy were properly deemed the priority.

An inflation target of 4–6 per cent, in the context of fiscal debt reduction, is more likely to lead to monetary policy that better accommodates economic and job growth than would be the case for a lower target (say 3 per cent), all else equal.

The 4–6 per cent inflation target was publicly communicated; it informed choices and would have been explicitly referenced in, for example, public-sector wage agreements to date. It is a medium-term target, and the BOJ, having missed it for June 2018 will need to 'wheel and come again' to achieve the target in a future period.

Before any reader believes that the Minister of Finance is giving away monetary policy direction (i.e., interest rates and liquidity, which are the purview of the Central Bank), let me add that the Central Bank's job is complicated by having to always consider that some portion of inflation is affected by external factors including weather conditions, which influence the movement in agricultural prices, and prices of imported commodities. Therefore, the worthiness of adjusting monetary variables in any particular direction can be tempered or supported by external conditions.

We continue to make substantial progress in fiscal reforms, delivering benefit to all Jamaicans. It is necessary that this is complemented by monetary reforms that increase transparency and accountability and improve market efficiency, which will assure all Jamaicans that low, stable, and predictable inflation is here to stay.

The Inflation Target

Published Commentary, September 2018

Economic reform is never easy. This is especially the case when the policy matters under consideration are highly technical in nature and the public space for informed and in-depth commentary is underdeveloped.

Monetary policy – the process by which the monetary authority, in our case the Bank of Jamaica (BOJ), varies money supply and sets policy interest rates – is one of those areas of our economy least understood by the public. This is partly the result of our torturous monetary history, which has been characterised by decades of sustained high inflation, high interest rates, and persistent devaluation. We have little experience with a 'normal' monetary environment. This makes monetary policy reform more challenging.

The Government of Jamaica has been gradually implementing reforms to transition monetary policy towards the explicit and sole objective of targeting specific levels of inflation, ushering in a new era of consistently low, stable, and predictable inflation. The most significant of these reforms, BOJ modernisation, will be tabled in October. This entails (a) changing the central bank mandate to make the preservation of purchasing power its primary goal, (b) improving BOJ's governance, (c) strengthening the BOJ's balance sheet, (d) enhancing the BOJ's accountability, and (e) institutionalising the BOJ's independence.

In the meantime, however, twelve-month inflation to April, May, June, and July was 3.2 per cent, 3.1 per cent, 2.8 per cent, and 3.2 per cent, respectively, and against the background of being told for years that 'low inflation' is good for Jamaica, why target a higher inflation rate of 5 per cent (plus or minus 1 per cent)?

An earlier version of this article appeared in the *Jamaica Gleaner*, September 7, 2018.

The fact that the monetary policy question in 2018 is whether the inflation target should be 3 or 5 per cent reflects a significant collective achievement that should not go unrecognised.

In response, we should first note that the definition of 'low inflation' must be understood by reference to Jamaica's historical experience. Inflation of 5 per cent or below is a very recent phenomenon. We have had inflation consistently at 5 per cent or lower for only the previous three of the last thirty years. In that context, an inflation rate of 5 per cent is low.

Second, there is a relationship between the policy interest rate set by the BOJ and future inflation outcomes that technocrats at central banks commonly call the 'monetary transmission mechanism.' This mechanism reflects local circumstances and can be complex. It describes how changes in the policy interest rate are transmitted through the economy and how they affect short- and long-term market interest rates, asset prices, market expectations, demand for goods and services, and other variables, including inflation.

With current inflation outcomes at approximately 3 per cent, a medium-term target of lower than 5 per cent (say, 3 or 4 per cent) would not allow the BOJ as much flexibility to keep policy interest rates as low as they are now. Due to BOJ forecasts of (a) recovery of agriculture prices and (b) oil prices remaining at current levels, inflation is projected to naturally trend upwards towards the current target of 5 per cent in the medium term.

To counteract this, as the BOJ would be obligated to do with an inflation target lower than 5 per cent, the Bank would need to consider raising interest rates to slow loan growth and curtail demand, which would dampen inflation prospects. Obviously, in the current economic environment, this would conflict with the larger policy objective of promoting conditions that favour economic and employment growth in the context of debt reduction.

The converse is true. An inflation target of 5 per cent, which, according to BOJ forecasts, will be naturally attained over the medium term, affords the BOJ some freedom and flexibility 'today' to not unduly worry about inflation exceeding the target 'tomorrow.' This allows the BOJ to maintain policy interest rates at current levels for longer than they otherwise could, all else equal, thereby promoting loan growth, rising employment, and an expanding economy.

The evidence suggests that the policy is bearing fruit. According to **BOJ** data, loans from deposit-taking institutions to the private sector have increased approximately 16 per cent as at June 2018 over the comparable figure for June 2017. This compares favourably with private-sector loan growth of 12 per cent as at June 2017 over June 2016. So we are witnessing an acceleration of loan growth, which augurs well for future economic growth.

Fiscal Sustainability, External Sustainability, and Price Stability

Published Commentary, December 2019

The international credit rating agency, Moody's, this week upgraded Jamaica's rating to the highest Moody's has assigned Jamaica in ten years. Standard & Poor's (S&P) also recently upgraded Jamaica to the highest credit rating S&P has ever assigned Jamaica since it started rating Jamaica's credit twenty years ago. These improvements in the assessment of Jamaica's economic resilience and future prospects reflect Jamaica's hard-earned macroeconomic stability.

Macroeconomic stability is necessary for sustainable long-term growth and development, though we know it is not sufficient. It is necessary because it provides the flexibility and policy space to absorb and respond to economic shocks without disrupting day-to-day activity. For higher and sustained growth, such stability must be accompanied by policies that raise labour and capital productivity, reduce structural impediments to investment, improve human capital, enhance efficiency of the public bureaucracy, and improve governance.

Many may now take this prerequisite of sustained macroeconomic stability for granted. But let me remind that such stability eluded Jamaica for approximately five decades. Today – in no small measure due to the work and sacrifice of the Jamaican people – we enjoy fiscal sustainability, external sustainability, and price stability that, together with financial stability, provide the foundation of macroeconomic stability. To be sure, vulnerabilities remain due to high levels of debt; but the stability achieved must be fervently safeguarded, even as we work on other reforms.

Fiscal Sustainability

Budgetary expenditure is typically financed from a variety of sources including tax and non-tax revenues. However, countries often

---

An earlier version of this article appeared in the *Jamaica Gleaner*, December 15, 2019.

spend well in excess of their collected revenue. The deficit that arises from excessive spending is financed with newly borrowed money, generating net increases in public debt. The question is whether we can sustainably service the stock of debt without crowding out basic public services or critical social and capital expenditure thereby stifling development. Prolonging a policy of excessive spending quickly leads to fiscal unsustainability – whereby the country borrows to pay interest, and debt uncontrollably spirals upwards, the private sector is crowded out, and living standards stagnate.

This has been Jamaica's history. In 2003–04, long before universal domestic acceptance of the unsustainability of Jamaica's prior fiscal path, interest costs of J$88 billion and salaries of J$61 billion – without adding social programme, and capital expenditure – totalled $149 billion in a year when total revenues were only $146 billion. We were effectively borrowing to pay interest. Against that background, it is no surprise that while it took forty-five years to incur our first trillion of national debt, in only seven more years the second trillion was accumulated. We put ourselves in an unsustainable debt spiral that only serious and painful reform could reverse.

The measures to place Jamaica on a sustainable fiscal path have been challenging and required sacrifices by the Jamaican people. They required the consistent maintenance of a very large surplus of revenue over non-interest expenditure. Today, though our debt remains high, we service it from current revenues, and we pay down more debt than we borrow each year. In other words, our fiscal accounts are on a path of sustainability, and we must stay the course to reach the debt-to-GDP target of 60 per cent by March 2026, as required under our Fiscal Responsibility Law.

External Sustainability

Fiscal sustainability as a necessary objective has never been clearer. Less clear, maybe, is why we need external sustainability.

External sustainability refers to Jamaica's ability to sustainably pay our collective external obligations as they come due, under a variety of benign and adverse scenarios. These obligations arise – in households, businesses, and the government – in the form of payments for goods bought abroad as well as in foreign interest and principal payments. In addition, foreign businesses operating in Jamaica have obligations to repatriate returns on their Jamaican investments.

Long-term external stability hinges on Jamaica's ability to meet all our external obligations in times of peace and war, in times of commodity price shocks (e.g., a sharp decline in alumina prices or a spike in the price of oil), in good times and bad.

The typical benchmark that reflects external sustainability is the Assessment of Reserve Adequacy (ARA) metric, a quantitative metric developed by the International Monetary Fund (and used to measure reserve adequacy for 189 member countries), which captures the level of reserves required to meet external obligations given the structure and size of the economy. Today, Jamaica's foreign currency reserves are in excess of 100 per cent of our ARA metric (up from 75 per cent in 2016), leaving comfortable room to absorb exogenous shocks.

This has not always been the case. Had Jamaica been externally sustainable in 2016, with an ARA metric in the region of 100 per cent, we may not have needed the IMF Precautionary Stand-By Arrangement. Furthermore, had Jamaica not achieved external sustainability in the years since, we wouldn't have been able to exit a programme relationship with the IMF in 2019. Our economic independence centres on this critical external-sustainability pillar.

The road to external sustainability has required implementation of various foreign-exchange market reforms, inclusive of revamped rules, procedures, and practises that have delivered a market-determined exchange rate where forces of demand and supply are resolved daily in two-way exchange-rate price movements. Reforms also included a transparent mechanism for the Bank of Jamaica (BOJ) to interact with authorised dealers in foreign-exchange transactions. Prior to these reforms, information on the price and times at which the central bank intervened in the market were not publicly available. Today, BOJ intervention is allocated in a transparent, competitive manner with full public disclosure to all Jamaicans.

Price Stability

For the past four years Jamaica has enjoyed inflation outcomes of 3–5 per cent, a distinct departure from the previous two decades when inflation averaged approximately 13 per cent and was highly variable. The relatively constant level of low inflation today, referred to as price stability, is a new experience for Jamaica.

It is easy to forget those days of high-inflation volatility when high, and extremely high, interest rates choked consumption and investment in a hopeless bid to tame inflation; the endless rounds of tax increases required for the government to operate in an unstable macroeconomic environment brought on by high inflation; the unwillingness of most investors to commit beyond a thirty- or ninety-day money-market instrument, due to uncertainty and risk; and how much lower the savings rate was in our high-inflation environment.

These days, the BOJ's easing of monetary policy has ushered in the lowest interest rates in Jamaica's history. The much-reduced interest bill and faster-than-programmed debt reduction has allowed the GOJ to implement the first net tax reduction for at least fifty years. Investors are committing to ten- and fifteen-year instruments at low rates, expanding and opening new factories, and constructing multi-storey buildings with optimism, while households are saving at a rate higher than in the past. These choices and actions of investors and households arise from, and are consistent with, the current environment characterised by price stability. Actions speak louder than words.

Jamaica has not experienced continued fiscal sustainability, external sustainability, and price stability, at the same time, for nearly fifty years. We now are. Vulnerabilities remain due to high debt, and so it is our duty to preserve, institutionalise, and protect our collective achievement of hitherto elusive macroeconomic stability. We now have the historic prospect of leveraging this stability, without compromising it, to build a new Jamaica with economic opportunity for all.

The Exchange Rate, Debt, and the Consumer Price Index

Published Commentary, December 2019

Jamaica has been undergoing profound change in economic policy and the accompanying institutional framework. However, Jamaica's politics, as practised, has not always incentivised public discourse that edifies. Instead the incentive has been to exploit gaps in both understanding and knowledge of relevant facts. While this may serve narrow interests at a point in time, it does not serve Jamaica over the longer term.

Over the past several weeks there has been public interest in the exchange rate, debt, and the Consumer Price Index (CPI), and I seek to add information that improves public understanding and aids public discourse.

The Exchange Rate

Jamaica has been through another cycle of depreciation that is now followed by appreciation. The Jamaican–US dollar exchange rate has gone from 142.23 three weeks ago to 134.95 on December 4, an appreciation of approximately 5 per cent. This two-way movement of our exchange rate is a departure from the 'one-way slide' of the past and represents the daily resolution of forces of demand and supply, reflecting how markets are supposed to work.

The fact that we only speak about the exchange rate on the depreciation cycle, and often do so in panicked tones without reference to underlying economic fundamentals, misinforms the public and distorts decision-making. Such rhetoric needs to change.

The Central Bank (BOJ) has gross reserves of US$3.6 billion and non-borrowed reserves in excess of US$2.5 billion, more than we have ever had. The data show that annual inflows of foreign exchange to Jamaica are more than sufficient to meet Jamaica's needs (or else BOJ's foreign exchange reserves could not have increased).

An earlier version of this article appeared in the *Jamaica Gleaner*, December 8, 2019.

Yes, we have a large trade deficit. However, this is compensated for by inflows from tourism, other services, and remittances. The sum of those items has resulted in a modest current account deficit of between 2 and 3 per cent of GDP for the past several years, which in turn has been more than adequately financed by inflows of foreign direct investment.

The challenge is that, like in every other country in the world, inflows and outflows are not balanced at every point in time. This is where market forces are best able to resolve short-term imbalances with price (i.e., exchange rate) movements, without the need for excessive central bank intervention.

The volatility that arises from two-way movement of the exchange rate presents an opportunity for private-sector innovation, with central bank support, in developing a forward market and other hedging instruments that allow businesses to plan.

Debt-to-GDP and the Exchange Rate

With respect to the sustainability of debt, the parameter that matters is not the absolute or nominal debt per se but the size of this debt relative to the size of the economy – i.e., the debt-to-GDP ratio. For instance, based on IMF data, Kenya's 2017 debt is nearly three times as large as Jamaica's, but its economy is also approximately five times larger. Thus, Kenya's 2017 debt-to-GDP of 52 per cent is smaller than Jamaica's at 95 per cent, implying that, assuming all else is equal, Kenya can service its debt more easily than Jamaica, even though its debt is larger in nominal terms.[10]

Jamaica has long had a majority of its debt denominated in foreign currency. For the past seven years the proportion of our debt denominated in foreign currency has hovered around 60 per cent of our total debt. When the exchange rate appreciates (or depreciates), the absolute size of the foreign-denominated debt converted to Jamaican dollars decreases (or increases). At the current mix of foreign-currency debt, a 1 per cent change in the J$/US$ exchange rate changes the total stock of nominal debt by approximately 0.6 per cent. But the story doesn't end there.

Inflation and growth have a role, too. In the same way that exchange-rate movements change the total stock of nominal debt, inflation and growth increase the nominal size of the economy. That is, the value of goods and services produced in Jamaica (Jamaica's GDP) increases in size due to inflation and growth. As a result, exchange-rate depreciation does not necessarily result in an increase of the debt-to-GDP ratio. An example makes the point: the foreign proportion of our debt has not changed substantially in recent years, and the exchange rate depreciated by 28 per cent from J$99:US$1 in March 2013 to J$126.5:US$1 in March 2019; yet our debt-to-GDP ratio declined from 145 per cent to 95 per cent over the same period. The reduction in debt by 50 per cent of GDP over this time reflected many factors: fiscal consolidation, inflation, growth, exchange-rate movements, and also liability management actions.

In addition, Jamaica's foreign debt is comprised of hundreds of loans that differ in interest and repayment periods. The times at which we pay interest and repay principal are diversified throughout the year. As a result, it is an average exchange rate over the year that affects Jamaica's debt service, not the spot exchange rate on any particular day.

The Consumer Price Index

The inflation rate is measured by changes in the Consumer Price Index (CPI), and the CPI is composed of a weighted measure of the prices of more than five hundred goods consumed in our economy. The identification of those goods and the weights applied are determined from an extensive Household Expenditure Survey (HES) conducted by the Statistical Institute of Jamaica (STATIN). The HES is a rigorous undertaking, conducted over twelve months to capture seasonality, and ranks only second to the national census in scale, complexity, and cost.

The weighting of a particular good or service is calculated by dividing the amount Jamaicans spend on that good or service, as determined by the HES, by the total consumption of all Jamaicans on all goods and services, also as determined by the HES.

STATIN endeavours to conduct a HES every ten years, consistent with international best standards for developing countries. A HES was conducted in 2005, and another was due in 2015. STATIN reports that a budget for the HES was submitted for consideration in 2014–15 but, presumably due to fiscal constraints, it was not approved. STATIN was therefore unable to conduct the HES in the year in which it was due.

An allocation was made in the 2016–17 budget for the HES, and it was completed in 2017. STATIN is currently engaged in the data analysis process, with a projected release of the CPI based on the revised basket of goods and services for April 2020 (published in May 2020).

History can provide more understanding and insight. Prior to the implementation of the current basket, which is based on the 2004–05 HES, the previous revision was undertaken in 1984. Between both surveys, the data revealed that the top three divisions remained the same despite minor shifts in their weight. Generally, 'Food and Drink,' 'Transportation,' and 'Housing, Electricity, Gas and other Fuels' are the larger categories of consumption.

STATIN has benefited from substantial technical assistance over many years and is subjected to periodic reviews by regional bodies, multilateral agencies, and peers in other countries. These independent reviews have consistently indicated that STATIN's work and output are technically robust and consistent with international standards and best practises.

Jamaica's market economy functions optimally with data, facts, and information used for decision-making. Our public discourse serves Jamaica and the Jamaican people when it is based on data and facts. To do otherwise is a disservice to Jamaica and only has the potential of serving narrow interests.

Jamaica is entering an exciting new period, with initial conditions anchored on hard-earned economic stability. Let our public conversation and rhetoric be based on facts and not misinformation.

Building Institutions for the Future –
Part I: An Independent Central Bank

Published Commentary, December 2020

Institution building is important for entrenching macroeconomic stability, as well as supporting policy predictability and transparency. Keeping these objectives in mind, this government has prioritised two complementary institutional reforms: legislation for the establishment of an Independent Fiscal Commission to strengthen Jamaica's Fiscal Responsibility Framework, and creation of an independent central bank with an explicit mandate for price stability.

Both Houses of Parliament recently enacted the Bank of Jamaica (BOJ) Amendment Act, which significantly amends the existing Bank of Jamaica Act.[11] In addition, the legislation to establish the Fiscal Commission was tabled in late November.

In a two-part series, I want to explain these developments and highlight why they are historic. This article focuses on the BOJ Amendment Act.

The BOJ Amendment Act – passed without much fanfare, including little coverage in the media – is a historic piece of legislation for Jamaica that benefited from the deliberations of a Joint Select Committee of Parliament.

The reform creates the institutional framework for a 'Full-Fledged Inflation Targeting' monetary policy strategy in which the achievement of the inflation target set by the government will be the unambiguous primary objective of the Bank of Jamaica. It also modernises the BOJ (Central Bank) through reorganisation of its governance to support greater accountability, transparency, and effectiveness in the discharge of its mandate.

The significance relates to our history. High and pervasive inflation in the past ruined tens, maybe hundreds of thousands of lives in Jamaica and devastated thousands of businesses. High inflation is the enemy of the poor, those without assets and those

---

An earlier version of this article appeared in the *Jamaica Gleaner*, December 13, 2020.

on fixed incomes. Meanwhile, those with real assets are insulated from high inflation and large (fixed-interest-rate) borrowers typically benefit. So, in that sense, high inflation deepens inequity and breeds social injustice. We have lived this. We know it.

Mandate and Accountability

The BOJ Amendment Act is a response to our experience. The primary objective of the central bank will now be the maintenance of price stability expressed as the achievement of the inflation target. This clarity will help anchor inflation expectations to guide decision-making across businesses and households.

After consultation with the BOJ the government will set the inflation target, expressed as a range, to be consistent with the government's growth and employment objectives. However, the BOJ Amendment Bill empowers the BOJ, and grants it the operational independence to achieve this target without external influence. Once a new target is set, the BOJ is expected to achieve it over the medium term (defined as not less than thirty-six months).

Such independence also requires that the Bank is held accountable to stakeholders for its actions and outcomes, and that the fullest transparency exists about its operations.

In that regard, the BOJ Amendment Act puts in place several measures, including notifying the public, through the Minister, on the reasons for any deviations of outcome from the target and any proposed actions to restore inflation within the target range. This notification will be published on the websites of the Central Bank and the Ministry of Finance. Furthermore, the public will have access to the minutes of Monetary Policy Committee (MPC) meetings where interest-rate and other monetary policy decisions are taken, within four weeks of the meeting. This level of transparency in policymaking is path-breaking for Jamaica.

Moreover, the MPC will submit semi-annual reports, that will be tabled in Parliament, on the performance of the BOJ in relation to its monetary policy and achievements in relation to the inflation target. In addition, the Bank's governor will be required to appear before the Standing Finance Committee of the House of Representatives to answer queries with respect to the reports.

Prohibited from Borrowing from the Central Bank

Jamaica suffered from fiscal dominance, over a long period of time. Fiscal dominance is defined as an economic condition resulting from unsustainably high levels of debt and persistent fiscal deficits. Under these conditions, monetary policy cannot successfully target inflation but instead is compelled to pursue the objective of keeping the government from bankruptcy. In effect, the primary objective of setting interest rates under conditions of fiscal dominance is to ensure, through sufficiently high interest-rate levels, that the government can continue to attract lenders, rather than any independent economic objective such as attaining a target inflation rate.

Jamaicans know this all too well.

While we have banished fiscal dominance through reform, and we are institutionalising its exile, another threat has remained. The government could unjustifiably and unreasonably cause the 'printing of money' by borrowing from the central bank.

The BOJ Amendment Act now prohibits the government from borrowing from the central bank, except in declared national emergencies. Even then, the procedure for securing a temporary advance from the BOJ requires transparency: a Ministerial Order, subject to affirmative resolution. That is, Parliament will have a role if the government is to temporarily borrow from the central bank.

With an independent central bank mandated to pursue monetary policy that is consistent with the achievement of an inflation target, and with the government restricted from borrowing from the central bank, the government will have little choice but to pursue a credible fiscal path in order to finance its operations, or risk bankruptcy.

Governance Structure

In keeping with the BOJ's independence and accountability, the board structure has also been significantly amended. It ensures effective oversight of the policymaking and management processes of the Bank, and it devolves the decision-making power of the governor to collective decision-making bodies that incorporate external expertise. The new law establishes two statutory committees for policymaking. The MPC will be responsible for monetary policy decisions, a power previously vested under the governor. There will also be a Financial Policy Committee that will determine the financial policies of the Bank, including with respect to prudential supervision and financial-system stability.

The board will comprise five external members in addition to three ex-officio directors including the governor. Terms of external board members will be staggered by two years to ensure that the entire board is not replaceable in a single five-year political cycle. Board members will have to pass 'Fit and Proper' criteria similar to those required for licensees under the Banking Services Act.

Balance Sheet Solvency

Anticipating passage of this modernisation bill, the BOJ was given the financial resources as required by the pending legislation, to ensure that it can engage in monetary policy operations necessary to achieve its mandate without imposing a cost on taxpayers through recurring losses. In other words, the legislation requires capitalisation of the Bank to ensure policy solvency. A well-capitalised and well-managed central bank will be able to generate profits for its shareholders, the government and people of Jamaica.

Why Is This Historic?

Recognising that it is insufficient to simply achieve macroeconomic stability, Jamaica is moving beyond this stage to the institutionalisation of stability. A credible institution is now legally tasked and empowered with the objective of preserving low and stable inflation within an accountable, transparent, and robust governance framework.

This institutionalisation reduces risk premia and borrowing costs over the long term as there is increased certainty about monetary policy into the future. Monetary policy, anchored around an inflation objective, becomes independent of the political cycle. This creates the conditions for longer-term planning, incentivises the deepening of financial markets, and supports greater financial inclusion. These in turn allow for higher economic growth and job-creation prospects, placing Jamaica on a strong and sustainable trajectory.

In the middle of the pandemic, when other countries are scrambling to finance current-year budgets, Jamaica is able to look ahead; to build and strengthen economic institutions for the future. There is certainly more to do. However, by building institutions, Jamaica will undoubtedly recover stronger.

Dividends from the Bank of Jamaica

Budget Speech Excerpt, March 2021

Madam Speaker, last year good policy delivered $90 billion of opening cash resources, at the right time, which assisted us greatly in financing the response to the pandemic, even as government revenues declined, without needing to borrow. This year, again, good policy is delivering a $33 billion dividend from the Bank of Jamaica (BOJ), straight into the consolidated fund in the first week in April. This could not come at a better time. Rarely are the fruits of right and appropriate policy so powerfully evident, in as short a time period.

My fellow Jamaicans, policy matters, and good policy matters even more.

Good policies expand opportunities and provide flexibility when we need to respond to crises. Without this historic dividend, unprecedented in size as a single payment, this year's budgetary process would have been an even more difficult exercise. But we need to have the courage and discipline to pursue good policy.

Central Banks are designed to be profitable, and in countries that pursue good policies – sustainable and prudent policies – central banks are indeed profitable. And they return these profits to taxpayers through dividends to the treasury or consolidated fund. The dividends can then be used to fund social support, finance infrastructure development, and support other worthy initiatives through an open and transparent budgetary process where everyone can see where the resources are going, and which groups are benefiting.

When policy results in central bank losses that taxpayers are called upon to fund, we know who bears the costs – you, the people. But the question of who benefits is not usually transparent.

Adapted from the opening budget presentation delivered in Parliament March 9, 2021.

To provide some examples of central bank dividend distributions: The Bank of England routinely paid annual dividends of 500 million pounds sterling to Her Majesty's Treasury for the period 2010–19. During the same period, the Canadian central bank paid dividends that averaged CAD$1 billion dollars annually; the Australian central bank averaged dividends over AUD$2 billion dollars annually; and the United States Federal Reserve paid dividends to the US Treasury that averaged US$75 billion per year.

What about Jamaica?

Over a similar period, between 2010 and 2017, the BOJ paid $0 dividends to the taxpayers of Jamaica who fund its operations, because it made huge losses.

Some of the losses were a result of debt exchanges, but they were also due to foreign-exchange losses from excessive intervention in foreign-currency markets. All told, from 2010 to 2017, the taxpayers of this country were called on to support the BOJ in the amount of over $31 billion because of losses it incurred over that period.

Now, you cannot hold an institution accountable if they are not provided with the resources specified and detailed by law. The law says that when the BOJ makes a loss, the government must cover that loss with taxpayer resources. But that did not happen. The BOJ merely had an IOU on its balance sheet for this amount. An IOU that they could not trade, they could not repossess. It represented a dead asset.

We rectified this in 2018 and 2019 by transferring the securities required by law to cover the cumulative losses BOJ made over the previous decade. This was particularly important in preparation for central bank independence and with renewed focus on the bank's new mandate, governance, and accountability. Prior to this, the BOJ was fighting with one hand tied behind its back.

The BOJ capital was stated as J$2 million in the original 1960 Bank of Jamaica Act. In 1976, the BOJ's capital was doubled to J$4 million. And BOJ's capital remained at the same paltry figure of J$4 million over the forty-two years between 1976 and 2018. That's like asking a man to paint a house without a paintbrush. So, we also injected $20 billion of permanent capital – which is capital that cannot be removed – into the BOJ in 2018 to empower the BOJ to fulfil its mandate.

And we made a deliberate shift in monetary policy towards inflation targeting which began in earnest in 2018, and away from the previous policy where a preoccupation with the exchange rate biased policy towards excessive interventions, which ultimately had a hidden fiscal cost. Inflation targeting has now been given the force of law with the BOJ Amendment Act, chiselled and passed with bi-partisan support.

This series of steps has led to a reversal of fortunes for the BOJ. They were able to reduce interest rates ten times since 2018. And after incurring a loss of $6.8 billion in 2017, the BOJ made a profit of $9.1 billion in 2018; $15.8 billion in 2019; and $9.9 billion in 2020. The vast majority (80 per cent) of these profits were from ordinary operations. Only about 20 per cent arises from realised foreign-exchange gains.

By law, these profits are to be distributed to the Consolidated Fund for the benefit of the Jamaican people. And there could hardly be a better time. Good policy cannot only consider today, it must also consider tomorrow.

At the end of calendar year 2020, the balance owed to the government increased further with profits made during the year. The amount BOJ is required by law to distribute to the Consolidated Fund, as confirmed by BOJ auditors, now equals three years of profits totalling $33 billion. Good policy pays dividends – literally and figuratively.

Madam Speaker, it is important to note that this distribution does not represent recurring revenue. This dividend is an accumulation of three years of profits.

Furthermore, going forward, when the BOJ Amendment Act comes into force, the dividend regime will be updated. BOJ dividends will not be paid if its capital at the end of their financial year (December) is less than 5 per cent of monetary liabilities, even if it makes a profit during that year. If its capital is between 5 per cent and 8 per cent of monetary liabilities, the dividend will be 25 per cent of profits. And when capital exceeds monetary liabilities, the dividend will represent 100 per cent of profits.

The **BOJ** is projected to have its capital at 5 per cent of monetary liabilities during this calendar year 2021.

Upgrade and Redesign of Banknotes:
Restoring National Heroes

Budget Speech Excerpt, March 2022

Our experience with fifty years of chronic macroeconomic instability, where our currency devalued by nearly 50,000 per cent, is chiselled into the deformation of our currency design, where a noble original intent has dissolved and is no longer recognisable.

While we continue to depend on physical cash, we need to make cash transactions more efficient. Technical studies have shown the need for a currency denomination between the $1000 note and the $5000 note. The Bank of Jamaica has advised that the introduction of a $2000 note would bring greater efficiency to the currency structure, allowing cash transactions to be settled easier, with fewer notes required to settle transactions.

In addition, the introduction of a new currency denomination allows us to leverage technology and material science improvements and upgrade the family of notes to achieve greater cost efficiencies. Today, our currency denominations use a mixture of material called substrates. The $50 and $100 notes use a hybrid substrate, which is a mixture of cotton and polymer. The $500, $1000, and $5000 are on varnished cotton. These are not the most durable materials available today.

The introduction of a substrate that offers a significant increase in the durability of banknotes will yield substantial benefits as it relates to the average circulation life of banknotes, which in turn will lead to lower order quantities with less frequency relative to current practise. There are substrates such as pure polymer, used by many countries such as the UK, that have a much longer life and are therefore more cost effective.

Banknote design is one of the methods used worldwide to deter counterfeiting and, as such, over the past decade banknote printers have developed more sophisticated security features to minimise

Adapted from the opening budget presentation delivered in Parliament March 8, 2022.

counterfeiting. It is important that the state-of-the-art technology currently used in the banknote-printing industry be incorporated in Jamaica's banknotes.

Although each of our current banknotes has one feature that caters to the visually impaired (either large numbering or tactile printing), the effectiveness of such features has been questioned by this community. An upgrade of the banknotes will therefore also provide the opportunity to implement enhancements which ensure that the visually impaired are able to easily identify all notes.

There are concerns among the Jamaican public that the colours of the $500 note and the $5000 note are not easily distinguishable, especially in low-light conditions, and this has resulted in individuals tendering $5000 instead of $500. We need distinct colour separation between notes, where you make them out even at night as you emerge from the taxi, and this is consistent with research and best practise. An upgrade of our banknotes will make this possible.

The Bank of Jamaica has therefore been engaged in an upgrade of the Jamaican banknotes to:

1. Introduce a new $2000 denomination;

2. Provide cost savings through increased durability of banknotes;

3. Enhance the security of banknotes to reduce the risk of counterfeiting;

4. Enhance banknote features to better meet the needs of the visually impaired; and

5. Ensure clear colour and other distinctions between banknotes of different denominations.

By policy, Jamaica's banknotes feature National Heroes and deceased prime ministers or premiers (in chronological order). However, currently, the existing five banknotes ($50, $100, $500, $1000, and $5000) feature only two out of seven National Heroes and three of four possible deceased prime ministers.

Of the five National Heroes not on notes, four are on coins: Alexander Bustamante on the $1 coin, Norman Manley on the

$5 coin, George William Gordon on the $10 coin, and Marcus Garvey on the $20 coin.

Paul Bogle, who led the Morant Bay Rebellion and was hung on the gallows for this, but whose sacrifice paved the way for representative government in Jamaica, is not presently represented on Jamaica's currency. He was featured on the $2 note until it was dematerialised in 1994. He was then placed on the ten-cent coin, but all denominations below $1 were dematerialised in February 2018.

This is an aberration that must be fixed. Paul Bogle and what he represents should be prominently reflected on Jamaica's currency. We will restore Paul Bogle to our national currency.

Similarly, the coins on which Alexander Bustamante, Norman Manley, George William Gordon, and Marcus Garvey appear do not give visibility consistent with the original intent. This, too, is an aberration that must be fixed. These heroes of Jamaica must be prominently placed on our banknotes. We will restore Alexander Bustamante, Norman Manley, George William Gordon, and Marcus Garvey to our banknotes consistent with the original intent.

When the Jamaican currency was first launched in the 1960s, our heroes were prominently represented on banknotes, with Sam Sharpe appearing on the $50 note in the 1980s.

A young Edward Seaga, still in his thirties, had responsibility for the launch of Jamaica's own currency for our new nation in the mid-1960s. In a seminal speech in 1965 he said the reason for representing our National Heroes on our banknotes was so we would 'focus attention on our history.'[12] Further in that speech he asked, 'But why should we ... look backwards over our shoulders to recognise the role of those who went before the modern development of our history in 1938?'

He answered his own question as follows:

A people who recognise their history recognise the role of those who went before them in thought and in action and understand to what extent those who went before them contributed to the things they have achieved and enjoy today. If we do not understand this and give credit where credit is due we are likely to give credit where credit is not due. We are likely to give all the credit of our achievements to foreign benefactors without understanding that

> *our own people played a significant role in achieving what we enjoy today.*
> *And when we do this we are naturally led to be influenced that our people*
> *and our country are not capable of achieving the things for which we fight*
> *for but that we must always look elsewhere for help, for assistance and for*
> *leadership.*[13]

So at the dawn of our nation, it was a deliberate, thoughtful act to prominently place our National Heroes on our banknotes to give credit where credit is due, and also to remind ourselves: of our capacity for self-determination, that we have agency and we can create the future we want; and that we can be self-sufficient, not dependent on foreign powers for basic needs.

Mr Seaga continued:

> *So the very first act is to understand that we have our leaders, past and*
> *present, and understand that they, together, past and present, achieved many*
> *things we enjoy today and because they have achieved these things we are a*
> *people capable of respect, capable of understanding our own potential and,*
> *therefore, one who understands that the meaning of the word independent*
> *is that it is to be a body of people in a nation that can do for themselves*
> *that which needs to be done. History plays a vital and important role in the*
> *creation of our society, in its development and in its progression.*

So, we have to upgrade our banknotes for the technical reasons given, and we have a new $2000 banknote to launch. But the Jamaica project has, in this regard, drifted from the original intent – our heroes no longer appear on our banknotes.

In this sixtieth year of Independence, this aspect of the national project must be restored. Our national heroes must, once again, appear on our banknotes. We must be constantly reminded of those who came before us and sacrificed so that we can enjoy what we have today. And in honouring our heroes we honour, in perpetuity, the thousands of Jamaicans who served with them.

As Mr Seaga said, give credit where it is due.

So we have seven national heroes and four deceased prime ministers,[14] including Mr Seaga, but only six banknotes: $50, $100, $500, $1000, $2000, and the $5000.

That is, we have eleven faces to fit onto six banknotes, where faces only appear on one side of each note. This means that we need to have two faces per note. Leaders should appear in chronological order subject to no leader appearing in a banknote of lower denomination than he or she was before.

In the newly designed banknotes, the Right Excellent Paul Bogle and the Right Excellent George William Gordon, who were on Jamaica's original banknotes, but who today are on none of our banknotes, will be restored and will appear together on the upgraded $50 banknote. United in the struggle for freedom, united in their sacrifice and execution. They, and those who sacrificed with them, will be honoured.

The Right Excellent Marcus Garvey, who was on Jamaica's 50¢ (half dollar) banknote, but who is on no banknote today, will be restored and will appear alone on the upgraded $100 banknote.

The Right Excellent Nanny of the Maroons and the Right Excellent Sam Sharpe will appear together on the upgraded $500 note.

The Right Excellent Sir Alexander Bustamante and the Right Excellent Norman Manley, who were founding fathers of modern Jamaica and who were contemporaries, serving over similar periods, and who were on Jamaica's original banknotes, are on none of our banknotes today. The Right Excellent Sir Alexander Bustamante and the Right Excellent Norman Manley will be restored and will appear together on the upgraded $1000 banknote.

Jamaica went through a near-civil war experience in the 1970s that deeply scarred the national consciousness. Electoral contests became overtly violent in nature. Remarkably, through great political and civil-society leadership, our country stepped back from the brink and reformed itself. Today, Jamaica's electoral system is a model for the world.

However, not all the scars of this period have healed. Persons active in that era are still with us. Families who lost loved ones, who were displaced, who lost homes and jobs due to the conflict are still here. They remember. They hurt. And, in many cases, those wounds and feelings run deep. We validate those experiences, wherever they exist, as authentic and sincere.

But are we to construct our affairs today in a manner that perpetuates this hurt, bequeaths unto future generations strife and division? Or are we to seek constructive, real, and symbolic ways of forging the unity, peace, and love for which our great philosophers, prophets, and artists advocate?

The latter path must be the way. We must restore unity in our society. Our symbolism must not seed division. Instead, it should forge unity and lift us all up in the process.

Therefore, with the backing of the prime minister and the Cabinet of Jamaica, and with the consent of the representatives of the families of the Most Honourable Michael Manley and the Most Honourable Edward Seaga, we are therefore pleased that:

The Most Honourable Michael Manley and the Most Honourable Edward Seaga, who were contemporaries and rivals, will appear together on the new $2000 banknote. We thank the families of Michael Manley and Edward Seaga for their consent. Our country must move forward, and move forward in unity, peace and love.

Jamaica's average income today is less, in real terms, than it was fifty years ago.

There is a mountaintop that we must climb, where milk and honey lie waiting on us ... but we can only get there together by climbing together.

To my fellow members of the Jamaica Labour Party, (JLP) and to those in the People's National Party (PNP) who are initially perturbed by this, I ask you to say to yourself: it is not about you, it's about all the children of Jamaica – including the multitude of the unborn. We cannot perpetuate hate and division and strife and expect that we will scale this mountaintop.

To Comrades and my fellow Labourites, I say that by co-locating images of great past leaders on our banknotes we do not deny anyone the unique identity of their contribution to Jamaica, nor do we shield them from the full introspection of history.

To my fellow Labourites in particular, I say the biggest respect we can show is by following the ideas of those to whom we want to show respect. It is ideas and not the placement of images that lasts the test of time. We don't really know what Moses of the Old

Testament looked like, but four thousand years later we remember the Ten Commandments he shared.

It was Mr Seaga's idea to have our National Heroes on our banknotes. We are restoring this, and in so doing honouring him.

Finally, the Most Honourable Donald Sangster and the Most Honourable Hugh Shearer will appear together on the upgraded $5000 note. These leaders presided over the greatest period of economic expansion this country has ever experienced.

This Government will restore our heroes to our banknotes; we will restore unity, and we will restore our country. The new and upgraded banknotes will be available late this calendar year. The Bank of Jamaica will be holding sensitisation sessions so that the new security features can be understood, and so that the visually impaired community can become familiar with the features that differentiate the banknotes.[15]

Fiscal Responsibility

Enhancing Jamaica's Fiscal Responsibility Framework

Policy Address, May 2018

In my first speech as Minister of Finance, I outlined the organising principles that will frame policymaking at the Ministry of Finance. I have learned that in public life important points require repetition.

I further outlined the view that a variety of interests with sometimes conflicting agendas seek to influence policy – sectoral interests, labour interests, capital interests, and even generational interests. I should have added media interests, too. I characterised this as normal.

Policymaking, therefore, requires balancing these interests. But as we seek to balance interests, there has to be an overarching vision that establishes priorities and frames decision-making.

For the Ministry of Finance, in an Andrew Holness administration, the organising principles are the pursuit of economic independence, the expansion of economic opportunity for all (i.e., economic growth), and the protection of the vulnerable. Today, I wish to speak about the first of these.

Jamaica's macroeconomic performance, as measured by key indicators, has been exemplary under successive programs with the International Monetary Fund (IMF): debt has reduced, fiscal health is being restored, interest rates are at record lows, unemployment has fallen to 9.6 per cent, inflation has substantially moderated, and jobs growth has been robust and sustained. Economic growth, however, has lagged.

How has this all happened? Well, success has many parents and, in this case deservedly so. Today, however, is not meant to deconstruct the period that we are still in but to prepare for what follows. Suffice to say, that with sound technical advice and financial resources from the IMF, Inter-American Development Bank, and World Bank;

Adapted from address delivered to stakeholders, May 10, 2018, at the Jamaica Pegasus Hotel, Kingston.

broad domestic ownership by diverse stakeholders; and responsible stewardship by successive administrations, much progress has been and continues to be made.

I would like, however, to spend time on just one of the many important components – the unprecedented level of public engagement and ownership of Jamaica's economic programme – that has characterised the last five years. This is symbolised in the Economic Programme Oversight Committee (EPOC).

The emergence of EPOC, however, would arguably not have been possible without the prior existence of the Partnership[16] and the Social Dialogue that it introduced. The Partnership saw a diverse group of stakeholders making the affirmative decision to collectively discuss challenges, share experiences and burdens, and brainstorm solutions in a collaborative spirit. Its distinctive features included mutual understanding, the predisposition to listen, and the courage to compromise.

The early successes of the Partnership and Social Dialogue built confidence and ushered in an era where stakeholders viewed government as critical but not necessarily the 'be all and end all.' The central lesson of the Partnership was that the consensus-building mechanisms of non-governmental bodies had, and continue to have, an indispensable role to play.

It was against this background that the previous administration approached members of the financial community with a second debt exchange and the unions with a multi-year wage freeze, as prior actions for entry into the Extended Fund Facility with the IMF. Both groups correctly insisted on the right to monitor Jamaica's economic programme in return for such sacrifices, to ensure that Jamaica maintained its commitments to the reforms embedded in the agreement.

And so EPOC was born, and it has been a success. So much so that it has been replicated in other countries with IMF programmes.

Given the success to date of our five-year engagement with the IMF, with the likely prospect of Jamaica graduating from a programme relationship with the Fund, it is important to consider the institutional arrangements that may assist in keeping Jamaica on the track towards greater economic independence.

Some have suggested 'legislating' EPOC. I don't take that suggestion literally nor do I understand it to have been meant literally. EPOC has no analytical capacity. It consists of fully occupied, hardworking leaders and was essentially created to monitor agreements between the Government of Jamaica (GOJ) and the IMF. In the absence of a Fund agreement, and without the Fund's analytical capacity and detailed published reviews, EPOC as constructed would not work.

What could work, however, is legislating for the institutional permanence of the *principles* on which EPOC and its companion entities have been founded:

1. Enhancing accountability of the policymaking process

2. Deepening transparency of government finances

3. Strengthening credibility of Jamaica's fiscal path

4. Promoting inclusiveness in the policy discussion space

5. Taking greater societal ownership of Jamaica's economic direction

The establishment of an institution that embodies these principles is crucial to the achievement and maintenance of Jamaica's economic independence.

I am therefore pleased to announce that Cabinet has endorsed the concept of an independent fiscal institution, such as a Fiscal Council [later legislated as the Fiscal Commission, though I have retained the term 'fiscal council' here for historical faithfulness], and the government has procured the services of very experienced international technocrats in this area to help Jamaica with the design.

What are fiscal councils?

Fiscal councils are permanent, independent institutions, staffed by competent, experienced, and technically proficient persons, that help promote economically sustainable fiscal policies across political cycles and that are created by legislation. Since the advent of the Global Financial Crisis of 2008–09, fiscal councils have proliferated as countries seek to implement measures to restore fiscal credibility.[17]

The establishment of a fiscal council, which can be constructed as an enhancement of the partnership models we now have, offers several advantages. Fiscal councils (a) foster greater transparency around fiscal policy by having legislated access to economic data, having sufficient analytical capacity, and providing unbiased information to the public; (b) deepen democratic accountability, as policymakers have to maintain credible policies or explain what appear as deviations; and (c) alter the incentive/disincentive structure in the political economy, raising the political cost of unsound policies or policy proposals. On the converse, fiscal councils reduce the political cost of complying with fiscal rules. Furthermore, fiscal councils help to keep the public and policymakers informed and educated, and by so doing reduce 'fiscal illusion,' where electorates and stakeholders wrongly believe that government has more resources than it lets on.

It is also important to note that credible fiscal councils are non-partisan in all their activities. They are not policy decision-makers, nor do they try to be; they only offer a second opinion. Fiscal councils are neither tsars nor gods; they are not a parallel Opposition, and they are not a parallel Government. Fiscal councils influence the public debate indirectly through the media impact of their reports but are not otherwise direct participants.

A most important feature of fiscal councils lies in their independence. Not only are they free from partisan influence, with independent access to the media and independence to choose their own communication strategy (except that communication should be scheduled to avoid the perception of partisan timing), they are operationally independent, and their independence is *enshrined in law.*

So, what does the Government of Jamaica propose that a fiscal council in Jamaica will do? A Jamaican fiscal council would be the guardian, interpreter, and arbiter of Jamaica's Fiscal Rules.

Jamaica adopted a Fiscal Responsibility Framework (the Framework) through the passage of legislation in 2010 and 2014. Among other things, this Framework promulgates the parameters of the budget calendar, provides for certain economic and fiscal reports and forecasts to be tabled in advance of the budget, and includes Fiscal Rules that establish prescriptive expenditure boundaries – and escape clauses from those boundaries in the event of natural disasters.

A Jamaican Fiscal Council could (a) monitor compliance with Jamaica's Fiscal Rules, (b) keep the public informed on economic matters according to a scheduled calendar, and (c) provide independent analysis on fiscal policy developments. Our Fiscal Council could do other things as well, subject to our ability to afford it.

Approached in this way, Jamaica's Independent Fiscal Council would embody the principles of credibility, accountability, transparency, inclusiveness, ownership, and permanence, which would help Jamaica maintain a path of fiscal prudence, enhancing our economic independence.

Now it is important to note that commonsense and the experience of other countries dictate that the establishment of a fiscal council requires, as a prerequisite or a parallel step, the strengthening of the macro-fiscal and public-financial management capacities of the Ministry of Finance. This is imperative. Also, in a country short on technical resources, a fiscal council cannot be made to cannibalise existing macro-fiscal capacity in the Ministry of Finance, for example, or in other agencies. Capacity-building therefore becomes strategically crucial.

We intend to have a consultative approach to the design of Jamaica's Fiscal Council involving all stakeholders: unions, private sector, financial sector, civil society, youth, academia, and Opposition. The government has engaged international experts who bring an appreciation of the theoretical foundations of such institutions, as well as the practical experience of having advised on the design and formation of these in many countries in the world. They will visit in June and meet with stakeholders so that we can incorporate the Jamaican experience into the design of our very own Independent Fiscal Council.

I use the word 'our' because, to be effective, it has to truly be ours in design and in implementation. Jamaica's Independent Fiscal Council will be an important cornerstone in Jamaica's Fiscal Responsibility architecture. It holds the promise of helping to keep Jamaica on a path towards the achievement and maintenance of economic independence long into the future.

Building Institutions for the Future –
Part II: An Independent Fiscal Commission
Published Commentary, December 2020

Previously, I wrote about the importance of entrenching macroeconomic stability by complementing its achievement with the building of institutions to preserve and maintain this stability. I elaborated on the historic enactment of the Bank of Jamaica Amendment Act, which creates an independent central bank with an explicit mandate for price stability, within an accountable, transparent, and robust governance framework.

Even in the midst of the pandemic, we are looking ahead, building economic institutions with the conviction that, in the long run, credible, durable, accountable, transparent, and robust institutions make the difference in the economic development process.

My focus this week is on the legislation recently tabled for the creation of the Independent Fiscal Commission. The policy and legislation benefited from local stakeholder consultations in addition to technical advice and support from Jamaica's multilateral and bilateral partners.

Bipartisan Fiscal Achievements

Under the IMF-supported Extended Fund Facility (EFF) of 2013 and the Precautionary Stand-By Arrangement (PSBA) of 2016, Jamaica achieved seven consecutive years of primary surpluses (revenue minus expenditure before interest) that exceeded 7 per cent of GDP, resulting in a decline of the national debt by more than 50 per cent of GDP. There is scarcely an international precedent for the means, scope, and time frame of this national, bipartisan achievement of fiscal discipline.

There are many factors, often overlooked, that account for this success, the analysis of which is beyond the intent of this article. But, undoubtedly, one crucial factor was the role played by the Economic

---

An earlier version of this article appeared in the *Jamaica Gleaner*, December 20, 2020.

Programme Oversight Committee (EPOC) across successive administrations.

EPOC members monitored macro-fiscal targets, as well as policy and legislative commitments under the programmes, and reported to Jamaicans on the country's performance. Of course, the IMF closely monitored programme performances through official reviews (more familiarly called IMF 'tests'); collected daily, weekly, and monthly fiscal and monetary data to publish detailed analyses; and provided technical assistance and policy support.

Fiscal Responsibility Framework

From the standpoint of the legal apparatus for fiscal responsibility, Jamaica first legislated our Fiscal Responsibility Framework (FRF) in 2010, when, among other things, the requirement to table a Fiscal Policy Paper (FPP) with the budget was introduced, as well as fiscal rules expressed as quantitative targets.

The FRF was strengthened in 2014, inclusive of the introduction of an algorithm that prescribes the fiscal balance (revenues minus expenditure) that the government ought to achieve in order to maintain a path consistent with achieving a debt target of 60 per cent of GDP by 2026. (Due to the pandemic and the associated economic fallout, this law had to be amended to push back the date to 2028.) By law therefore, this debt anchor in our FRF ought to guide fiscal policy.

Independent Fiscal Commission

However, laws alone do not assure fiscal responsibility into the future. We need institutions, too. The goal, therefore, is to have a domestic institution fit for Jamaica's purpose that combines the independent fiscal review and analysis that the IMF provided, along with the domestic monitoring, ownership, and reporting embodied by EPOC – all of which contributed to Jamaica's internationally recognised fiscal transformation. This domestic institution we seek to establish is an Independent Fiscal Commission, joining more than forty other countries that have established similar institutions.

Consistent with international best practises, the Independent Fiscal Commission's mandate will be to provide the public with an informed, independent opinion on the soundness and sustainability of Jamaica's fiscal policies and positions, in keeping with Jamaica's Fiscal Responsibility Framework.

Key operational aspects proposed in the legislation include:

1. *The Commissioner.* The Commission will be headed by a fiscal commissioner, appointed for a maximum, non-renewable term of seven years by the governor general, after consultation with the prime minister and the leader of the Opposition. The commissioner – who will be identified by an open recruitment process – is expected to be a person of high integrity who possesses the knowledge, expertise, and experience in public finance, macroeconomic forecasting, and fiscal-policy management and assessment required to discharge the functions of the office efficiently and effectively. Dismissal of the commissioner is possible only for cause. It is expected that the Commission will be staffed with professionals who support the commissioner in fulfilling the Commission's mandate.

2. *Quarterly Reports.* The Commission will issue two 'Economic and Fiscal Assessment Reports,' published within ten days of the release of the FPP and the Interim FPP, in February and September (or October) each year. These reports will include the Commission's opinions on the soundness of Jamaica's fiscal position in the context of the FRF, while also assessing long-term debt sustainability. The latter would, for example, stress-test the interest- and exchange-rate assumptions, debt composition, and economic and fiscal risks, similar to the IMF's debt-sustainability analysis. The Commission will not, however, assess the policies underlying the FPP, which are social policy choices of the government in place.

The Fiscal Commission will also produce two 'Statements on Fiscal Performance,' in respect of the June and December quarters, which assess the government's achievement of the budget and fiscal targets pursuant to the FRF. These reports are analogous to EPOC's updates on fiscal outcomes versus targets. The reports will be subject to a corrections policy, to prevent disclosure of market-sensitive information and factual errors.

3. *Accountability and Funding.* The Commission will be accountable to the people of Jamaica and to Parliament. The Commission will publish its reports on its website, and concurrently submit them to both Houses of Parliament. Funding for the Commission will be

approved by Parliament as a line item in the budget, with annual reports to be audited by the auditor general.

4. Advisory Committee. An advisory committee, comprising a group of five stakeholders with experienced and qualified representatives from academia, the private sector, trade unions, and civil society will support the fiscal commissioner by providing periodically their views on the fiscal and economic outlook – while not encroaching on the operational independence of the Commission. For full transparency, the meeting schedule with the advisory committee will be disclosed a year in advance, and minutes of meetings will be published within six weeks or prior to the next meeting, whichever is earlier.

While the Fiscal Commission will act as a check against unrealistic budgeting, fanciful assumptions, and creative accounting inclusive of arrears and deferred financing, its role only provides an informed 'second opinion' with its statements, forecasts, and analyses. It will have no power to legislate, nor to make, change, or implement policy. The Fiscal Commission monitors, analyses, informs, and reports. With an engaged citizenry, as is increasingly the case in Jamaica, that can go a long way to incentivise adherence to responsible fiscal policy, as our experience under the EFF and PSBA demonstrates.

Finally, while the Fiscal Commission will assume some roles of the Auditor General under the FRF, the auditor general will continue to assess and report on the contingent liabilities that accrue to government under public-private partnerships.

Why Is This Important?

Economic independence requires that we invest in the technical capacity of Jamaicans and build domestic institutions that allow us to responsibly chart our own course, through good times and bad, and responsibly pursue our national objectives.

High levels of debt that crowd out productivity-enhancing capital expenditures and squeeze spending on education, health, and social support threaten our economic independence. Furthermore, high debt levels remove policy flexibility when this is most needed – at the bottom of the economic cycle. With lower and lower debt, we can more easily achieve longer and longer unbroken periods of economic growth, sustainably lifting more people out of poverty, while retaining the policy flexibility to implement counter-cyclical measures to influence shorter and shorter recessions at the cycles' bottom.

The graduation of Jamaica from an IMF programme in 2019 and the experience with EPOC opened an opportunity to create our own Independent Fiscal Commission as the permanent guardian and arbiter of Jamaica's Fiscal Responsibility Framework. In passing the legislation to establish the Independent Fiscal Commission, we aim to normalise fiscal responsibility into the future by institutionalising the critical analysis, review, and reporting that proved instrumental in Jamaica's fiscal transformation.[18]

The Tax Write-Off System is Transparent

Letter to the Editor of the Jamaica Gleaner

October 2, 2020

Dear Editor,

The tax write-off system is transparent. We will make it more transparent.

The GOJ's policy of tax write-offs was overhauled in 2013 as part of the first suite of staff-level structural benchmarks agreed with the IMF under the Extended Fund Facility.

Previously, tax write-offs were at the discretion of the Minister, and these write-offs were never made public. In addition, there were no written rules that governed the circumstances on which taxpayer arrears could be written off. The new system transferred the power to determine taxpayer accounts that should be written off from the Minister to the Commissioner General of Tax. Furthermore, the regulations approved by Parliament list the specific criteria to be used by the Commissioner General to determine a tax arrear uncollectable. The Commissioner General has no flexibility outside of these rules and, rightly, the Minister has no power to determine a tax arrear uncollectable. The final step requires the Minister to publish an Order in the *Gazette* of the determination made by the Commissioner General. This publication details the taxpayers and amounts.

This reform, and the resulting laws and rules, benefited from the technical advice of Jamaica's international partners who are experts on transparency in governance. With (1) an explicit, legislated, rules-based approach, (2) the exclusion of the Minister in the write-off determinations and the devolution of this responsibility to the Commissioner General of Tax and (3) the publication of taxpayer names and amounts written off, the system meets international transparency criteria.

However, it could be made more transparent. As the *Gleaner* and others have suggested, the publication ought not to paint all taxpayers with the same brush if circumstances differ substantially. Also, though the *Gazette* is an official public document, and the 'newspaper of record' for the Government, it is not in wide circulation. The publication could therefore be made more accessible.[19]

We will immediately improve the system. Going forward, I will direct that where an Order is published in the *Gazette* on the tax write-off determinations made by the Commissioner General, we will upload that issue of the *Gazette* to the Ministry's website within thirty days of it being printed. We will also examine whether the write-offs can be categorised by the specific criteria in the Regulations on which the Commissioner General made the write-off determination.

It is in the public interest that this process, which has been in place since 2013, is properly understood and enjoys the confidence of the Jamaican people. I will therefore shed further light on the legislation, the regulations, the rationale, the related policy matters, and the total tax arrears written off since 2013 in a follow-up letter to you.

Sincerely,

Nigel Clarke
Minister of Finance and the Public Service

Understanding the Complexity of Jamaica's Tax Arrears and Write-Off System

Published Commentary, October 2020

A country's tax records fossilise its economic history. The chronic economic instability and turmoil that Jamaica experienced over much of the past three decades, that affected public and private sectors, and the struggles of under-resourced tax authorities to keep up, are indelibly expressed in our tax-record metadata.

As a society we have no better choice than to attempt to understand and reckon with this historical reality, even as authorities endeavour to transparently resolve the legacy consequences.

In 2011, when a policy was being developed to address the untenable issue of uncollectable tax arrears, there were 70,245 taxpayers accounting for approximately $230 billion of tax arrears. By 2013, when the proposed legislative amendments were submitted to Cabinet for approval, more than $408 billion was owed by 145,271 taxpayer accounts, which demonstrated the ballooning nature of the problem.

How Tax Arrears Arise

Tax arrears consist of taxes, of all types, that are, in the estimation of Tax Administration Jamaica (TAJ or Revenue Authority), lawfully due and payable but that remain unpaid. Tax arrears are made up of the original principal amount of the tax plus interest, penalties, and surcharges added with punitive and dissuasive intent.

When public and private-sector taxpayers experience severe financial duress, they sometimes skip tax payments and become delinquent, thereby increasing the stock of tax arrears. There are other instances when financially stable taxpayers do not comply and are then assessed to be liable for taxation, and this adds to the volume of tax arrears outstanding. There are more egregious cases

---

An earlier version of this article appeared in the *Jamaica Gleaner*, October 4, 2020.

of foreigners absconding, having previously established business in Jamaica.

On occasion, otherwise compliant taxpayers receive assessments that claim they are liable for more taxes than they have declared or paid. Once the due date of the tax assessment passes without payment the stock of arrears increases. A balanced account must acknowledge that not all of what the Revenue Authority records as tax arrears results from taxpayer delinquency. It is sometimes the case that what is recorded as a tax arrear by the Authority is the subject of a legitimate objection by the taxpayer. In other words, some of the inventory of tax arrears represent contested claims.

The Composition of Tax Arrears

The stock of tax arrears declined from J$403 billion in 2013 to J$159 billion in 2020, on account of collection activities, write-offs of uncollectable tax arrears, and lower net annual increases of new tax arrears.

The public tends to think of tax arrears as only being associated with the private sector. It would therefore probably surprise readers to learn that just under 40 per cent of current tax arrears are on account of 2,029 government sector taxpayers (state-owned enterprises, public bodies, public schools, departments, agencies, ministries, etc.,) and 60 per cent of tax arrears are on account of 143,840 non-government taxpayers including individuals, professionals, businesses, private schools and colleges, as well as NGOs. Furthermore, TAJ reports that government-sector taxpayer arrears constitute, by far, the largest individual taxpayer arrear balances, with only nine government-sector taxpayer arrear balances accounting for 25 per cent of the entire stock of arrears.

It is also useful to note that approximately 66 per cent (or J$104 billion) of the arrears balance originates from automatically applied interest, penalties, and surcharges and 34 per cent (or J$55 billion) represents the original principal tax arrears balance. That is, the original principal tax arrears balance represents about 10 per cent of annual tax revenues.

A Large Stock of Tax Arrears Creates Problems

A large stock of tax arrears leads to an over-estimation of revenue forecasts and an over-commitment of expenditure, resulting in an accumulation of debt.

A large stock of uncollectible taxpayer arrears creates even bigger problems. Prior to 2013, large numbers and amounts of taxpayer arrear balances generated mountains of discretionary waiver requests that engulfed resources. Systems for processing these requests were not rules-based and depended on ministerial discretion with the obvious governance pitfalls. Furthermore, there was no mechanism for informing the public of the particulars of these ministerial tax arrears write-offs.

Collectability of Tax Arrears

During the 2019–20 fiscal year, approximately J$18 billion (or 3 per cent) of the revenue collected came from taxpayer arrears. However, in some instances tax arrears are uncollectable. Tax arrears may be uncollectable if the taxpayer no longer exists, is bankrupt, or does not have the income or assets that could finance payment. Tax arrears may also be uncollectable if the legal basis to collect does not exist, or if it so old that the records are compromised. Also, it may be the case that the cost of collection of the arrear is not justified by the likely yield.

Despite these realities, pre-2013 legislation allowed the Revenue Authority to indefinitely expend resources to collect taxes that had been assessed – even if they may have become impossible or impractical to collect. There were no statutory criteria on which a tax collector could properly refrain from continuing the collection pursuit. This contributed to ballooning arrears, which, at the time, could only legally be deflated by ministerial discretion.

Tax Collection Reform and Write-Off

When the Government of Jamaica (GOJ) entered into the Extended Fund Facility with the IMF in May 2013, in addition to strengthening tax collection powers, one of the first staff-level structural benchmarks set for October 2013 was to achieve '… Parliamentary approval of the legislation for the introduction of a write-off policy for tax and customs duties arrears inclusive of interest, penalty and surcharge consistent with FAD advice....'[20] (FAD is the Fiscal Affairs Department of the IMF).

The Fund immediately recognised the self-defeating nature of perpetually carrying a large stock of uncollectable tax arrears and the weakness in tax administration legislation that did not provide the avenue for transparent write-off of uncollectable tax arrears.

The solution, by way of new legislation, included:

1. abolishing the discretionary power of the Minister to grant waivers in relation to tax arrears matters;

2. amending the Tax Collection Act to introduce a rules-based procedure for the Commissioner General of Tax to determine a tax arrear as uncollectable;

3. introducing the Tax Collection (Write-off) Regulations of 2013;

4. prescribing in the Regulations the specific circumstances under which the Commissioner General can determine a tax arrear as uncollectable;

5. including in those Regulations the circumstances where the Commissioner General is prohibited from determining an arrear as uncollectable;

6. requiring that taxpayer write-off determinations made by the Commissioner General are made public through an Order signed by the Minister and published in the *Gazette*; and

7. giving the Commissioner General the power to recover the debt written off in the future, if any information becomes available to the Commissioner General that the sum can in fact be collected.

To operationalise this process, the Commissioner General relies on a Tax Write-Off Committee of senior GOJ tax officials, chaired by a non-TAJ member, who meet monthly to consider the Commissioner General's recommendations. Unanimous agreement that each case meets the criteria set out in the Regulations is required before the Commissioner General makes the write-off determination.

Operation 'Broad Brush'

The problem of uncollectable tax arrears, however, was so acutely, densely, and intractably complicated that the case-by-case approach was insufficient to resolve the problem. A brute force approach was also necessary.

To clean up the tax ledger the Regulations include a provision that allows for non-government tax arrears as at Dec 31, 2010, and for public-body tax arrears as at Dec 31, 2012, to be written off in a 'Broad Brush approach' (the actual name of the project). The 'Broad Brush' approach bypasses the specific circumstances-based criteria in Section 5(1)a of the Regulations and uses a cut-off date criterion as per Section 5(1)b of the Regulations. The basis of the 'Broad Brush' approach is the impracticability collecting these tax arrears. This was the only practical approach given the scale of the problem.

Under this approach, over $250 billion in tax arrears were written off in 2014 and 2015, in batches. Totals were published in the *Gazette* but neither government nor non-government taxpayers were itemised as this was deemed impractical. Listing each 'Broad Brush' taxpayer arrears write-off would easily exhaust 10,000 pages.

The Way Forward

Since passage of the legislation in 2013, more than $288 billion of uncollectable taxpayer arrears have been written off. Going forward with the reforms pledged in my letter to the *Gleaner* last Friday, and the further reforms committed to in this article, we will continue to strengthen the transparency of the tax arrears write-off system.[21]

Fiscal Responsibility Matters When the Stakes Are High

Published Commentary, March 2023

I think it is safe for readers to assume that, at heart, the *Gleaner* supports fiscal responsibility in general, and Jamaica's fiscal rules in particular, adherence to which its editorial page has championed across political administrations.

If that is so, sections of last Sunday's *Gleaner* Editorial gave us reason to question the due diligence it employs before arriving at its positions on matters of a technical nature.

Weighing in on the public-sector wage restructuring is fair game. However, on a day (Sunday, March 12) when the voting membership of teachers and doctors were gathered to make critical decisions, the promotion of impractical and irresponsible fiscal choices by the *Gleaner* Editorial, and the resulting trivialisation of Jamaica's rigid fiscal realities, stained the *Gleaner*'s otherwise strong record of upholding fiscal truth in Jamaica.

If fiscal targets do not matter, then of course, the Government of Jamaica (GOJ) can take on any expenditure, at any time, and the GOJ can even ignore the revenue implications of its decisions.

The GOJ has J$30 billion of budgeted 'back-pay' resources in this fiscal year for teachers, doctors, and police. Since November, I have been explaining that if this large volume of expenditure goes unpaid this fiscal year, it would most probably need to be paid over a number of years beginning in 2024–25. Revenue received this fiscal year, if not spent during the year, cannot be utilised for any 'above the line' expenditures (expenditures that go into determining the fiscal balance) in a succeeding period given that under our fiscal rules, Jamaica is required to run a modest positive fiscal balance at this time. If the J$30 billion is unspent, it could only be utilised

---

An earlier version of this article appeared in the *Jamaica Gleaner*, March 16, 2023.

in the next fiscal year for 'below the line' expenditures such as the repayment of debt.

The 2023–24 budget has no provision for J$30 billion of payments relating to the first year of restructured compensation. (However, it makes provisions of $32 billion for the second year of payments).

Couldn't 2023–24 expenditure be rearranged to accommodate the unbudgeted expenditure?

Budgetary expenditure for 2023–24 is programmed at just over J$1,000 billion. Of this amount, three line items – wages and salaries, debt service, and pension payments – consume approximately J$700 billion or 70 per cent of the budget.

Add the next eight largest categories of recurrent expenditure:

1. PATH Programme (school nutrition, school transportation, and all PATH grants),
2. drugs and supplies for hospitals,
3. subventions to our universities,
4. subvention to the university hospital,
5. allocation for the Judiciary,
6. subvention to the JUTC (Jamaica Urban Transit Company),
7. recurrent maintenance of roads and bridges,
8. streetlights, books, and materials for schools,

and we are just below J$800 billion or approximately 80 per cent of the budget. To this add the non-wage operating expenses of the police, correctional services, the Major Organised Crime and Anti-Corruption Agency (MOCA), regional health authorities, and laboratories, and we surpass J$850 billion.

The capital expenditure budget envelope, which is used to improve standards of living, is considered less than optimal at 2.2 per cent of GDP or J$75 billion. This brings our total to J$925 billion.

The approximate J$75 billion that remains must cover all other remaining expenditure across ministries, departments, and agencies (MDAs). It is therefore virtually impossible to force-fit a block of J$30 billion of unplanned expenditure into such a structure without precipitating a crisis.

Misleading Solution of a Supplementary Budget

The *Gleaner* Editorial made the misguided suggestion that the J$30 billion could be accommodated by invocation of a supplementary budget: 'the administration might consider tabling a supplementary budget.... Supplementary budgets are a norm for governments, which have to react to developments during the financial year....'

I consider this misleading and deeply troubling.

If fiscal targets matter, then supplementary budgets that accommodate additional unbudgeted expenditure can only be consistent with fiscal rules if additional revenues finance them. We have had seven supplementary budgets over the past two fiscal years. Most of these revised expenditure significantly upwards.... However, the dramatic over-performance of GOJ revenues in this period was the only reason these large supplementary additions to expenditure were feasible.

Now that the economy has surpassed pre-COVID-19 levels of economic output, and with inflation declining, the scope for significant revenue over-performance that could accommodate $30 billion as a single line item of unbudgeted expenditure, is extremely limited. Contrary to the *Gleaner* Editorial suggestion, the chances of a supplementary budget process 'magically' creating space for $30 billion, in a fiscally responsible manner, are slim to nil.

The *Gleaner* Editorial also suggested:

> While funds are fungible, monies can be segregated and escrowed, as the Government did with the amounts that it was prepared to pay the Venezuelan government for its 49 per cent share of the Petrojam oil refinery that Caracas refused to accept. A similar approach might be contemplated with respect to the bargain units that haven't accepted the administration's offer.

I only have space to mention two of several challenges with this suggestion.

Warrants for payments can only be drawn against specific budgeted activities. In this case, the budgeted activity that relates to the $30 billion provision is compensation allocated across all MDAs. The Petrojam-Venezuela example involved a single beneficiary. With teachers, doctors, and police, we have approximately forty thousand individual beneficiaries!

Furthermore, the law requires that the employer withholds statutory payments relating to compensation and pay these over to the tax authority. If funds are placed into an escrow account, how would the employer handle the withholding of statutory payments? And, at what point would the statutory payments become legally due and payable, since the actual employee would not be in receipt of the funds at the point of expenditure by the government?

Anticipated receipts of statutory payments from additional compensation have naturally been factored into revenue. If the programmed compensation were paid out into escrow without the simultaneous inflow of related statutory payments, the fiscal balance target would be missed. The suggestion is therefore unworkable as the achievement of fiscal targets is actually very important.

Championing fiscal responsibility matters most when the numbers are big and the stakes are high. The *Gleaner* Editorial has usually been well informed, and on point, at these junctures. Not this time, unfortunately. Thankfully, though, teachers and doctors, who turned out in record numbers to vote on Sunday, ignored the misguided musings of last Sunday's Editorial.

Prioritising Economic Policies That Take Responsibility for Our Vulnerability

Budget Speech Excerpt, March 2023

One of the lessons of [our] experience, Madam Speaker, is the critical importance of ensuring that we put in place adequate resource buffers to protect ourselves against unexpected shocks. Jamaica is a small, open economy in a vast world.

Cross-border trade in goods and services account for 80 per cent of GDP in Jamaica as compared with, for example, the United States where this ratio is less than 30 per cent. Economic openness reflects the degree to which foreign actors affect and participate in the domestic economy. What this means is that economic life in Jamaica is easily affected and often disturbed by what happens outside of Jamaica, which is not under the control of anyone in Jamaica. So adverse international events – such as war, economic sanctions, and trade tensions – can often result in economic shock to Jamaica.

Our economic openness is also related in part to our dependence on foreign-imported food and energy. For example, adverse movements in the prices of wheat, soya beans, corn, and energy commodities have contributed to economic shock in Jamaica. In addition, tourism is such a significant source of foreign exchange in Jamaica that economic dips in the United States, Canada, and the UK can result in declines in our foreign exchange receipts. To top it off, we live in a climatic zone where we are susceptible to hurricanes, excess rainfall, and other natural disasters that interrupt, delay, and reduce economic activity.

These are simply the realities we face. And a careful review of our economic history reveals that these have long been our realities. Madam Speaker, members of this Honourable House, and my fellow Jamaicans, please reflect on the serious economic impact on Jamaica of various adverse external episodes such as:

- the oil-price shock of 1974;

Adapted from the opening budget presentation delivered in Parliament March 7, 2023.

- the oil-price shock of 1979;
- the crash in world alumina prices in the mid-1980s;
- Hurricane Gilbert in 1988;
- the September 11 terrorist attacks in 2001;
- Hurricane Ivan in 2004;
- Hurricane Dean in 2007;
- the Global Financial Crisis of 2008–10;
- the oil-price shock of 2008;
- Hurricane Gustav in 2008;
- Hurricane Sandy in 2011;
- the oil-price shock of 2010–14;
- Hurricane Matthew in 2016;
- the global COVID-19 pandemic of 2020;
- the Ukraine war of 2022;
- the oil-price shock of 2022; and
- the global inflation crisis of 2022.

This list is by no means complete.

Here is the bad news: Jamaica will certainly continue to suffer from adverse external events and economic shocks in the future. We cannot control them. We cannot stop them.

Here is the good news: we need not leave our social and economic development hostage to these outside forces – and indeed we must not.

Sadly, this is largely the approach that we in Jamaica have taken over the past fifty years. What we must do – what this administration has been committed to doing, and what this administration has been doing – is to ensure that our economic policies take account of our vulnerabilities and adequately prepare us to respond quickly and effectively to adverse external events and shocks, whenever and however they occur.

We must take responsibility for our own vulnerabilities and prepare for them. We are proud to say that we have done so, with the support of the Jamaican people. That is how we can ensure quick recoveries from economic shock, and that is why Jamaica has recovered as strongly and as quickly as we did from the most recent, unprecedented 'mother of all shocks,' the COVID-19 pandemic.

Over the past fifty years, sadly, Jamaica has been hit frequently by a variety of economic shocks, and our recovery periods have been far too long. To avoid this fate in the future, we must ensure that we maintain above-adequate foreign exchange reserves; reduce our dependence on imported food and energy; put in place fiscal buffers to counter the economic impact of natural disasters; and keep our debt levels low. These efforts will provide the flexibility needed to respond to economic shocks, protect the vulnerable in the society, and ensure strong and speedy recoveries.

We must put in place economic and social policies that are appropriate for our size and position in the world economy and which prioritise building up and maintaining resource buffers, as well as strengthening and deepening our economic and social resiliency.

Establishment of a Fiscal Research Centre

Budget Speech Excerpt, March 2023

The benefits of pursuing sound public financial management are so significant that it cannot be left to the Minister of Finance alone. It cannot even be left to the Ministry of Finance alone. It cannot be left to the Cabinet alone, or to Parliament alone. Sound public financial management, appropriate for our circumstances, must become an instinct that permeates our entire society.

Jamaica's own Professor Patterson, reflecting on his time as an advisor to former Prime Minister Michael Manley, wrote in his book *The Confounding Island* that 'the tragedy of radical change is that you cannot implement it without able management….' Noble economic and social policy goals cannot be sustainably achieved without sound public financial management that takes into account all of our circumstances.

Madam Speaker, there is an appalling lack of opportunity for public financial management research and training in the Caribbean. If we are to command our own ship, independently and sustainably, then a large increase in the supply of graduates specialising in public finance is a national imperative. In addition, generations of public sector leaders will need better exposure to, and training in, public financial management.

For these reasons, I am pleased to announce that the Government of Jamaica will supplement the budgetary grant extended to The University of the West Indies (UWI) in the amount of $200 million as a down-payment to endow a Fiscal Research Institute (or Centre) within the Department of Economics. This will be followed by further endowments to establish the Centre, which we expect will be financed from the returns on its endowment. I intend to secure the

---

Adapted from the opening budget presentation delivered in Parliament March 7, 2023. The Fiscal Research Centre was launched at UWI on October 22, 2024, in partnership with the Inter-American Development Bank and Canada's Institute of Fiscal Studies. The promised GOJ contribution was transferred that week.

support of the private sector in endowing the chair of this centre as part of the government's initiative in collaboration with The UWI.

The Fiscal Research Centre will be a non-partisan think tank engaged in conducting rigorous, high-level research, teaching, and training in public finance and public policy. The Centre will offer courses in public finance and public financial management at both the undergraduate and graduate levels. The Centre will also analyse and inform economic and social policy decisions – particularly those involving public expenditure, taxation, and fiscal sustainability – to help policymakers and the general population understand the impact of public choices on individuals, households, firms, the government's financial position, and the overall interaction between the domestic and global economies.

While we will always be able to benefit from the advice of our multilateral partners, the Jamaica project becomes unsustainable without increased domestic capacity for public finance management training, analysis, and research.

The Importance of Reducing Debt

Budget Speech Excerpt, March 2023

Earlier, I spoke about Jamaica's debt being lower today than it was prior to the pandemic. In fact, we are on track to achieving the lowest level of debt in over twenty years! Our goal is that by this time next year, Jamaica's debt level will be lower than it was prior to the domestic economic shock known as FINSAC.

For the younger generation, FINSAC stands for the Financial Sector Adjustment Company, a massive entity established by the Jamaican government to address the financial-sector crisis in the 1990s. FINSAC resulted in a massive increase in debt – from approximately 74 per cent of GDP to more than 110 per cent in a few short years – which has dogged Jamaica ever since and which no doubt has also compounded other crises since that time.

It will have taken us an entire generation to rid ourselves of the FINSAC debt accumulated in the 1990s financial-sector crisis. Almost thirty years.

Almost thirty years, Madam Speaker.

Thirty years!

That is the central lesson of debt: it is easy to put on and very hard to take off. A single policy can add mountains of debt that strangles the chances of a generation and takes decades to remove.

Another problem with debt is that it increases the rigidity of the budget – you end up with high fixed expenses to service and repay that debt, which cannot be altered even in times of crisis.

High debt makes economic crises worse.

High debt makes economic shocks more severe.

High debt also reduces the fiscal space and flexibility needed to respond to economic shocks.

Adapted from the opening budget presentation delivered in Parliament March 7, 2023.

And, as such, initial economic shocks can lead to other crises, which complicate and lengthen economic recovery. Lengthy, decade-long periods of economic recovery impede social, economic, and national development.

And high debt is not the metric itself. Debt is a proxy for the more relevant metric, which is the cost of servicing that debt as a proportion of GDP. We live in a world which prices money based on the perceived ability to repay. Those who are viewed as having the least ability to repay get charged the most. That is the reality of our world.

We cannot follow the United States of America, for example, whose debt is over 100 per cent of GDP. Despite this relatively high debt ratio, the average cost of their debt is still only 2 per cent. Even though Jamaica's debt ratio is projected to be quite a bit lower than in the United States at 80 per cent of GDP, it costs us approximately 6 per cent of GDP to service. Jamaica's debt ratio is 80 per cent of the United States' debt ratio, but the cost of our debt takes up 300 per cent more of our fiscal space. Even though the US has a higher debt ratio, they have much, much more fiscal flexibility than we do.

Shakespeare wrote in *Hamlet*, 'This above all: to thine own self be true.'

We must 'know ourselves and be true to ourselves' by internalising our own realities and maintaining a policy posture that is relevant and optimal to our circumstances.

Given our level of openness and our level of vulnerability, our debt must be maintained at levels substantially lower than what we hope to achieve in the upcoming fiscal year for us to have a meaningful chance at sustainable development.

Jamaica is part of CARICOM, which is an extremely high debt zone, and we have been in this paradigm for so long that high debt has become normalised. The reality, however, is that there are many successful small countries with open economies that have very low levels of debt-to-GDP. For example: the Dominican Republic (44 per cent), Ireland (42 per cent), Latvia and Lithuania (both at 36 per cent), New Zealand (23 per cent), and Estonia (9 per cent).

We can and must do better to continue reducing our debt as a percentage of GDP, to ensure that we have the fiscal space and flexibility to [allow us to] recover quickly and effectively from economic shocks whenever and however they occur in the future. We must preserve and maintain the gains of our economic recovery.

149

Credit Ratings Matter because the Cost of Credit Matters

Published Commentary, October 2023

Standard & Poor's (S&P), the international credit-rating agency, recently upgraded Jamaica's sovereign debt from B+ to BB-. This is the best credit rating that Jamaica has received from S&P since they started rating Jamaica's sovereign debt in 1999.

Many Jamaicans intrinsically understand the significance of this development. Others wonder, *Why does this matter?* Credit ratings matter because the cost of credit matters. And credit-rating upgrades matter because they support improvements in the relative cost of credit.

Credit Ratings Influence a Country's Relative Cost of Credit

Governments rely on loan financing to plug seasonal cash-flow gaps and to fund projects and programmes. Bond investors provide loan financing to governments and price these loans primarily through the interest rate (i.e., the 'yield') they require the borrowing government to pay.

For bonds issued in international capital markets, the yield can be thought of as consisting of two components. The first is the prevailing yield on similar securities issued by the United States government (i.e., US Treasury Bonds and US Treasury Bills, collectively referred to hereinafter as US Treasuries). These are traditionally regarded as the safest investments one can make. The second component is the spread above comparable US Treasuries that represents the perceived riskiness of lending to the borrowing country. The riskier the economy, the higher the spread over US Treasuries that investors will demand.

However, international government bond investors do not all have the capacity, nor the inclination, to keep track of the riskiness of all the

---

An earlier version of this article appeared in the *Jamaica Gleaner*, October 1, 2023.

countries they lend to. As such, international credit-rating agencies, who have tremendous scale in research and analysis, perform the service of closely tracking countries and ascribing periodic credit ratings that represent their view of the country's creditworthiness. These ratings play an influential role in determining the spread over US Treasury yields that investors demand for lending to the particular country.

Here I present historical data to show that during the thirteen-year period between 2010–23, across all outstanding emerging-market bonds rated 'B' by S&P, investors demanded an average spread of 600 basis points (i.e., 6 percentage points) over US Treasuries, while over the same time horizon bonds from 'BB' rated emerging-market countries required an average spread of 295 basis points (i.e., 2.95 percentage points) over US Treasuries.

So, for illustrative purposes, if US Treasuries yielded an average of 2.5 per cent over this period, the 'B' rated bonds, of similar maturity profile, would have yielded an average of 8.5 per cent over the same period, while 'BB' rated bonds would have yielded 5.45 per cent. These yields reflect the prices that countries with a 'B' rating, and others with a 'BB' rating, would have had to pay, on average, on new bonds issued over that period.

Over time, this 305-basis point (3.05 percentage points) differential between what the 'B' rated country pays on its debt and what the 'BB' rated country pays, adds up to substantial amounts that the 'BB' rated country could deploy to other activities better aligned with development, such as education, health, and infrastructure spending.

Jamaica's Relative Cost of Credit is Now Better Than Regional Peers

We can bring the point closer home by examining the trajectory of the spread over US Treasuries that investors required to hold Jamaica's bond maturing in 2025 (Jamaica's 2025 bond), which was issued in 2005. In early 2013, when Jamaica had a credit rating of CCC from S&P, investors required a spread of approximately 700 basis points (7 percentage points!) over US Treasuries to hold Jamaica's 2025 bond. By early 2016, Jamaica's credit rating was single B, two notches above CCC, and bond investors reduced this spread to 500 basis points (5 percentage points). Today, Jamaica's credit rating is **BB-**, two notches above single B, and the spread on the Jamaica 2025 bond hovers at just over 100 basis points (1 percentage point) over similar US Treasuries. The dramatic reduction in this spread, from 7 percentage points to 1 percentage point, vividly portrays the improvement in Jamaica's risk profile and relative cost of financing over the period.

Today, investors require an even lower yield on Jamaican bonds than our credit rating would suggest. A snapshot of data on emerging-market bond-yield spreads for September 21, 2022, reveals that on this date, investors were requiring compensation of 1,992 basis points (19.92 percentage points) above US Treasuries to hold Sri Lanka's government bonds, 705 basis points (7.05 percentage points) above US Treasuries to hold Bahama's government bonds, and 370 basis points (3.7 percentage points) above US Treasuries to hold Barbados' government bonds – but only 119 basis points (1.19 percentage points) above US Treasuries to hold Jamaican government bonds of similar tenor.

Also, the spread over US Treasuries that investors require to hold Jamaican bonds is even less today than investors require to hold similar bonds issued by the governments of Mexico, Panama, and Hungary even though these countries are designated 'investment grade' by rating agencies, which represents a credit rating three notches above Jamaica's.

At the same time, the yield on the ten-year US Treasury bond has increased from 1.7 per cent at the beginning of 2022 to about 4.5 per cent today, which means yields on all government bonds, globally, have increased over this time frame. However, Jamaica's relative cost of financing has never been cheaper. The market data above suggest that, today, Jamaica can raise financing on international capital markets more cheaply than the vast majority of our regional peers.

Credit Rating Upgrades Improve the Cost of Doing Business

This improvement in the GOJ's credit profile also has a positive impact on the cost of credit for Jamaican businesses. A higher credit rating improves the terms of trade that Jamaica has with the rest of the world. This matters, as we imported approximately US$7.7 billion of goods in 2022 which represented approximately 40 per cent of GDP. Commercial importers need to negotiate credit terms with suppliers who assess the risk of being repaid, and the credit risk of the GOJ features prominently in such assessments. Depending on the industry, commercial importers may have to post bonds, or secure credit insurance to satisfy suppliers. These become more affordable the higher the credit rating of the GOJ. The more competitive the industry, the more these savings flow to consumers.

In addition, project financings and public-private partnerships (PPPs) become more financeable and hence more feasible the higher a country's credit rating. Similarly, the signals transmitted from a higher credit rating make Jamaica more attractive for foreign investment in general.

Important to Continue to Improve on Factors That Influenced Jamaica's Upgrade

In upgrading Jamaica's credit rating, S&P would have taken into consideration the following, among other factors: (a) Jamaica's improved and more robust institutional framework, including an independent central bank, a new fiscal commissioner, and the independent fiscal commission; (b) Jamaica's monetary-policy framework of inflation targeting within the context of a market-determined exchange rate; (c) Jamaica's improved disaster risk financing framework that improves fiscal resilience through an independently sponsored catastrophe bond, a capitalised contingency fund for natural disasters, and a credit contingency claim; (d) Jamaica's commitment to debt reduction and our dramatically improved debt-to-GDP, which is projected to be 74 per cent by March 2023, down from 110 per cent at the height of the pandemic; (e) the existence of a credible fiscal path for attaining debt-to-GDP of 60 per cent within the timeline specified in Jamaica's fiscal rules; and (f) Jamaica's improved net international reserves (NIR) of US$4.4 billion – significantly more than the US$3 billion when Jamaica was last upgraded to B+ in 2019, and double the US$2 billion in NIR in early 2016.

These policy reforms and achievements contributed to the historic S&P credit upgrade, and it is vitally important that we continue to build on these, to lower Jamaica's cost of credit and create even more fiscal space for development.

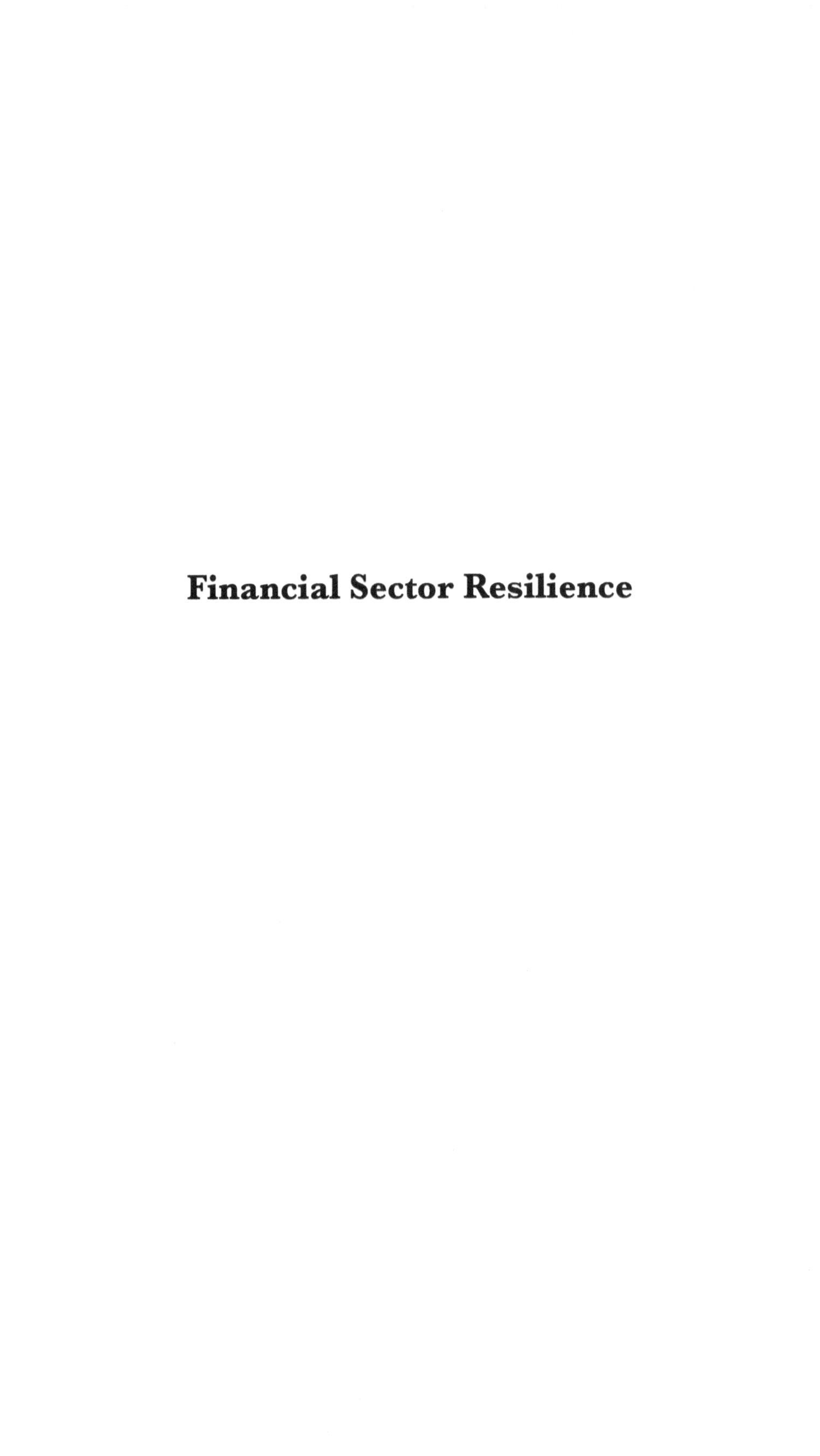

Financial Sector Resilience

Jamaica's Grey-Listing by the Financial Action Task Force

Q&A Session, February 2020

On February 25, 2020, the *Jamaica Observer* broke the story that the Financial Action Task Force (FATF) had placed Jamaica on its list for enhanced follow-up, otherwise known as the 'Grey List.'[22] I took questions from journalists at the *Observer* to explain the significance of this development.

Question: What does being added to this list mean for Jamaica?

This means that Jamaica's progress towards improving its framework for combatting money-laundering and terrorist financing will be monitored by the Financial Action Task Force (FATF). Among the matters that Jamaica has to address are (a) completing an assessment of the money-laundering and terrorist-financing risks that Jamaica faces, (b) implementing new laws and amending existing ones to improve the effectiveness of our AML/CFT framework, and (c) ensuring effective risk-based supervision by appropriate regulators for designated non-financial businesses and professions, such as the accounting profession, real estate dealers, the legal fraternity, the gaming industry, and trust and company service providers.

Question: How will the Jamaican Government respond in meeting the requirements to be removed from the list?

By prioritising and implementing the range of reforms to remedy Jamaica's strategic deficiencies within the time frame agreed with the FATF. Some reforms will take up to two years to implement.[23] Others can be done more quickly. The key is to ensure that the reforms are not only achieved as quickly as possible but are sustainable.

We have established a secretariat at the Bank of Jamaica to coordinate the actions. We have reached out to our bilateral and multilateral partners who have agreed to assist with technical resources that will be useful in implementing the required reforms.

National Effort Required to Improve Jamaica's Anti-Money Laundering and Counter-Terrorist Financing Framework

Published Commentary, February 2020

Jamaica has engaged in structural reform of our fiscal and monetary institutions, laws, and policies with much success. This reform effort benefited from a high level of public awareness of the serious national interests at stake and from social consensus around the reform effort. A similar unified national effort is required to improve Jamaica's Anti–Money Laundering and Counter–Terrorist Financing (AML/CFT) regime.

Benefits to Jamaica of a Strong AML/CFT Regime

Implementation of a strong AML/CFT framework will mean that Jamaica is intent on undercutting the primary, profit-making motives related to crime along with any avenues used to conceal the proceeds of such crime or to further the reach of criminal enterprise.

A strong AML/CFT framework will mean that Jamaica is no longer willing to allow such activities to generate financial flows that involve the diversion of resources away from economically and socially productive uses.

It also means that Jamaicans from all walks of life recognise that a well-designed and implemented framework is a way to limit the corrosive, corrupting effect stemming from 'profitable crime' on society and the economic system as a whole. AML/CFT controls, when effectively implemented, mitigate the adverse effects of criminal economic activity and promote integrity and stability in financial markets.

In addition, a robust AML/CFT framework is increasingly a requirement for participation in the global financial system. Jamaica cannot function without access to, and participation in, the global financial system. That access is threatened by the deficiencies in our AML/CFT regime.

An earlier version of this article appeared in the *Jamaica Gleaner*, February 9, 2020.

Financial Action Task Force's Assessment of Jamaica

The Financial Action Task Force (FATF) is the global standard-setter for rules that address money-laundering and terrorist-financing, and FATF has increased its scrutiny of countries' implementation of its forty recommendations. FATF is also taking increased steps to penalise countries for falling short of these requirements. These penalties can eventually lead to countries losing access to the global financial system.

FATF recognises that in addition to the financial sector, non-financial sectors such as law, accounting, real estate, gaming, jewellery, and non-profit sectors, among others, are exposed to significant AML/CFT risks.

FATF measures the effectiveness of a regime not only with respect to the laws and regulations in place but, more importantly, the use of those laws to regulate, investigate, prosecute, and convict, in addition to interrupting or preventing criminals from benefiting from the proceeds of their crime.

The strength of Jamaica's AML/CFT framework was assessed in 2005 and again in 2015, through mutual evaluation exercises spearheaded by the Caribbean Financial Action Task Force (CFATF), a FATF-styled regional body. Substantial deficiencies were identified.

Some Progress Has Been Made

Legislation such as the Companies (Amendment) Act 2017, the 2019 Proceeds of Crime (Amendment) Act, the United Nations Security Council Resolution (Implementation) (Amendment) Act, and the Terrorism Prevention Act, among other recent laws and regulations, have improved our AML/CFT regime. The micro-credit bill to regulate the microfinance sector has also been tabled.

More than twenty-five hundred law enforcement personnel, including investigators and police officers, were trained in the areas of AML/CFT. Increased training resulted in several money-laundering investigations, charges, and convictions over the period from 2016 to 2019.

Data from the Financial Investigations Division confirms that 117 persons were charged with money-laundering offences over this period. In the update to FATF, Jamaica's Financial Intelligence Unit reported that the number of intelligence reports disseminated to law enforcement agencies for money-laundering and other criminal activities also increased substantially, resulting in increased investigations and charges.

Delays

However, despite this progress, FATF has observed that further amendments are required in our AML/CFT legislative framework. Also, institutions that regulate the real estate, legal, accounting, jewellery, gaming, and pawnbroker sectors need to be resourced to implement risk-based supervision.

One delay merits highlighting. In June 2014, the order bringing attorneys under the Proceeds of Crime Act as Designated Non-Financial Institutions (DNFIs) was passed. The General Legal Council (GLC) was designated the competent authority and issued its guidance from May 2014 with accompanying regulations to follow. In October 2014, the Jamaica Bar Association instituted an action against the GOJ and the GLC to declare the regime unconstitutional. Pending determination of that action, in November 2014, an injunction was granted which had the effect of suspending the operation of the AML regime, including the suspension of the GLC's power to monitor compliance.

The action was heard in March 2015, and the Full Court dismissed the action in April 2017. Consequent on the dismissal of the action, the GLC proceeded in 2017 to promulgate further regulations that had been put on hold with the grant of the injunction in 2014, and attorneys were notified that the GLC would commence inspections in 2018 to ascertain and monitor compliance.

The Jamaican Bar Association appealed the decision of the Full Court, and that appeal was heard as a matter of urgency in July 2017, when judgment was reserved. In January 2018 the Court of Appeal reinstated a limited injunction, the effect of which is to again prevent the GLC, as competent authority, from monitoring AML compliance by attorneys. That order remains in effect.

The effect of the protracted Court proceedings and injunctions is that the GLC's power to supervise and monitor AML compliance by attorneys has been suspended.

Commitment to AML/CFT Action Plan Developed with FATF

Significant work remains to be done to improve the deficiencies in our AML/CFT framework and by so doing to enhance the security of our financial system and satisfy our obligations to the CFATF and the FATF. To this end, Jamaica will be required to commit to the FATF on an action plan that addresses these weaknesses. This action plan will include, among other things:

1. Finalising a more comprehensive national risk assessment to identify risks associated with the financial, legal, accounting, real estate, jewellery, remittance, pawnbroking, car dealership, and non-profit sectors, among others. Without a comprehensive understanding of the AML/CFT risks, Jamaica cannot adequately develop policies and strategies.

2. Finalising the inclusion of all designated non-financial institutions and designated non-financial businesses and professions in the AML/CFT regime, including the legal profession (subject to the court's decision), and ensuring these professions are subject to effective risk-based AML/CFT supervision.

3. Completing the necessary legislative amendments to bring the microfinance sector under AML/CFT requirements and start implementation to ensure that adequate risk-based supervision of the sector is in place.

4. Ensuring an increase in money-laundering investigations that use financial intelligence information and effective cooperation with other jurisdictions, along with corresponding resourcing of the justice system.

5. Amending the Companies Act to ensure, among other things, updating beneficial ownership disclosure standards to be consistent with the FATF standards, along with effective, proportionate, and dissuasive sanctions for legal entities in breach of their beneficial owner disclosure obligations.

6. Amending laws governing the regulation of trusts and the non-profit sectors to improve AML/CFT compliance.

7. Remedying deficiencies in Jamaica's framework for addressing UN-targeted financial sanctions related to terrorism and terrorist/proliferation financing and demonstrating that these targeted, financial-sanction designations are given effect without delay (i.e., within 24 hours) and communicated to obliged entities.

Committed National Effort Required

We need a committed national effort, involving public- and private-sector stakeholders – ministries and departments involved in AML/CFT as well as bankers, remittance companies, cambios, lawyers, real-estate practitioners, gaming operators, microfinance companies, and their umbrella organisations to significantly improve Jamaica's Anti–Money Laundering and Counter–Terrorist Financing Framework.

The good news is that our multilateral and bilateral partners have confirmed their commitment to providing critical technical assistance designed to support Jamaica in satisfying all elements of the Action Plan. Progress will be tracked and publicly disclosed.

While compliance with our FATF obligations is important, far more important is the significant benefit to Jamaica and Jamaicans of a strong AML/CFT framework.

Substantial Progress in Improving Jamaica's AML/CFT Regime

Statement to Parliament, December 12, 2023

This statement is intended to provide a brief update on Jamaica's AML/CFT compliance. Madam Speaker, there are forty Financial Action Task Force (FATF) recommendations[24] that constitute the international standards by which jurisdictions' preventative measures to combat the risks posed by criminals to launder the proceeds of crime and finance terrorism and proliferation of weapons of mass destruction are assessed.

Substantial Improvement in Compliance

Jamaica's Fourth Round Mutual Evaluation, conducted in 2015 by the Caribbean Financial Action Task Force (CFATF) and published in 2017, concluded that Jamaica was compliant or partially compliant in only seventeen of these forty recommendations. Against this background, I am pleased to provide the interim update to the House as follows:

Jamaica has applied for re-rating [of its compliance] on three occasions: in 2019, 2022, and the last such occasion in 2023. With the 2023 re-rating, in aggregate, Jamaica's performance has now resulted in twenty recommendations being upgraded to 'Compliant' or 'Largely Compliant' since the 2015 mutual evaluation. This means that Jamaica is now compliant or largely compliant in thirty-seven out of forty FATF recommendations.

The last round of re-rating (in 2023), where Jamaica sought upgrades for four recommendations, was driven by bringing lawyers in under the AML/CFT framework. Accomplishing this allowed Jamaica to become 'largely compliant' with Recommendations 22, 23, and 28. Additionally, with comprehensive amendments to the Companies Act, Jamaica was upgraded to 'compliant' with Recommendation 24. On the date of my delivery of this news to Parliament, Jamaica was one of only two countries in the entire FATF global network compliant with Recommendation 24, and the only country compliant with both Recommendation 24 and

Recommendation 25, which cover Transparency and Beneficial Ownership of Legal Arrangements. This progress in Jamaica's AML/CFT legislative framework is critically important for Jamaica and Jamaican citizens as we wage a multiple-decades-long struggle with organised crime.

Moving from 'compliant' or 'largely compliant' in only seventeen recommendations, to now thirty-seven recommendations required the amendment of many laws and the passage of new ones, in addition to the passage of many amended and new regulations. And this required the resolve of this administration, and this Parliament. As such, on behalf of all Jamaicans, I acknowledge the support of my parliamentary and Cabinet colleagues.

Three Remaining FATF Recommendations

With these encouraging results, Jamaica must now quickly address the three remaining FATF recommendations with which we are 'Partially Compliant' [namely, Recommendation 7, 'Targeted Financial Sanctions Related to Proliferation'; Recommendation 8, 'Non-Profit Organisations (NPOs); and Recommendation 15, 'New Technologies'].

It is imperative that Jamaica swiftly address these three remaining pieces of legislation as the window for getting them in place is very narrow. Jamaica's Fifth Round Mutual Evaluation is scheduled for mid-2026. However, the date for submitting the self-assessment of our legal framework against the FATF Forty Recommendations (Technical Compliance Template), is December 2025.

One important requirement for the legislation submitted for review is that it should have been in force for at least six months, indicating the need for proper implementation of the law. This means that Jamaica must complete its AML/CFT legislative agenda by March 2025 at the very latest.

FATF Grey-Listing

This progress is also important to return Jamaica to compliance with international standards on AML/CFT so that international counterparts are not required to engage in enhanced due diligence when conducting business with Jamaica.

In addition to being assessed as 'Compliant' in only seventeen of FATF's forty recommendations as at 2015, Jamaica was, at that time, found to have: (a) 'substantial level of effectiveness' in only one of eleven possible Immediate Outcomes; (b) 'moderate level of effectiveness' in four of the eleven Immediate Outcomes; and (c) 'low level of effectiveness' in six of the eleven Immediate Outcomes.

While compliance with FATF recommendations measures existence of the legislative framework in the country to address specific risks, the Immediate Outcomes measure the effectiveness of the laws on the books: Are they being enforced? Is enhanced due diligence being conducted when required?

Due to deficiencies in the effectiveness of Jamaica's AML/CFT regime, and due to the size of Jamaica's economy as measured by a money-supply metric that was arbitrarily changed, Jamaica was placed under enhanced monitoring and follow-up by FATF, otherwise known as 'grey-listing.' This resulted in Jamaica committing to a thirteen-point Action Plan to address deficiencies in the effectiveness of our regime.

Jamaica has accomplished an impressive body of work since entering the FATF's Grey List, especially considering that it agreed to the thirteen-point Action Plan, covering five Immediate Outcomes, in February 2020, just ahead of the pandemic. Only one point now remains outstanding – which is to demonstrate the effective implementation of Jamaica's framework for the Transparency and Beneficial Ownership of Legal Persons.

Given the work being undertaken by the Companies Office of Jamaica, and its parent ministry, we are optimistic that Jamaica will clear the final hurdle by February 2024, when the FATF will determine if Jamaica has effectively implemented its framework for the Transparency and Beneficial Ownership of Legal Persons.

Concluding Remarks

Madam Speaker, in concluding, I want to reiterate thanks to members of both Houses who have accommodated the passage of legislation to improve Jamaica's AML/CFT.

With the tremendous progress we have made, it is important that we keep it up, as the international standards are under constant review and will be updated from time to time. Having had the experience of being assessed as deficient in 60 per cent of FATF Recommendations in our Fourth Mutual Evaluation in 2015 and spending the better part of the next decade trying to catch up, Jamaica must have a substantially improved showing in the Fifth Mutual Evaluation slated for 2026.

With the results achieved so far, we are on that track, as whatever Jamaica focuses on, Jamaica can do.

FATF Removes Jamaica from Grey List

Ministry Press Release, June 2024

KINGSTON, Jamaica (Friday, June 28, 2024) – The Minister of Finance and the Public Service, Dr the Honourable Nigel Clarke, led the Jamaican delegation to the Financial Action Task Force (FATF) meetings in Singapore this week. On the conclusion of the meetings, Minister Clarke issued the following statement from Singapore:

I am proud to share that the Financial Action Task Force (FATF), at its Plenary in Singapore on Friday, June 28, 2024, removed Jamaica from its 'Grey List' of countries that are assessed as having deficiencies in their Anti–Money Laundering/Countering the Financing of Terrorism (AML/CFT) Regimes.

In a statement released by FATF on the conclusion of the Plenary in Singapore, FATF welcomed 'Jamaica's significant progress in improving its AML/CFT regime.'

The FATF's release further stated that 'Jamaica strengthened the effectiveness of its AML/CFT regime to meet the commitments in its action plan regarding the strategic deficiencies that FATF identified in February 2020.'

As such, FATF concluded that Jamaica is 'no longer subject to FATF's increased monitoring process.'

This is a significant achievement for Jamaica.

In February 2020, Jamaica was placed on the Grey List by FATF. Placement on FATF's Grey List signals to international financial and other institutions to take special care [engage in enhanced due diligence] when transacting with entities and individuals from a FATF 'Grey Listed' country. This makes transacting with FATF 'Grey Listed' countries more expensive. In the aftermath of the FATF 'Grey Listing,' the Government of Jamaica (GOJ) agreed to a thirteen-point action plan with FATF to address Jamaica's AML/CFT deficiencies.

Despite the dislocating onset of the COVID-19 pandemic shortly after we agreed to this action plan, Jamaica delivered on the full range of legislative and regulatory reforms detailed in Jamaica's action plan and ensured that the implementation of these was effective.

A Joint Group from FATF visited Jamaica six weeks ago for an on-site visit to assess the effectiveness of Jamaica's implementation of our action plan. The Joint Group confirmed to FATF that Jamaica has a robust and comprehensive understanding of its money-laundering and terrorist-financing risks, and in its report to FATF, the Joint Group highlighted that, in some instances of the implementation of its AML/CFT framework, Jamaica was an example of global good practise.

This has not been an easy process. It has required painstakingly detailed and comprehensive work across the GOJ mostly during the very demanding and difficult time of the COVID-19 pandemic and its aftermath.

On behalf of a grateful nation, therefore, I would like to express gratitude to:

The Prime Minister of Jamaica, the Most Honourable Andrew Holness, who provided me with the space and support to do what was necessary to ensure the achievement of these results, and to my Cabinet colleagues for the collaboration and teamwork that made this achievement possible.

All the hardworking and committed public servants who serve on the multi-agency National Anti–Money Laundering Committee (NAMLC), which is a multi-agency committee that we strengthened in 2021, and which has responsibility for the general oversight of the AML/CFT policy in Jamaica and ensuring adherence to the FATF 40 recommendations, and for which I have the privilege of serving as Chairman. Supported by the work of the NAMLC Secretariat, this body has been instrumental in facilitating the coordination required to achieve these results.

The FATF, the Caribbean Action Task Force (CFATF), and our bilateral and multilateral partners, without whom Jamaica would have been hard-pressed to achieve these results; and

Jamaica's Prime Contact to CFATF, former Deputy Governor, Maurene Simms and the NAMLAC Secretariat hosted at the BOJ.

As Jamaica prepares to assume the Chair of the CFATF in December 2024, when we host the organisation's 59th Plenary, we pledge our unwavering commitment to ensuring that Jamaica builds on this achievement and maintains up to date with the latest global standards in the AML/CFT and Countering Proliferation Financing (CPF) spaces. So, while we celebrate this milestone achievement, we have to look ahead to ensure we never again give the global standard-setter for AML/CFT/CPF matters reason to 'Grey List' Jamaica.

As such, Jamaica, like other countries, is now preparing for the globally applicable Fifth Round of AML/CFT/CPF mutual evaluations scheduled to take place in mid-2026. Before end of 2025, Jamaica will therefore need to amend or introduce new laws to (a) regulate virtual assets and virtual asset providers, (b) make the registration of non-profit organisations mandatory, and (c) promulgate regulations that address certain targeted financial sanctions related to proliferation.

Back to today. The central lesson from today's achievement is that it is a demonstration of the fact that whatever Jamaica focusses on, Jamaica can achieve.

The Resolution of Non-Viable Financial Institutions: Fixing the Institutional Gap

Published Commentary, September 2023

While Stocks and Securities Limited (SSL) was a relatively small financial services firm, representing less than 0.7 per cent of total financial-sector assets, its demise, the related investigations, and the public reaction hold disproportionately large lessons for Jamaica. For example, the experience has exposed gaps in the institutional framework for the resolution of non-viable financial institutions – and in particular how such resolutions ought to be financed.

The Government of Jamaica (GOJ) has been unequivocally clear: the GOJ will not 'bail out' clients or shareholders of SSL, as occurred in some past financial-sector failures. Unfortunately for them, the financial losses experienced by clients and shareholders of SSL are theirs, and theirs only.

Where the government has responsibility, however, through its regulatory and financial-crime investigative bodies, is to (a) safely resolve the SSL quagmire, (b) seamlessly unwind and return the approximately $30 billion in client funds across 8,000 client accounts, (c) conduct a thorough investigation into the alleged fraud at SSL, bringing perpetrators and conspirators before the courts, and (d) where criminal verdicts or civil settlements are reached, to recover any proceeds of crime that can be identified.

Fulfilment of these resolutions and investigative responsibilities is in the public interest. However, under the current institutional framework, the responsibilities of the respective state agencies cannot be discharged without state financing. I have explained that the Financial Services Commission's (FSC's) short-term support of SSL employee costs and other expenses facilitates the GOJ's fulfilment of its investigative and temporary management responsibilities, and this support will be financed by the FSC from its own resources, and not from the Consolidated Fund.

An earlier version of this article appeared in the ***Jamaica Gleaner,*** **September 10, 2023.**

I have also explained that the Financial Investigations Division (FID) is using the proceeds of assets confiscated under Jamaica's Proceeds of Crime legislation to fund the extraordinary expenses it incurs in pursuing [its] investigation into the SSL fraud. These funds do not constitute tax revenue. Rather, these funds arise from the confiscation of ill-gotten gains.

But we are only dealing with a failure of SSL, a tiny firm in which a large fraud allegedly occurred. Let us engage in a thought experiment. Suppose, God forbid, it were a larger firm that became unviable, maybe for different reasons. With the current institutional arrangements, could the FSC and the FID discharge their responsibilities in such a scenario, without recourse to taxpayers?

Taxpayer-funded financial-crime investigations, inclusive of taxpayer-funded engagement of overseas specialists, are, in the normal course, completely justifiable. However, my views fully align with public sentiment on the funding of the resolution of non-viable financial services firms: resolution of non-viable financial institutions should be seamless; financial stability should be preserved, but taxpayer funds should, ideally, not be touched in the pursuit of these objectives.

The challenge for Jamaica is that the institutional mechanisms to deliver resolution of non-viable financial sector entities on these terms do not exist. While we have a well-funded deposit insurance scheme in place to pay out retail depositors to a maximum cap, the only resolution option currently available after taking control of a non-viable deposit-taking institution via temporary management, is the acquisition (vesting) of the entity by the government.

As such, the responsibility for the recapitalisation of a failed deposit-taking institution under the relevant legislation resides with the government, which would expose the taxpayer to significant potential cost. There are other deficiencies. The current legislative framework is fragmented, which impedes timely intervention and resolution. Furthermore, the conditions for intervention are also not clearly and comprehensively defined. Also, the ability to effect a merger or transfer of assets or [use] other resolution tools is limited, given the overriding rights of shareholders. Finally, there is a loophole in the law regarding the winding-up of financial institutions, as the insolvency provisions in the new Insolvency Act do not cover the winding-up of deposit-taking institutions and insurance companies.

There is a public interest in financial system stability due to (a) the vital role that the financial sector plays in the functioning of an economy (e.g., facilitating payments, providing credit, transmitting monetary policy, etc.) and (b) the vulnerability of financial-sector businesses to public 'loss of confidence' – even in otherwise healthy institutions. Indeed, experiences around the world in recent decades, including in Jamaica, have vividly demonstrated the direct linkage between a loss of financial system stability and economic ruin.

However, the resolution of non-viable financial institutions costs money. The services of accountants, lawyers, bankers, and other professionals are required. The non-viable entity needs to retain staff to service customers, maintain records and accounts, and support investigations. In addition, the failed entity will have other expenses that also have to be financed.

Due to the strong public interest in financial system stability and early resolution, governments across the globe have, for several decades, through regulators or special resolution trusts, intervened directly and fiscally in the process of resolving insolvent or distressed financial institutions.

For example, in Jamaica, the government's intervention, with taxpayer funds, to resolve the financial sector crisis of the 1990s cost 40 per cent of GDP, which is $1 trillion in today's money. In the 2008–10 Global Financial Crisis, the US Government intervention, funded by US taxpayers, cost 9 per cent of GDP, and there are many other examples.

Despite the intentions of governments, these types of interventions have often generated significant backlash. This makes perfect sense. The privatisation of profits in good times and socialisation of losses in bad times is unfair and can never be popular. In fact, the negative reaction to the numerous government interventions designed to rescue national financial systems during the Global Financial Crisis was so severe that, in 2011, the G20 mandated the Financial Stability Board (FSB), an international body that monitors and makes recommendations on global financial stability, to develop robust alternatives to the common practise of publicly funded resolution of financial institutions.

In 2014, the FSB delivered on its G20 mandate through the publication of the Key Attributes of Effective Resolution Regimes for Financial Institutions, which are the international standard for financial sector resolution regimes. As the FSB says:

> The aim of the Key Attributes is to make it possible to resolve any financial institution in an orderly manner without severe systemic disruption or exposing taxpayers to the risk of loss, by protecting the firm's functions that are critical to the financial market or the real economy and ensuring that losses are borne by shareholders and creditors of the failing firm, as they would be in insolvency.[25]

The SSL experience has reaffirmed the strong alignment of Jamaican public sentiment with these global best-practise objectives.

The good news is that all members of the FSB, including Jamaica, are committed to pursuing the implementation of international financial standards in the resolution of non-viable financial services entities. As such, Jamaica has made an explicit high-level policy commitment, under the Precautionary Liquidity Line with the IMF, to submit a Special Resolution Regime (SRR) law to parliament in 2024 that would serve to strengthen the GOJ's ability to resolve non-viable financial institutions while protecting financial stability and taxpayer funds.

The objective of Jamaica's SRR will be 'to make feasible the resolution of financial institutions without severe systemic disruption and without exposing taxpayers to loss, while protecting vital economic functions through mechanisms which make it possible for shareholders and unsecured and uninsured creditors to absorb losses in a manner that respects the hierarchy of claims in liquidation.'

The SRR will be explicitly structured such that the funding of future resolution activities will not be borne by the taxpayer.

The work involved in delivering on this policy commitment is being collaboratively advanced by many agencies of government working together. We do not have the SRR in place for the resolution of SSL, which makes this task more challenging. But the lesson from the SSL case is that Jamaica's Special Resolution Regime cannot come too soon.

Financial Sector Regulation: Moving to a 'Twin Peaks' Model of Supervision

Policy Address, January 2023

An institutional structure for regulation should reflect the structure of the industry that it is called upon to regulate. With the intention of supporting the continued growth of the financial sector, while preserving the safety and soundness of the financial system, we need a regulatory structure that is appropriate for our circumstances and responsive to our needs.

In Jamaica, financial groups that include deposit-taking institutions account for close to 90 per cent of financial system assets. That is, the Jamaican financial landscape is characterised by financial conglomerates spanning banking, securities, insurance, and pensions that account for all but 10 per cent of financial system assets. Fragmented supervision can lead to regulatory gaps in a landscape such as ours, where financial conglomerates dominate. In addition, there is often duplication of effort, duplicate oversight, and sometimes coordination challenges. The natural institutional silos that emerge detract from the nimbleness needed to comprehensively regulate financial groups.

The Twin Peaks Model

The GOJ will pursue a unification of prudential supervision and regulation. The prudential supervision and regulation of deposit-taking financial institutions (commercial banks, building societies, merchant banks, and credit unions) and non-bank financial institutions (securities dealers, insurance companies, and pension funds) will be consolidated into one institution – the Bank of Jamaica (BOJ) – and a second ('twin') regulator for market conduct and consumer protection for the full spectrum of financial services will be established separately.

Adapted from policy address delivered on January 23, 2023, in the auditorium of the Ministry of Foreign Affairs, Kingston.

Market-conduct and consumer-protection regulation refers to the oversight of financial institutions to ensure that they are engaging in fair and ethical business practises. This includes monitoring compliance with laws and regulations related to consumer protection, anti-money laundering, and anti-fraud measures. It also includes monitoring the sales and marketing practises of financial institutions to ensure that they are not engaging in deceptive or misleading conduct. The goal of market-conduct regulation is to protect consumers and maintain the integrity of the financial marketplace.

Today Jamaica has a sector-by-sector based regulatory approach where the BOJ regulates deposit-taking institutions and the FSC regulates non-bank financial institutions. Under the Twin Peaks regulatory model that we will pursue, the prudential mandate of the FSC with respect to the non-deposit taking financial sector would be fully taken over by the BOJ, and the new FSC would become a highly visible market-conduct and consumer-protection supervisor for all financial-service providers.

While some of the issues outlined in having sectoral regulators could be resolved by close coordination and cooperation of sectoral supervisors, an integrated single prudential supervisor will be in a better position to address them. In particular, the coordination and exchange of information will be smoother within one institution, as well as the effort to close existing regulatory gaps within the regime.

Implementation of a single prudential regulator (under the Twin Peaks model) for deposit-taking institutions and non-bank financial institutions has several advantages. A single authority would: (a) provide economies of scale in supervision, (b) allow for sharing of specialist knowledge across the supervisory spectrum, (c) help preserve scarce management resources, and (d) facilitate delivery of the much-needed system-wide oversight and effective supervision. It would help promote a consistent, harmonised framework of regulatory requirements (where applicable) and of supervisory methodology, reducing regulatory arbitrage and gaps. A single authority would generate cost savings relative to current arrangements, through the rationalisation of management and support functions.

More significantly, it would create options for more effective organisation of resources, facilitating risk-based allocation of staff to emerging supervisory risks and different approaches to conglomerate supervision (these could include the creation of a single team for one or more groups, maximising the synergies from the integrated model). Coordination of supervisory work would be greatly facilitated. It would create a richer, more dynamic scope for employees, allowing for development and sharing of expertise while offering more challenging career paths for supervisory staff.

Timeline and Capacity Building

We will need technical advice and time to consult with industry participants on the details. We expect to fully implement a unified financial-sector regulator and a separate market-conduct [and] consumer-protection regulator for the financial sector in eighteen to twenty-four months.

Even with an upgrading of the regulatory structure to reflect the industry, Jamaica needs to continuously and sustainably strengthen and renew its regulatory and supervisory capacity. The BOJ currently has a range of international partnerships that provide training. This could be expanded and formalised. The economies of scale of a consolidated supervisor would allow the BOJ [to create its own staff training] for supervisory and prudential regulators.

Update on the Implementation of 'Twin Peaks' Supervision[26]

Statement to Parliament, June 11, 2024

Madam Speaker, I wish to update this Honourable House on the progress that has been made in the process of the proposed transition to the Twin Peaks model of supervision and regulation of the financial sector. You will recall that on January 23, 2023, I announced the intention of the government to reform and enhance the system of supervision and regulation of the financial sector in Jamaica. The Bank of Jamaica (BOJ) was charged with leading a collaborative process for the introduction of the legislative framework and operational arrangements necessary to bring about this important change.

Under the Twin Peaks model, BOJ will assume full responsibility for prudential supervision of all bank and non-bank financial institutions; and the Financial Services Commission (FSC) will be transformed into a new regulatory entity that will supervise all bank and non-bank financial institutions from the perspective of market conduct and the protection of consumers of financial services.

The system of financial-sector supervision that emerged after the meltdown of the 1990s is now in urgent need of a radical overhaul, and significant strengthening. It is clear from the escalation of public complaints about banking services, for example, that it is imperative for there to be the introduction of a comprehensive and robust consumer-protection framework for financial-sector services. We are committed to addressing this gap as a matter of urgency. It is clear, from the high-profile instances of fraud involving financial institutions and the funds of depositors and investors, that there is a need to strengthen the supervisory framework for all financial institutions to address this.

The adoption of the new Twin Peaks model will change the existing bifurcated supervisory architecture and sector-by-sector regulatory approach. This approach presently sees BOJ as regulator for Deposit-Taking Institutions (DTIs) only, with the FSC having regulatory oversight for non-DTIs only. The new regulatory architecture, once implemented, will see the prudential regulation of commercial banks, building societies, merchant banks, micro-credit institutions, and eventually credit unions, along with non-DTIs (comprising securities dealers, insurance companies, and pension funds) being consolidated into one regulatory peak under the supervision of the BOJ. Similarly, all market-conduct and consumer-protection regulation will be consolidated in the other peak under a proposed Financial Services Conduct Authority (FSCA), which will be a successor agency to the FSC. The FSCA, on full implementation of the Twin Peaks model, will be responsible for market-conduct regulation and financial consumer protection for all operators in the financial sector, whether they are DTIs or non-DTIs.

I want to commend the team led by BOJ Governor Richard Byles, and involving staff of the BOJ and FSC, as well as the Ministry of Finance and the Public Service, for the ardent, concerted, and focussed work that they have been undertaking since I made that announcement.

They have consulted with the financial sector on the Twin Peaks concept for Jamaica and have updated me regularly. They have studied the implementation and operation of the Twin Peaks model in other jurisdictions such as the UK, Australia, New Zealand, Belgium, the Netherlands, and South Africa. The process has benefitted from the sharing of experiences by institutions around the world that are already managing the Twin peaks model, including the Bank of England, the South African Reserve Bank, the Reserve Bank of New Zealand, and the Financial Sector Conduct Authority of South Africa. As we seek to implement a new regulatory system to meet the highest standards in the world, there have also been consultations regarding technology implications with the Bank of Lithuania.

The team has benefitted from technical expertise provided by the World Bank and the International Monetary Fund. Discussions are currently underway with the Inter-American Development Bank for the provision of additional technical assistance.

Implementation of the Twin Peaks model is expected by 2026. A Twin Peaks Concept Paper, which sets out the legal and operational contours of the model, was prepared and submitted for my approval by the BOJ–FSC Twin Peaks Steering Committee, chaired by the BOJ governor in 2023. The Concept Paper has been approved, and we are now in the final stages of preparing a Cabinet Submission for the consideration and approval of Cabinet, following which formal drafting, instructions will be issued for the development of the Bill [that will eventually] give effect to the Twin Peaks model of financial regulation in Jamaica.

Development of the Twin Peaks legislation is receiving the required urgency and priority. We believe it would be better at this time to focus our limited resources on developing the legislation for a comprehensive and robust regulatory framework that the Twin Peaks model will deliver, rather than developing interim legislation to address gaps relating to consumer protection for financial services.

However, Madam Speaker, we are not waiting on all that time to pass before we begin to address urgent issues affecting the financial sector – especially those pain-points experienced by members of the public who need to use the financial services.

Given the timelines and the urgent need to begin addressing some of the deficiencies identified, the BOJ–FSC Twin Peaks Steering Committee has proposed that a period of Practise of the Twin Peaks arrangements takes place, within the constraints of the existing statutory provisions, before the legal cut-over from the current framework to the Twin Peaks model. This approach was adopted by the United Kingdom.

Further, for the Twin Peaks model of financial regulation to be successful, and to facilitate a smooth transition once the anticipated changes to the legislative framework are passed, the BOJ–FSC Steering Committee has recommended that during the 'Practise Period' both organisations collaborate in a structured way to allow a seamless transition for the financial sector and the public. The Twin Peaks Practise Period is scheduled to commence in this quarter and will run through to the appointed date when Twin Peaks legislative changes come into effect.

The Twin Peaks Practise Period is intended to enable capacity-building and closer collaboration between the regulators, pending the passage of the legislation. In anticipation of the legislative changes proposed, the objective of the Practise is to prepare team members for Twin Peaks implementation by providing opportunities for real-world experience in the supervision and regulation of DTIs and non-DTIs, within the constraints of the existing regulatory frameworks.

It will also help to lay the foundation of a smooth transition at legal cut-over to the Twin Peaks Regime. It is important to repeat and emphasise that during this Practise Period, the two regulatory entities – the BOJ and the FSC – will collaborate and operate within the confines of the existing laws.

A tangible example of the Twin Peaks Practise includes a comprehensive set of Service-Level Standards – jointly developed by the BOJ and the FSC and issued by the BOJ to its licensees on April 2 this year – for the management of Automated Banking Machines (ABMs) by DTIs. The performance of commercial banks against those Standards is now being published so that there can be full transparency, and the public can help to hold the institutions to account.

The laws governing the BOJ and the FSC do not at present provide them with legal authority to enforce such standards related to consumer protection through the imposition of fines. It is proposed that this will be addressed in the future dispensation under the legislative changes proposed under the Twin Peaks model. In the meantime, the Service-Level standards for ABMs were developed and issued to address an urgent problem, through consultation. It is anticipated that standards such as these will be incorporated as legally binding regulations when the market-conduct and consumer-protection framework is passed into law as part of the Twin Peaks Regime.

The various institutions and umbrella associations in the financial sector are now being provided with detailed information on the proposed Twin Peaks Practise, which will occur in the following phases:

1. Preparation Phase – The aim of this initial phase is to build capacity of the members of the FSC and BOJ teams assigned to market-conduct and prudential regulation, through training.

2. Pilot Phase – This phase will seek to further deepen the capacity-building process by (a) carrying out simulation

exercises involving the application of proposed requirements and supervisory models that will be implemented when Twin Peaks goes live, in order to mimic real-life regulatory cases, both prudential and market conduct; (b) commencing a joint examination of selected conglomerates that have both DTI and non-DTI operations; and (c) publication of joint-standards which will govern the behaviour of licensees of the BOJ and FSC under both the prudential and the market-conduct and consumer-protection 'Peaks.'

3. Practicum Phase – During this phase, staff from the BOJ will be seconded to FSC and vice versa in order to gain deeper exposure in the supervision and regulation of all segments within the financial sector.

4. Implementation Phase – This phase will allow for seamless transition to Twin Peaks by implementing in both regulators the operational structure that is anticipated will exist after legal cut-over. Until legal cut-over, the two regulators will continue to utilise existing laws in terms of approvals/rejections, on-site examinations, off-site monitoring, risk mitigation/prompt corrective action, and enforcement.

In conclusion, I want to remind the members of this House and all Jamaicans, that the challenges faced by our country are many and varied. Some are complex. These challenges cannot all be solved overnight. Solutions to the nation's problems require co-operation across the aisle in this House and across various sectors in the society at large. It is hoped that the measures being adopted by the BOJ and the FSC, to prepare the way for the Twin Peaks model of financial regulation in Jamaica once the legislative amendments proposed are adopted, will allow for a seamless transition to this new framework that will strengthen the regulatory environment from both the prudential and market-conduct perspectives.

In our relentless quest for prosperity for all, peace and good order in our nation, this government will continue to adopt a collaborative approach and seek to find common ground with all sectors of the society and ultimately with the people, whom we are sworn to serve and represent. I believe that adopting this collaborative and consultative approach as we develop and move towards implementing the Twin Peaks Model of Financial Sector Regulation and Supervision in Jamaica, will help to build a stronger financial sector and a better Jamaica for all.

PART FOUR

CRISES

As islanders, we innately understand our vulnerabilities to the natural world. Flood rains, tropical storms, hurricanes, and earthquakes have forever been part of the Jamaican experience. Natural disasters have huge fiscal impact. They have the potential to sharply reduce government revenues in the immediate aftermath of an event, and for months thereafter – just when they are needed the most. At the same time, the expenses of government increase as emergency response is required. As a result, space shrinks for spending on other critical areas, and funds otherwise available for capital expenditure are diverted to address the crisis.

Also, as we learned most dramatically in March 2020, weather-related disasters are not the only threat to our health and safety, as individuals or as a nation. It is therefore the duty of a government to prioritise, intentionally, the principles of stability that allow an economy the flexibility to accommodate an appropriate, compassionate response – that does not jeopardise stability – and to quickly recover.

The COVID-19 Pandemic

The COVID-19 pandemic was the most serious global public health threat in a century and caused the most damaging global economic crisis since the Great Depression of the 1930s.[1]

Every country in the world was gravely affected, and Jamaica was no exception. The contraction in employment and economic output reached historic proportions. The precipitous decline in the government's revenues were accompanied by a dramatic increase in public expenditure pressures. Ongoing and essential public health measures and the resulting economic dynamics severely disrupted the normal flow and pattern of life and strained the social fabric.

Uncertainty surrounding the depth and duration of the pandemic compounded the challenges. We had to wait for the development of a vaccine, and for large numbers of persons to be inoculated, before any approximation of a normal, pre-COVID-19 life could resume. However, we could not afford to wait to begin to chart an economic recovery. Recovery efforts on the part of the Government of Jamaica (GOJ) had to start immediately, just as we had to adapt to living with the realities of COVID-19.

The crisis unveiled social fragilities that needed to be addressed for Jamaica to recover sustainably and with greater resilience. Although pre-COVID-19 unemployment sat at historical lows, most households lacked an income stabiliser, which motivated the successful completion of a feasibility study on unemployment insurance and the engagement of the World Bank to assist in its implementation. However, back in 2020, GOJ social-support interventions needed to increase in the short term, even as social safety institutions were strengthened for the medium term.

The sub-optimality of the relative size of the informal economy, for State and citizen, was brutally exposed by the pandemic. Similarly, the economic, social, and educational barriers imposed by a lack of individual identification, absence of access to a bank account, and lack of an Internet connection became even more evident.

On March 10, 2020, I had delivered the good news of our nation's strong economic position in an upbeat, positively soaring annual budget presentation to Parliament. That afternoon, however, COVID-19 came to our shores. In April, as the gravity of the pandemic unfolded, the prime minister commissioned the COVID-19 Economic Recovery Task Force (for which I became the chairman), with the objective of charting Jamaica's economic recovery from the fallout and devastation likely to be caused by the pandemic, with the input and participation of diverse stakeholder groups. The Task Force's report, with recommendations, was publicly disseminated at the end of June 2020.

Importantly, the COVID-19 Economic Task Force aimed not simply to fix 'what has been broken by COVID-19,' returning Jamaica to pre-COVID-19 reality, but to go beyond – to also 'address the fundamental gaps that have been exposed by COVID-19 and exploit the opportunities' afforded by the crisis.[2] In other words, we needed do better. We needed to embrace reform with ambition to be on a better footing for when recovery took hold.

Every crisis will generate a plethora of suggested solutions. Some of these will be distortionary, some will be unmoored from sustainable economic principles, some will be blunt and wasteful, and others may only serve the interests of the proposer's interest group. Many will have the potential to achieve the intended effect but ought to be rejected after considering the unintended consequences. The inclination to weigh policy advice, to accurately assess trade-offs, and the courage to act decisively are among the most important qualities of the policymaker.

As we considered policy responses to this crisis, it was therefore important to set expectations, and to provide reassurance through clear communication about the adjustments that the GOJ would and would not make. So, I began as early as March 2020 to address the pandemic in articles published in the *Gleaner* and in publicly available speeches and Task Force reports, laying out the principles that would guide our economic policymaking during the COVID-19 crisis. From the suspension of our Fiscal Responsibility Rules and their timely readoption, to the design of targeted interventions such as the CARE Programme, the COVID-19-related selections in the following pages show how the intentionality and stability of prior chapters, coupled with transparent, principled, and rules-based use of resources in response to a crisis unfolding in real time, allowed Jamaica to make a recovery that outpaced other countries – without touching the Capital Development Fund encountered in the introduction to 'Stability.'

Building Resilience to Natural Disasters

Even if we might consider that COVID-19 has now faded into the fabric of everyday life and no longer constitutes a crisis, who is to say that another health emergency could not shake the world? And even if we have successfully weathered this devastating pandemic and might perhaps be lucky enough to not see another like it in our lifetimes, this would of course not spare us from the enduring reality of our geographic location, and thus our exposure to catastrophe in the form of natural disasters.

Personally, I have understood this all my life. From the point of view of a policymaker, however, I experienced a jolt while serving in my role as Ambassador of Economic Affairs, working out of the Office of the Prime Minister and functioning as the primary interlocutor with the IMF post-February 2016.

At the time, Jamaica had successfully completed the thirteenth review under the IMF's Extended Fund Facility programme, launched under the prior administration. Looking ahead, we were now scheduled to hold a press conference to announce the then-new US$1.6 billion Precautionary Stand-By Agreement (see page 27). The head of the IMF's Western Hemisphere Department was to come for that.

Well, Hurricane Matthew intervened, and for forty-eight hours this Category 5 hurricane was headed directly towards Jamaica. Emergency plans were in high gear, and nine hundred shelters were opened across the country. The Fund staff who had set up camp in Jamaica were eventually ordered to leave (like many others) and took the last flight out of Kingston before the airport closed in anticipation of the hurricane's arrival. Of course, the Western Hemisphere director could no longer come.

It was a surreal experience, coming to terms with the economic exposure over those anxious forty-eight hours. Jamaica was very exposed. The programme we had just negotiated with the IMF, and that we were set to announce, had not yet received final approval by the IMF Executive Board – and even if it had, the funds would have been woefully insufficient had a direct hit of that hurricane occurred as seemed likely in those moments. Furthermore, much of the fiscal progress under the Extended Fund Facility would have been completely erased.

Luckily for Jamaica – but at the tragic expense of our Caribbean neighbours, with whom we stand in sympathy – Hurricane Matthew veered sharply north at the very last minute. As a result, more than five hundred persons died in Haiti, where much of the country was destroyed, causing billions and billions of dollars in damage.

At that time, I resolved to do my best, given all the work Jamaica had done to reform our economy, and given all the hope this engendered, to ensure that Jamaica would never again remain extremely exposed, from a fiscal point of view, in the event of serious natural disaster. And since then, with the support of the prime minister and of Cabinet, stakeholders have come on board with the absolute necessity of always having financing in place specifically for the risk of natural disaster.

With the assistance of our multilateral partners – including the IMF, the World Bank, and the Inter-American Development Bank – Jamaica's Disaster Risk Financing Framework is now the most advanced in the Caribbean region. We have implemented a multi-layered strategy, with a menu of financial instruments to manage the financing of disaster risk. At the end of this section on 'Crises,' three pieces of commentary, previously published in the *Jamaica Gleaner*, provide details on the Government of Jamaica's framework and the parameters of the various financial tools in place to address crises arising from natural disasters.

Of course, the wisdom of proactively planning and increasing the government's ability to respond to human suffering in the aftermath of a natural disaster needs no ongoing explanation. Even as I worked to compile this book, in early July 2024, Hurricane Beryl – the strongest hurricane to strike Jamaica in almost seventeen years[3] – battered our country with high winds and rain, causing widespread devastation, leaving hundreds of thousands to suffer without power or other basic necessities, and yet others to lose the roofs off their homes, everything. It is always the most painful reality to see this suffering.

More Than Rebuilding

Crises such as these – whether a global pandemic or a more localised natural disaster such as a hurricane – put a spotlight on inequities and vulnerabilities and magnify the scope and complexity of policy responses required.

The balance-of-payments and debt dynamics unleashed by the COVID-19 pandemic meant that there was little room for policy errors. To avoid repeating our historical experiences with prolonged economic recoveries, the durations of which are measured on generational timescales, we needed to engender social consensus around a coherent policy agenda and create bias towards implementation with unity of purpose. This is, and will be, true of any crisis response.

But challenging times also show the true value of economic reform and prudent policies. The success of our collective efforts over the seven years preceding the pandemic in terms of fiscal, monetary, and structural reforms – which allowed us to reduce debt, increase foreign exchange reserves, restore macroeconomic stability, privatise state enterprises, and reintegrate public bodies – in addition to our fiscal over-performance, provided buffers and a head start for a quicker recovery.[4]

Jamaica's resilience has been tested time and time again, and neither COVID-19 nor Beryl will be the last crisis our nation faces. By embracing reform with ambition, Jamaica endured a pandemic – absorbing its adverse social and economic effects, restoring lost jobs and output – and not only 'rebuilt' but attained even higher levels of economic and social development. The same can be true in a post-Beryl Jamaica. We are, after all, one of the most resilient nations on Earth.

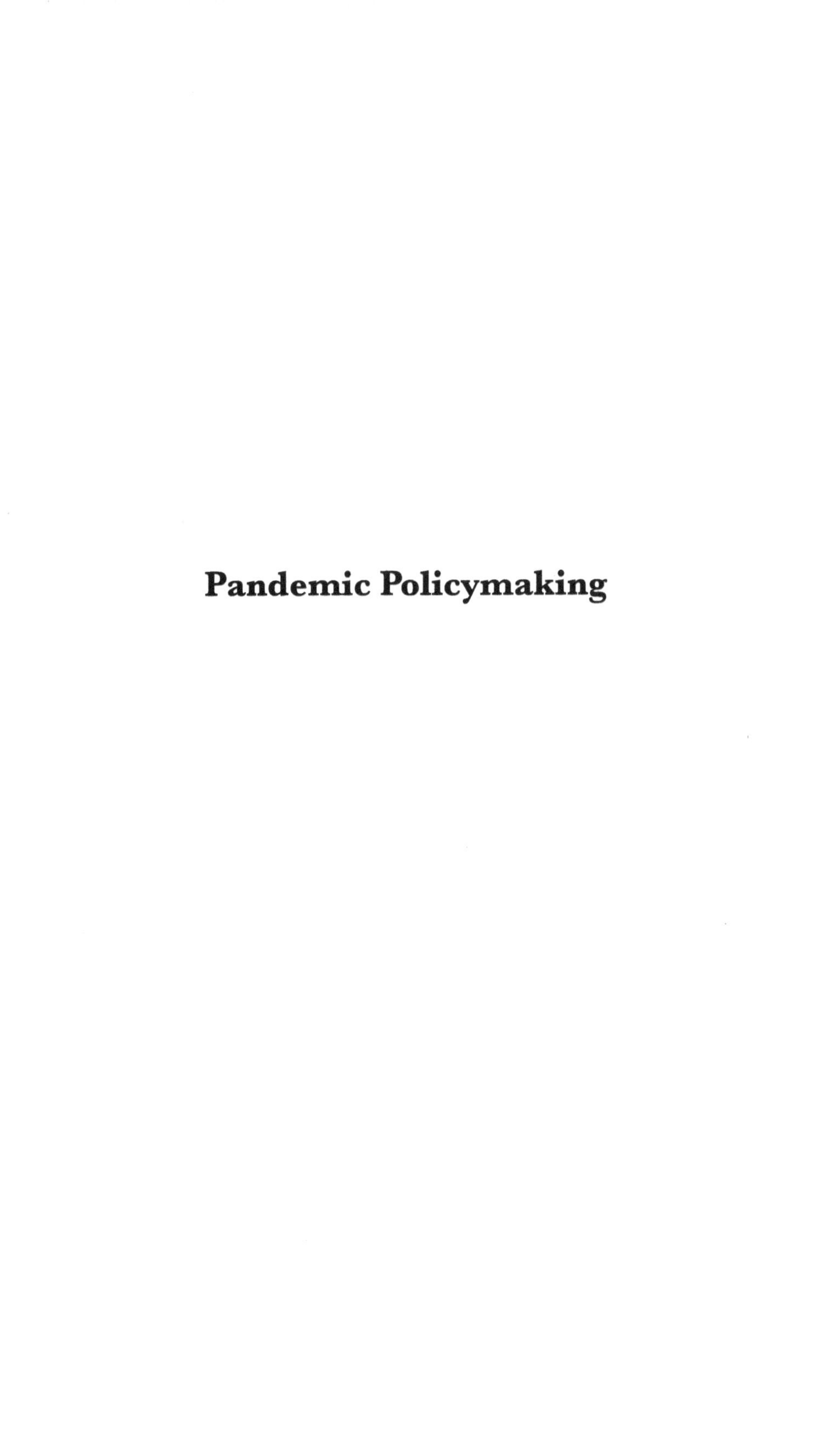

Pandemic Policymaking

Economic Policy Response to COVID-19

Published Commentary, March 2020

The COVID-19 global health crisis, recently declared a pandemic by the World Health Organisation, has led to severe disruptions in the usual pattern of life around the world. These disruptions will no doubt depress economic activity and suppress world growth; those magnitudes are still evolving. Jamaica's economy will not escape the effects of this global shock.

The channels through which the COVID-19 global shock are likely to affect Jamaica include a sharp decline in stop-over and cruise visitor arrivals to Jamaica, shorter length of stay for those who do come, and significantly less expenditure in restaurants and on attractions by tourists. In fact, cruise lines are likely to suspend their arrivals for at least thirty days. The tourism sector will be hit hard in the short term.

In addition, sectors closely linked to tourism, including transportation, will likely be affected. The entertainment industry is experiencing blanket cancellation of public events as social distancing, the most effective tool in flattening the spread of the virus, is at odds with such gatherings.

Other sectors may be impacted, too. Commodity prices have declined steeply due to the anticipated fall in global consumer demand. While Jamaica benefits from the large drop in the price of oil, further falls in the price of alumina could impact our bauxite/alumina industry.

The disruption to global supply chains, and the closure of schools and universities are also expected to impact businesses across many sectors.

Furthermore, an overall contraction in short-term (i.e., quarterly) economic growth seems inevitable. While Jamaica is acting decisively

---

An earlier version of this article appeared in the *Jamaica Gleaner*, March 15, 2020. Jamaica's Ministry of Health confirmed the first case of COVID-19 on March 10, 2020.

to slow the spread of the virus and contain its effects, the pace of the eventual economic recovery will depend, in large part, on global factors. That is, the speed at which our major trading partners including the United States, the United Kingdom and Europe, and China are able to reverse the spread of COVID-19 will determine how quickly the global economy recovers from the shock.

Along with the rest of the world, Jamaica is heading for challenging times. However, the good news is that, while the economic impact is inevitable, Jamaica is in a better economic position today to respond to global economic shocks than we have been in decades. Our debt is substantially reduced and on a downward trajectory, and our expenditure profile over the medium term can be sustainably financed. We have also had several successive years of low inflation, and the level of foreign exchange reserves in our central bank provides a meaningful buffer.

Furthermore, the Government is providing an $18 billion tax stimulus to the economy – the largest stimulus package in Jamaica's history – which could hardly come at a better time. The stimulus is financed by an acceleration in the repayment of debt in the amount of $73 billion or 3.3 per cent of GDP. Reducing debt by this amount allows for a reduction in the annual fiscal savings required to meet our legislated debt target of 60 per cent of GDP, and this reduction in fiscal savings is being returned to the Jamaican people in the form of a series of tax cuts.

Effectively pumping $18 billion into the economy at this time of uncertainty helps to support domestic economic activity. This is always desirable when the global environment weakens. The $14 billion General Consumption Tax (GCT) reduction supports consumption; the $3 billion reduction in asset taxes applied to financial institutions incentivises a lowering of fees and interest rates;[5] the $1 billion Medium, Small, and Micro Enterprises (MSME) tax credit provides critical cash-flow support to MSMEs; and the dramatic reduction in regulatory fees for coconut, coffee, cocoa, and spice farmers incentivises greater production.[6]

In this time of need for the country, it is also important that Jamaicans support our domestic economy by buying Jamaican. This would further enhance the effect of these measures by supporting domestic production and domestic economic activity.

In addition to the $18 billion stimulus, the government has carved out $7 billion as a contingency for the potential health and economic impact of COVID-19. This could be applied in the form of temporary fiscal stimuli.[7]

At this time the government's policy choice will be weighted towards intervention that (a) reduces disruption to employment in the most affected sectors, and (b) preserves productive capacity. Possibilities include, for example, various forms of temporary and targeted wage subsidies to keep workers employed. Another possibility is temporary debt-service support and other forms of cash transfers for MSMEs and workers in targeted sectors, to lessen chances of COVID-19 related bankruptcies. While we will not be able to implement every suggestion offered, we will work with various stakeholders in the design and implementation of the forms of fiscal intervention to ensure that maximum impact is achieved with taxpayer dollars.

On the monetary side, non-borrowed foreign exchange reserves increased by US$1 billion since October 2016, and the Central Bank has limited its interventions to periods of market dislocation. This policy, which preserved our reserves for moments of real need, was instituted with times like these in mind. Our gross foreign exchange reserves, which stand at approximately US$3.5 billion, exist to protect Jamaica when the external environment deteriorates or when Jamaica is affected by a global economic shock. We are now in such a time. The Central Bank governor has already signalled the Bank of Jamaica's ability and readiness to provide support in the event that traditional inflows of foreign exchange are reduced, and to provide liquidity to the financial system as required.

Should conditions worsen beyond current expectations or be extended for a time longer than apparent at this point, the Government has other economic policy tools at its disposal. The Government is already considering other downside scenarios and drafting responses to these should signs emerge of these scenarios materialising.

An adverse and sharp economic impact from COVID-19 is unavoidable. However, the government has the capacity to, and will, employ a range of economic policy tools calibrated to cushion against the effects of this global health crisis and the resulting global economic shock. This cushion will provide the best opportunity for eventual economic recovery.

Principles to Guide the Fiscal Policy Response to the COVID-19 Economic Shock

Budget Speech Excerpt, March 2020

When visibility of the path ahead is unclear, it is useful to rally around a set of principles for future action. As part of my speech delivered at the closing of the 2020–21 budget debate in Parliament, just two weeks after the emergence of COVID-19 in Jamaica, I outlined the following principles to guide our fiscal policy response to the pandemic.

1. *The Government of Jamaica will subsidise people, but it is not reasonable to expect the government to subsidise profits.* People, businesses, and the government will experience losses from this pandemic. Our first objective will be to protect the neediest people from the worst effects of this COVID-19 crisis. We will also have to make preparation for the government to absorb the hits to its own revenue, but we won't be able to protect businesses from all losses.

2. *The public interest is served by doing all we can to maintain productive capacity.* Lost productive capacity takes years to rebuild. We know that from our own experience in Jamaica. When a hotel or a factory is mothballed, it takes years and much capital to get it going again. Over the past few years, we have had an explosive growth in the number of small businesses in operation and the number of start-ups. Preserving that productive capacity is a critical objective even as we aim to work together with financial sector institutions and others to maintain the productive capacity in our hotels, attractions, tours, and restaurant space.

3. *Fiscal measures must be transparent.* This is three-fold: (1) The method of intervention should be easy to understand, and its cost should be easy to estimate, if not calculate, and should be available to the government, recipients, and the public; (2) Intervention will be resourced with taxpayer funds and should be designed so that the public knows its cost; and (3) Fiscal

Adapted from the closing budget presentation delivered in Parliament March 24, 2020.

measures should be implemented in a rules-based approach with equal opportunity among eligible beneficiaries.

4. *The government will do all that it can, but the government cannot do it all.* We will have to prioritise and channel our intervention first to the neediest segments of our society, whether individual or business. For those with personal and corporate reserves, who operate businesses affected by the effects of the pandemic, we expect that these reserves will be put to work. Those with undrawn lines of credit from financial institutions and those with cash balances, we expect that the government should not be your first call.

5. *Any fiscal stimulus will necessarily be of finite duration.*

6. *We will favour simplicity where simplicity does not violate any other principle.*

7. *If conditions deteriorate and further actions, beyond measures already announced, are required to support businesses, we will favour market-based solutions.* With respect to any particular case, to the extent that market-based solutions are not feasible, any intervention by the government with taxpayer dollars must be for value.

I want to be very clear on this principle. The government will not put taxpayer dollars at risk without the prospect of a commensurate return. If it is necessary for the government to invest, we will invest with the view of making a return.

These principles will guide our approach to the targeted fiscal stimulus [to address the pandemic] and to any escalation of fiscal intervention that could become necessary in the future.

Fiscal Stimulus: The CARE Programme
Budget Speech Excerpt, March 2020

Mr Speaker, we introduce the COVID-19 Allocation of Resources for Employees (CARE) programme. The CARE programme represents the Jamaican society coming together to assist those who are most affected by the economic impact of the COVID-19 pandemic, to put us in the best position to recover and to be stronger than we were before the crisis. We have the best chance to recover if we support companies to remain connected with their employees and we support employees who have been disconnected. Mr Speaker, we care. We care about employees across Jamaica who could be affected by this pandemic.

> Following are highly condensed descriptions of the principal elements of the *initial* fiscal stimulus package proposed and delivered by the Government of Jamaica to help Jamaican workers, households and businesses, and especially the most vulnerable members of society, cope with the impact of the COVID-19 pandemic. For greater detail, I refer readers to the full text of the presentation sourced in the bibliography (Clarke, 'We Care'). These measures were *greatly* supplemented by other measures as the pandemic intensified over the course of the months and years that followed this speech. In presenting these points before Parliament, the overriding message from the Ministry of Finance and the Public Service was, 'We CARE and help is on the way.'

We will introduce:

Cash Transfers and Grants

1. Business Employee Support and Transfer of Cash (BEST Cash) – which will provide temporary cash transfers to registered businesses operating in the hotel, tours, attraction companies,

---

Adapted from the closing budget presentation delivered in Parliament March 24, 2020.

and segments of the tourism industry who are licensed with the Jamaica Tourist Board, based on the number of workers they keep employed who are under the income tax threshold of $1.5 million.

2. Supporting Employees with Transfer of Cash (SET Cash) – Recognising that employers will not be able to retain all employees on the payroll, and understanding that employees from industries other than tourism will be laid off, we will implement SET Cash to provide temporary cash transfers to individuals from any sector where it can be verified [by matching applicant data to employer forms] that they lost their employment after March 10, the date of the first COVID-19 case in Jamaica, and before June 30. SET Cash is directed towards individuals who earn below the income tax threshold of $1.5 million, who constitute more than 80 per cent of the working population and who are most vulnerable to the effects of being suddenly laid off.

   Jamaica has never had a direct transfer electronic programme such as this and we have a multi-disciplinary team from the Ministry of Finance, the Accountant General's Department, Tax Administration Jamaica and eGOV who are working overtime to quick design and launch the online interface processes and protocols.

   We expect the BEST Cash and SET Cash elements of the CARE Programme to cost approximately $5.9 billion.

3. COVID-19 Grants for Marginally Self Employed and Informally Employed-the unfortunate reality is that the employment status of many Jamaicans is informal and there are no statutory payments made on their behalf. These are challenging cases but no less deserving and perhaps more in need. We will allocate $1 billion in additional funding to the Ministry of Labour and Social Security and work with them [on verification of applicants] as they seek to implement this element of the CARE Programme.

4. PATH Grants – The poor and vulnerable on PATH will be affected by this crisis in ways that may not be readily visible. They are characterised by having income that is supplemented by various irregular flows, which are likely to be interrupted

by the pandemic and its effects. We wish to channel the fiscal intervention in a manner that assists these members of our society through this time, so we will be channelling $1.1 billion in additional funding to the Ministry of Labour and Social Security to increase PATH cash grants paid during the period of April through June.

5. Small Business Grants – Over the past few years we have seen a growth in the number of micro- and small enterprises operating in Jamaica, and they account for a substantial amount of employment. The health of these sectors is important to Jamaica. We need to step in with direct support to our small businesses. All small businesses with sales of $50 million or less who file taxes in the 2019–20 financial year, and who filed payroll returns indicating they have employees, will be eligible for a one-time COVID-19 Small Business grant of $100,000. This measure is expected to cost $800 million.

6. Tourism Grant – our tourism industry consists of many small hotel operators, attraction companies, tour operators, transportation companies, and entertainment companies, among others. These businesses will be under severe financial stress over the next three months with near zero revenues while enduring fixed operating costs in the hope of reopening shortly. There is a public interest in maintaining this productive capacity, as it would give us the best chance of a quick recovery once conditions improved. As such, Mr Speaker, the government will make $1.2 billion available in the form of grants to businesses operating in tourism and related sectors. In consultation with the Jamaica Hotel and Tourist Association, we will establish the maximum grant that any one business can receive, among other criteria.

7. COVID-19 Compassionate Grants – the poor and vulnerable are not limited to the PATH beneficiary population.

Many small farmers have crops in the field about to be harvested, where the intended market was the hotel sector. I have had consultations with Minister Shaw, and we will reallocate expenditure in the MICAF [Jamaica's business ministry] budget to provide $200 million for relief to small farmers.

Importantly, the COVID-19 Compassionate Grants, which total $650 million, will be financed by reallocations of existing budgets.

There was a time that government was seen as 'Babylon,' where government was seen as something to escape from. This is the moment Mr Speaker, where we see [the Government of Jamaica] as provider of assistance when it is needed. This is the moment where those who play by the rules win: Those small businesses who have filed the information that allows us to engage in this counter-cyclical stimulus to small business. Those registered with the Jamaica Tourist Board, or with Jamaica Union of Travellers Association (JUTA), or with the metropolitan authority, are in line for assistance.

This is the moment when we realise that we are all in this together. When you think that the financial institutions volunteered the give-back of the asset tax reduction, and we are using that to provide stimulus to small businesses, as well as the poor and vulnerable across all sectors, you realise that something very special is happening in Jamaica.

Reduction of the General Consumption Tax (GCT)

In addition to the above, as previously announced, GCT will be reduced by one and a half (1.5) per cent, effective April 1, 2020. The COVID-19 pandemic will depress aggregate demand, which will affect all sectors of the economy and all consumers. There is no better time than now to return $14 billion to the Jamaican people. After years of fiscal consolidation, and $185 billion in tax increases (2020 dollars) over the past two decades, it is a moral imperative that it be manifestly evident that all Jamaicans have benefited from the improvement in the Jamaican economy to date. With the broad-based nature of this last measure, we are certain that every Jamaican will have benefited to some degree from the improvement in the Jamaican economy.

Yes, we face the economic fallout of the pandemic. It will be tough, but it will pass. After that we will still need to maintain fiscal discipline as we march towards our debt-sustainability goals. We are just over halfway there, in terms of time. It will be important as we continue that journey for all Jamaicans to know, and for all of us in this House to be aware, no matter what side you may be on, that all Jamaicans have shared in the economic improvements to date.

That is the eternal contract between the Jamaican State and the Jamaican people that keeps the fabric of our liberal democracy intact.

COVID-19 and the Suspension of Jamaica's Fiscal Rules

Published Commentary, June 2020

This week the Houses of Parliament approved, by affirmative resolution, an Order to suspend Jamaica's fiscal rules for the initial period of this fiscal year ending March 31, 2021, consistent with the provisions of the Financial Administration and Audit Act.

Jamaica's Fiscal Responsibility Framework

Jamaica's fiscal rules were given the force of law in 2010 and updated in 2014 to provide for an escape clause in times of crisis among other amendments.

Embedded in this Fiscal Responsibility Framework is the objective of attaining a debt-to-GDP target of 60 per cent by 2027–28, a target date that, with the endorsement of the IMF and local stakeholders, has been pushed back by two years given the materially negative economic impact of the COVID-19 pandemic.

Furthermore, our Fiscal Responsibility Framework prescribes the minimum level of annual fiscal savings consistent with this debt-reduction objective, given prevailing economic parameters. It also provides limits on the aggregate level of public sector wage expenditure as a ratio of GDP.

Under the framework, the circumstances that can trigger an escape are outside the control of government. These events are: a severe economic downturn, natural disaster, health and other disasters, and public emergencies. Importantly, however, the fiscal rule suspension can only be activated after an independent verification by the Auditor General that the fiscal impact of the triggering event exceeds the threshold of 1.5 per cent of GDP and after the Houses of Parliament approve, by affirmative resolution, an Order for suspension.

An earlier version of this article appeared in the *Jamaica Gleaner*, June 7, 2020.

COVID-19 and the Fiscal Rule Suspension

Jamaica was declared a disaster area on account of the COVID-19 pandemic. The Auditor General subsequently validated that the fiscal impact of the pandemic is above the threshold of 1.5 per cent of GDP. This validation was tabled in parliament along with supporting economic data provided by the PIOJ and the Ministry of Finance.

We need to suspend the fiscal rules for the following reasons:

First, the COVID-19 pandemic has led to the need to deploy significant additional fiscal resources, primarily in the form of (a) social and economic support through the CARE Programme, (b) health expenditure on new personnel, equipment and supplies, and (c) other critical expenditures which together total $34 billion. It will not be possible to accommodate these additional expenditures unless the fiscal rules are suspended.

Second, economic activity will contract significantly this fiscal year as a result of the COVID-19 pandemic. The contraction is a consequence of the economic spillovers from actions that other countries have taken, as well as actions we have had to take in Jamaica, to slow the spread of the coronavirus. We expect economic contraction this fiscal year in the region of 5.1 per cent.

This anticipated shrinking of economic output means that the government is likely to have much less revenue this year than originally planned. Estimates are that revenues will be lower by approximately $81 billion. This loss of revenue means that it will neither be possible, practical, nor desirable to achieve the level of fiscal savings that the fiscal rules would otherwise imply. For these reasons, the fiscal rules need to be suspended.

The Road to Suspending Fiscal Rules

The journey towards the suspension of our fiscal rules has involved dialogue and consensus on the critical issues. I first mentioned fiscal rule suspension as a likely course of action in my closing budget presentation on March 24. In my opening remarks during the tabling of the First Supplementary Estimates on May 13, I confirmed this direction and further proposed that we needed to extend the target date for attainment of our 60 per cent debt-to-GDP objective.

In response to my remarks, the Opposition voiced its support for both objectives: fiscal rule suspension and extension of the debt reduction timeline by two years. Discussions have also been had with other stakeholders locally and internationally, including with the IMF. (The *Gleaner* was among the first local stakeholders to support a suspension of the fiscal rules and an extension of the debt-reduction timeline).

On approval of the disbursement of approximately US$520 million under the Rapid Financing Instrument, the Executive Board of the IMF endorsed Jamaica's move to suspend our fiscal rules and to extend the 60 per cent debt target timeline by two years. Their report was published on May 18. Given how recently Jamaica emerged from successive Fund programmes, it was important for this report to be published before beginning the fiscal rule suspension process.

The Need to Amend the Fiscal Responsibility Law

However, the avenue for the suspension of the fiscal rules did not exist. Use of the 'economic contraction' trigger was not possible, as the Fiscal Responsibility Law (FRL) is written in a manner that requires that the contraction has already happened. In addition, quarterly GDP contraction has to exceed 2 per cent to trigger the process.

Last week, the PIOJ projected a 1.7 per cent contraction for the quarter ending March 2020 and a 12 to 14 per cent contraction for the quarter ending June 2020. The 'economic contraction' trigger would therefore be unavailable until the anticipated June contraction is measured and confirmed by STATIN, around September 2020.

We therefore had to amend the FRL to create an avenue for suspension consistent with the principles that (a) the circumstances that can trigger an escape are outside the control of government, and (b) activation of the suspension would still require independent verification of the fiscal impact by the Auditor General. (The Government and Opposition disagreed on the urgency of this amendment.)

Other Countries Have Had to Amend Their Laws, Too

Other countries have had to amend their fiscal rules to allow for suspension in this unprecedented crisis. In Panama, the National Assembly adopted new legislation to modify their fiscal responsibility law's deficit limit for 2020, allowing for larger deviations. Peru went even further. Instead of using their escape clause, the Peruvian government enacted new legislation to bypass the fiscal rule altogether. Presumably the formal escape route would have included conditions for fiscal recovery measures post-suspension.

Most Countries with Fiscal Rules Are Suspending Them Because of COVID-19

Many countries of the world do not have fiscal rules. For example, among CARICOM members, only two – Jamaica and Grenada – have fiscal rules in place. However, most countries that have fiscal rules, are suspending them due to the effects of COVID-19.

The European Union has activated the 'general escape clause' of their fiscal rules, which allow EU member states to undertake measures to address the impact of the pandemic. These measures will allow departure from the budgetary restrictions that would normally apply under the EU fiscal framework.

In addition to the EU supranational escape clause, European countries have individually activated their own national escape clauses for additional flexibility. Austria, Bulgaria, Croatia, Czech Republic, Germany, Estonia, France, Greece, Italy, Lithuania, Latvia, Portugal, Romania, and Slovenia have all already activated their national escape clauses.

Closer to home, Grenada, which had a public debt-to-GDP ratio of 60 per cent in 2019 and has been the fastest growing Caribbean economy in recent years, announced plans to invoke suspension provisions under their Fiscal Responsibility Law.

Panama and Peru were mentioned earlier. Costa Rica enacted a National Emergency Decree and is expected to activate their emergency escape clause to permit a growth in expenditure higher than the allowed threshold for 2020. In Honduras and Paraguay, governments have announced plans to trigger their fiscal rule escape, allowing for increased spending and a larger deficit this year, and Brazil declared a state of 'public calamity,' which allows for a relaxation of restrictions under their fiscal responsibility framework.

Concluding Remarks

These are unprecedented times, here in Jamaica and around the world. We can be proud that Jamaica has an institutional framework that supports the sustainability of our public finances. We can be even prouder that this framework requires a formal and transparent process for its temporary relaxation in times of crisis.

Economic Recovery from COVID-19

Published Commentary, July 2020

The COVID-19 pandemic is the most serious global public health threat in a century and is easily the most damaging global economic crisis since the Great Depression of the 1930s. It is wreaking health, social, and economic havoc in every country; Jamaica is no exception.

The challenge is, *how do we cope with this crisis and recover stronger than before?* As Chairman of the COVID-19 Economic Recovery Task Force, it has been my privilege to work with a team of committed Jamaicans to develop a strategy for coping and recovering from the crisis. The idea is not just to recover, but to recover stronger and reset to a new version: Jamaica 2.0.

Jamaica's condition, on entry into this crisis, was characterised by a strong economic foundation with deep social capital built together by the Jamaican people. We also have the benefit of lessons learned from our historical experiences with previous crises. Jamaica therefore has what it takes to absorb this enormous shock and bounce back stronger.

My focus, in this first article in a series, is on why we need to sustain macroeconomic stability and introduce the structural reforms needed for a resilient recovery. While this alone is not sufficient for economic recovery, it is absolutely necessary.

Together, We Have Built Buffers

There is no doubt that the impact of COVID-19 on the Jamaican economy will be severe. Economic activity has dropped precipitously, government revenues have declined sharply, foreign exchange inflows from tourism have dried up, foreign direct investment will decline, our external balance of payments will be negatively impacted, economic output will contract significantly, and employment gains will be eroded.

An earlier version of this article appeared in the *Jamaica Gleaner*, July 19, 2020.

However, we have built buffers through our collective efforts, which helps to preserve our hard-earned macroeconomic stability:

1. Jamaica's debt pre-COVID-19 was still quite high in relative terms. However, after years of fiscal consolidation our public debt had fallen by over 50 per cent of GDP, providing more policy room than we would otherwise have had.

2. Continuous liability management has allowed us to lengthen the maturity profile of our external debt. Today, 77 per cent of our foreign debt matures after five years, 46 per cent after ten years, and 22 per cent after twenty years. A single round of liability management transactions in September 2019 increased the latter two buckets from 36 per cent and 1 per cent, respectively. Our current maturity profile greatly reduces liquidity and refinancing risks. Some countries, with appreciably less debt than Jamaica's, face more severe problems due to external refinancing challenges.

3. In addition, the Government of Jamaica (GOJ) entered the crisis with an opening cash balance of $87 billion, or 3 per cent of GDP, which came from fiscal over-performance, privatisation of state-owned enterprises, and reintegration of public bodies.

4. Monetary reforms introduced two-way movement of the exchange rate and decreased the footprint of the Bank of Jamaica (BOJ) in the foreign exchange market, which increased non-borrowed foreign exchange reserves by US$1 billion between 2016 and 2019.

5. Policy reform that made inflation targeting the anchor of monetary policy, in addition to the introduction of a two-way foreign exchange market, allowed for sustained monetary easing prior to the COVID-19 pandemic. The policy interest rate was reduced ten times since 2018 and was at 0.5 per cent pre-COVID-19. While room for further lowering has been reduced, easier monetary conditions mean that firms and households can access credit at more affordable prices.

6. In the last two financial years, the BOJ's balance sheet has been significantly strengthened to pursue open-market operations and relax the reliance on blunt prudential tools for liquidity management. The Bank of Jamaica has been capitalised in the

amount of $20.6 billion and the GOJ has settled central bank losses of an additional $33.2 billion.

7. For thirty years prior to fiscal year 2018–19, the constitutionally provided Contingencies Fund had a maximum of $100 million for emergencies or disasters. In March 2019, the GOJ added $2 billion in capital, and in March 2020 an additional $2.4 billion, raising the amount in the Contingencies Fund to $4.5 billion. As the pandemic unfolded, the GOJ was able to draw down on the Contingencies Fund to make an immediate and timely counter-cyclical response by advancing $4.2 billion in CARE social and economic support grants, well before the passage of the Supplementary Budget.

8. In addition, the GOJ quickly accessed US$520 million from the IMF's Rapid Financing Instrument, which provided a boost to Jamaica's official foreign reserves.

Sustaining Macroeconomic Stability is Critically Important

Based on our historical experiences with crisis, sustaining our macroeconomic stability will be critically important. In the past, structural imbalances and macroeconomic instability have impeded, complicated, and prolonged Jamaica's economic recoveries.

For example, it took fourteen years for the Jamaican economy to return to 1975 levels of economic output after the major economic contraction in 1976, when annual GDP declined by 6.5 per cent, the largest annual decline on record to date. More recently, it took approximately eleven years for the Jamaican economy to return to 2007 levels of economic output after the Global Financial Crisis of 2008–2009, when annual GDP declined by 3.2 per cent in 2009. In both instances, deep macroeconomic instability before and during the crises compounded the economic challenges and stymied economic recoveries.

To avoid history repeating itself, we need to push for and provide the environment that can accommodate a swift recovery for which we will need to preserve a sustainable fiscal and debt trajectory, financial sector stability, adequate foreign exchange reserves, and low and stable inflation. Economic recovery cannot be attained without macroeconomic stability. There will therefore be little room for policy errors.

Building a Resilient Jamaica 2.0

Building Jamaica 2.0 will also require pursuing a host of structural reforms. We will need to accelerate macro-fiscal reforms and public sector transformation, strengthen our governance architecture, improve the business climate, boost competitiveness, deepen local supply chains, strengthen economic and social resilience, press forward on education to build our future, increase economic formalisation, improve financial inclusion and access to finance, strengthen the social safety net, pursue productivity enhancing labour market reforms, increase the GOJ technical resource capacity, and invest in our people and communities.

Broadening opportunity, making Jamaica fairer and more equitable even as we prepare for the opportunities of the fourth industrial revolution, will be critical. Promoting universal broadband access, accelerating investment in math and science education, digitising public and private sector services, provision of a national identification for all Jamaicans, rolling out a universally accessible digital payment platform, and full transition to an online economy will be transformational.

Pursuing these reforms concurrently will require ambition, drive, and working together. The GOJ has an important role to play. But the days where the GOJ serves as the engine of growth are long gone. The GOJ will provide the enabling environment, but we continue to need the private sector to lead the way. We need unions, academia, civil society, and other stakeholders to all play their constructive roles.

Jamaica has shown the world that effective social dialogue can create transformative changes. The COVID-19 Economic Recovery Task Force was conceived in that tradition and lays out policy proposals for a resilient Jamaica 2.0.

One Year into COVID-19:
The Economic Impact
Budget Speech Excerpt, March 2021

This past year has been one of the most difficult and challenging years on record for Jamaica, for Jamaicans, and for all of humanity. Up to yesterday, more than 117 million persons around the world, including nearly 27,000 Jamaicans, have contracted the virus, which has caused severe illness, hospitalisation, and death around the world. More than 2.6 million people have died, including 454 Jamaicans, making this most devastating pandemic in over one hundred years.

I pause to express solidarity with all the individuals and families who have been impacted by this deadly disease, with those who have lost loved ones, those still in hospital, and with others in isolation.

Over the past twelve months, many have been unable to attend the funerals of close associates due to gathering limits. Others have had to restrict the attendance of loved ones for their most treasured celebrations: weddings, the traditional Christmas dinner, and special family occasions. And just when normality seemed to be gradually returning, the government found it necessary to impose restrictive measures over a three-week period as COVID-19 case volume mounted, hospitalisations surged to worrying levels, and intensive care capacity approached its breaking point.

As Prime Minister Andrew Holness has said, these decisions are never easy There are always those who suffer far more than others and those who pay a steep, often painful, price. On behalf of the Government of Jamaica, I want to take this opportunity while opening the budget debate to say that this government does not take these decisions lightly, and they often involve many hours of wrenching, agonising debate. I want to use this opportunity publicly to let the people of Jamaica know that we hear you, we understand your concerns, we share your pain, and we will remain steadfast in

---

Adapted from the opening budget presentation delivered in Parliament March 9, 2021.

our commitment to act in the best interests of all Jamaicans as we seek to balance the objectives of protecting both lives and livelihoods.

Though it is often darkest right before dawn, from all we can see, it certainly looks like we are about to enter the phase of the health crisis that can be described as the beginning of the end. For the economic crisis, however, we may only be at the end of the beginning.

Our objectives and our goals are to have a faster economic recovery than we have ever had before and to recover stronger than before. We will achieve this through disciplined policy choices, prioritising within priorities, maintaining a keen awareness of risk, and by modernising our economy. To do so, it is important that we first consider the impact of the COVID-19 pandemic, thus far, on the Jamaican economy.

Growth

The economic impact of the COVID-19 pandemic on Jamaica can be expressed in a staggering set of numbers that boggle the mind.

The PIOJ expects the economy to contract by approximately 12 per cent this fiscal year ending March 31, 2021. This is, by far, the worst economic contraction in Jamaica's history. No previous economic decline comes close.... The closest comparisons were the declines of 6.5 per cent in 1975; 5.7 per cent in 1980; 4.6 per cent in 1985; 3.9 per cent in 1974; and 3.2 per cent in 2009.

In 2020–21, the economic decline was driven by a massive 70 per cent contraction in the tourist industry. With the exception of the construction sector, which PIOJ expects to show modest growth for 2020–21, all sectors of the economy have declined during the fiscal year.

During April to June 2020, construction declined by 14.5 per cent but grew by 7 per cent in the July to September 2020 quarter, and is forecasted by PIOJ to grow by 6.2 per cent in the October to December 2020 quarter.

Yes, madam Speaker, the construction sector is growing despite the COVID-19 pandemic. This growth is a reflection of the belief of those builders and developers that this, too, shall pass, and that there is a brighter future ahead for Jamaica.

It is also a reflection of the importance of good policy. For example, central bank modernisation, inclusive of the policy shift to inflation targeting, provided the space for interest rates to be reduced ten times to record lows, which allowed these builders and developers the ability to access the capital needed, at attractive prices, to fuel construction. In addition, the reduction and abolishment of transaction taxes on real estate under this government provided a further fillip to development. So even the pandemic could not blunt the impact of good and disciplined policy in this regard.

Company and Business Name Registrations

In the biggest economic crisis in nearly eighty years, more new companies and more new businesses were registered than the previous year, and more than at any time in our history. Now clearly this, by itself, is not an indicator of current economic activity, but it is an indicator of intentions and of possibilities. And it is a great thing that more companies are being formed than at any time in the past.

Our policies of abolishing Minimum Business Tax and abolishing the Asset Tax and going in the opposite direction of providing a Tax Credit to micro and small business and providing benefits to registered entities is increasing formalisation and strengthening the institutional fabric of our country.

Government Revenues and Expenditure

Even after factoring in inflation, government revenues are expected to decline by $70 billion or 12 per cent in this fiscal year 2020–21 as compared with the previous year. Yet the government continued with the provision of goods and services even as expenditures also increased by a net amount of $24 billion on account of the COVID-19 pandemic.

However, direct COVID-19 related expenditures far exceeded this amount and, as a result, we had to reallocate programmed expenditure, mostly capital expenditure, in Supplementary Budgets during the year. Inclusive of the amount spent in the Third Supplementary Estimates of 2019–20, the central government spent approximately $40 billion responding to the impact of the

COVID-19 pandemic, consisting of the CARE Programme, health expenditure, support of Public Bodies affected by the pandemic, and incremental compensation expenditure – in particular in health and security.

This $40 billion does not include the COVID-19 expenditures for programmes implemented by the National Housing Trust, the Student Loan Bureau, and other public bodies to help cushion the pandemic's impact.

Jobs

Madam Speaker, it took four years between 2016 and 2020 for Jamaica to add 100,000 jobs to the economy, and in the first *four months* of the COVID pandemic more than 130,000 jobs were lost. The Jamaicans who lost jobs in the pandemic could fill every seat in the national stadium four times over. When we talk about economic recovery, we are talking about eventually getting every single one of those Jamaicans back in a job. That is our goal and our mission.

Jamaica experienced the lowest level of unemployment in Jamaica's history (7.2 per cent in October 2019) just four months before the onset of the COVID-19 pandemic, and the unemployment rate was 7.3 per cent in January 2020. By July 2020 the rate of unemployment jumped to 12.7 per cent. The good news is that the unemployment rate has improved, and as at October 2020 it was 10.7 per cent. It is still way too high, Madam Speaker, but we are headed in the right direction.

Foreign Exchange Inflows – Tourism

As you know, Jamaica's two largest sources of foreign exchange are tourism and remittances. COVID-19 has decimated Jamaica's foreign exchange inflows from tourism. And again, there is no parallel in Jamaica's history for what has occurred. During the 9/11 terrorist attacks, tourism earnings declined by 14 per cent. In the global financial crisis, tourism earnings declined by 5 per cent As a result of the COVID-19 pandemic, Jamaica's foreign exchange inflows from tourism are projected to fall by 74 per cent, or US$2.5 billion in 2020–21. In 2019–20 we earned US$3.4 billion from tourism, but in 2020–21 we are expected to earn only US$874 million or approximately one quarter of 2019–20 earnings. The last time our foreign exchange inflows were this low was approximately thirty years ago, in 1992–93.

Foreign Exchange Inflows – Remittances

There is a silver lining; Jamaica's diaspora rose to the occasion, and although they face their own COVID-19 related challenges, faithful Jamaicans abroad sent US$600 million more to their family members and friends in Jamaica, which is 23 per cent more than the previous year. I have reviewed thirty years of remittance data, Madam Speaker, and never before have remittances increased by US$600 million in a single year, nor by 23 per cent in a single year.

On behalf of all Jamaicans, I would like to use this opportunity to both recognise and thank all those kind, considerate, and caring members of the larger Jamaican family in the United States, Canada, the United Kingdom, the Caribbean, and throughout the world who never forget their loved ones in the country of their birth, and who stepped up to embrace the command outlined in the Holy Book that we should not forget to do good and share with others.

I should point out quickly that some of this increase in remittances might actually be an unintended consequence of the COVID-19 pandemic. Because many members of the diaspora who are used to travelling to Jamaica and putting money in the hands of their loved ones directly were not able to do so, many chose to send money through traditional channels, which get captured in the formal balance of payments statistics.

However the money comes, we are grateful for it.

Foreign Exchange Outflows – Imports

On the basis of the available data to September 2020, the Bank of Jamaica estimates that outflows related to merchandise imports fell by close to US$1.4 billion for the fiscal year impacted by the related reduction in oil prices and the contraction in GDP. Some of the import reduction also reflected lower demand for certain products like imported food and manufactured goods by the tourism sector, due to hotel closures and significantly lower occupancy levels.

Current Account Deficit

As a result of these factors, the Bank of Jamaica estimates the current account deficit at only 1.7 per cent of GDP 2020–21, an extremely small increase from the [prior year].

This is a remarkable achievement for Jamaica. The current account deficit is our foreign exchange deficit with the rest of the world before you add foreign direct investment. So we have had the worst economic crisis in our history, where tourism revenues fell by US$2.5 billion, and the current account has remained well within the bands of sustainability.

Prior to this experience no one would have thought that Jamaica could have withstood a US$2.5 billion collapse in tourism receipts while retaining macroeconomic stability.

Debt

Over the past few years, this government has pursued a prudent policy of building up our cash reserves to pay down debt. Because of these decisions, we opened the 2020–21 fiscal year with cash reserves of approximately $90 billion, or more than 4 per cent of GDP. As a result, when the COVID-19 pandemic came we were able to finance a 3.5 per cent fiscal deficit without materially increasing nominal debt. Few countries can report similarly. In fact, the stock of foreign-currency-denominated debt *decreased* during the fiscal year. The central government lent Clarendon Alumina Partners (CAP) US$140 million to repay a loan obligation due to the Noble Group, which has lowered CAP's interest costs. This allowed CAP to renegotiate its marketing agreement with Noble, improving the pricing it receives for alumina. We also swapped US$50 million of IDB US$ denominated debt into J$ debt in an innovative transaction pioneered by the IDB.

Both of these transactions contributed to a lowering of the nominal US$ denominated debt during the fiscal year 2020–21. This compares with previous economic crises where nominal US$ debt increased during the crisis. This time around, in the worst economic crisis in our history, nominal US$ debt actually decreased.

Credit Rating

Notwithstanding the historically savage nature of this COVID-19 economic shock, Jamaica has maintained its international credit rating.

Early in the crisis, we took the initiative to contact the credit rating agencies and provided them with an assessment of the crisis, the principles that would ground our response, and our actions. As compared with the credit rating *downgrades* of other countries, the highest credit ratings that Jamaica has had – in twenty years from Standard & Poor's and in fourteen years from Fitch – have thus far been maintained, although we have experienced the worst economic crisis in our history.

Innovations of the CARE Programme

Budget Speech Excerpt, March 2021

Madam Speaker, in the execution of the CARE Programme, we did something novel. We asked the Auditor General to perform concurrent audits of the CARE Programme. That is, to audit while the programme was being executed and before each batch of payments was made. So applications for each CARE grant type were validated, and then processed and batched for payment, subject to audit. Prior to the files being transferred for payment, the Auditor General's Department, which had access to the system and all of its data, audited the eligibility, validation, and other processes, and produced reports allowing for any errors to be identified and corrected prior to payment. Those reports were tabled in Parliament for the people's representatives to review and ask questions, and for the world to see.

This had the effect of slowing down payments as we had to process grant types one at a time – compassionate grant, general grant, small business grant, SET cash grant, BEST cash grant, and so on – and also, within grant types, each discrete batch.

This caused delays and some backlash, but the transparency of this process, and the openness of the programme to the highest level of immediate scrutiny, provided the public confidence that allowed the programme to scale to $20 billion.

In this programme, similarly situated Jamaicans had equal access to government benefits, which, importantly, did not depend on race, class, gender, or political affiliation.

Your CARE benefit did not depend on who you voted for. Your CARE benefit did not depend on whether you were PNP, JLP, or No Party. If you were eligible, and your identity could be established, you could receive this benefit from the government.

Adapted from the opening budget presentation delivered in Parliament on March 9, 2021.

There was no paperwork, no human interface. You applied online or on your mobile phone, tablet, or computer and eventually you collected your benefit from the Jamaican State at the remittance company or the bank.

In the end more than 440,000 Jamaicans benefitted from one of a number of CARE grants through the We CARE digital portal.

I will be the first to admit that it was not perfect. There were glitches that we had to overcome and areas that could be improved.

However, there are some powerful lessons in the experience of the CARE programme that I would like to share. These are by no means exhaustive:

1. Digital means of processing and delivery offer the opportunity for quick, efficient, rules-based, and scalable programmes. As the Prime Minister is on record saying, we must make the transition to a fully digital society. The potential benefits to Jamaica and Jamaicans are huge. This is our goal and our mission.

2. The Member of Parliament and local government Councillors have a legitimate and important role to play in assisting the citizen to navigate the State bureaucracy to access benefits offered by the State. Without the role of Members of Parliament, supported by Councillors, who helped to sign people up, and made representation on their behalf when there were problems, the programme would not have reached as many persons, despite the convenience of the digital platform, and it would not have been as successful. The key is to ensure that the Member of Parliament and Councillor cannot unduly influence the results. A digital solution that is auditable and rules-based helps achieve this.

3. Openness and transparency in the use of public resources, and open, transparent, and equitable processes for the distribution of the resources of the State, ultimately empower the State to do more for the people. It is a virtuous cycle.

Since that time we have moved with alacrity to: deepen transparency in monetary policy with the passage of central bank modernisation legislation; deepen fiscal transparency with the passage of the independent fiscal commission legislation; deepen transparency around the execution of the Government of Jamaica's public investment programme with the launch of the Public Investment Map; and deepen openness in the public policy formation process with the launch of the Open Government initiative.

It is important to make the connection. We are institutionalising transparency in policy execution and applying transparent principles in the use of public resources. We remain committed to making policy decisions that provide greater openness, transparency, and fairness in the distribution of government resources. That is our goal and our mission as we aim to recover faster and stronger than before.

Lessons Learned from the COVID-19 Economic Crisis

Budget Speech Excerpt, March 2021

Madam Speaker, when we learn, we grow. So it is always good to distil the 'lessons learned' from our significant or important experiences. This is true at the level of the individual, and it is also true at the level of the country.

For a young nation experiencing a painful economic shock of historic proportions, it is useful to take stock and distil some of the main economic lessons thus far.

The Lesson of Buffers – Never Leave the Cupboard Empty

One lesson, at the policy level, is the importance of having buffers that result from an awareness of risk. Economic shocks happen. Sometimes, huge economic shocks happen. From time to time, we experience economic shocks arising from commodity price volatility, geopolitical tension, social tensions, natural disaster, and yes epidemics and pandemics. Sometimes, unfortunately, we experience more than one of these shocks at the same time.

As a small, open, developing, and relatively undiversified economy, Jamaica is particularly vulnerable to a variety of economic shocks. This is our reality.

What has happened to us in the past is that economic shocks have set us back years, even decades. The economic shock in the 1970s led to six years of economic decline between 1974 and 1980, and it took us fourteen years to recover to pre-crisis levels of economic output.

The economic shock arising from the global financial crisis 2008–2009 led to three years of economic decline, where the economy contracted for eleven out of twelve fiscal quarters, and it took us ten years to recover to pre-crisis levels of economic output.

Adapted from the opening budget presentation delivered in Parliament March 9, 2021.

Our recoveries have taken too long. They have fit on a generational timescale. We are determined to change that. That is our goal and our mission.

The biggest hurdle on our development path since independence has been that, as compared with more successful economies, our periods of economic expansion have been too short, while our experiences of economic declines have been too long. Proverbially, moving two steps forwards, and one step back.

If you move two steps forward and one step back, it takes you three times as long to reach your destination. It is like building a house: you lay three bricks, and two slip off, and you lay three bricks, and two slip off again. If every time you lay three bricks, two slip off, the house 'nah go finish' for now. What you want to do is build the house brick, by brick, by brick, steadily, brick by brick.

When you build the house steadily brick by brick, rain or shine, brick by brick by brick, the resources become available to sustain the levels of social investment that can counter the decay and erosion of Jamaica's social fabric.

Our biggest challenge is to fundamentally change our approach. The economic cycle of expansion and decline is an eternal condition of humankind. We will always have periods of economic decline. But we want the periods of economic decline and recovery to be shorter and shorter, with our periods of our economic expansion longer and longer. That is, we want to ensure we have quick economic recoveries. We have made it our mission from the very outset of this crisis to defy our history and, relative to this history, to have the quickest recovery from our worst economic crisis.

So how do we ensure that our economic expansions last longer and our declines are shorter?

First, our policies must incorporate the reality of the economic risks we face. We must ensure that we are always adequately prepared. For the foreseeable future, we will remain vulnerable to the economic impact of commodity price shocks, geopolitical tensions, and natural disaster events. We must ensure that we always have buffers.

We should never, ever, have the cupboard empty.

Second, we must continue to prioritise and preserve macroeconomic stability. That is, policies and institutions that are consistent with low inflation, adequate foreign exchange reserves, financial sector stability, and debt sustainability.

We remain committed to these objectives of providing a buffer for the future through the pursuit of good policy. That is our goal and mission as we aim to recover faster and quicker than before.

The Lesson of Agency – We Can Shape the Future We Want

The most powerful lesson is that through disciplined policy choices, and effective implementation, we have the capacity to bring into reality the Jamaica we want. The most powerful lesson is that we have agency. We are, in fact, in control of our destiny.

Jamaica's history includes hundreds of years of colonisation and domination. Through the persistent forces of history, we sometimes subtly adopt, embrace, internalise, and pass on an identity where our existential frame is a world where things happen to us: 'A just so it go. A just suh di ting set.' That is, we sometimes act as if we are not in control of our destiny. As if there are forces at work that are too big for us to confront.

Marcus Garvey did not think like that. Norman Manley did not think like that. Alexander Bustamante never thought like that. Neither did any of our national heroes. And it was Jesus himself who warned us with the parable of the talents. Jesus rejected the man in the parable who was given one talent, but who lacked vision and was too afraid and thought he could not transform his environment.

So far, we have weathered this crisis better than others in the past, though it's the worst economic crisis in our history – not by magic, but because of the policy choices we as an independent people have made.

With that as my reference, and in the spirit of the parable I referred to you, I say to my fellow Jamaicans that, with God's help, and with disciplined policy choice, we, as a nation, can bend the future to our will.

We can win. And we will win.

That is our goal and our mission.

Jamaican Economy Rolls with the Punches to Get Back Up Again

Interview, April 2021

This interview that I granted, and that appeared as sponsored journalism in *Foreign Policy* on April 15, 2021, a little more than a year after the start of the COVID-19 pandemic, highlights the way in which Jamaica's 'positive financial history cushions the nation from ill economic effects due to the pandemic and stages a platform for further growth.'

Question: Given Jamaica's dependency on its tourism industry, how has the COVID-19 pandemic affected the economy?

COVID-19 has had a significant impact on the world economy, and Jamaica is no exception. Jamaica is an open economy, and the trade of goods and services is a huge part of our gross domestic product (GDP). The pandemic introduced demand and supply shocks. The Jamaican government's revenues declined by approximately 16 per cent from April to December 2020 based on a year-by-year comparison. We are expecting a contraction in economic activity of about 12 per cent of our GDP this fiscal year, the worst in our history.

Another variable affected by the pandemic is foreign exchange inflows. Jamaica derives much of this from exports of commodity items, finished goods, and tourism receipts and remittances. Because airports, cruise ports, and hotels were shut, our foreign exchange inflows declined substantially.

After factoring in the trade balance, the overall balance of payments saw a deterioration of approximately 1.7 per cent of our GDP this fiscal year. The good news is that this is not a significant deviation from 1.6 per cent the previous year. We had a sustainable account deficit for several years leading up to this crisis, about 2 per cent of GDP, which was easily financed by foreign direct investments and capital inflows.

Unemployment increased dramatically. Only 7.2 per cent of our population was unemployed in January 2020, the lowest unemployment rate in our history. However, by June 2020, the unemployment rate went up to 12.8 per cent. About 10 per cent of the workforce lost their jobs, mostly those working in the service economy.

Luckily, our historic fiscal responsibility provided buffers. For the seven financial years prior to the pandemic, Jamaica had budgets with primary surpluses of 7 per cent of GDP. This had resulted in a dramatic decline in Jamaica's debt. As a result, Jamaica could be flexible in responding to the crisis. We also divested some state enterprises by making them public. We had cash reserves of over 3 per cent of GDP, which is very unusual for a government.

Rating agencies such as Standard & Poor's and financial institutions such as Jamaica's central bank, the International Monetary Fund, and the Caribbean Development Bank expect Jamaica to bounce back in the next year. However, it will take a few years for economic output to re-attain pre-COVID levels. Structurally, the economy is still intact.

Question: What programs has the public sector created to support poverty created by the crisis?

The Government of Jamaica introduced the COVID-19 Allocation of Resources for Employees (CARE) Programme, our social and economic support programme to cushion the economic impact on individuals and businesses. This is the largest programme based on annual expenditure in Jamaican history. A large-scale electronic system had to be built from scratch as we could not have people physically lining up to apply and sign in. This number of persons who lost their jobs and required monthly payments from the government has never happened before.

The programme consists of two separate components. The first, Supporting Employees with Transfer of Cash, supports workers with cash transfers. The second, Business Employee Support and Transfer of Cash, supports business employees, directly targeting the tourism sector. Tourism operators who maintained people on their payroll (earning below a threshold) received cash stipends. We also provided grants to small businesses and sole traders, people in the disabled community, and those who were long-term unemployed and not registered in the formal system. Additionally, the central bank intervened with liquidity support by purchasing treasury and government bonds from the main financial institutions. This allowed financial institutions to provide temporary forbearance to customers. The government will continue to prioritise health and education. We will also focus on investment in the country to support growth and the return of jobs. The country will continue with our foreign direct investment and big construction projects. Construction planned for Jamaica's north coast will continue. We expect big investments in logistics, business process outsourcing, and manufacturing.

Question: What advice would you give to foreign investors looking to participate in the market?

Jamaica's direction is unmistakably positive; our momentum is unaffected by the pandemic. Jamaica is building durable, transparent, and accountable economic institutions. We have fulfilled our commitment to become independent of the central bank, despite the pandemic. The central bank has been legislated to maintain price stability as its primary mandate.

We have tabled legislation for an independent fiscal commission, which gives assurance that fiscal responsibility is institutionalised. Investors looking at Jamaica can be confident that we have a long-term macroeconomic environment that is hospitable to investment. We expect tremendous momentum in the future.

On the Path of Economic Recovery

Budget Speech Excerpt, March 2022

Over the past year, the Jamaican economy has begun an impressive recovery from the devastating impact of the COVID-19 pandemic. Across several metrics – such as economic growth, job growth, debt reduction, and credit ratings – the Jamaican economy has been recovering from COVID-19 well ahead of most of our peers.

Let me remind you, when we gathered here last year this time, [the Opposition] never believed we could recover this fast. When we forecasted 5 per cent growth, they questioned it.

I don't blame them, because the kind of economic recovery we experienced over the last year has never been experienced before. So how could they have seen it? It is difficult to see and recognise what you have never experienced.

While other economies in our region wobbled in fiscal year 2021–22, Jamaica staged a strong, robust, and historic recovery. That was no accident.

With the blessings of God Almighty and good policy choices, the historic shock delivered by the pandemic did not lead to a balance of payment crisis, as in the past; did not lead to a debt crisis, as in the past; and did not lead to a fiscal crisis, as in the past. Any of these knock-on effects would have complicated Jamaica's recovery.

Instead, the Jamaican economy came roaring back with 14 per cent growth in the first quarter of the fiscal year – the highest quarterly growth rate ever recorded in Jamaica….

And, the 'dance' dem, and 'weddy, weddy' don't roll in yet!

Prime Minister, I know you are working on something for the entertainment sector. Don't tek too long PM, 'cause I want them

---

Adapted from the opening budget presentation delivered in Parliament March 8, 2021.

to come out. When we have a 'dance,' a 'round robin,' a 'fish fry,' a 'cake sale'....

We talking 'bout the 'Cane man,' 'Soupy,' and all 'Nutsy' eat a food out of that.

Young Keisha who get her 'pardner draw' and convert that into buying some liquor to sell, add some ice and she borrow a igloo, and two case on top of 'di' igloo on top of di ice....

Is Keisha weekend dinner 'dat'!

So is when Brogad 'bus all dem people deh,' that is when you really going to see and feel the recovery!

The Cause of Economic Growth

There was great policy coordination across the major economies of the world. That coordination helped, but cannot be considered the major factor for country experiences, because there is great divergence in economic recovery among countries of the world.

Among other factors, our economic recovery benefited first from putting in place buffers:

- Fiscal buffers – we took the strategic decision to increase cash cushions through privatisations, reintegration of public bodies, and targeted fiscal over-performance

- Monetary buffers – we took the strategic decision to increase non-borrowed reserves by US$1 billion since 2016 through the policy choices of exchange-rate flexibility and inflation targeting (which also brought the period of lowest annual percentage depreciation of any administration in the last thirty years)

- Resilience buffers – we took the strategic decision to put away resources in 2018 and 2019 in disaster funds that we were able to draw down in the first few months of the pandemic

- Capitalised Central Bank – we took the strategic decision to capitalise the Bank of Jamaica with $20 billion in 2018 and 2019, which allowed it to make unprecedented liquidity injections into the banking system

And second, by making sustainable and internally consistent policy choices during the crisis, and having the discipline to reject ideas that fell outside of that criteria.

As a result, our economic recovery in Jamaica has been faster and stronger than the vast majority of our peers in the Caribbean, quite a few of whom had the unfortunate experience of a second year of economic decline in 2021. The forces unleashed by good policies, including abolishment of distortionary transaction taxes, could not be stopped by a mere pandemic!

It is worth noting that after a dreadful and painful 2020, the Tourism sector returned with a bang, growing over 300 per cent in the second quarter of 2021, over 100 per cent in the third quarter, and over 75 per cent in the fourth quarter. There is still, however, much more recovery necessary.

It is also worth noting that for the last three quarters of 2021–22, all sectors of the economy recovered strongly and grew with the exception of mining. And the reasons for mining's decline are well understood.

Employment Growth

I am pleased to report that during 2021–22, we recovered jobs at a rapid pace: There was a growth of one hundred thousand jobs between July 2020 and July 2021, and there was a growth of seventy-five thousand jobs between October 2020 and October 2021. In fact, the unemployment rate in October 2021 fell to the lowest level in Jamaica's history, 7.1 per cent – even lower than the pre-Pandemic unemployment rate!

Now, the labour force participation rate was slightly lower as more persons stayed home and out of the job market due to various factors, including school closures and taking care of children. There are those who will try to undermine job growth and belittle hard working people in jobs. But let me tell you, every one of the one hundred thousand families that benefited from the recovery of a job – they know the value of stable government with good policies. They have an income again. They are independent again. For those one hundred thousand Jamaicans who were at home and now have income – they appreciate the strong recovery.

Of course, we want an economy with higher paying jobs. [Much as Singapore drove their economic growth by using the jobs they had, and not spending more than they earned….] We, too, will use what we have. We won't curse it. We will use what we have to get to where we want to go.

Again, we were ready and prepared to bring people back to work after the crisis.

Debt Reduction

Jamaica's debt-to-GDP ratio was 94 per cent in March 2020 and, due to the COVID-19 pandemic and the measures necessary to slow its spread, this critically important ratio climbed to approximately 110 per cent by March 2021.

For Jamaica, given our vulnerabilities, this was a high and risky level of debt, as I articulated in my budget presentation last year. Well, a year later I am pleased to report that along with strong GDP growth and strong jobs growth, we have also significantly reduced our debt-to-GDP ratio, which is projected to be 96 per cent by March 2022.

With God's help, and barring any major surprises and exogenous setbacks, by the end of the upcoming fiscal year, we could see this ratio go below 90 per cent for the first time in what would be twenty-three years! An entire generation!

There is a chart in the IMF's 2021 Article IV Consultation on Jamaica, for countries in Latin America and the Caribbean, which shows the change in the debt-to-GDP ratio in percentage points of GDP, between 2019 and 2021. Jamaica ranks second among thirty countries of the region in restoring the national debt level – the debt-to-GDP ratio – to almost pre-COVID-19 levels by 2021. Most countries in the region have debt-to-GDP ratios that are still ten, twenty, thirty, forty, fifty, and even sixty percentage points higher than their pre-COVID-19 levels.

This is Jamaica's achievement. This is your achievement. And this achievement lowers the risk of the Jamaican economy and provides better protection for turbulence.

But let's not get carried away. We are not yet out of the woods, by any means. Due to very high levels of debt that now prevail around the world we are likely to see a debt crisis emerge globally and even in the Western Hemisphere.

With God's help, we will steer clear of that so that we recover and restore. And we can continue to build an economy where real per capita Income increases steadily over time.

On Our Way to Achieving Economic Recovery from the COVID-19 Pandemic

Budget Speech Excerpt, March 2023

Madam Speaker, I am pleased to report to this Honourable House and to the people of Jamaica that the Jamaican economy is projected to have expanded by 3.4 per cent in the fourth quarter of 2022. As compared with the corresponding quarters of 2021, in 2022 the economy officially expanded by 5.8 per cent in the third quarter, 4.8 per cent in the second quarter, and 6.5 per cent in the first quarter. This follows economic expansion of 6.7 per cent in the fourth quarter of 2021, 5.9 per cent in the third quarter of 2021, and a record 14.2 per cent in the second quarter of 2021.

I am pleased to update this House, and indeed all Jamaicans here and in the diaspora, that by December 2022, Jamaica not only achieved, but also surpassed pre-pandemic levels of quarterly economic output for the quarter ended December 2019.[8] This, is an achievement of which all Jamaicans can be proud. This is a result of our collective efforts, and it comes one fiscal year ahead of expectations. And for those who question whether this rapid growth in 2021 and 2022 is simply a product of the steep decline in the economy in 2020, I simply ask this:

After a 6.7 per cent decline in 1976, why didn't we grow in 1977?

After a 4.5 per cent decline in 1985, why didn't we grow in 1986?

After a 3.2 per cent decline in 2009, why didn't we grow in 2010?

In our history, economic decline has often been followed by further decline, sadly.

Together, we, the Jamaican society, broke that cycle this time. Hopefully and prayerfully, a new template has been established for the future. The significance of this achievement is evident by reference to our own economic history, and also to what is happening elsewhere in the world today. It took fourteen years to recover from

---

Adapted from the opening budget presentation delivered in Parliament March 7, 2023.

the economic shocks of the mid-1970s. When economic output registered negative growth of by -6.5 per cent, -2.4 per cent, -1.8 per cent, and -5.7 per cent in 1976, 1977, 1979, and 1980, respectively, it was not until 1989 that economic output, in real terms, surpassed 1975 levels.

It took eleven years to recover from the economic shock delivered by the global financial crisis when economic output registered negative growth of -0.8 per cent, -3.4 per cent, and -1.4 per cent in 2008, 2009, and 2010, respectively. We suffered a devastating economic shock of -10 per cent in 2020. Importantly, and unlike times past, although we lost US$2.5 billion of foreign exchange inflows, this historic economic shock did not precipitate a balance of payment crisis.

Little Jamaica survived a decimation of foreign exchange inflows of US$2.5 billion. This is an amazing show of resilience by our country.

I would like to take this opportunity to formally recognise the role of the diaspora who in 2020 sent over US$600 million more than in the previous year, an increase of 23 per cent. On behalf of the Jamaican people here on the island, I thank you. And, of course, I encourage you to continue supporting your family and friends and helping to build our nation. Importantly, and unlike times past, although our debt increased dramatically to approximately 110 per cent of GDP, we were able to avoid a fiscal crisis through prudent policy choices and the tremendous support of the Jamaican people.

And, it is critically important to note that our financial services sector – the lifeblood of the economy – remained strong, robust, and resilient through the COVID-19 economic shock, and even through the inflation crisis that followed.

Any one of these crises – a balance of payments crisis, a fiscal crisis, or a financial sector crisis, triggered by the COVID-19 shock or the inflation shock, or both as happened in many countries across the world – would have seriously complicated and significantly delayed prospects for economic recovery. And it would have been easy to have happened here in Jamaica. Look around the world: countries in the Caribbean, in Central America, in sub-Saharan Africa, in Asia are battling serious fiscal crises, debt crises, and balance of payment crises triggered by the onslaught of the COVID-19 pandemic and the subsequent inflation shock.

Many countries will not recover to pre-COVID levels of economic output for five years. Some for ten years or more, while Jamaica, today, stands as a shining example to the world.

Jamaica is recognised internationally for our music, sports, and the vibrancy of our culture. Madam Speaker, though we have many challenges, Jamaica is also becoming known and recognised globally for the successes of our economic reforms and recovery. Not only has economic output now surpassed pre-COVID levels, but levels of unemployment are also lower today than the historic lows achieved immediately prior to the pandemic. Since we have been measuring it, unemployment in Jamaica has never been lower than the 6.0 per cent rate achieved in April 2022. This is more than a full percentage point lower than the 7.2 per cent achieved in January 2020, prior to the onset of the pandemic. Again, this is an achievement that all Jamaicans can take pride in. Over 150,000 persons lost their jobs during the pandemic, but more than 150,000 jobs have already been created or restored since that time.

We are also pleased to report that the number of employed persons in April 2022 of 1,269,300 is the highest number of persons ever employed in Jamaica's recorded history.

In my 2021 budget presentation I shared the view that many countries in the emerging markets, and even several developed nations around the world, would be impacted by a major debt crisis. I made those remarks before Sri Lanka, before Pakistan, before Ghana, and before several other countries made headlines for their fiscal distress. It is in that context that our next achievement as a country is particularly significant; not only have we recovered lost economic output and recovered jobs lost in the pandemic, but also, despite the fact that our debt attained the worrying level of 110 per cent of GDP in the aftermath of the pandemic, I am pleased that our debt level in Jamaica is also lower than it was pre-pandemic.

Data from the International Monetary Fund (IMF) confirms that there are few countries in the Western Hemisphere that can claim all three of these things occurred at the same time in the last quarter of 2022:

1. Higher economic output in real terms in the last quarter of 2022 than the last quarter pre-COVID levels;

2. Lower unemployment than pre-COVID levels; and

3. Lower debt than pre-COVID levels.

In fact, this trinity of macroeconomic achievements puts Jamaica in rare company in the entire world. This is our collective achievement.

I salute and thank the Jamaican people and, even as I do that, I also want to say thanks to God Almighty.

Financing the Risk of Natural Disasters

Addressing the Fiscal Risk of Natural Disaster: Jamaica's Catastrophe Bond

Published Commentary, September 2021

Implementation and maintenance of a strategy to counter the fiscal risks of natural disaster are as important to Jamaica's economic security as the preservation of foreign exchange reserve adequacy and debt sustainability.

The Ministry of Finance and the Public Service therefore elevated natural disaster risk financing to a strategic priority, and we have since made important strides in the implementation of a multi-layered strategy.

GOJ's Multi-Layered Strategy

Consistent with past practise, we provide budgetary space, in annual and supplementary budgets, to enable a response to high frequency, low-impact natural disaster events.

However, in 2019 we went beyond this traditional approach and capitalised our Contingency Fund with J$4 billion (US$27 million) – a historic move at the time, given that the Contingency Fund had, for decades, only held a maximum of J$100 million. By parliamentary resolution, we also increased the Contingency Fund cap from J$100 million to J$10 billion, signalling future intent.

Prior to this, in 2018, we entered into a US$285 million (J$43 billion) Contingent Credit Claim with the Inter-American Development Bank (IDB) that disburses in the event of a hurricane catastrophe, and we renewed the Caribbean Catastrophe Reinsurance Facility (CCRIF) which provides approximately US$81 million (J$12 billion) of coverage against hurricanes, approximately US$125 million (J$19 billion) of coverage against earthquakes, and approximately US$ 31 million (J$5 billion) of coverage against excess rainfall.

An earlier version of this article appeared in the *Jamaica Gleaner*, **September 25, 2021.**

In July, we further advanced Jamaica's strategy with the successful placement of a US$185 million (J$28 billion) catastrophe bond in global capital markets, through the World Bank.

These layers – budgetary provisions, Contingency Fund capitalisation, the Credit Contingent Claim, the CCRIF, and now the Catastrophe Bond – address different layers of natural-disaster risk: from high frequency, low-impact to low frequency, high-impact events.

We expect to cover high frequency occurrences such as annual rainfall, below a certain threshold, but at a level that sometimes leads to flooding, from budgetary allocations and reallocations. At the other end of the spectrum, in a low frequency, high-impact natural disaster occurrence we expect all layers to be triggered in part or in whole.

Fitch's Assessment

Natural disasters generate the need for governments to engage in emergency public expenditure. The layers in Jamaica's strategy collectively provide buffers for the fiscal shock that natural disasters inevitably cause. These buffers increase Jamaica's resilience and strengthen our ability to recover from natural disasters without too significant an impairment to our economic trajectory. This lowers Jamaica's risk and lowers the cost of investment.

Fitch, the international credit rating agency, in their published analysis of our catastrophe bond earlier this week, reported that the catastrophe bond 'significantly strengthens (Jamaica's) disaster risk mitigation strategy.' Fitch further noted the fact that this is the first catastrophe bond ever to be independently sponsored by a small country. More significantly, Fitch commented that of all the catastrophe bonds the World Bank has issued, this is the largest in relation to the size of the sponsoring country's economy.

What Is a Catastrophe Bond?

A catastrophe bond transfers catastrophic natural-disaster risk from a sponsor (in this case Jamaica) to international capital-market investors. It is a form of insurance that achieves our objectives by creating securities in which investors can invest principal, enjoy the premiums paid during the term of the contract, and accept the risk that – in the event of a natural disaster that breaches thresholds – some, or all, of the principal amount they put at risk is paid over to the sponsor. (Though the 'bond' terminology is convenient, a catastrophe bond does not add to Jamaica's debt stock).

In traditional insurance, after a natural disaster event, loss adjusters first assess the amount of damage, before paying out. This can be a complicated process that takes many months, sometimes up to two years. A catastrophe bond is a form of parametric insurance where payout is triggered if/when observable and measurable features of the natural disaster event breach pre-agreed thresholds. As a result, a catastrophe bond pays out within weeks of a natural disaster without the need to assess the real loss sustained.

Jamaica's Catastrophe Bond

Jamaica's catastrophe bond is globally pioneering the 'cat in a grid' trigger approach, as we are the first in the world to use this. The 'cat in a grid' trigger places a grid over Jamaica and surrounding waters, with each grid having a centralised air-pressure threshold. Payout is triggered if a hurricane passes through a grid and has centralised air pressure at or below the threshold for that grid. (Note: The lower the centralised air pressure, the higher the intensity of the hurricane).

The size of payout is related to how many such grids are breached. This granular approach allows us to optimise and, for example, provide higher thresholds for geographical areas where losses are likely to be higher from a direct hit, e.g., Kingston and Montego Bay.

The World Bank Treasury acts as an intermediary between Jamaica and our catastrophe bond capital-market investors. They collect the premiums from Jamaica and remit these funds to the investors in the form of bond coupons. They also hold custody of the principal invested by the investors and will pay this out to Jamaica if a natural disaster event breaches the established thresholds.

The Governments of the United Kingdom, Germany, and the United States are assisting Jamaica with grants that pay the entire premium for the catastrophe bond across the three hurricane cycles it covers, including the current one. The commitment and expectation is that Jamaica will finance the premiums on renewal as our fiscal dynamics improve.

It is important to note that Jamaica's multi-layered strategy for the management of fiscal risk of natural disaster only works for the people of Jamaica if it is consistently maintained, over the long term, beyond the life of any administration. For this reason we are institutionalising the approach, including by providing updates on Jamaica's disaster-risk financing in the annual and interim fiscal policy papers, which are tabled in parliament, alongside standard commentary on economic, fiscal, and monetary outcomes.

Addressing the fiscal risk of natural disaster should be a permanent strategic priority for Jamaica.

Jamaica's Disaster Risk Financing Framework: The CCRIF Layer

Published Commentary, July 2024

In September 2004, Hurricane Ivan demolished Grenada, submerged Cayman, and battered Haiti and Jamaica. In the immediate aftermath of the passage of this devastating hurricane, CARICOM Heads of Government met in an emergency session and, according to Grenada's then-Prime Minister Keith Mitchell, 'issued a clarion call to international financial institutions to develop affordable and effective catastrophe risk instruments.'[9]

The international community responded by providing the technical and financial resources that led to the establishment of the Caribbean Catastrophe Risk Insurance Facility, known as CCRIF.

As CCRIF shares on its website: 'the CCRIF was developed under the technical leadership of the World Bank and with a grant from the Government of Japan. It was capitalised through contributions to a Multi-Donor Trust Fund (MDTF) by the Government of Canada, the European Union, the World Bank, the governments of the UK and France, the Caribbean Development Bank and the governments of Ireland and Bermuda, as well as through membership fees paid by participating governments.'

These donors contributed US$47 million for the initial capitalisation that allowed the CCRIF to open its doors to Caribbean governments in 2007. As a legal entity, CCRIF is domiciled in Cayman, has no physical offices, and operates virtually with its CEO based in St Lucia.

Over the ten hurricane seasons between 2007 and 2016, Jamaica was impacted by five natural disasters: Hurricane Dean (2007), Tropical Storm Nicole (2008), Tropical Storm Gustav (2008), Hurricane Sandy (2012), and Hurricane Matthew (2016). Despite

---

An earlier version of this article appeared in the *Jamaica Gleaner*, July 14, 2024.

the impact of these disasters, Jamaica received *no* payout from the then-CCRIF policies.

By 2016, the Ministry of Finance had only J$94 million in the Contingencies Fund and insurance policies with the CCRIF. For practical purposes, this was a single layer of disaster-risk financing (i.e., the CCRIF policies) that had the unrealistic burden of covering the full breadth of natural disasters, from low frequency to high frequency, as well as from low intensity to high intensity.

Against this background, the CCRIF sustained cynical and negative press in Jamaica. Even Parliamentarians lost faith in its potential. In the last month of the PNP administration, in January 2016, then-Minister of Local Government Noel Arscott is quoted in the *Gleaner* as frustratingly expressing 'dissatisfaction with CCRIF' and advocating for it to be 'renegotiated.'

In 2017, the Public Administration and Appropriations Committee (PAAC), under the Chairmanship of then-Opposition Member of Parliament Wykeham McNeil, grilled Ministry of Finance officials about lack of payouts from Jamaica's CCRIF policies and called for a 'review of the arrangements with CCRIF.' The minutes of that May 17, 2017, PAAC meeting detail that 'Mikael Philipps recommended that going forward consideration should be given to self-insurance [as a replacement for CCRIF] to which Messrs. Phillip Paulwell and Fitz Jackson agreed.'

By the time I became Minister of Finance in early 2018, the sentiments about CCRIF were therefore very negative. As such, the Ministry of Finance faced pressure to terminate or reduce our arrangements with the CCRIF.

Here was my approach. In my maiden budget presentation, I advanced the view that 'the pursuit of economic independence requires an institutional response to the financial risk of natural disaster.' I committed that the Ministry of Finance would develop a policy for 'Public Financial Management…for Natural Disaster Risk,' which would be submitted to Parliament for its approval and adoption as the national policy. Furthermore, I outlined that our strategy for disaster-risk financing would rely on multiple layers, instead of only a single layer, and these layers would include accumulated fiscal savings, a contingent credit facility, a catastrophe bond, as well as the CCRIF, which is not static but whose policies are renewed and optimised each year.

We accomplished all these goals, including additional layers, long before Hurricane Beryl, with the design philosophy that every storm would not trigger all instruments; however, fiscal resources would always be available from some instruments for every storm.

So, we heard the critics. We engaged with the CCRIF. And we chose to do the opposite of what the critics suggested. We stuck with, and advocated for the CCRIF, increased coverage limits, and optimised parameters within budgetary constraints.

Today, Jamaica's policies with CCRIF have completely different parameters from the CCRIF policies of 2007. For example, Jamaica's tropical cyclone policy now has a significantly lower Attachment Point which is defined as 'the minimum severity of an event loss which gives rise to a payment and therefore is the loss value at which the policy contract is triggered,' and is analogous to the deductible in a home insurance policy. Today's policy also has a much lower Exhaustion Point, which is defined as 'the severity of the event loss at or above which the maximum payment is triggered.'

In 2020, the first ever payout from the CCRIF to Jamaica was triggered in the amount of US$3.5 million by Tropical Cyclone Eta in relation to our excess rainfall policy. The second payout from CCRIF will be made in 2024 in relation to Hurricane Beryl in the amount of US$16.5 million as our tropical cyclone policy has triggered. And there may yet be a third payout from CCRIF in 2024, in relation to our excess rainfall policy.[10]

The CCRIF provides model-based parametric insurance. This allows for faster payouts than indemnity insurance, which requires loss adjusters to go into the field and verify the value of actual losses which can take several months.

CCRIF policies are not triggered by actual observed losses. Instead, payouts are made against modelled losses. CCRIF maintains huge amounts of data about the distribution, location, and value of assets in insured member states. Once a tropical cyclone passes, and its descriptive quantitative parameters are known, CCRIF simulates the passage of the hurricane on its computers, incorporating the database of asset distribution, and calculates the value of the damage sustained in the modelled event. For the policy to trigger, these 'model losses' must exceed the Attachment Point in the policy.

Sometimes, as in the past, modelled losses have not exceeded the Attachment Point agreed to in Jamaica's CCRIF policy, and, as such, there has been no payout. It is also possible for deviations to exist between modelled losses and actual losses, as no model provides a perfect description of reality even though the CCRIF updates its models periodically to ensure that this basis-risk is minimised.

Based on the totality of the 2007–24 experience, the reader should see that it would be sub-optimal to rely on the CCRIF as the only real disaster-risk financing instrument as Jamaica did for the first eleven years of this period. CCRIF may not be triggered by many natural disaster events that cause damage to Jamaica. Furthermore, the maximum payout under tropical cyclone is US\$84 million, which would be insufficient for the relief and recovery efforts in the event of a direct hit, where the centre of the hurricane passes over some of the landmass of Jamaica.

In response to these realities, the Government of Jamaica has adopted a proactive approach to pre-financing emerging expenditures that arise from natural disasters by assembling a multi-layered suite of financial instruments calibrated to provide fiscal resources to finance the relief and recovery. As such, Jamaica has never been better fiscally prepared for a hurricane as it was for Hurricane Beryl.

Building a Robust Disaster Risk Financing Framework

Published Commentary, July 2024

The Government of Jamaica's (GOJ) relief and recovery responses to Hurricane Beryl are well advanced. So why am I still writing about multi-layered disaster-risk financing? Because there isn't a better opportunity to further advance public understanding of this national policy than through the demonstration of its necessity, benefits, and efficacy.

Last week, the Minister of Labour and Social Security, Hon. Pearnel Charles, Jr, announced interventions of up to J$400,000 for marginal and low-income persons whose homes were destroyed by Hurricane Beryl. This compares with the Hurricane Sandy vouchers of a maximum of J$60,000 per person, approved in 2012, for the same purpose. Adjusted for compounded inflation over the period, this represents a more than three-fold real per capita increase in the GOJ's response to the most vulnerable, and worst affected, in the aftermath of a hurricane.

The GOJ will tap $5 billion from our disaster-risk financing resources to provide housing grants; to finance the repair of schools, health clinics, and hospitals; to support farmers and fishermen; and to clean Jamaica's drains and gullies, among other hurricane-related expenditure.

Fiscal improvements aside, the enhancement of the GOJ's capacity to respond has only been possible because the GOJ had saved funds annually for this purpose and maintained an optimised suite of financial products.

Disaster Risk Financing Policy

Jamaica faces a variety of natural disaster risks. As such, Jamaica's disaster-risk financing framework needs to be responsive to the full range of potential natural disaster outcomes – from low

---

An earlier version of this article appeared in the *Jamaica Gleaner*, July 28, 2024.

intensity to high intensity events, and from low frequency to high frequency disasters. No one layer of protection can cover this range of possibilities. We need multiple layers. However, such a strategy is only effective if it is sustained over the long term and across successive political administrations.

For this reason, in 2022, with the approval of Cabinet, the Ministry of Finance and the Public Service (Finance Ministry) tabled a Green Paper in Parliament titled 'The National Natural Disaster Risk Financing Policy' (DRF Policy). The Finance Ministry, supported by leading dancehall artistes, then engaged in public consultations in 2023 across Jamaica, in William Grant Park, Downtown Kingston, Mandela Park, May Pen, and Montego Bay.

After the required period of consultation, the Finance Ministry tabled the corresponding White Paper, which was adopted by Parliament. The DRF Policy is now, therefore, the policy of the country as it relates to disaster-risk financing. We all own it.

As it states, the DRF Policy 'promotes a risk-layered approach to funding disaster relief, recovery and reconstruction through the establishment of adequate reserves to address the costs associated with high frequency, low severity events such as floods or heavy rainfall, and the transfer of risks related to low-frequency, high severity events such as major hurricanes and earthquakes through a portfolio of financing instruments.'[11]

Multi-layered Strategy

Domestic savings will ordinarily not be sufficient to finance relief and recovery from the most intense hurricanes, and most insurance products will not trigger for lower intensity events. Consistent with the DRF Policy, therefore, Jamaica retains the risk of higher frequency events, which it finances through domestic savings, a credit contingent claim, and by retaining the option to reallocate budgets. For lower frequency events, which are often also of high intensity, Jamaica transfers the risk to third-party insurance and capital markets.

Contingencies Fund

The Contingencies Fund is provided for in the Constitution and is intended to provide financial support for genuine contingencies, including natural disasters. In 1962, the maximum limit of this fund set by legislation was J$10 million. This limit was increased to J$100 million in 1992 and remained at this level for nearly three decades. In 2019, however, we increased the Contingencies Fund limit one hundred-fold from J$100 million to J$10 billion and injected a historic capitalisation of J$4 billion into the Contingencies Fund. The GOJ has further added to this amount annually, and the balance in the Contingencies Fund stood at J$5.3 billion as at March 31, 2024.

The National Natural Disaster Risk Fund

Only a month ago, in June 2024, with unanimous consent in Parliament, we amended the Financial Administration and Audit Act to create the National Natural Disaster Risk Fund (Disaster Fund).

The Disaster Fund is intended to be the principal pool of domestic savings accumulated specifically to finance natural disaster relief and recovery. It will also become the repository of proceeds from disaster-risk instruments that trigger payments. Importantly, the GOJ is legally mandated to save annually and contribute to the Disaster Fund. In the 2024–25 budget, we made provisions to capitalise the Disaster Fund with J$1 billion.

Jamaica's Catastrophe Bond

Jamaica placed its first catastrophe bond in 2021, with the assistance of the World Bank. I devoted an entire Op-Ed in the *Gleaner* to describing this instrument, which also applies to its 2024 successor.

To review, a catastrophe bond transfers catastrophic natural-disaster risk from a sponsor (in this case Jamaica) to international capital-market investors. Jamaica's catastrophe bond globally pioneered the 'cat in a grid' trigger approach, which places a grid over Jamaica and surrounding waters, with each grid having a centralised air-pressure threshold. Payout is triggered if a hurricane passes through a grid and has centralised air pressure [as measured by the National Hurricane Centre in the United States] at or below the threshold for that grid. (Note: The lower the centralised air pressure, the higher the intensity of the hurricane). The size of payout is related to how many such grids are breached and the materiality of such breaches.

Each of these grids is associated with a centralised air-pressure threshold. For instance, the threshold applicable to grids 5, 6, 7, and 8 are 958 milli bars (mb), 945mb, 947mb, and 932mb; the threshold in grids 10, 11,12,13, and 14 are 920mb, 940mb, 960mb, 969mb, and 940mb, and the thresholds applicable to grids 16, 17, 18 and 19 are 920mb, 926mb, 950mb, and 920mb (*see* Figure 1).

Hurricanes are generally categorised using the Saffir-Simpson Scale, which classifies hurricanes into five categories. A hurricane designated as a Category 2 will have centralised air pressure between 979mb and 965mb. The corresponding ranges of air pressures for Category 3, 4, and 5 hurricanes are 964mb–945mb, 944mb–920mb, and lower than 920mb, respectively.

As such, Hurricane Ivan, which ravaged Jamaica in 2004, and which recorded centralised air pressures of 924mb and 923mb as it rampaged through grids 18 and 17, would have triggered Jamaica's catastrophe bond with a 100 per cent payout of US$150 million, or approximately J$24 billion today.

Similarly, Hurricane Dean, which pummelled Jamaica in 2007, and which recorded centralised air pressures of 927mb and 926mb as it barrelled through grids 18 and 17, would have triggered Jamaica's catastrophe bond with a 92 per cent payout of US$138 million, or approximately J$22 billion today (*see* Figure 1).

Hurricane Gilbert, which made landfall in 1988, breached grids 12 and 13 with recorded air pressure of 960mb and would also have triggered the catastrophe bond with a US$103.5 million payout.

The centralised air pressure of Hurricane Beryl, which also traversed through grid 18, was recorded by the National Hurricane Centre as 959mb – higher than the 950mb threshold required to trigger our catastrophe bond. Beryl was also recorded as having air pressure of 960mb as it moved through grid 10 – again higher than the trigger threshold for that grid.

Our catastrophe bond covers Jamaica for the 2024, 2025, 2026, and 2027 hurricane seasons, and the trigger mechanism is simple and transparent. Anyone with internet access can retrieve hurricane trajectories and air pressures from the National Hurricane Centre website and determine, with a fair degree of accuracy, whether the catastrophe bond has triggered.

Jamaica has to continuously and consistently build on the existing DRF framework to ensure we are always fiscally prepared for the possibility of natural disaster events.

Figure 1: Centralised Air-pressure Threshold Bond Grid

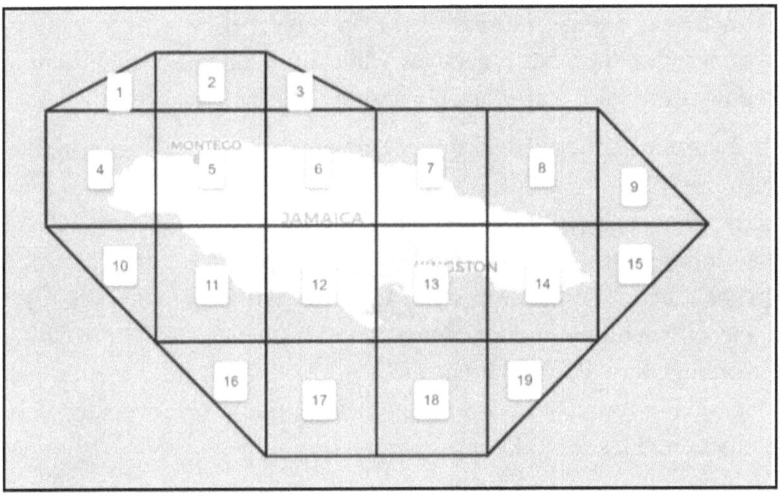

Source: Prospectus Supplement, International Bank for Reconstruction and Development, US$150,000,000 Floating Rate Catastrophe-Linked Capital at Risk Notes due December 29, 2027, Hong Kong Exchange, published April 25, 2024.

Having Buffers is Vital to Sustained Development

Published Commentary, October 2024

Following Hurricane Beryl, we are here again, once more. Events beyond our immediate control are projected to have a significantly adverse impact on economic growth, and, by extension, on the government's revenues. The impact of this growth shock is such that we will need to draw on buffers if we are to achieve planned development objectives while simultaneously maintaining a downward debt trajectory, consistent with Jamaica's fiscal rules.

External shocks frequently visit Jamaica's shores. In the past, they also interrupted growth, but buffers to offset the fiscal impact were often unavailable. As such, economic shocks would either suspend development or deepen instability through increased debt, or both. In the current era, however, the Government of Jamaica's (GOJ's) focus on economic independence, fiscal resilience, and the building of buffers, has allowed Jamaica to absorb a significant growth shock this year without compromising development or reversing debt reduction. This should not go unnoticed.

In the first quarter of this fiscal year (April to June 2024), the economy grew by only 0.2 per cent. The major explanatory factor for this deviation from expectation was the sub-par tourism performance for that quarter. For the previous four quarters, tourism grew by between 7 and 8 per cent per quarter as compared with same quarter in the previous year. However, for the first quarter of this fiscal year, tourism growth cratered to 1 per cent, which pulled overall growth down considerably. Availability of airline seats into Jamaica declined during the quarter, which tourism policy experts link with the earlier unfavourable US Travel Advisory on Jamaica.

If that were not enough, Jamaica experienced Hurricane Beryl in July 2024. This Category 5 system was the most intense hurricane to impact Jamaica since Hurricane Dean seventeen years ago. While

---

An earlier version of this article appeared in the *Jamaica Gleaner*, October 13, 2024.

we were more prepared than ever to finance the related emergency relief and recovery costs, Jamaica remained exposed to the impact of this climate event on economic output. Hurricane Beryl decimated agricultural output in the breadbasket of the country. Anecdotally, too, economic output related to the generation of electricity and water declined, and economic activity was disrupted for several weeks.

These developments combined led the Planning Institute of Jamaica (PIOJ) to forecast a decline in economic output, or negative growth, of -2.1 per cent in the July–September 2024 quarter. Sadly, this projected quarterly decline in Jamaica's GDP will break the stretch of thirteen consecutive quarters of economic growth between the April to June quarter of 2021 and the April to June quarter of 2024. Let us recall that it was another shock, induced by COVID-19, that broke nineteen consecutive quarters of economic growth (the twentieth quarter was flat) between the January to March quarter of 2015 and the October to December quarter of 2019.

The good news is that these periods represent the two longest periods of consecutive quarterly economic growth since Jamaica started measuring growth quarterly, twenty-seven years ago. While the GOJ's economic reforms have not yet delivered an increase in the absolute level of average growth, Jamaica's reforms have undoubtedly delivered a much greater stability of growth.

But back to 2024. With a growth outturn of 0.2 per cent in the first quarter and a projection of -2.1 per cent in the second quarter, it will be difficult to recover lost ground in the third and fourth quarters at a level that fully offsets the negative growth shocks. As such, the PIOJ forecasts that Jamaica will experience an economic contraction of -0.2 per cent for the full 2024–25 fiscal year. This compares with prior growth projections of 1.8 per cent for the fiscal year. The growth shock therefore represents a two-percentage-point deviation – huge by fiscal standards.

Tax revenues, for the most part, bear a relationship of proportionality to economic output. The higher the level of economic output, the higher tax revenues are likely to be. The converse is also true. Economic decline drags tax revenues lower. Given that our economy exceeds $3.2 trillion in size, a growth shock of two percentage points represents a potentially profound adverse revenue impact of over $64 billion on an annualised basis. In other words, a growth shock quickly becomes a fiscal shock.

Faced with a fiscal shock of this magnitude, absent any cushion, the GOJ would have had the unenviable choice of borrowing more, thereby compromising Jamaica's debt trajectory (which in turn would make Jamaica more vulnerable to economic shocks in the future), or else delaying major development projects in health, transportation, and/or roads, in an effort to adjust one-off expenditure to fit the updated revenue profile. That is where buffers come in.

Jamaica's buffers, or shock absorbers, for this fiscal year primarily consist of having $75 billion of inflows from the successful execution of the GOJ's first securitisation in international capital markets (detailed in Part Two). In this transaction, Jamaica generated resources by selling its share of revenues from the recently privatised Norman Manley International Airport.

The parallel with the much more serious COVID-19 economic shock is worthy of examination. Immediately prior to that historic shock, the GOJ had harvested substantial inflows from a series of transactions involving the privatisation of Wigton Windfarm and TransJamaican Highway Limited (see 'Broadening the Ownership Base of the Jamaican Economy' in Part Five) that included historically large initial public offerings on the Jamaica Stock Exchange. While these flows were initially intended for an explicit acceleration of debt repayment, they instead assisted Jamaica in maintaining a modest fiscal deficit in 2020 as compared with peers, even after accounting for plunging GOJ revenues and surging COVID-related expenditure. The proceeds of these transactions proved vital to Jamaica's debt reduction in the sense that they limited the country's reliance on borrowings to finance our way through the difficulties of 2020.

In 2024, transaction inflows will again come to Jamaica's assistance at a time of external economic shock. Despite the projected GDP contraction this year, Jamaica will still be able to maintain its flagship infrastructure development programs – for example, the SPARK (road improvement) Programme, the REACH (road improvement) Programme, the buildout of multiple hospitals, and further investments in public transportation. Despite the projected

GDP contraction this year, we still maintain a balanced budget, and Jamaica's debt-to-GDP ratio is projected to fall from 73 per cent to 68 per cent or lower by the end of this fiscal year, the lowest level in nearly fifty years.

This is fiscal resilience in action. Without these transaction inflows, none of the above would have been possible this year in light of the sizable economic growth shock. We are sustaining development, even while passing through the valleys of repeated growth setbacks.

So, What Are the Lessons?

Clearly, we had no premonition of COVID-19 when we planned and executed the series of Wigton and TransJamaican Highway transactions in 2019 and early 2020. Similarly, we would not have been aware of Hurricane Beryl when we embarked on the securitisation transaction process more than a year ago.

So first, it is always helpful to maintain a disposition towards the harvesting of resources. In times of adverse GDP shock – as with COVID-19 and Hurricane Beryl – we can then strategically deploy these resources to maintain capital-expenditure policy priorities while preserving fiscal sustainability through crisis, and as an alternative to debt accumulation. And in benign times these resources can be used to generate further fiscal space by reducing debt.

The second lesson is that the experience this year should be seen as yet another timely reminder of Jamaica's vulnerabilities and the pernicious fiscal exposure that arises from these vulnerabilities. It could not be clearer. If Jamaica is to experience uninterrupted, sustained development as an independent country, we must maintain low debt, adequate foreign exchange reserves, strong economic institutions, and fiscal buffers.

Third, having built a disaster-risk financing framework, we must maintain it. However, the GOJ will need to improve physical resilience, too, by having disaster-proofed power supply for water storage, processing, and distribution systems, and for telecom towers, as well as better drainage and more resilient road infrastructure.

Fourth, we will need to enhance our GDP resilience. Our economic base is too narrow. We are over-reliant on a few sectors for most of Jamaica's foreign exchange: tourism, business process outsourcing, agriculture, and mining. We must further diversify over the next decade.

Jamaica has a strong privatisation and transaction pipeline that, if strategically executed, will continue to enhance resilience and build buffers for sustained development and economic stability. Policymaking must be deliberate. Given Jamaica's vulnerabilities, complacency is not an option.

PART FIVE

OPPORTUNITY

Jamaica is a small, climate-exposed, undiversified, open economy. These properties render Jamaica highly vulnerable to frequent occurrences of economic and climate-related shocks. As such, Jamaica needs stability and resilience to achieve sustained growth within the context of its structural realities.

Despite the entrenchment of macroeconomic stability in Jamaica, however, faster economic growth has remained elusive. While the fiscal profligacy of yesteryear resulted in neither stability nor strong growth, the pursuit of economic reforms entrenched stability and delivered the advantage of low growth-volatility – but without meaningfully improving average growth levels. The latter should not be entirely surprising. The same fiscal consolidation policies that have allowed Jamaica to stabilise the economy and reduce its riskiness can have a dampening effect on growth. For example, in addition to reducing debt, the pursuit of a high primary balance has constrained capital spending that otherwise may have boosted growth further. (Spending that boosts consumption has little impact on growth for Jamaica, because the goods and services consumed have such high import content.)

But failure to reduce debt would have made it impossible for Jamaica to recover from, or weather, the recent economic shocks as well as we have. There is a trade-off between stabilisation and the opportunity for short spurts of higher growth. While the level of average growth does matter, given Jamaica's economic history, in the long run, the volatility of growth matters more. Short periods of higher growth are helpful, but sustained development requires sustained growth.

Pre-stabilisation, higher growth was possible, but it did not last. The environment was volatile. Between the beginning of 1997, when Jamaica started measuring growth quarterly, and the last quarter of 2007, a period during which our debt-to-GDP ratio escalated from 74 to over 130 per cent, we endured seven quarters of economic decline and then a flat quarter, followed by seven quarters of growth, followed by a quarter of decline, and then three quarters of growth and three quarters of decline, followed by nine quarters of growth, another three quarters of decline, and again nine quarters of growth, and ending the period with a quarter of decline.[1]

Since stabilisation, Jamaica has been able to achieve an elongation of the business cycle, with longer periods of consecutive quarterly economic growth. In this era, we have experienced an unbroken twenty consecutive quarters – five years, between the January-to-March quarter of 2015 and the September-to-December quarter of 2019 – without economic decline (the twentieth quarter was flat).[2] This was only broken by the COVID-19 pandemic. Previously, the longest stretch of unbroken economic growth was nine consecutive quarters, or just over two years, from the June-to-September quarter of 2002 to the June-to-September quarter of 2004,[3] and again between the June-to-September quarter of 2005 and the June-to-September quarter of 2007.[4] So, Jamaica has made a conscious decision to favour macroeconomic stability accompanied by sustained growth and economic resilience, over short spurts of higher growth but higher volatility that leave the country exposed and vulnerable to economic shocks, with no better long-term average growth.

If the first piece in this set of readings, 'Jamaica at Sixty – Taking Responsibility for Our Vulnerabilities,' touches on this relationship between vulnerability, volatility, and Jamaica's economic growth and development, the next, 'Pursuing Growth with Equity,' invites the questions: What kind of growth does Jamaica need? Who will benefit?

Higher levels of long-term, sustained growth will only come from revolutionising education outcomes and increasing the proficiency and attainment in mathematics and science, while improving the levels of technical skills in the population, all of which are beyond the scope of this book. However, there will very shortly come a time when Jamaica will have the opportunity to deploy significantly more resources into growth-inducing capital expenditure. And meanwhile, much has been done – and remains to be done – to enable more Jamaicans to receive the benefits that come from a stable economy.

The Role of a Fiscal Policymaker

Jamaica's pursuit of economic stability is not an end in itself, but merely a means to an end. So how does the fiscal policymaker confined by choice to a narrow, stability-defined corridor of fiscal manoeuvrability, best use fiscal policy to support growth and increase prosperity for the citizens that he (or she) has promised to serve? This was my challenge upon entering the Ministry of Finance and the Public Service.

The writings presented in this part of the book reveal my approach, which relied on the conviction that fiscal policy is more than the dollars given up, or taken in, through tax and expenditure-policy decisions. The *signals* sent by fiscal policy are equally important and must remain so. I began by focusing on areas where taxes distorted economic activity and worked to abolish such distortionary taxes using fiscal gains to target areas of importance in people's lives and livelihoods. Often the cost of rectifying the distortion was small, in the grand scheme, but the signal was huge: the government cares about start-ups; the government cares about micro and small businesses; the government sees value in the construction and real estate sector, and so forth.

We used fiscal gains from public-body reintegrations which released trapped funds, from de-earmarking of flows to public bodies, and from privatisations to accelerate debt reduction. This resulted in being as much as a year ahead of our debt-to-GDP target under the then-in-force IMF programme.

Given the heavy tax packages (levied in the fiscal years beginning 2009, 2012, 2013, and 2015) which were needed to kick-start and later boost fiscal consolidation, once we got ahead of our targets we recalibrated the debt-sustainability requirements and returned dividends to the people through tax reductions. These, in turn, would spur further fiscal gains.

Generating gains through fiscal consolidation takes on new meaning when those gains are translated into benefits for citizens. And we have found that fiscal consolidation can be sustained if it is evidently seen to generate tangible policy dividends along the way. The benefits of Jamaica's newfound stability that we have worked to share with as many stakeholders and constituents as possible may be generally grouped into three main purposes: Empowering the Private Sector, Reforming the Public Sector, and Strengthening the Social Safety Net.

Empowering the Private Sector

Simplified, the private sector consists of two arms: the 'real' sector (meaning corporate Jamaica and smaller enterprises, or 'businesses') and the financial sector. If a country's policies are encouraging to business activity, these arms work together to carry the country forward, supporting growth in a dynamic ecosystem of commercial activity. The focus of my work here has been to use fiscal policy to strategically deploy reintegration, de-earmarking, and privatisation gains in ways designed to send signals for businesses, provide policy dividends, and empower the private sector to stimulate economic activity. In this area, readers will encounter budget excerpts showing how we abolished distortionary taxes and delivered a Medium, Small, and Micro Enterprises (MSME) tax credit.

Given the openness of the Jamaican economy to trade in visible and invisible goods, border procedures have an outsized impact on economic vitality. I have therefore also advocated for modernisation of customs procedures and introduced a customs fee threshold.

And with the end of Jamaica's period of fiscal dominance and the success of the government's programme of rapid deleveraging, institutional investors also needed new places to invest. We therefore sought to support and accelerate the creation of investible domestic assets through privatisations, by way of direct listings on the Jamaica Stock Exchange and broadening the category of assets in which pension funds could invest.

While a term such as 'private sector' can sound academic and cold, it is important to remember that policy positions relate to people's hopes. Giving hope and financing options to entrepreneurs so that they can build and sustain their businesses, and to corporations for their profitability, is transformative for our economy. And when our economy is stable and more hospitable to business, yet simultaneously focussed on the daily needs of our population, we can begin to entertain new, more ambitious development possibilities – improving infrastructure with structured transactions such as Public-Private Partnerships (PPPs), for example.

Properly structured PPPs allow for more optimised allocation of government resources and for acceleration of investment that will improve public services and generate jobs. Properly structuring these transactions at scale, and attracting global bidders, requires the best technical expertise, international transaction experience, and access to networks. In a testament to our progress to date, Jamaica's requirements of the multilateral community have therefore changed. Financing will always be important. But now we need vast amounts of technical advice and support even more than we need financing.

A historic, simultaneous visit to Jamaica in summer 2023 by the presidents of the World Bank and the Inter-American Development Bank marked the beginning of this new period of opportunity for Jamaica. 'Empowering the Private Sector' and 'Reforming the Public Sector' contain thoughts on leveraging the unrivalled knowledge-power of these institutions to help accelerate Jamaica's development – from assisting us with structuring infrastructure PPP's to advising on human capital development and the reforming of public-sector systems.

Reforming the Public Sector

Economic growth also requires the support of a competent and efficient public sector. Over decades, Jamaica's public sector grew without check. As encountered in the 'Intention' section of the book, in each decade following Independence, the government added significant numbers of public bodies until the volume became unsustainable and had to be reduced. We achieved this reduction through mergers, de-earmarking, privatisation, and closure of public bodies. 'Reforming the Public Sector' contains short pieces on this policy area, with an example of its application and two pieces relating to significant public-body governance reforms. Strong public institutions are macro-critical, and strong institutions require strong governance.

Additionally, government expenditure, inclusive of public-body expenditure, accounts for nearly 50 per cent of GDP. As such, government systems, such as systems for public investment, have a decisive impact on economic outcomes. An efficient public investment management system can help oil the engines of the economy. Thus, I have also advocated for a robust public investment management system (PIMS). But no matter how streamlined or robust a government and its systems become, the public service will be ineffective if it cannot attract and retain the talent it needs.

I came to terms with the scale of this problem when five of seven vacancies in the economics unit within the Ministry of Finance went unfilled for two years, despite robust advertising. This unit produced macro-fiscal forecasts, maintained debt sustainability analyses, and assisted greatly in budget preparations. While we were in IMF programmes, understaffing of this unit mattered less since we could lean on Fund resources. Out of Fund programmes, however, with an independent central bank and imminent operationalisation of an independent fiscal commission, understaffing in this area created a frightening liability.

The situation was not unique to our unit or ministry. In a world where the public service needs to develop apps, transition services online, and accommodate digital payments, the public service needs IT talent, for example. The government's inability to attract and retain talent created a serious impediment to Jamaica's development. I am exceptionally proud, therefore, of our government's announcement of the Marcus Garvey Public Sector Graduate Scholarship (see page 330). In creating opportunities such as this scholarship, or in implementing new policies for family leave (page 347), a government can express its values.

The most complicated piece of our public sector transformation, however, has flowed from the need to restructure our compensation in a manner that is transparent, equitable, and encourages employee retention. Over decades of chronic instability, public-sector compensation had evolved its own logic. Distrust in the stability of economic arrangements bred short, two-year agreements, putting the government in constant negotiation mode, given the fragmented public-sector wage-bargaining framework, with forty distinct public-sector unions and bargaining groups. It would therefore often take substantially more than two years to conclude all forty agreements.

This cycle, repeated over decades, left little time for work on structural issues affecting public-sector compensation. Meanwhile, allowances proliferated, some of which masked the reality of our performance against targets for wages embedded in Jamaica's Fiscal Rules, enacted in 2010 (and amended in 2014).[5] Chief among these was the tax-free travel allowance, which was problematic for several reasons, explained in 'Appeal for Reasonableness' (see page 349).

But the public sector's patience was wearing thin. Most painfully, since 2010, compression in the real value of wages has been a key driver in the fiscal-consolidation effort, given Jamaica's social-policy choice to refrain from cutting public-sector jobs as a goal in itself. As a result, up to 2022, public-sector wage increases had not kept pace with cumulative inflation.

As if to add insult to injury, returns to capital often precede returns to labour in market economies where economic adjustment and stabilisation have been successfully implemented. This was certainly true in Jamaica, where the Jamaica Stock Exchange distinguished itself with the Bloomberg Award for Best Performing Stock Exchange in the World in 2015 – which was early in our stabilisation journey – and again in 2018. Seeing this while feeling left behind in terms of their own (lack of) prosperity would have been disappointing, disheartening, and disempowering, and would have worked against the overall reform agenda had we not signalled that we would take steps to ensure that gains from economic reform were equitably shared – to labour, to capital, and to the vulnerable – and then followed up with decisive action to implement same.

The balance of writings in this section reveals my advocacy regarding compensation reform and presents some context and complexities of the reform as well as the response to speedbumps encountered along the way. This was a once-in-a-lifetime comprehensive reform of public-sector compensation implemented concurrently across all of government. It is critical that the principles that underpinned the reform are retained long into the future.

Strengthening the Social Safety Net

The health of a country's economy depends critically on maintaining citizens' confidence that economic stability and fiscal sustainability serve their interests. This was a constant preoccupation and explains my focus on social-protection policy, often approached from a fiscal perspective. Throughout my time as Minister of Finance, I have operated on the premise that any gains of policy must flow into growth-inducing capital expenditure, human-capital development, and social-protection frameworks.

For example, as a Member of Parliament, I had the experience of serving elderly constituents who played by the rules, laboured during their working lives, and contributed to Jamaica only to end up destitute with no regular income in their senior and most vulnerable years. Structural inequities are embedded in the informality of our arrangements. Though we have a National Insurance Scheme, the penetration is low, as many workers in the informal economy are not enrolled.

The section on 'Strengthening the Social Safety Net' includes a piece that describes the social pension we developed through collaboration with the World Bank – with the consent and support of consecutive Ministers of Labour and Social Security – in response to this gap in our social-protection framework, while ensuring that the parameters would not provide a disincentive for enrolment in the National Insurance Fund (NIF). I also worked with the Ministry of Labour and Social Security (MLSS) to improve the sustainability of the NIF, advancing the requirements to extend its life. Other pieces present the development (also with the World Bank and MLSS) of social pension and unemployment insurance – the urgency for this accelerated by the COVID-19 experience of a significant unemployment shock.

Finally, but in no way of least concern, throughout my public service I often encountered students from poor and marginalised backgrounds who excelled in high school but whose families did not see tertiary education as a feasible option due to a perceived absence of funding. In each of these cases I could not help but feel a profound sense of sadness at the lost opportunity for citizen and country. There were visible and invisible institutional barriers to accessing available public financing for tertiary education through the Student Loan Bureau (SLB).

Again, policy signalling is sometimes as or even more important than explicit revenue and expenditure decisions. And sometimes, the most far-reaching and consequential policy changes do not even require significant additional funding. This was the case with the SLB. In 2019, I authorised the abolishment of the practise of publishing photographs of delinquent student loan borrowers in the national newspaper. While this national shaming may have prompted the individual delinquent to repay (where this was feasible), scores more potential customers, especially from poorer backgrounds, would have been dissuaded from engaging the SLB for financing due to the culture that this practise bred.

This section concludes with pieces on similarly simple yet impactful reforms to the SLB. There was a restructuring of how payments are applied to delinquent balances, as well as a policy that abolished the requirement of guarantors for student loan access. These policy changes, which had a profound impact on tertiary financing accessibility, were financed by internal efficiency gains and did not require increased allocations to the SLB.

Through social-protection innovations, our government has demonstrated that the fiscal gains from our economic reforms would serve the people's interest.

Jamaica at Sixty: Taking Responsibility for Our Vulnerabilities

Published Commentary, August 2022

As we celebrate 'Jamaica 60,' it is only fitting that we highlight our many achievements as a nation. As one of the few countries on the planet to introduce and propagate a universally popular genre of music and one of a handful of nations to spawn a globally recognised religion, Jamaica has an authentic and unique voice in the world.

Economic Development Has Lagged

However, it is also a useful time to reflect on key development lessons from our journey thus far. Despite our many achievements, it is widely acknowledged that our economic development has lagged.

As the IMF noted in its Article IV Consultation published in February 2022, Jamaica's real per capita GDP, or average income per person adjusted for inflation, is '20% less today than it was in 1970.'

This compares with several of our Caribbean neighbours where real per capita GDP has grown significantly over the same period. For the Dominican Republic, real per capita GDP growth over this period exceeds 220 per cent. For St Lucia, it exceeds 230 per cent.

Domestic policy choices explain much of our under-performance. But this is not the complete picture.

Economic Volatility Has Delayed Development

We often describe economic data using common statistical measures such as 'mean' or 'average' and 'standard deviation' or 'volatility.' In commenting on our economy we most often use the average, for example, 'The average growth over the last fifty years was 1 per cent.' Arguably a far more consequential measure that captures the constraints on the pace of development is the level of volatility associated with that growth.

An earlier version of this article appeared in the *Jamaica Gleaner*, August 7, 2022.

Economic volatility measures the frequency of the turnover between growth and decline, or in other words, how often we walk forwards only to walk backwards again in quick succession.

Jamaica's sixty years of independence have been characterised by a profound level of economic volatility that has interrupted, delayed, and sometimes reversed our human, social, and physical development. Furthermore, exogenous economic shocks have both initiated and compounded economic volatility.

Exogenous Economic Shocks Are Here to Stay

Reflect on the impact on Jamaica of various adverse external episodes such as the oil-price shock of 1974, the oil-price shock of 1979, the alumina world market crash of the mid-1980s, Hurricane Gilbert in 1988, the September 11 terrorist attacks of 2001, Hurricane Ivan in 2004, Hurricane Dean in 2007, the Global Financial Crisis of 2008–2010, the oil-price shocks of 2008 and 2010–14, Hurricane Gustav in 2008, Hurricane Sandy in 2012, Hurricane Matthew of 2016, the COVID-19 pandemic of 2020, and the [start of the] Ukraine war in 2022. And, this list is by no means complete.

Here is the bad news: these adverse events and economic shocks will continue to punctuate time. We cannot control them. We cannot stop them. And we cannot leave our social and economic development hostage to them. We have to take the exogenous realities we cannot change as given and build and maintain robustness and resilience in our economic arrangements.

If we are seriously committed to improving our development prospects over the next sixty years, we will have to dramatically reduce economic volatility. To do so we must internalise that economic volatility is fertile in a land that is vulnerable to exogenous economic shocks.

Addressing Our Vulnerabilities

To reduce economic volatility, therefore, we must take responsibility for, and – with a national, bipartisan focus – commit to addressing our vulnerabilities. Some of Jamaica's historical and current economic vulnerabilities, which [expose us to] exogenous economic shocks, arise from the following:

- We are, and have been, an energy importer. Energy imports accounted for as much as 16.7 per cent of GDP in 2011–12 and just over 11.4 per cent of GDP in 2021–22;
- We are heavily dependent on food commodities imported from abroad;
- We have a narrow economic base and an even narrower foreign exchange earning capacity. Only a handful of sectors earn meaningful foreign exchange;
- We have very high levels of debt, which make us vulnerable as it reduces fiscal flexibility in times of crisis and high interest costs crowd out social expenditure and growth-inducing capital expenditure;
- We live in a climatic zone prone to hurricanes and tropical cyclones.

Securing our continuous development, with as little interruption as possible, requires that we address these.

We must very rapidly diversify away from fossil fuels as a source of energy. This is a national economic imperative. We can no longer leave ourselves open to the vagaries of global fossil fuel markets. If I can be permitted to say so, the recent adjustment to fiscal policy on electric vehicles and solar batteries, along with the GOJ's policy on renewables, are therefore encouraging. However, the GOJ will likely need to consider further legislative or other means to quickly accelerate this transition.

We must significantly diversify our sources of foreign exchange. Tourism, remittances, business-process outsourcing, and bauxite/alumina/other minerals accounted for more than 90 per cent of our foreign-exchange inflows, pre-pandemic. The GOJ's development of logistics, animation, film, and agriculture sectors offers the prospect of increasing the resilience of foreign-exchange inflows.

We must climate-proof our economy and maintain a suite of risk-transfer instruments that will provide liquid resources in the event of a natural disaster event beyond a prescribed threshold.

And, we must continue to reduce our debt-to-GDP ratio consistent with our fiscal rules. For a small, open, vulnerable economy our debt is way too high, and this compounds our fragility and imperils our development. There has been a national bipartisan consensus on this approach for more than ten years. This needs to continue. Given our realities, we have to always be prepared for the next crisis.

COVID Economic Recovery and New Economic Shocks

Jamaica's recovery from the COVID-19 crisis began with 8.2 per cent growth in the 2021–22 fiscal year. Unemployment is at a historic low of 6 per cent and approximately 100,000 jobs have been restored and added. The pace of this recovery, thus far, represents a substantial positive change from our historical experience. It is possible that we could recover to pre-COVID levels of economic output by the end of 2023. This recovery matters and impacts lives daily. With our approach, unlike in the past, we have been able to increase public-sector salaries throughout the crisis, though modestly, in 2020 and 2021, while other countries in the region have held public-sector salaries fixed for the last four years. Even as we move to implement the restructuring of public-sector compensation, which will [increase] public-sector pay, public-sector employees in Belize, for example, had to absorb a 10 per cent salary reduction in 2021.

Amidst recovery, new clouds of global uncertainty are gathering. Historically high levels of global inflation exacerbated by the Russia-Ukraine war are inflicting local pain as prices move out of reach. Central banks around the world have raised interest rates and tightened financial conditions to ensure that high inflation does not become entrenched.

This has led to a decline in bond prices and an increase in interest rates for mortgages and car loans around the world, including in Jamaica. This is a source of discomfort and discontent. The GOJ has committed approximately $7 billion of expenditure, above and beyond amounts ordinarily budgeted for social protection, and has targeted this expenditure at vulnerable segments of the population who are most impacted by the inflation crisis.

Robust, Resilient, and Strong

After this crisis passes, the developed world will return to low inflation. Jamaica cannot afford to be stuck with high inflation when this time comes. The Bank of Jamaica has communicated that it is acting today with a time horizon beyond the next eighteen months which is already set with respect to inflation. The actions today are necessary to reduce our future vulnerability.

There is concern, and some evidence, that the trade-off between the response to inflation and growth will tip some large economies into recession. This would be yet another exogenous economic shock for Jamaica. We have to be prepared for that, too.

Taking responsibility for our vulnerabilities is an organising principle we take seriously. As such, we will continue to pursue a path that keeps Jamaica resilient, robust, and strong so that our human, social, and physical development can advance even amidst exogenous economic shocks.

Pursuing Growth with Equity
Budget Speech Excerpt, March 2019

On my appointment as Minister of Finance, I established the economic policy direction of the government as (1) the pursuit of economic independence, (2) the promotion of economic opportunity for all, and (3) the protection of the vulnerable. This is the policy architecture that is required for us to achieve growth with equity.

The struggle for greater levels of equity has occupied the Jamaican consciousness for hundreds of years. And rightly so. Over that time, we have made incredible progress on the march for greater levels of equity and social justice, and we continue that march. However, no society is disconnected from its past and historical inequities have undoubtedly cast a long shadow.

Our two major political parties at their inception, and through the course of their histories, identified with the struggle of Jamaican people.

We are one of few countries in the world where the trade-union movement is represented and entrenched on both sides of the political aisle, with both major political parties allied with major labour unions.

As for the Jamaican Labour Party (JLP), it grew out of the first and oldest union movement in the Caribbean that was formed to agitate on behalf of the Jamaican working class. Today, the Bustamante Industrial Trade Union is the largest multi-industry trade union in the Caribbean.

'Equal Rights and Justice' has been the rallying cry of the JLP for seventy-five years, repeated at every meeting of the JLP wherever two or three are gathered. Jamaica Labour Party administrations, from the 1940s to the present time, have advanced the cause of equity and justice in Jamaica.

Adapted from the opening budget presentation delivered in Parliament March 7, 2019.

I am sure the other side would make a similar claim.

As a result, the issue of equity has always been in the political economy and springs from the unique foundation and alignments of our major political movements. This is our source of strength, yet it is often undermined by the political class itself.

Much of our political discourse is about trying to deny this unique historical reality, and worse, denying our respective contributions in this struggle. This is nationally self-defeating. It is nationally disempowering. It is empty and only serves the narrow interest of some politicians, not the long-term interest of the people.

On the other hand, the quest for economic growth has not always been part of the political economy, even though the expansion of our economy is a necessary condition for us to achieve the aspirations and dreams of all Jamaicans.

Growth and equity are not mutually exclusive. Rather they go hand in hand and are mutually reinforcing. Higher levels of growth provide the means through which greater levels of equity can be achieved. Greater societal equity increases the productive potential of our people and fosters greater social harmony, both of which are conducive to higher economic output.

Equity is multi-faceted, too. We need equity for all members of our society. For basic school children and tertiary students, for civil servants and even for politicians, for inner-city youths and for small business, for men and women, for children and for pensioners, for the 92 per cent of Jamaicans employed in the private sector and for the 8 per cent of Jamaicans employed in the public sector, for rural and urban, for able and disabled, and even for Jamaicans who find themselves behind bars. We need equity for all Jamaicans.

However, we often speak about equity from our own perspectives without recognising the legitimate equity aspirations of others or of the broader public good.

One of the lessons of our history is that some policies that seek to address issues of equity in a current time frame have had devastating impact on future generations, through the accumulation of unsustainable debt or through high inflation, both of which create severe inter-generational inequity. The debt incurred by prior generations is a chain that has limited the prospects of successive generations.

In order to guarantee equity across generations, we can only sustainably finance the march for greater equity from the dividends of economic expansion. Over our forty-year period of low growth, successive administrations have refrained from implementing bold pro-growth fiscal policy that serves the public good and that ultimately advances the cause of equity. That is about to change.

What I will lay out today is a budget crafted to maintain a path of economic independence, that provides economic opportunity for all, protects the vulnerable, and, by so doing, will deliver growth with equity. Our ability to achieve our aspiration of growth with equity is enhanced by economic independence. It is the goal of the Andrew Holness government, the goal of this generation, that Jamaica be an economically independent country.

Jamaica, though politically independent, became serially dependent on the international community for economic support and assistance beginning in the 1970s. This dependence has continued for a majority of the nearly fifty years since then.

Economic independence means that we as a country are empowered to chart our economic destiny, to set well-thought-out economic priorities, and to provide the framework, rules, and environment that will allow our citizens to freely pursue economic activities in a way that promotes growth and well-being for all.

Economic independence *does not* mean a withdrawal from the global economic and financial system. It does not mean that we cannot benefit from external financial flows, technology, and know-how. But it *does* mean that we responsibly take our destiny into our own hands.

This is important, as otherwise we fit into the vision of others for ourselves and will not have the chance to pursue our own dreams. While we may be at a certain stage of development now, our vision is not to be 'hewers of wood nor drawers of stone.'

Rather, we are a people of destiny, a nation of purpose with a unique role to play in this world.

With policies that achieve and maintain economic independence, provide economic opportunity for all, and protect the vulnerable, sustained over time, we will eventually produce aircraft components and medical devices right here in Jamaica. We will lead in artificial intelligence and internet security. People will come here for jobs, rather than us migrating there.

That is the vision.

A necessary and fundamental principle to abide by, if we are to achieve this vision, is to manage our financial affairs so as to maintain a sustainable economic path that guarantees stability for future generations.

Jamaica is now in the best shape, as compared to any other period over the last fifty years, to achieve economic independence.

Empowering the Private Sector

Private-Sector Foundations for Jamaica 2.0

Published Commentary, August 2020

In this column, which belongs to a multi-part series on the 'Rebuild Jamaica' COVID-19 Economic Recovery Task Force Report, I want to highlight the key role of the private sector in supporting Jamaica's robust recovery from COVID-19 and beyond. The report includes recommendations to enable the private sector as the engine of growth for Jamaica and features the role of the financial sector in providing the necessary support to realise this vision. Reference to the term 'private sector' should be understood to include every economic entity in Jamaica, outside of those in the public, voluntary, and diplomatic sectors. The term includes micro, small, medium, and corporate enterprises in addition to households.

In earlier columns, I reflected on the imperative of maintaining macroeconomic stability as the foundation for Jamaica's sustained economic recovery, while noting the need to concurrently address the various structural bottlenecks that continue to impede growth. I also wrote about the need to address Jamaica's social challenges, including pursuing economic formalisation, strengthening the social safety net, and digitising public- and private-sector services.

A critical pillar of economic growth is of course the private sector. While Jamaica has the broad strokes of a market economy where the private sector should drive growth, various hurdles have muddied the ability of the private sector to attain what's truly feasible. The reasons are well documented – crime, weak business environment, financial exclusion, weak competitiveness, and historical fiscal dominance, to mention a few.

The Task Force considered and made several recommendations to enable a strong private sector as the way forward to support a dynamic and flourishing economy. Note that crime was not part

---

An earlier version of this article appeared in the *Jamaica Gleaner*, August 9, 2020.

of the Task Force's terms of reference. There are separate ongoing efforts in that dimension.

Private and Financial Sector Involvement

The private sector, including the financial sector, is the cornerstone of economic growth. For an economy to thrive with economic opportunities and fulfilling jobs, the private sector needs to thrive.

In a simplistic way, there are two arms to the private sector – the real sector and the financial sector. The real sector comprises, inter alia, corporate Jamaica and Micro, Small, and Medium-Sized Enterprises (MSMEs) including manufacturers, producers, farmers, entertainers, retailers, Business Process Outsourcing businesses, mining operators, distributors, craftsmen, repair garages, personal service providers, restaurants, tourism attraction operators, hotels, etc. They constitute the heartbeat of the Jamaican economy.

But sole traders, companies, and MSMEs don't operate in isolation – there is a very large support network that works together. The financial sector is a critical part of that support. Without financing, there is not much scope for businesses to grow. A significant push is needed on both fronts for the Jamaican economy to sustainably reach a higher potential growth.

Expanding Private-Sector Opportunities and Competitiveness

The Government of Jamaica (GOJ) is committed to expanding opportunity for private-sector investment by, among other things, advancing public-private partnerships (PPPs) to develop public infrastructure. For example, there is scope for PPPs in water (e.g., storage and treatment plants), roads (e.g., various North Coast bypass projects), healthcare (e.g., centres of excellence for oncology and nephrology), sewerage (e.g., Soapberry), and waste management (e.g., NSWMA). Likewise, the GOJ could catalyse private-sector-run private equity vehicles that have the goal of recapitalising and investing in companies affected by COVID-19. If conditions allow, GOJ's capitalisation could come in the form of a first-loss tranche, with commensurate return on investment for this risk designed to incentivise further private subscription.

Jamaica's competitiveness needs a shakeup, which we cannot achieve until some of the deeply entrenched structural hurdles are resolved. Competition drives technology investment and innovation, and vice versa, which in turn improve productivity and economic growth. Among other preconditions, competition thrives when information is readily available and accessible by market participants.

The Task Force recommends creation of a transparent GOJ land bank, where all investors – local and overseas – are aware of investment opportunities for land purchase or lease. There should be a strong and effective claw-back mechanism applied if such land is not developed within a specific time frame.

Furthermore, the Task Force recommends a comprehensive GOJ land divestment policy that is transparent, simple, and applies across all government agencies, rather than just the National Land Agency, thereby enhancing predictability of the process around purchase, sale, lease, and other land-related transactions with government.

The Task Force also recommends accelerated completion of the National Business Portal that would host a multitude of business-to-government (B2G) transactions, allowing MSMEs, local corporates, and foreign investors to (a) submit applications online for various licenses, permits, and other approvals, (b) have them reviewed by the relevant government entities, and then (c) obtain decisions online, all in a timely manner that can be transparently tracked. This single policy achievement would greatly enhance competitiveness and productivity of the Jamaican economy.

In addition, customs reform will greatly simplify procedures, creating a level playing field for large and small businesses, and reforms to the government electrical regulatory system will improve access to and speed of obtaining electricity.

Financial Deepening and Inclusion

The COVID-19 pandemic exposed economic impediments that result from low levels of financial inclusion. The interface between the CARE Programme and the banking sector exposed the large number of persons who have bank accounts that they do not regularly use. These accounts often lapse into dormancy, making them ineffective. Another factor rendering tens of thousands of accounts ineffective is the needed 'Know Your Customer' (KYC) documentation. In addition, access to credit is constrained, leaving MSMEs hungry for capital, and slowing growth. Pursuing reforms in these areas could be transformational for Jamaica.

So, what exactly can be done?

Streamlining KYC requirements would make it easier for Jamaicans to open bank accounts. Digital and portable KYC and remote onboarding for low-value transactional accounts would help, including allowing financial institutions to collect and share digital identities.

Fintech, which refers to technological innovations in the delivery of financial services, offers huge opportunities to modernise Jamaica's economy, deepen financial inclusion, and lower the cost of financial services. The Bank of Jamaica's Fintech Regulatory Sandbox – within which fintech innovations offered by fintech companies in partnership with regulated entities will be tested, including payment solutions and central bank digital currency – is an encouraging start.

Accelerating private credit growth will also benefit from further building the existing collateral registry to increase the attractiveness of asset-related products (e.g., mortgages, leasing, receivables finance) and ensure that the same collateral is not being used for cross-purposes. Sharing of credit information could also be mandated through regulation to remove information asymmetries. Financial information-sharing platforms could support this objective. Calculations for loan-loss provisions, currently based on a conservative rules-based approach (e.g., automatic triggers for loan classification, minimum provisioning percentages for each category), could also be reconsidered.

All lenders should be required to include transparent, understandable, and comparable information in their product listings and documentation, such that customers can easily choose between financial providers. Such information must reflect the true cost of lending, including the annual interest plus any fees, charges, etc., to enable informed decision-making.

And finally, initiatives are needed to promote greater financial literacy in schools and through partnerships with community-based organisations.

Diversify the Economic Base

Jamaica's economic vulnerability to natural disasters and commodity-price shocks is exacerbated by its narrow economic base. A few sectors account for most of the economic output. Greater emphasis must be placed on further diversifying the Jamaican economy. This, of course, is not an overnight operation. But we need to begin to push for achieving higher output and value-added from logistics, agro-processing, animation, medical-supply manufacturing, music and entertainment, sports, and other sectors and sub-sectors.

The COVID-19 pandemic has undoubtedly set us back. However, it also offers the opportunity for us to build back stronger. By embracing reform with ambition in our macroeconomic institutions, our social infrastructure, and our business environment, Jamaica can endure this pandemic, absorb its adverse social and economic effects, restore lost jobs and output, and not only 'rebuild Jamaica,' but reset to a Jamaica 2.0 that attains even higher levels of economic and social development in the years to come.

'Economic Opportunity for All':
Abolishment of Distortionary Taxes
Budget Speech Excerpt, March 2019

There was a time when revenues would always underperform. Over the eighteen-year period from 1997–98 to 2015–16, only once did we collect the budgeted revenues. In the last three years under this administration, not only have budgeted revenues been attained, but they have been surpassed. I will remind you that in the first two of those three years the bold direct-to-indirect tax reform was implemented.

For three consecutive years we have seen revenue over-perform budget by the equivalent of 0.8 per cent of GDP per year. In this 2018–19 financial year, we were able to use that over-performance to pay off long-standing government arrears … and we have increased the payments of tax refunds outstanding to businesses. After almost twenty years of consistent tax increases, and no new taxes last year, it is now time to give back, and it is the right thing to do.

We still have the challenge of high debt, and growth below what we want. Therefore, the way we give back must be calibrated to have a stimulative impact on growth. As a result, our first priority in giving back is to phase out taxes that are most distortionary to economic activity and that cut across all sectors of the economy.

We also want to phase out distortionary taxes in a fiscally responsible way, where we remain on track to achieving our debt-to-GDP target of 60 per cent by March 2026.

Abolishing the Minimum Business Tax

Mr Speaker, the Minimum Business Tax is distortionary. It imposes a tax of $60,000 a year on every company, without regard to whether it is struggling or performing, whether it is a start-up or is mature, whether it is making a loss or a profit. It is an indiscriminate tax that discourages business formation and activity. The business

---

Adapted from the opening budget presentation delivered in Parliament March 7, 2019.

owner just starting their catering business, or their small farm, or their cleaning business – before they have even one dollar of revenue, they become liable to pay the Minimum Business Tax. That is no way to encourage small business. The student leaving the University of Technology or Northern Caribbean University or The University of the West Indies with ideas to start a business becomes liable for Minimum Business Tax on the first March after incorporation. That is no way to encourage entrepreneurship. Your business is in trouble. It was going well, but then you lose a contract. The government still wants its Minimum Business Tax. The Minimum Business Tax is so indiscriminate that it applies whether the company is active or dormant.

We want to encourage incorporation, and we want the holding of assets in corporate form to be an attractive option. Hitting dormant companies with a Minimum Business Tax works against a Jamaica that wants to grow. For these reasons, effective April 1, we will *abolish* the Minimum Business Tax.

This is Economic Opportunity for All.

Abolishing Ad Valorem Stamp Duty on Financial Transactions

The Government of Jamaica currently imposes stamp duty and transfer tax on a wide variety of transactions. Some stamp duties are charged at a flat rate of five hundred or five thousand dollars, and others are ad valorem, which means it varies according to the value of the transaction.

Stamp duties, transfer taxes, or both are applicable to almost all asset transfers and the documentation that accompanies these transfers. Transfers of land, transfers of mortgages, transfers of loans, and transfers of securities all attract these taxes. In addition, supplying security for loans attracts ad valorem stamp duty, whether the security offered is inventory, land, equipment, receivables, shares, or other types of assets.

Trading of shares on the Jamaica Stock Exchange and on the Junior Market is exempt from ad valorem stamp duties and transfer taxes. The reason is because these taxes impede the proper and efficient function of the equity market. Similarly, if we want markets for loans, mortgages, securities, receivables, and land to function effectively, for transaction volumes to increase, for economic and business activity to thrive, which in turn provides a foundation for economic growth, the government should not be taxing these transactions.

Interest rates have been lowered seven successive times and are at record lows today. Some banks lower at faster rates than others. It's through competition among financial institutions on loan rates that the customer ends up with the best deal. However, competition in the loan market is hampered when customers incur high transaction costs to switch lenders, due to the government taxes that have to be paid to give new security to the new lender. To enjoy increased productivity gains from lower interest rates, increased economic and business activity from higher transaction volume, and higher rates of growth, we must reduce the burden of government transaction taxes.

The business that has a debenture over its assets and gets a better bank offer should not have to pay the government high stamp-transaction taxes to accept that better offer. The public-sector employee who has a mortgage with a bank and who wants to take advantage of a better offer, should not have to pay the government high transaction taxes to accept that better offer from another lender. The small business that goes to a micro-credit firm and grants a bill of sale over its equipment to facilitate a loan, should not have to pay the government high transaction taxes to accept a better offer from another micro-credit firm. The construction company that needs to register a performance bond to compete for a contract, should not have to pay the government high transaction taxes in order to have this done.

Similarly, the small business that wants to assign some of its receivables to obtain financing should not have to pay a hefty sum to the government for the privilege. Receivables are the largest pool of assets held by businesses, especially small businesses. We want an environment where businesses can raise capital by pledging receivables and having those registered, but this is not feasible if the government stands in the way with high transaction taxes.

The manufacturer that wants to increase its share capital to ensure that it can fund its expansion, should not have to pay the government high transaction taxes to do so.

And the Jamaican who has been on land owned by her parents and grandparents, and now wants to have that land registered so she can have a title – so she can have a piece of the rock, a place within Jamaican that she owns, that is recognised by the State as her own – the government should not stand in her way with high transaction taxes. We want her to register the land. We want there to be a title, and for her to have her name on the title. Greater formalisation is in the public interest. So why discourage it with high transaction taxes?

These stamp duties are distortionary. These stamp duties disincentivise the very activities we want to encourage.

These stamp duties discourage transactions.

They discourage competition.

These stamp duties impede access to finance.

They discourage business activity.

They discourage capital formation.

They discourage formalisation.

These ad valorem stamp duties are anti-growth.

The worst part is that at the time in the life cycle of a company – small, medium, or large – when it may be stumbling and in need of restructuring, even this restructuring is impeded by high transaction costs. High transaction costs lead to an inefficient and distorted allocation of resources and capital.

For these reasons, effective April 1, we will *abolish* distortionary ad valorem stamp duties applicable to the processes of registering land, issuing a bond, assignments, registering a debenture, registering a mortgage whether for primary land or other land, refinancing a mortgage whether the amount is the same or higher, discharging a mortgage, and other stamp duties involved in the granting and perfection of other forms of securities in addition to stamp duties for increasing share capital, rental or lease agreements, and other transactions. We will replace these with nominal processing fees that do not disincentivise these transactions. These fees will be a flat five thousand dollars per transaction which, when multiplied by existing volume, reflects the approximate cost of providing the stamping service.

So, when you hear that interest rates are moving down, but yours is not moving and some other institution offers you a better rate, phase the financial institution out – the government will not stand in your way.

This is Economic Opportunity for All.

Abolishing Ad Valorem Stamp Duty on Property

This government has firmly resolved to increase home ownership in Jamaica. We have made important progress, with the most housing starts of any administration in at least two decades. NHT housing starts in the first two years of this administration were greater than what the previous administration completed in four years. In addition, in the upcoming financial year, the NHT has plans for 8,640 more housing starts – more than all four years of the previous administration.

And we want to do more. How many times have you heard of instances where the mortgage loan is available, the deposit is available, but the closing costs were not anticipated, and the young couple has difficulty closing or has to defer their dream of owning a home? How many Members of Parliament recognise this account in the stories of their constituents? I had the privilege of chairing the board of NHT, and I know these stories exist in abundance for NHT-financed, open-market purchases. The closing transaction costs on homes often make it difficult for low-income earners to purchase homes. Even if a home is 100 per cent financed, and the buyers' incomes can cover the debt service, coming up with the funds to finance the transaction costs is difficult for many individuals. On a $5 million house, assuming 100 per cent financing, at current rates, the closing government transaction costs could be over $156,250 before legal fees. The high stamp duty and transfer tax on property affects the mobility of labour as labour becomes less willing to move in search of employment opportunity due to the high transaction costs of switching homes.

High stamp duty and transfer tax on property discourages downsising. For the retired couple on fixed income, with grown children, it does not make sense to sell their house, incur large transaction taxes, purchase a smaller unit and incur more transaction taxes. With an ageing population in a country that has suffered from stagnant growth for forty years, with limited land availability, this does not make sense. The society benefits from a recirculation of the housing stock to those who can maximise use of space. Our tax system should encourage, rather than discourage, being able to choose the right home for their circumstances.

High stamp duty and transfer tax on property also increases the risk to property developers. Higher transaction costs compound errors of judgement and create unforeseen adverse changes in business parameters. With high transaction taxes, individuals and institutions are more hesitant; they wait after forty years of low growth, we can't afford the hesitancy. We cannot afford waiting. We can't afford government-induced high-risk premia on property.

High transaction costs for property also have distortive impact on capital allocation in the economy. Whereas equities on the stock exchange do not attract high government transaction taxes, property purchases currently do. If we continue to do this, we create a bias towards investment in public equities over real estate, even for primary homes, which can have unintended consequences.

For this reason, we will *abolish* ad valorem stamp duty on properties on April 1, and we will replace it with a fee that approximates the value of providing the service.

This represents Economic Opportunity for All.

Addressing Transfer Taxes on Property and Estates

We strengthened property taxes in 2017, and the time has now come to reduce property transfer taxes. Like stamp duty, these taxes increase the cost of buying and selling property. We want to make it easier and cheaper for everyone to buy and sell property. As such we will reduce transfer tax on property from 5 per cent to 2 per cent on April 1. There is also a lot of property tied up in the estates of those who have passed away, where Jamaican families who want to sell the property and use the proceeds in a straightforward way for varied economic purposes are unable to do so because of the estate transfer tax. Successive governments have recognised this concern. However, we need to go further. The exemption threshold was first set at $10,000 in 1974. It was raised to $100,000 in 2005 and has been at that level since. Mr Speaker, we will raise the exemption threshold on estate transfer tax from $100,000 to $10 million, effective April 1.

This will allow for greater mobility of assets, which is consistent with our drive for economic growth.

This is Economic Opportunity for All.

Mr Speaker, too many Jamaicans in 2019 are still unable to afford home ownership, to own a place of their own, to build upon it, to borrow against it, and to pass it along to their children and grandchildren. The sum of these policies announced today are designed to address this problem which dates to our foundation as a country.

Impact of the Tax Stimulus

The abolishment and lowering of these distortionary transaction taxes means that the government will forgo approximately $14 billion or 0.7 per cent of GDP. This is the first time in decades – in living memory – that any Government of Jamaica is giving back taxes on a net basis to the Jamaican people.

And it is well overdue. After more than $130 billion in tax increases over the last twenty years and approximately $90 billion in tax increases over the last ten years, and with decades of sluggish economic growth, the time is right for a tax reduction.

This is a $14 billion tax stimulus that abolishes or lowers various distortionary transaction taxes to catalyse increased transaction volume, increased business and economic activity, and increased economic growth.

These measures will stimulate micro business, stimulate small business, stimulate the credit market, stimulate the construction sector, stimulate the real estate market, stimulate formality, and stimulate overall economic activity.

These measures will lead to a more liquid real estate market, will support more agents, more valuators, more property transactions, more property turnover, more plumbers, more carpenters, and more masons who prepare properties for purchase and sale.

This will have second-order effects for manufacturers who make household furnishings, household goods, and building materials. More cement, more sand, more stone, more windows, more doors, more furniture, more economic opportunity, and, very importantly, more jobs.

This is Economic Opportunity for All in action.

Introducing an MSME Tax Credit

Budget Speech Excerpt, March 2020

Mr Speaker, small and medium-sized businesses are the backbone of the economy, accounting for significant employment. We need an environment that is hospitable to MSME growth and development. We also wish more and more young people to see starting a business and pursuing an entrepreneurial path as a viable option.

We want to remove obstacles that stand in the way of a vibrant MSME sector in Jamaica. In last year's budget presentation, we announced the abolishment of the asset tax, the abolishment of the minimum business tax, and an increase in the General Consumption Tax threshold from $3 million to $10 million. Following those tax reforms, do you know that incorporation of new companies increased by an incredible 95 per cent in the period of March 2019 to December 2019 as compared to the corresponding period in 2018?

By encouraging the starting up of new businesses, *Jamaica is moving in the right direction.*

This year, we are going further. We are going to give back to small business. In the past, we had the backwards practise where the small business operator would have to pay taxes to the government, whether or not they made a profit. We did away with that, and this year we say to small business: we don't wish to burden you with worrying about taxes from your first dollar of earnings. This year, effective calendar year 2020, we introduce, for the first time in the history of Jamaica, the MSME Tax Credit that will provide a tax credit of $375,000 to every micro, small, and medium-sized business that files taxes. The potential revenue loss of this measure is expected to be $1.01 billion. Thousands of small businesses are struggling to get by, and the obligation to pay tax from their first dollar of profit imposes a burden – very often a cash-flow burden. Small businesses

---

Adapted from the opening budget presentation delivered in Parliament March 10, 2020.

should know that the government wants the small businesswoman, the micro-businessman to succeed. We are also saying to young people who are leaving university, go start your business, knowing that the government has got your back and is invested in your success.

By reducing the overall tax burden on MSMEs, we will also reduce the incentives for informal operation. MSMEs are an integral part of Jamaica's economic activity and growth; the more we incentivise formalisation, the more we capture their contribution to growth. By reducing the tax burden on our small businesses. *Jamaica is moving in the right direction.*

Reducing the Rate of the General Consumption Tax

Budget Speech Excerpt, March 2020

Mr Speaker, as I have said in this presentation and repeated many times, Jamaica's economic recovery is attributable to the resilience, the resolve, and the sacrifice of the Jamaican people. The Jamaican people came together and have owned the economic reforms, and today Jamaica is a shining example to the world.

We are creating fiscal space this year not through an expected over-performance of revenues. We are creating fiscal space by deliberate and strategic acceleration of debt repayment that has taken careful planning and execution, across a wide range of initiatives.

Last year, with debt still quite high at 94 per cent of GDP and plans to recapitalise the Bank of Jamaica that year, we had to be careful not to erode the tax base. We therefore chose to abolish or reduce distortionary taxes to boost economic activity and investment. The early evidence is that those policies are working. Company incorporations were up 94 per cent in the period of March to December 2019 over the period March to December of 2018, and mortgages over land are up 74 per cent between March and December 2019. By reducing the cost of transacting property and making it easier to start and grow a business, *Jamaica is moving in the right direction.*

With debt-to-GDP now at 90.2 per cent,[6] and having advanced our policy to accelerate debt repayment to the point that we can now implement it with a significant reduction in nominal debt in 2020–21, which is forecasted to contribute to the lowering of the debt-to-GDP ratio to 83 or 84 per cent by the end of the upcoming financial year, our policy choices can be broadened to include other measures. This economic recovery belongs to all Jamaicans, and we wish to reduce tax that virtually everyone has to pay. Quite apart from any economic argument, there is a moral imperative to do this.

Adapted from the opening budget presentation delivered in Parliament March 10, 2020.

The government's focus has been on jobs and growth. We have had one hundred thousand jobs created in the last four years; however, growth is hampered by our susceptibility to one-off shocks. We will be relentless in seeking new ways to stimulate growth. The monetary channel has been used extensively with an unprecedented eleven consecutive reductions in interest rates, and I have just announced a measure that will improve the transmission of the Bank of Jamaica's monetary decisions. Through the fiscal channel, we have reduced distortionary taxes to promote investment, and I have just announced other fiscal measures designed to boost investment.

Effective April 1, 2020, the standard rate of General Consumption Tax (GCT) will be reduced by 1.5 per cent, from 16.5 per cent to 15 per cent. The potential revenue loss is estimated to be approximately $14 billion, or 0.67 per cent of GDP. This is the first cut in the GCT rate that is not accompanied by GCT being applied to new areas. By reducing the GCT taxes which all Jamaicans pay and allowing Jamaicans to keep more of their hard-earned money in their pockets, *Jamaica is moving in the right direction.*

Introducing an Exemption Threshold for the Customs Administrative Fee

Budget Speech Excerpt, March 2021

Madam Speaker, we do not print US dollars in Jamaica. Every US dollar you purchase in Jamaica was earned by someone, borrowed from someone, or sent by remittance to someone here. For US dollars to be available, there must be a supply. Arguing in our society about how this scarce commodity is allocated, and the level at which it is available, has been a preoccupation for much of the last forty years. And it has been politicised by both sides, which is unfortunate, as it misses the real issue.

Some countries have foreign exchange controls where the central bank effectively rations foreign exchange and tells you how much you can buy and at what price. We rejected that long ago. Jamaicans do not want such a system. However, if we don't want exchange controls and want to be able to freely buy or sell foreign exchange with minimal restrictions, then clearly, for any given level of supply of US dollars, a market system is the best means of allocating those resources.

A subsidised system would result in losses for the central bank, non-transparent benefit transfers towards the largest users, and a huge bill for taxpayers. We are better off focusing our time, thought, and energies on how we can increase the supply of US dollars to our country, which is the real issue that, for too long, we have been skirting around. And there is no better time to focus on this than now, when our foreign-exchange earnings are at the lowest levels in twenty years.

Today, we earn foreign exchange primarily through the export of goods or services. Our biggest export of services is in the tourism sector, and I know Minister Bartlett has a solid recovery strategy. With respect to the export of goods, since 2013, Customs has levied a Customs Administrative Fee (CAF), which replaced the Customer

---

Adapted from the opening budget presentation delivered in Parliament March 9, 2021.

User Fee, a levy which was not deemed compliant with the rules of the World Trade Organization. The CAF was set at J$3,000, per customs export declaration, and has remained at that level for the past seven years.

With the improving economic environment over the past four years, pre-COVID, and with the advances in technology, an entire ecosystem of firms has mushroomed and is engaged in the manufacturing and export of small-value shipments. These companies, most of which are small businesses, are a very important part of the productive ecosystem. They contribute to the economy through employment, taxes, and foreign-exchange earnings. They export candles, specialty garments, craft items, processed food, homemade sauces, ceramics, paintings, hand crafted jewellery, cosmetics, soaps, coconut and other oils, and hundreds of other items that consumers throughout the world want to buy from our local manufacturers and artisans.

However, when a shipment has a value of J$1,500 and the government charges a CAF of J$3,000, we have an absurd situation in which the CAF is higher than the value of the product itself. The customer will often absorb shipping costs, but more often than not the exporter has to absorb these disproportionately high government fees. This has been the case since the CAF was introduced in 2013. When a shipment has a value of J$5,000 and the government levies a CAF of J$3,000, that shipment becomes uncompetitive as the CAF is 60 per cent of the value of the shipment. This has been the case since the CAF was introduced in 2013. When a shipment has a value of J$20,000, a J$3,000 CAF is 15 per cent of the value of the product. This administrative fee imposed by the government falls disproportionately hard on the backs of our small-business manufacturers and artisans. This has been the case since the CAF was introduced in 2013.

Jamaica cannot be competitive in exports with this setup. We can't increase foreign-exchange earnings while forcing our exporters to operate with their hands tied behind their backs. In 2019–20, the Jamaica Customs Agency processed just under forty-three thousand export-good declarations. Of this number, 73 per cent were for export by air, which represented 6 per cent of the value of exports;

and 27 per cent were for export by sea, which represented 94 per cent of the value of exports.

So, what we have is an emerging industry of exporting small-value shipments for quick delivery. These data are descriptive of an emerging e-commerce export sector, which anecdotally we know to be the case. Of the approximately forty-three thousand export declarations, just under eleven thousand were for value less than US$50 or J$7,000[7] and each of these exports required a payment of J$3,000. Another almost eleven thousand of the export declarations were between US$50 and US$500. So, a total of twenty-two thousand of the export declarations, or more than 50 per cent were valued less than US$500.

The government will support the emergence of the e-commerce export sector and the manufacturers and artisans that are earning foreign exchange for our country through this modality. In today's Jamaica, with the opportunities available and the need to encourage and support export, the CAF for small-value exports is, frankly speaking, ridiculously counter-productive, and needs to be abolished. It belongs in the same rubbish bin as the Minimum Business Tax and the Asset Tax for non-financial businesses that this government abolished a few years ago.

As such, this government will abolish the Customs Administrative Fee for permanent exports of value less than or equal to US$500. This is estimated to cost $70 million, an amount we can afford, even at this time, and is one of the best investments of $70 million we could ever make.

Brick by brick, Madam Speaker, we will recover stronger.

The New Customs Act:
Enhancing Economic Activity

Published Commentary, June 2024

Jamaica's trade in goods and services accounts for approximately 80 per cent of GDP. As such, there are few single pieces of legislation that have a greater impact on economic activity than the Customs Act. Yet Jamaica's Customs Act dates to 1941! It is complex, uses language that is out of step with modern trade terms, and is not easily understood. The Customs Act is antiquated, with cumbersome procedural requirements that do not readily facilitate the global, interlocking, just-in-time nature of modern international commerce and supporting logistics.

Furthermore, with scores of amendments over decades, the Customs Act and its schedules do not exist in any single compendium. One therefore must reference many separate documents, which are not always readily accessible, to gain a full understanding of Jamaica's customs laws, regulations, and procedures. For these and other reasons, Jamaica's eighty-three-year-old customs legislative regime has long been sub-optimal.

The good news is that Jamaica is one step closer to a transformed customs legislative architecture with the passage in the Lower House of Parliament last Tuesday, of the Customs Act (2020), which is designed to repeal and replace the 1941 Customs Act. It now goes to the Senate.

The proposed new Customs Act, which benefited from a vigorous, consultative, and collaborative joint-select-committee process, consists of just under three hundred clauses, across two hundred pages, with a further eight hundred pages of schedules, all in a single document. The consolidation of all this legislative material into a single publication is enormous even without considering the updating of the substance of the law. The customs rates applicable to every conceivable product are included in the schedules, organised

---

An earlier version of this article appeared in the *Jamaica Gleaner*, June 2, 2024.

by logical categories and prefaced by an easy-to-understand table of contents. This levels the playing field between large, well-resourced businesses and micro-enterprises with respect to the ability to independently navigate Jamaica's customs laws and to reference customs rates.

The existing customs legislation dates to the Second World War and uses outdated language that often alienates the twenty-first-century Jamaican. The proposed new Customs Act, by comparison, introduces modern terminology with simple, clear language which will make Jamaica's customs law truly accessible to every Jamaican. In addition, the updated language uses internationally accepted terms and definitions, which will facilitate Jamaica's improved interaction with the international trading community. More specifically, the UN-sponsored global integrated customs management system for international trade (ASYCUDA) enshrines internationally accepted customs terms, which our proposed new Customs Act incorporates. This promises to make our customs architecture more globally compatible.

A More Efficient, Predictable and Productive Customs Regime

The proposed Customs Act (2020) is forward-looking and promotes efficiency, predictability, transparency, and accountability – principles that align with and advance Vision 2030. For instance, the pre–adult-suffrage customs law was designed for a pre-electronic and pre-digital era. By contrast, the new Act lays a robust foundation for a range of electronic customs systems which will save time, enhance transparency, reduce the cost of paper, and significantly reduce crowding in physical facilities, thereby improving efficiency and productivity.

Predictability in customs procedures lowers transaction costs. The proposed new Customs Act includes a procedure through which an importer may receive a binding decision regarding how Customs will treat their goods before those goods are even imported. This is a significant step in advancing trade predictability. The proposed Act also improves customs clearance processes, which will allow goods to pass through Jamaica's airports and seaports with enhanced efficiency.

The new Customs Act also creates a framework for voluntary disclosure: under specific terms and conditions, a person who voluntarily discloses non-compliance and pays any outstanding duty and tax, will legally avoid penalties or prosecution. This will allow Jamaicans to quickly move on from genuine mistakes.

In addition, the new customs legislation includes mechanisms that reward those who comply with the customs laws through enhanced application of risk management and audit-based controls. Specifically, a person's or entity's record of compliance may result in the grant of special authorisations and pre-approvals, which may enable goods imported by that person or entity to be cleared with reduced Customs interventions.

Furthermore, in the new customs architecture, the posting of security will be risk-based, instead of rigidly and inflexibly determined. Accordingly, the amount of security that a person would be required to provide will depend on their record of compliance, and any risk factors related to the specific type of goods. It is also proposed that the Jamaica Customs Agency facilitates a wide range of security. The intention is to ease the burden faced by some members of the trading community regarding the obligation to provide bonds and bank guarantees when doing business with Customs.

Supports Growth of New Industries

Importantly, the proposed new Customs Act facilitates the growth and development of Jamaica as a destination for globally connected logistics activity. Jamaica's geographic position, in relation to global trading routes, has long made Jamaica an ideal location for logistics-related economic activity. This requires goods, or parts of goods, to be able to enter Jamaica's borders through one transportation modality (e.g., sea); be processed, altered, and/or stored in Jamaica; and then leave later through the same, or another, transportation modality (e.g., air) all in a seamless fashion, with minimal regulatory transactions costs. This is challenging to achieve with our existing antiquated customs framework that could not, and did not, anticipate the intricacies of modern global supply chains. By contrast, the new customs framework is specifically designed to support the growth of Jamaica's logistics industry.

Similarly, there is huge scope for growth of Jamaica's tourism in the under-tapped segment of meetings, incentives, conferences, and exhibitions (known by the acronym MICE). In this segment, scores or hundreds of individuals travel to attend a seminar, conference, meeting, trade show, or exhibition in a convenient, attractive destination. While Jamaica has the hotels, atmosphere, and people to compete in this market segment, our outdated customs laws represent an inhibiting factor. It is cumbersome to obtain the permissions to import the pens, writing pads, memorabilia, and paraphernalia, which are not intended to stay in Jamaica but are essential to these events, without payment of duties. This makes Jamaica a less attractive destination for MICE activities than it would otherwise be.

The new Customs Act provides a simple incentive structure to support Jamaica's ability to compete in and grow the MICE market segment. Goods imported for a MICE event approved by the tourism ministry that are 'imported for consumption, otherwise than by sale, at a meeting, incentive, convention or exposition' will be imported free of duty. This will allow Jamaica to be promoted as an ideal destination for MICE activities and will set the stage for the growth of the MICE tourism market.

Similarly, promoters of music festivals, and the consuming public, also stand to benefit. Today it is exceedingly complicated to bring equipment into Jamaica, that is not intended to remain in Jamaica, for music concerts, music festivals, and the filming of movies. Under the new Customs Act the procedures for importing and re-exporting equipment for these purposes will be greatly simplified. This will make Jamaica a more attractive and convenient international entertainment destination.

There is much more. The Customs Act (2020) is, simply, transformative. This week, we achieved an important milestone towards its implementation that ought not to go unnoticed.

Broadening the Ownership Base
of the Jamaican Economy
Published Commentary, March 2020

The Government of Jamaica aims to broaden the ownership base of the Jamaican economy by listing state assets on the Jamaica Stock Exchange and catalysing broad participation, and by encouraging more young people to go into business. Broadening the ownership base of the economy – that is, having more Jamaicans participate in the risk and reward that comes with the ownership of productive assets – increases economic opportunity, equity, and social cohesion.

The government's Wigton Windfarm Initial Public Offering (IPO) generated more than thirty-one thousand applications. Never had so many persons applied to purchase shares in an IPO on the Jamaica Stock Exchange.[8] Furthermore, the Jamaica Stock Exchange reported that approximately eleven thousand of those applicants had never before invested on the Exchange. Among the applications, public-sector employees purchased over \$1.1 billion of the Wigton shares on offer. Also, the 'bottom up' allocation ensured that all small investors were successful in their applications.

The application window for the TransJamaica IPO, by far the largest IPO in Jamaica's history,[9] closed on March 2. TransJamaica was a private-sector company that started construction of the East–West Highway in 2001 and that owned and operated it since then up to December 2019. During this eighteen-year period, all ordinary shares of TransJamaica were owned and controlled by foreign investors with the government owning preference shares. The government acquired all the ordinary shares in TransJamaica from the consortium of foreign investors and made them available for Jamaicans to purchase by listing TransJamaica on the Jamaica Stock Exchange. Preliminary results of the TransJamaica Highway IPO, which aimed to raise two and a half times what was raised in Wigton Windfarm IPO, suggest that the records established by

---

An earlier version appeared as a wrapper for the *Jamaica Observer*, March 10, 2020.

Wigton have been surpassed. The official results are expected to be released shortly.

Up until now, the energy and infrastructure sectors have largely been dominated by international investors. We are grateful for their investment. However, now, ordinary Jamaicans can also, if they so choose, invest in energy and infrastructure opportunities. Not only are we broadening the base of ownership of the economy, we are also opening access to sectors in which ordinary Jamaicans have thus far been underrepresented. In other words, we are expanding economic opportunity.

Broadening the ownership base of the economy is also being pursued by implementing policies that encourage young people to go into business. In April 2019, we abolished the Asset Tax[10] and the Minimum Business Tax and increased the threshold for General Consumption Tax from $3 million to $10 million with the small businessperson in mind. We also wanted to remove the obstacles that young people, without family money, face in starting and owning businesses. Early indications are that the policy is bearing fruit, and Jamaicans are responding in a manner consistent with the policy thrust. In the six months to December 2019, company incorporations increased by an incredible 95 per cent!

Medium, small, and micro enterprises (MSMEs) are considered the backbone of the economy. With the technical and financial assistance of the Inter-American Development Bank and the World Bank, the government is also channelling more funds through the Development Bank of Jamaica to improve MSMEs access to finance.

The government is increasing the access of MSMEs to debt financing, and, by removing the restrictions that prevented pension funds from investing in venture capital, the government is paving the way for the emergence of MSME-focussed providers of equity financing. Of course, the vibrancy of the Jamaica Stock Exchange's Main and Junior markets also provides further avenues of financing available to Jamaican businesses including MSMEs.

The government has made broadening the ownership base of the Jamaican economy a central plank of its policy platform. Along with the entrenchment of macroeconomic stability, this policy position greatly expands economic opportunity for all Jamaicans.

Permitting Pension Funds to Invest in Private Market Securities

Policy Address, February 2019

As we engage in a variety of fiscal, monetary, and other structural reforms, we are essentially widening the scope of the non-government sector – that is, the private sector broadly defined; the business community, comprised of thousands of businesses across Jamaica – so that those businesses, as economic agents, can play an ever-increasing role in Jamaica's economic growth and development.

The development financing required to build the social and physical infrastructure that Jamaica will need cannot be financed by the government alone. There is no way that government revenues – tax revenues – are going to be able to finance all the water plants, and sewerage plants, and all the infrastructure that we need. For that reason, the private economic agents – individuals, institutions, businesses, financial institutions – are going to have a large role to play in Jamaica's growth and development going forward.

As we enter this period, we must ensure that our economy is characterised by three core principles: (1) competition, (2) deep markets, and (3) transparency of pricing. Economic agents in a market economy interact through capital markets. For Jamaica to achieve its social and economic development, and for us to maintain and advance our social and economic infrastructure, the capital markets of Jamaica will have a fundamental role to play. But we want capital markets that are characterised by competition, by transparency as far as prices are concerned, and by depth, that is, liquidity.

The non-bank financial sector, as we know, is larger than the deposit-taking institutions – by assets. The last time I looked, and I admit this was several months ago, the non-bank financial sector – consisting of the securities dealers, pension funds, and life insurance companies after you take out crossholdings – had assets in

---

Adapted from an address to the Jamaica Securities Dealers Association on February 13, 2019.

excess of $1.7 trillion. The deposit-taking institutions had assets of approximately $1.6 trillion. This means that the non-bank financial sector is absolutely crucial for our growth and development, because a considerable amount of the private resources of Jamaica, are held within the institutions that make up the non-banking financial sector. This is something that demands our attention.

One thing we are doing in this area is amending and updating the legislation around the permissible investments for pension funds. The amendments were tabled in Parliament, and I expect them to be passed next week. These amendments will broaden the pool of assets that pension funds are able to invest in. Today, pension funds cannot invest in unsecured debt, for example, which does not really make sense if you think about it. Pension funds invest in equities on the stock exchange, and equities are junior to debt, so why on earth would we preclude pension funds from investing in unsecured debt? It doesn't make sense at all – it is just an aberration that has existed for a long period of time and needs to be changed.

In changing it, we are mindful of the fact that pension funds have $500 billion of assets, and that we want to move in moderation – and that we are prepared to change, again, in twelve months or twenty-four months, as the case may be. So, the amendments that are before the House today will allow pension funds the ability to invest in unsecured debt. Let me back up a bit. The amendments around debt are geared towards what I mentioned earlier as well: incentivising price discovery, which is crucial to a market. A market that does not have price discovery – and I want this to be something that the securities dealers champion – a market that does not have price discovery is a market that is not in our interest. In all markets we want prices to be available, to be transparent, and for everybody to see the same set of prices.

Investors exist who are willing to take on the various degrees of risk – Type A, B, C, D, and even junk – provided that investments are calibrated to provide returns that are commensurate with the risks undertaken. What we don't want is for people to be investing in what they think is A, but then turns out to be E. That is not in the interest of the investor; it not in the interest of the issuer; and it is not in the interest of Jamaica. It does not aid price discovery or transparency – in fact it blocks all those things and potentially chokes the system, leading to results that we don't want.

We want to incentivise pricing discovery and transparency, but we also want to incentivise risk disclosure and risk discovery. When you go to the supermarket, and you want to buy oranges – you get oranges. It doesn't mean that oranges don't spoil. But at least you get oranges.

For that reason, for unsecured debt that is either rated or listed on the exchange, pension funds will be able to invest without limit. It will be the responsibility of trustees and of investment managers to ensure that investments accord to the principles of the pension fund. You must accord with the investment principles and objectives of the pension fund. Once you are within the investment objectives of the fund, then the trustees and investment managers together, depending on what they decide in detail, have discretion and will be able to invest in unsecured debt that is listed or rated. For unsecured debt that is neither listed nor rated, the ability will still exist to invest, but it will be prescribed to an aggregate amount of no more than 5 per cent of the assets of the pension fund.

We expect that this change will lead to greater competition in all our markets, including our debt and loan markets. We believe that as the government signals its need to not borrow as much from the investing public, and as government risk declines and government yields come down, pension funds are going to have to find other sources of investment that provide yields that are appropriate for the liabilities they are trying to finance. Pension funds will be able to seek out the best opportunities as far as debt is concerned from private issuers; and private issuers, through their broker dealers, will have access to a larger pool of funds and will have access to more choices than simply bank debt. We see this as a change that will encourage and catalyse the kind of financing that is required for growth and development.

There are other changes. Private equity, which was precluded before, will be a permissible investment. Private equity is a broad category that includes venture capital and other forms of private equity. Private equity will be allowable to the extent that the combination of private equity and unrated, unsecured debt investments does not exceed 5 per cent of the market value of the pension-fund assets. Again, pension funds have $500 billion of investments, so we believe that is a good start, and the authority (the Financial Services Commission), will watch to see how the market develops and the kinds of decisions that investment managers and trustees make. Dependent on that and other further demand, those limits can be revisited. These are geared towards ensuring that we have deep markets, transparent pricing, and competition.

The economic variables are aligned in a way that they have not been aligned before. The opportunities are tremendous. The number of people who are earning, the number of people who are employed, creates opportunities for all of you. The number of persons in Jamaica who have accounts with the institutions represented in this room is a small proportion of the working population, and that working population is expanding – which means there is tremendous opportunity. So, we want all Jamaicans to be able to access the kinds of financial services that your organisations provide. And so, for that reason, we are working to ensure that the markets in which you operate – operate efficiently, fairly, and smoothly so Jamaica can grow, prosper, and develop.

Venture Capital and Private Equity Ecosystem

Budget Speech Excerpt, March 2023

Madam Speaker, the importance of venture capital and angel investors for early-stage businesses is well known across the world in innovation-led economies, as these sources of funding have been the fuel behind the startup of many of the world's leading businesses, most notably the major technology companies. The absence of these alternative forms of financing in Jamaica has resulted in under-investment in innovative enterprises, as well as many ideas being stillborn, or start-up businesses not getting off the ground. Under the Development Bank of Jamaica's (DBJ's) Boosting Innovation, Growth, and Entrepreneurship Ecosystems (BIGEE) programme with the Inter-American Development Bank, the Angel Fund was launched in December 2022 to invest $232.5 million, alongside eligible angel investors, in early-stage, sometimes pre-revenue companies. This is a historical first for Jamaica.

Through the efforts of the DBJ, and with financing from the Ministry of Finance and the Public Service, and from the World Bank, three Small and Medium-Sized (SME) private-equity funds have been established with a total investment of $5.325 billion, including $1.775 billion from the Government of Jamaica through the DBJ.

If you are a small or medium-sized enterprise looking for equity financing, there are at least three options available to assist you if you meet their criteria:

1. Vertex SME Holdings, managed by JMMB Securities Limited;

2. Stratus Private Equity & SME Fund, managed by NCB Capital Markets; and

3. JASMEF 1, managed by Victoria Mutual Investments and Actus Partners.

Adapted from the opening budget presentation delivered in Parliament March 7, 2023.

I am pleased to report that, through the policies of this government, new funds, with a total capitalisation of $13.45 billion have been established to provide equity funding to Jamaican businesses – primarily small and medium-sized businesses, and startups. In addition, through the BIGEE programme, which is being executed with funding from the Inter-American Development Bank and the European Union, the Government of Jamaica, through DBJ, has established: an Innovation Grant Fund that provides grants for innovation; a Patent Grant Fund to help inventors to protect their intellectual property; three Incubator (and Pre-Incubator) programmes which are expected to provide training, mentorship, and incubation support services to approximately one hundred high-potential Jamaican startup companies; and two Accelerator programmes, which are expected to provide acceleration services to one hundred scalable Jamaican startup companies in the coming year.

Madam Speaker, there has never been a better time to be an ambitious entrepreneur – especially a young entrepreneur – in Jamaica.

Advancing Jamaica's Development with the World Bank and IDB

Published Commentary, June 2023

Eleven days after taking charge of the World Bank Group (World Bank), Mr Ajay Banga, the new president, is scheduled to make a historic trip to Kingston this week. The World Bank is the world's largest multilateral development bank, owned by 189 member countries, which promotes long-term economic development and poverty reduction.

President Banga will visit Jamaica on his very first overseas trip. This will also be the first visit of any World Bank President to Jamaica. This is significant. Among other things, it speaks volumes about the opportunities for development that Jamaica has earned for herself.

This is a historic moment for another reason, too. Kingston will also host, at the same time, the new president of the Inter-American Development Bank (IDB), Mr Ilan Goldfajn. The IDB is the largest multilateral financial institution in the Western Hemisphere, owned by forty-eight member countries. Jointly, the combined assets of the two institutions amount to over three-quarter trillion US dollars.

These simultaneous Jamaican visits by the leadership of two vast multilateral institutions come at a time of great uncertainty for many of the world's emerging-market economies, as the world is hit by shock upon shock. In many countries, an overhang of debt from the policy responses to the COVID-19 crisis, and the global inflation shock, threaten economic and financial stability. The developing debt crisis is compounded by tightening global financial conditions, through rising global interest rates and other monetary policy actions focussed on taming inflation, making it more difficult for many countries to access market financing at a time when policy space has been mostly exhausted.

An earlier version of this article appeared in the *Jamaica Observer*, June 10, 2023.

Against this background, Jamaica's economic performance through these crises has garnered international attention. Jamaica's policy interventions have been targeted, and economic recovery has been swift. During 2022, employment surpassed pre-COVID levels, and the level of economic output in real terms at end December 2022 surpassed output at end 2019. While some countries can rival these achievements, Jamaica stands in rare company for attaining this economic recovery while also having reduced debt substantially relative to end December 2019.

However, Jamaica's differentiation is not limited to the pace and quality of our economic recovery. We also used the time during the crisis to strengthen institutions, build resilience and pursue reform. COVID-19 did not derail our plans for central bank independence. Rather, in a global environment of social distancing, working from home, and almost universal mask-wearing, we completed the legislative processes that institutionalised inflation targeting and monetary policy independence. It could not have come at a better time. The Bank of Jamaica used its independence to [make us] one of the first countries to mount an early, credible, forceful response to the inflation crisis even as some segments of the business community pushed back. Point-to-Point inflation cooled to 5.8 per cent in April 2023, inside the target window, after nineteen months of inflation outcomes that have been higher than the upper bound of the target range. While the central bank has cautioned that it's too early to declare victory, the reversal of Jamaican inflation to target range ahead of advanced countries, such as the UK, is a staggering demonstration of the transformative power of policy discipline.

Also, during the COVID period, Jamaica became the first small country to launch an independently sponsored catastrophe bond with the assistance of the World Bank and the support of bilateral partners: the US, UK, and Germany. While much of the world was in COVID-19–induced lockdown, we also passed legislation to create an independent fiscal commission.

At this time, though risks remain, the Jamaican macroeconomic story is unlike any other in the world, and positively so. As such, while we have long been known internationally for our music, culture, and sport, Jamaica is now experiencing international acknowledgement for our macroeconomic performance. This performance has delivered tens of thousands of new construction, tourism, and Business Process Outsourcing jobs, supported record growth in company incorporations, and provides the platform for further achievements that improve quality of life.

A legacy of Jamaica's past macroeconomic instability, in the context of a globalised labour market for the highly skilled, is the loss of much of the locally well-trained technical talent to overseas markets. An important implication of the newfound macroeconomic stability is that we are likely to have the opportunity to take on development projects over the medium term that are outside of Jamaica's institutional experience in size, scope, and/or focus. This introduces risks with the potential to derail our hard-earned stability. While this is a natural phase of the development cycle, we have to be humble about our current national limitations, to avoid costly errors. In addition, the capital required for infrastructure-development projects exceeds the capacity of government many times over.

We have an opportunity now to significantly advance Jamaica's development agenda through strategic partnerships and deeper engagements with the World Bank and the IDB. There is no other institution with more technically skilled and globally experienced development-policy talent than the World Bank. And within our hemisphere the IDB is unmatched in development expertise with globally competitive practises in many sectors.

We therefore intend to leverage Jamaica's macroeconomic stability, and our credibility with these technically resourced institutions, to accelerate Jamaica's pace of development. Across the medium term we intend to crowd-in up to US$1.5 billion of private-sector infrastructure investment through Public-Private Partnerships (PPPs) and other infrastructure procurement modalities – through open, competitive, and transparent processes. As a transaction advisor with a development bias, the private-sector arm of the World Bank, the International Finance Corporation (IFC), has unparalleled global expertise. The opportunities are ripe to partner with them to bring to market, possibly, highway, broadband, healthcare, water, sanitation, and other infrastructure projects.

The IDB also has tremendous PPP advisory capacity and has provided Jamaica with a project-preparation grant window to assist in bringing such projects to market. In addition, the IDB is raising capital from its forty-eight member countries to expand the capacity of its private-sector window. We intend to position Jamaica to benefit from this increased firepower. Meanwhile, we are 'doubling up' with the IDB's innovation arm, IDB Labs, to nurture entrepreneurial capacity within the small- and medium-sized enterprise space.

Our development will be hampered without significant improvements in education outcomes. At the Government of Jamaica's (GOJ's) invitation, the World Bank completed an insightful public expenditure review on education spending, benchmarked against global peers. The GOJ hopes to continue to work with the World Bank on improving learning conditions in schools, the application of information technology in the education sector, and on the implementation of the Prime Minister's vision of STEM schools.

As we strive to improve domestic value-add, and so boost growth and incomes, the GOJ aims to again partner with the IDB on round two of the global-services skills project, even as we work with them to achieve greater food security with impactful agriculture projects. The GOJ also hopes to work with the IDB to transform healthcare delivery through the construction and upgrade of hospitals and health centres.

Digitisation of government services promises to lower costs, reduce processing times, and boost productivity. It provides the best chance for leapfrogging traditional phases of development. However, this is an awesomely complex undertaking with many pitfalls. The IDB is ideally positioned to assist, and the World Bank has valuable global experience to share.

Our partnership with the World Bank recently delivered the social pension product, which now benefits thousands of elderly Jamaicans. The GOJ intends to build on this collaboration to produce an unemployment insurance scheme for the Jamaican people as well as meaningful social welfare reform.

As global interest rates rise, multilateral borrowing becomes more attractive as a source of funding as compared with international capital market alternatives. However, Jamaica and other middle-income countries, as determined by GDP per capita, have more limited access to concessional multilateral funding. The Caribbean has long argued that, in the allocation of multilateral financing opportunities, vulnerability ought to incorporate a multivariate perspective rather than the singular focus on GDP per capita. The IMF responded, and Jamaica recently accessed a low-interest US$764 million Resilience and Sustainability Facility.

There is therefore much to discuss in Kingston this week, and we welcome Mr Banga and Mr Goldfajn, as we work with them and their teams to advance Jamaica's agenda during this defining period of development opportunity.

Reforming the Public Sector

De-Earmarking of Public Bodies

Remarks, March 2017

Jamaica has approximately 190 public bodies. Countries with economies several times the size of Jamaica's economy have less than a quarter of this number of public bodies. There are currently a number of licenses, taxes, and fees that are collected directly by public bodies or earmarked for them (i.e., collected by the central government and turned over to them). The total revenues of these public bodies, including taxes, fees, licenses, and contributions were as high as approximately J$74 billion in 2015 – equivalent to approximately 20 per cent of central government tax revenues at that time! – while the expenses of those entities in that year were approximately $54 billion.

In an ideal world, the best public financial management principles support an efficient allocation of public resources, where all revenues first flow to the Consolidated Fund, with the central government allocating to each depending on the needs of the day. The advantages of this approach are:

1. Public bodies are not, by definition, fully included in the macro-fiscal plans and thus can present unexpected demands on the budget. In fact, much of Jamaica's debt – tens of billions of Jamaica's debt – arose as a result of several public bodies that found themselves in difficult times.

2. This type of financial management introduces rigidities and does not allow the government of the day to properly respond to the urgent problems of the day. It does not allow the government to prioritise and make choices. It therefore weakens government.

3. Resource allocation is inefficient, as earmarked public revenues and expenditures are not subject to the same public evaluation and scrutiny as the budget process for ministries, departments, and agencies.

Remarks delivered while Ambassador of Economic Affairs as part of a policy forum at the Office of the Prime Minister, March 21, 2017, Kingston.

4. Public bodies incur higher costs as small public bodies cannot achieve efficiencies in scale.

The history behind these public bodies and segregated funds relates to the lack of trust that the public has had in the administration of the county's finances over decades. The historical lack of fiscal discipline and accountability has undermined trust in central government, and therefore as a society we have preferred to warehouse funds in segregated entities.

However, the Government of Jamaica is entrenching fiscal discipline, and across two administrations deep structural reforms have been and are being made. Now is the time therefore to make public financial management more efficient by de-earmarking *eligible* public bodies.

This does not mean that the public bodies are not funded. It just means that the public body needs to justify its programme of expenditures each year like all other departments and agencies of government. Some years they may end up with more than they have now, and other years it may be less. However, at all times, the needs and priorities of all Jamaica are taken into account when Jamaica's money is being allocated and spent.

Public-Body Governance
Policy Address, June 2018

Ladies and gentlemen, good corporate governance is just as important in public enterprises as it is in the private sector. I posit that effective corporate governance is *even more critical* in the public sector since public funds are being utilised for the common good.

Public sector entities make a vital contribution to our social and economic circumstance by providing a range of essential public services in areas such as infrastructure development, public utilities, employment creation, social welfare, and economic growth. The effectiveness with which they provide those services and the efficiency with which they utilise the significant public resources at their disposal are matters of deep public interest.

As the Government of Jamaica pursues a comprehensive programme of public sector transformation and modernisation, the broad goal is to achieve greater efficiency, effectiveness, and economy in resource utilisation and service delivery, and, critically, to address perennial concerns of poor performance and management, financial irresponsibility, and weak mechanisms for monitoring accountability in government.

In January 2017, Cabinet approved the implementation of a Competency Profile Instrument for the boards of public bodies. It was recognised that for public sector boards to be high performing, their membership needs to be diverse, having a mix of experience and qualification as well as technical and interpersonal skills.

The Competency Profile allows for the selection and appointment of members who collectively possess the skills and experience deemed necessary for the effective functioning of the public body. This will promote greater effectiveness in board selection and composition processes and establish the government's benchmark for the oversight of public bodies. Permanent secretaries in the various

---

Adapted from a public policy address delivered to stakeholders at the Montego Bay Chamber of Commerce and Industry.

ministries have been sensitised by the Ministry of Finance and advised to encourage their relevant ministers to use this instrument when selecting board members.

In April 2017, Cabinet approved implementation of the Board Performance Evaluation Instrument for boards of public bodies. It is essential that there is in place a formal and rigorous process for regularly reviewing the performance of the board, its committees, and individual directors and purposefully addressing any issue that may emerge from those evaluations. The implementation of the Board Performance Evaluation Instrument signals the importance of transparency, accountability, integrity, and stewardship – all key to improving governance and transforming the public sector.

There will be a phased implementation of this instrument, and for this fiscal year a sample of twenty public bodies (comprising large, medium, and small), will test the instrument in their board performance evaluations for the 2017–18 period. This pilot will be undertaken with the assistance of the corporate secretaries and will test the adequacy of the training and support processes and facilitate learning that can be applied to a broader roll-out of the initiative.

The critical next phase towards improving board effectiveness is to formalise the processes – which are objective, transparent, and efficient – for the nomination, selection, and appointment of board members. To that end, the Office of the Cabinet, in collaboration with the Ministry of Finance and the Public Service, retained the Management Institute for National Development (MIND) to develop the appropriate policy guidelines.

Development of the policy guidelines benefited from consultations with diverse stakeholders through questionnaires, focus groups, and personal interviews. Stakeholders consulted included: permanent secretaries, academia, trade unions, parliamentarians, private sector organisations, professional bodies, NGOs, public commentators, and former and current senior public officers, among others.

The consultations were geographically diverse and included rurally based stakeholders. This dialogue revealed a general consensus that the current approaches to nominating, selecting, and appointing boards are in need of reform to reflect best practises.

There exist approximately 190 public bodies, each with board membership ranging from a low of seven to a high of seventeen persons. Problems do arise in the selection of appropriate board members, and a procedure for selection allows for membership to be developed in a planned, systematic, and coordinated way.

Ladies and gentlemen, I am pleased to announce that last week, on May 28, 2018, the Cabinet, in its commitment to public sector reform, good governance, and gender equity, approved a set of 'Policy Guidelines for the Nomination, Selection and Appointment of the Boards of Public Bodies.'[11]

The Policy Guidelines articulate comprehensive and transparent processes based on best practises and approaches for the nomination, selection, and appointment of board members. The Guidelines also refer to support mechanisms needed to ensure greater accountability of board members. Adherence to and reporting on this process is expected to lead to greater confidence in corporate governance for public bodies.

The Guidelines apply specifically to board appointments for public bodies as defined by the Public Bodies and Management and Accountability Act, which excludes the appointment of school boards and the advisory boards of executive agencies. Individuals appointed ex-officio by virtue of the office they hold under certain legislation, will also not be subject to the Guidelines.

The new process for nomination, selection, and appointment will be guided by five key principles which include: (1) merit/competence; (2) accountability and integrity; (3) transparency; (4) efficiency and effectiveness; and (5) commitment and capacity to serve.

The processes are to be followed in the event of a change of administration; a change of portfolio minister; the resignation or removal of an individual director or entire board; or the end of term of appointment for an individual director or the entire board.

Given that the lack of continuity on the boards of public bodies was identified as an issue during the consultations, the Policy Guidelines indicate that ministers should reappoint at least one-third of the outgoing board. All directors would be required to resign upon a change of administration or change of portfolio minister.

Meanwhile, reappointments are to be guided inter alia by the results of board member evaluations.

This is a culture change.

It is imperative for a board to acknowledge that it is the primary decision-making authority for its public body and thus is collectively responsible for governance, strategic management, and oversight. The board should also recognise that the CEO is primarily responsible for the day-to-day operation of the entity.

Ladies and gentlemen, it is to be noted that Cabinet remains the final approving authority in the appointment process, as Cabinet approval is required before board members can be appointed. This excludes the case where boards are appointed by the Governor General in consultation with the Prime Minister and the Leader of the Opposition, as defined by the statute (e.g., Early Childhood Commission and Broadcasting Commission).

Cabinet also approved, last week, the issuance of drafting instructions to the Chief Parliamentary Counsel for Regulations, under the Public Bodies Management and Accountability (PBMA) Act to be informed by sections of the Policy Guidelines.

Cabinet approval was further granted for strengthening the existing capacity within the Public Enterprises Division of the Ministry of Finance and the Public Service to support cabinet ministers in the nomination, election, appointment, and termination process for boards. The unit is expected to be tasked with: developing and maintaining a database of current directors and of persons with the required competencies to serve on boards of public bodies; conducting due diligence of prospective board members; facilitating the conduct of 'Fit and Proper' tests for some board members; facilitating board performance evaluations.

The database will be confidential and used only for the purposes of identifying, screening, and shortlisting prospective directors. The Secretariat will populate the database using various mechanisms including stakeholder recommendations and nominations; references; and applications to serve in response to targeted advertisement or other forms of invitation.

Ladies and gentlemen, in closing I must emphasise that the priority in the appointment process is to have the best mix of skills, qualification, and experience for boards of public bodies. The government anticipates that, in accordance with the guidelines to be implemented, there will be a huge change in how public bodies function. This will result in better public service to support growth of the Jamaican economy and help build greater investor confidence.

Nomination, Selection, and Appointment of Public Body Boards

Budget Speech Excerpt, March 2023

Madam Speaker, the Public Bodies Management and Accountability (Nomination, Selection and Appointment) Regulations 2021 came into full effect on January 20, 2023. What this means is that all appointments to public body boards should be made in accordance with the Regulations.

Let me remind you that the new process facilitated by the Regulations will seek to improve corporate governance within our public bodies. This includes enabling the selection of prospective directors who have satisfied the respective board competencies and, to a larger extent, the selection of the best-suited skillsets to aid in the overall functioning of the public bodies.[12]

As a further reminder, the main objectives of the Regulations are to improve the efficiency and effectiveness of our public bodies; to promote transparency in the nomination, selection, and appointment process for persons to public body boards; and to facilitate the inclusion of persons from a wider pool of professional competencies to help drive the strategic output of our public bodies.

The Ministry of Finance and Public Service has been involved in the development of an electronic portal to facilitate online applications of persons interested in serving on boards of public bodies, as well as applications from existing board members. Once applications are made via this online portal, the team at the Ministry will conduct a due diligence check, and thereafter the applicant will become part of the database for future selection. We at the Ministry recognise the importance of data protection, and as such, security protocols have been established and built into the electronic database.

Once a board vacancy arises – whether from a change of government, end of tenure, or any other reason – the database will be used by the Secretariat to generate a directory of persons with

---

Adapted from the opening budget presentation delivered in Parliament March 7, 2023.

matching competencies for the respective board. This directory will be used by the appointing authority to select and shortlist candidates. In some circumstances, persons may be appointed to the boards of select entities, which will necessitate a 'Fit and Proper' check to be conducted prior to final selection.

The online portal will be available April 1, 2023, and we will be relying on professional bodies, business associations, unions, and political parties, among other groups, to encourage their members to make themselves available for inclusion by completing the online application.

Introducing the Marcus Garvey Public Sector Graduate Scholarship

Budget Speech Excerpt, March 2020

Jamaica is entering a new era. An era of economic stability that allows us to plan and invest for the future. From the dawn of civilisation until the current time, all civilisations and countries that have achieved greatness have also had highly efficient and competent public services.

As other countries have done in modern times, Jamaica must make strategic plans to ensure that, to the best of our ability, we have a public sector resourced with highly qualified and technically proficient persons. In addition, we need a public service where there is an appreciation for how challenges and problems in respective fields are addressed and resolved by other countries around the world. International exposure and context in our public sector are critical for our small island developing state with ambitions to move forward and get ahead.

It was Marcus Garvey who exhorted us to 'Accomplish What We Will.'

The scholarship programme [that we seek to establish in his name] will be used as a tool to help attract, motivate, and retain qualified and high-potential staff. It will give public-sector employees an added incentive to remain in the government service, and it will include a mechanism to ensure that the scholarship recipients commit to adequate time in the government service to allow them to employ, and transfer where applicable, their new skills and qualifications. The Marcus Garvey Public Sector Graduate Scholarship will be a curated scholarship programme that will provide high-potential public-sector employees the opportunity to pursue graduate studies at our local universities and at the best universities in the world, thereby advancing their careers.

Adapted from the opening budget presentation delivered in Parliament March 10, 2020.

There are several existing scholarship opportunities available to Jamaicans for post-graduate studies. The more prominent of these include the Rhodes Scholarship, the Commonwealth Scholarship, the Chevening Scholarship, and the Fulbright Scholarship, all of which are externally funded. Other international scholarship programmes are also offered by our bilateral partners and the private sector.

With respect to public-sector employees specifically, the Education Grant for Public Sector Workers is a financial assistance programme that covers tuition costs up to a maximum of JM$150 thousand per annum for undergraduate or post-graduate programmes, certification courses, or Caribbean Secondary Education Certificate/Caribbean Advanced Proficiency Examinations. In 2018, this grant supported 1,073 public-sector workers. However, it is important to note that this programme does not meet the standards of a scholarship.

Currently there is no established post-graduate scholarship programme for public-sector employees. According to data from the Scholarship Unit of the Ministry of Finance and the Public Service, in 2017 there were two public-sector employees among the nine awardees of scholarships funded by bilateral partners and administered by the Unit; in 2018, out of nineteen awardees, two were public-sector employees.

The proposed Marcus Garvey Public Sector Graduate Scholarship Programme would be unique in that it is exclusively geared towards funding graduate studies for high-potential public-sector employees in strategic areas aligned with government priorities. Mr Speaker, the Marcus Garvey Public Sector Scholarship will provide thirty fully funded graduate scholarships each year, at the best universities in the world, for each of the next five years – that is 150 fully funded, exclusive graduate scholarships as we invest in and build the capacity of our public sector. These scholarships will support specific programmes aligned with government's priorities at universities including The University of the West Indies, University of Technology, Oxford University, Harvard University, Kings College, and John Hopkins University – entirely funded by the Government of Jamaica.

We say to ambitious, high-potential graduates of our universities: consider a public service career and you could win one of these prestigious Marcus Garvey Graduate Scholarships. We say to the hard-working members of our civil service: advance your career, expand your horizons, and develop your competencies by applying for one of these graduate scholarships.

These scholarships will cost $1 billion over five years and will be funded from the reserves of the Student Loan Bureau. Scholarship awardees will be required to work with government for a minimum period after completing their scholarships. Many countries including China, Chile, Brazil, Mexico, India, and Indonesia have successfully utilised [similar] graduate scholarship programmes to help build and improve the capacity of their public sector.

This is an initiative that I have been working on with the President of the Jamaica Civil Service Union, Mr O'Neil Grant, who is present in the Gallery, who represents the Government of Jamaica investing in the public sector. Thank you, Sir.

There has never before been a programme like this to develop the capacity of the public sector. We are not here simply to win elections, Mr Speaker, we are here to build a nation. I say to the members of the civil service of Jamaica who want to advance their careers, and to all well-thinking Jamaicans committed to strengthening the capacity of the public sector and building our nation: *Jamaica is moving in the right direction.*

Restructuring Public-Sector Compensation

Published Commentary, February 2022

Jamaica is experiencing a rapid economic recovery from the sharp and historic contraction of 2020–21 induced by the COVID-19 pandemic. For economic growth to continue at levels higher than our historical average, however, it will be necessary for the Government of Jamaica (GOJ) to continue to implement reforms that reduce the cost of business, improve labour and capital productivity, and increase resilience.

Transformation of the Public Sector

One of the central reforms aimed at boosting productivity is the transformation of the public sector. An efficient public sector is essential to sustained economic expansion. The GOJ is pursuing reforms to improve public-sector efficiency through five pillars: (1) rationalisation of public bodies; (2) introduction of enterprise systems for human resource management; (3) implementation of shared services; (4) digitising public-sector services; and (5) restructuring of public-sector compensation.

Through the GOJ's public-body rationalisation exercise, the number of public bodies has reduced from approximately 190 in 2016 to under 150 at the beginning of 2022. There have been mergers, divestments, and closures of public bodies, as well as reintegration of some bodies into parent ministries, with net fiscal savings of approximately $2 billion annually. Jamaica still has too many public bodies relative to the size of our economy, and public-body rationalisation needs to continue.

Our human resources represent the most important asset of the GOJ, yet we continue to rely on manual, paper-based HR systems. This compromises strategic decision-making at the policy level, leads to poor people decisions at the operational level, and results in sub-

---

An earlier version of this article appeared in the *Jamaica Gleaner*, February 6, 2022.

optimal employee experiences at the individual level. As such, the GOJ is implementing My HR+, a web-based integrated human resource management and payroll system across two hundred ministries, departments, and agencies (MDAs). This will bring synergies and efficiencies across MDAs, improve resource allocation, and produce better outcomes.

Jamaica risks falling further behind if we do not accelerate digitalisation. We either seize the opportunities for leapfrogging offered by this fourth industrial revolution or risk being outcompeted by other nations. Improving public-sector efficiency, and therefore Jamaica's productivity, will require that public services are accessible online, through digital and mobile platforms. The Jamaican citizen will then be able to file taxes, apply for and receive licenses and permits, and trade across borders in less time, boosting productivity. To achieve this, the GOJ is investing in communication infrastructure to connect MDAs. This network, GovNet, will provide the platform to automate processes within the GOJ.

The GovNet infrastructure will also facilitate implementation of shared services in the GOJ. Today, human resource administration, IT, internal audit, procurement, and other services are replicated across all MDAs. With the technologies available today, this replication is unnecessary and costly. The opportunity exists to make the required investments to organise the delivery of these internal services more efficiently. Standalone shared-service centres will specialise by service (e.g., HR) and will deliver across MDAs. This will offer greater professional scope for the service professional and better-specialised service for customers in a government MDA.

These are critically important reforms that form part of the public-sector transformation initiative. A most ambitious and challenging aspect of public-sector transformation is the restructuring of public-sector compensation.

The Existing Public-Sector Compensation System is Unsustainable

We know, anecdotally, that many nurses, teachers, doctors, police, and others migrate annually, seeking better terms overseas. In addition, we have technical, analytical, and managerial jobs across MDAs that are difficult to fill and remain vacant for extended periods, due to uncompetitive compensation. A modern state needs to attract and retain first-class management, IT, accounting, engineering, legal, public policy, data analysis, and other professionals. Among other staff needs, our hospitals need critical-care nurses, our schools need math and science teachers, and our police force needs detectives and patrol officers. We have shortages in these areas largely on account of remuneration levels.

Our public-sector compensation system is burdened by 325 salary scales that evolved from using multiple job-evaluation tools. By comparison, there are seven grade levels in the UK civil service. In addition, our compensation system incorporates 185 allowances. This is utterly unmanageable. This structure also leads to glaring real and perceived inequities, which are the source of much discontent. Our compensation system lacks transparency, and employees need spreadsheets to calculate their total income. Given the complexities, the GOJ has difficulty determining its total wage bill and, during periods of negotiation, it is challenging to keep track of the aggregate increase in the wage bill implied by claims and responses. The system exposes Jamaica to fiscal risks and is untenable.

We did not get here overnight or by design. Decades of tinkering with the systems, putting in place short-term measures to offset wage freezes, and appeasing bargaining units with allowances have contributed to this cumbersome compensation system. Today's system is unsustainable and needs to be restructured.

To the credit of public-sector unions, they have long realised and advocated for this. However, the two-year wage cycle, which had its origins in Jamaica's history of chronic economic instability, high inflation, and lack of fiscal prudence, worked against substantial reform. Historically, by the time the GOJ concluded its engagement with forty unions and bargaining groups, the two-year period would have long expired, and we would be halfway through, or at the end of, a new two-year cycle. Again, to the credit of Jamaica's public-sector unions, they agreed to a four-year wage settlement with the understanding that the GOJ would use the time to hire the required consultants and build the internal capacity to undertake the necessary analysis, data mining, costing, and planning towards a completely restructured compensation system.

Principles Guiding the Restructuring of Public-Sector Compensation

Four key principles guide this work. First, the new compensation system must be *simple and easily understood*. This means that we make compensation as clear, clean, and coherent as possible, so that public-sector employees can easily see the value of their total compensation package. This requires that we move away from a system based on allowances and towards a new structure that transparently contemplates total compensation. No longer will there be a basic salary with a plethora of allowances layered on top. That structure has not served the best interests of public-sector employees nor the GOJ.

Second, the new compensation system must be *fair and equitable*. This means we must have a consistent way of determining pay across the public service, which reflects the value we place on the work our public officers do. Consistency across the service requires that we significantly reduce the number of salary scales, eliminating the duplicity of scales that relate to what is essentially the same job function or jobs of equal value.

Third, it must *recognise and reward performance*. There should be a clear link between performance and pay progression, with transparent mechanisms for recognising and rewarding good, and especially excellent performance. So, we must move away from incremental progression based on length of service to progression based on performance that is grounded in the provision of increased incentives to perform.

Fourth, the system must be *sustainable and affordable*. While it is important to maintain competitive compensation levels, to build a strong public sector, we cannot defeat ourselves and throw away the fiscal sustainability we have achieved from ten years of sacrifice. A restructured compensation system must therefore be fiscally consistent with the debt-reduction objectives enshrined in our fiscal rules, which underpin the stability we enjoy, without compromising the levels of capital spending required to catalyse growth and improve the quality of life.

Implementation Time Frame

We had originally committed to begin implementation of this reform in April 2021. However, COVID-19 intervened, and the severe economic contraction and health crisis decimated and diverted resources. The GOJ therefore proposed a one-year delay to public-sector unions, with a modest increase in the interim.

The 2022–23 budget will be tabled in a few days. While the GOJ will continue to focus on economic recovery, restoring education, and improving security, this year's budget will prioritise implementation of restructured public-sector compensation. We plan to complete consultations with unions and other stakeholders and to engage in sensitisation and information sessions with public-sector employees. Thereafter implementation will begin, as soon as possible in the new fiscal year, with an effective date of April 1, 2022. It cannot all be achieved in one year, however, and will, in all likelihood, need to be phased in over three years.

Wage-to-GDP

This reform is happening in a context where Jamaica is not yet out of the woods. Our debt is still very high, and our economy remains vulnerable to shocks. The implementation of restructured public-sector compensation will lead to a significant rise in the wage bill, which will likely breach the 9 per cent wage-to-GDP target in Jamaica's fiscal responsibility law unless growth surprises on the upside.[13] However, if one were to incorporate the subset of allowances, (e.g., travel upkeep) that have not previously been included in the wage bill based on legal definitions, the breach would be smaller.

It is important to note that from debt-sustainability modelling and analysis, the higher wage bill associated with the planned restructured public-sector compensation will not compromise Jamaica's debt targets. Furthermore, capital investments as a proportion of GDP will increase in the upcoming fiscal year and continue to increase across the medium term. Notwithstanding the above, the higher wage bill will significantly diminish fiscal buffers and room for error.

The reduced fiscal flexibility implied by a higher wage bill makes it imperative that we accelerate implementation of other pillars of the transformation agenda, inclusive of the pursuit of higher growth, that can bring compensation as a percentage of GDP to more sustainable levels across the medium term. The restructuring of public-sector compensation is an ambitious, complex, yet necessary reform.

With Patience Let Us Allow Daylight to Finally Emerge

Published Commentary, May 2022

Restructuring public-sector compensation was never going to be easy, though the necessity of such a reform has long been obvious. The inordinate complexity of the exercise, the sheer breadth and range of its application, the magnitude of the changes required, and the risk to any government that embarked on such a process convinced many that this would never actually happen. However, with the support of public-sector unions, and the dogged determination of many, we are now within striking distance of some of the most profound and comprehensive structural changes to public-sector compensation by any administration. These changes are designed to simplify public-sector compensation overall, improve transparency, increase equity and fairness, and improve compensation levels while retaining the sustainability of Jamaica's finances.

At the point of delivering on an ambitious reform that promises improvement to tens of thousands, and that was once seen as remote and impossible, we are experiencing dislocation outside of recent experience. How can that be? An old proverb offers some insight: it is always darkest before dawn.

Our Torturous Fiscal History has had Unspoken Costs

Jamaica has had a tortuous economic and fiscal experience over the last several decades and, as a society, we have not fully accounted for the impact. As we teetered on bankruptcy, with unsustainable public finances, public-sector wages – the single largest GOJ expense – were frozen for five years between 2010 and 2015. Unimplemented provisions of pre-existing Memoranda of Understanding, which had a fiscal impact, were suspended. This, however, was not enough. Our fiscal rehabilitation required even more effort and yet more years of sacrifice.

An earlier version of this article appeared in the *Jamaica Observer*, May 14, 2022.

For the next five years, between 2015 and 2021, in an admittedly benign inflationary environment, wages moved by an average of 4 per cent, with a freeze applied to most allowances, while fiscally impactful sections of pre-fiscal-crisis MOUs remained unfulfilled by necessity. And public-sector workers were asked to accept, and have accepted, a 4 per cent increase for a further year (2021–22), with allowances frozen, which the economic onslaught of the global pandemic made necessary. The point is not the level of these increases but the fact that these agreements represented a long 'standstill.' A plethora of structural inequities remained intact throughout this period.

Achieving these agreements of restraint with public-sector unions over the past twelve years, across multiple administrations, has not been easy. In fact, it has been excruciatingly difficult. And there have been unspoken costs. For one, faith and trust in government, as a permanent institution across time, to deliver for public-sector employees, has suffered. Despite the success of heads of agreements, signed between the GOJ and union leaders, the trust deficit between government and the public-sector employee widened. In addition, the wells of public-sector dissatisfaction with respect to compensation, swelled. Just recall and reflect. Year after year, for twelve years: a very familiar gloomy message on matters related to compensation.

A Long Period of Wage Restraint Has Been Necessary

To be clear, wage restraint has been necessary for Jamaica's economic survival. And for completeness, Jamaica made a conscious and explicit social policy choice to retain the employment base of the public sector and instead pursue fiscal wage-adjustment through sustained wage restraint instead of through workforce reduction. Barbados, for instance, chose a different path, as their conditions are different. In the first year of their fiscal adjustment, in 2018, in response to their fiscal crisis, which was quite similar to ours, the Barbados government laid off approximately fifteen hundred public-sector employees (proportionally equivalent by relative public-sector sizes to more than ten thousand public-sector jobs in Jamaica!) and maintained social peace. Barbados laid off even more public-sector workers in 2019. They will likely have a different experience in the evolution of real public-sector salaries as a result of these reforms. In our experience of twelve years of wage restraint, therefore, while it is legitimate to acknowledge its impact, it is important to not see ourselves as victims. In the face of an existential fiscal crisis we, as a society, consciously and explicitly chose, and have since reaffirmed, our own path, with its set of advantages and disadvantages relative to other choices that existed.

The Forces of Tension at Work

I played an integral role in the process for the past six of those twelve years, first as Ambassador of Economic Affairs, then as Minister of Finance. We were only able to secure the agreements of restraint over the past six years, sometimes by slender margins, with repeated assurances, in the face of natural doubt, that the GOJ will implement comprehensive compensation reform. As such, much rides on this reform.

The credibility of unions, who persuaded employees to hold strain for twelve years and wait, is at stake. There is concern, too, and speculation, about the intended future of the public-sector collective bargaining process, in the context of the absence of 185 allowances, the presence of which fuels advocacy and which, in the current paradigm, provides existential justification for the fragmentation of bargaining groups.

For public-sector employees who have experienced an erosion of purchasing power over a decade and who have grown wary from a history of unimplemented promises there is an instinctive distrust that provides fertile ground for misinformation to grow. And when you have waited as long as public-sector employees have, and you now sense that this change is imminent, but worry that it could adversely affect you, anxiety overflows.

For the government and elements of non-public-sector civil society, there is great concern that opening the door to this reform, after more than a decade of steely containment, does not inadvertently send false messages that lead to runaway expectations that threaten hard-earned fiscal sustainability and macroeconomic stability. The government cannot be the only stakeholder in the conference room that sees the absolute necessity of preserving Jamaica's gains.

Understanding Dynamics Unleashed by the Imminence of a Long-awaited Reform

With the sense that implementation is imminent, these dynamics have the potential to create an unstable cocktail, as we have seen. This is complicated by the misfortune of having to implement the restructuring of public-sector compensation after a debilitating global pandemic, during a period of economic recovery, and during the worst global inflation in forty years, which has inflamed passions.

There is the further complication of sequencing of implementation. Who should be first: central government entities (civil servants, teachers, nurses, police, etc.) or public bodies? Everyone has waited just as long. Now that the reform is imminent, this question has taken on real significance.

In some cases, over the past several years, bargaining groups representing public bodies such as the National Water Commission (NWC), National Irrigation Commission, Civil Aviation Authority, Petrojam, and Broadcasting Commission, among others, were actually ahead of the rest of the GOJ in their agitation for reform (i.e., reclassification exercises). However, acceding to these requests, agency by agency, department by department, would only have entrenched and perpetuated the problem of multiple compensation systems, incompatible job evaluation bases, and a plethora of salary scales across government. What was needed instead was a comprehensive, across-all-of-government compensation reform. At various points over the last five years, and with much effort, we have been able to secure the support of multiple unions and bargaining groups representing these and other public bodies, to wait on the government-wide compensation reform.

That reform is now here. It is not yet complete, however. Only through consultations can it approach a semblance of completion (though it will, by definition, still fall short of perfection). These consultations are underway. In this phase, the Ministry of Finance and the Public Service (MOFPS) has had first-round consultations with forty-five of forty-seven public-sector unions and staff associations that represent central government groups. In these meetings, vital information has been shared with the unions and staff associations including new salary bands for their members, the slated actions for allowances, and a revised approach to benefits. We have asked our union partners to formally give us their feedback, which will inform the second round of consultations and provide an opportunity to clarify misconceptions and address any problems they may have.

As this phase of the process has proceeded, in April and May to date, and with round-the-clock meetings at the MOFPS with forty-five central government groups, it has fed the misconception among many public bodies that they are being left out. After all, their managements and bargaining groups are, as yet, unable to supply reliable information on how the exercise will affect them, even as they are aware that colleagues in many other parts of the government have received information. Though we are closer than ever before, for some public bodies which were persuaded, years ago, to subordinate their own attempts at reclassification to the across-all-of-government reform effort, the perception that progress is underway for some, that they are not experiencing, has led to palpable discontent.

But consultation with all groups will take time. And we have to sequence these consultations. For better or worse we have made a decision to conclude consultations with forty-seven central-government unions and bargaining groups first, to be followed by the 140 public bodies. Conditioned on progress with central government that facilitates timely implementation, we project to engage public bodies by November, more or less consistent with the timeline provided to the NWC.

We Ask for Patience

We therefore ask for patience. We need the same patience which allowed the hardworking teams to complete four years of work, setting up the policy framework for this reform, engaging the public sector about its key elements, procuring and engaging the services of multinational consultants, collecting and analysing data on 110,000 jobs, designing and completing surveys, modelling, forecasting, and communicating. After enduring the road phase of this reform marathon, we have now entered the stadium and are actually on the home stretch, in full visibility of the finishing line. It is supreme patience that got us here. As close as we are, we cannot now afford to collapse on the track. Instead, fuelled by that same patience, for just a few more months, we can make it across the finish line.

For other groups, as desirable as progress with the compensation restructuring is, it has only served to highlight that other issues are outstanding. The imminence of the compensation restructuring has intensified anxiety and frustration around these issues with the insistence that they be completed prior to implementation of the comprehensive reform. There is an eagerness to squeeze in other changes through what is seen as the wide door of comprehensive compensation reform. This is natural. However, while some of this is achievable, we must remember that we cannot make 'perfection the enemy of the good.' There are practical limits as to what this reform can achieve.

As our consultations have progressed, despite the efforts of our partners in unions and bargaining groups, partial and out-of-context information – along with, in some cases, gross misconceptions – have percolated in the employee space and aroused concern. Given the complexity of this exercise and the breadth of its applicability, we can only address these inaccuracies, some of which are local and specific, with time.

What 'No One Will Be Worse Off' Means

In the meantime, the blanket assurance, repeated over and over, that 'no public sector employee will be worse off' has been misconstrued to mean that we are inhospitable to consideration of what employees correctly or incorrectly see as detrimental. What the assurance instead means is that we expect thoughtful, analytic, rational, objective, reasoned, and expeditious feedback around the conference table in the next round of consultations, and, where it can be proven that someone would indeed be worse off, we will endeavour to find a fix that does not violate fundamental principles of the reform. Of course, a most fundamental principle is maintaining sanity in the trajectory of Jamaica's public finances, as erosion of this would only undermine the sustainability of these reforms.

This Is Our Country

In many ways, as a society, we have inherited and propagated the frames and narrative of oppression that emerged from power relations of a previous era – and sometimes misapplied these frames, and the associated language, to situations that are structurally different.

Contemporary violations by the State of fundamental rights, including the right to life, has unfortunately provided justification. Inequitable access to quality education and other services, which are at the root of many social ills, undermines the sense that we have progressed from colonial times. And partisan competition, where labels and accusations are hurled with reckless abandon by all sides to seek advantage from distress, ignorance, or confusion, is also a factor that often disguises the tremendous opportunity we have.

This is our country. We all own it. We are all privileged to have entrenched liberal, democratic traditions, free elections, a free press, and an independent judiciary. Unlike many other countries, it is those with the least resources who power our politics. Just view the membership roll of our political parties or visit an annual political conference. More importantly, through electoral and economic reforms that have defied international expectations, we have demonstrated the capacity to change our circumstances. We have agency, and the government works for you, for all Jamaicans. Unlike in times past, we are your brothers and schoolmates, we are your daughters and neighbours, we are your children and share the same church family. We are available and accessible.

A perceived slight, real or imagined, by an under-appreciated and hardworking Financial Secretary, even with emotions running high, ought not to kick the can over. The grotesque unfairness and inequity of public-sector compensation affects her more than many. She, like thousands of others, has endured this with dignity and served her country with distinction through an excruciatingly difficult period. You may not know her pain, but it resembles yours.

Chronic deficiency of resources, and inefficiency of our systems, explains much of our problems, and not indifference. This is why this compensation-restructuring reform is so essential. The efficient use of resources is a developmental imperative. A fair and equitable compensation system is essential to attracting and retaining the talent needed to design and manage an efficient bureaucracy. A compensation system that delivers liveable pensions is a key component of generational equity. A simple compensation system is critical to accomplishing more in the same time, a boost to national efficiency and productivity. And a transparent compensation system is important for employee satisfaction and an economically stable Jamaica.

We have approached this reorganisation of compensation with ambition. The public sector has been through a long night, and the day of reform finally approaches. But it is always darkest before dawn. Let not the darkness of this brief pre-dawn period lead us to stumble as a society. Kicking the can over, even if unintended, will only further delay the emergence of daylight, and even then, with spilt milk, daylight could not be sustained. Patience and orderly discourse, on the other hand, will allow a sustainable dawn to emerge.

Expanding Leave: Paternity, Maternity, and Family Leave in the Public Service

Press Statement, July 12, 2022

As you are aware, the Government of Jamaica (GOJ) is in the process of restructuring public-sector compensation. Compensation consists of not only wages and salaries but takes into account benefits like pension, and terms and conditions such as leave entitlements.

In 2018 we amended the Pension Act to make public-sector pensions equitable, fair, simple to administer, and sustainable.

As previously indicated, our discussions about the details of the compensation restructure take place with public-sector unions and bargaining groups around the conference table. That has been going well. We have completed first-round consultations with all public-sector unions and bargaining groups, and we are progressing with the second round of consultations.

Sometimes, however, it is necessary for me to signal to the country the direction of the reform, as I did a few weeks ago when I said that persons at the bottom of the compensation ladder in the public service – i.e., those earning $500,000 per annum and $600,000 per annum, and even lower amounts – can expect a significant adjustment to their compensation. Today, I intend to similarly signal the direction of this reform as it pertains to maternity leave, paternity leave, and family leave.

Coming out of the Compensation Restructure, and in reviewing the terms and conditions of service, the GOJ has decided to update the terms of maternity leave and to introduce a provision for paternity leave and leave for adoptive parents in the public service. All of these are components of total compensation.

The GOJ intends to update the Public Sector Staff Orders of 2004 to increase maternity leave from forty days to three calendar months.

The GOJ also intends to update the Public Sector Staff Orders of 2004 to introduce paternity leave for the first time in the public service, for fathers of newborns, for a specific time and on specific terms to be finalised.

The GOJ also intends to update the Public Sector Staff Orders of 2004 to introduce family leave for adoptive parents who are bringing a new child into the home.

We are working to modernise our public service. Modernisation is multifaceted. It includes pursuing efficiency and simplification; it embraces fairness and equity in compensation; it involves the application of technology to boost access and productivity; it requires better customer service; and it also embraces changes in terms and conditions that better reflect our values.

To give effect to these changes, the appropriate circular will be sent out to members of the public service by September 30.

Appeal for Reasonableness

Budget Speech Excerpt, March 2023

Madam Speaker, change is never easy. The public-sector compensation we are moving away from cannot take Jamaica forward. *We need a compensation system that is simple and easy to understand.* The old compensation system is not.

There is a separate salary scale for: health record officers, meteorologists, videographers at JIS, secretaries, drivers, legal officers, office attendants, public health inspectors, social workers, pharmacists, clerical officers, accountants, and librarians. There are 325 separate salary scales altogether, which is overly complex and utterly unmanageable.

The new compensation system has a core salary scale with sixteen bands, which introduces simplicity and efficiency. There are three additional salary scales for teachers, security forces, and health practitioners that are aligned to the core scale.

We also need a compensation system that is fair and equitable. The old system was not. The old compensation system was characterised by 185 separate allowances which made compensation difficult to understand. With a plethora of tax-free and taxable allowances, public officers sometimes are not able to make like-for-like comparisons.

Pensionable public officers suffer in retirement with pensions that bear little similarity to pre-retirement income, even after thirty-three years of service. That is so as non-pensionable allowances made up 40 to 60 per cent of income in many instances.

The structure of allowances made compensation non-transparent in that allowances totalling 1 per cent of GDP were included under programmes, but not salaries and wages. The structure of allowances

---

Adapted from the opening budget presentation delivered in Parliament March 7, 2023.

introduced inequities within and across public sector groups in other ways as well.

One of the largest allowances in aggregate was the travelling allowance. Introduced decades ago, it was designed to reimburse public officers who travelled for their job. Not for travelling to and from work but travelling done in the performance of one's public duties. Over decades, however, the rules around who could be designated a travelling officer, and therefore be in receipt of the travelling allowance, became lax, and this travelling allowance morphed into a kind of allowance that symbolised the status of the job or, in some public bodies, it was used to supplement pay.

As such, it should be no surprise that travelling became the single largest allowance in the public sector. But, along the way, it lost its purpose. Thousands of public-sector employees received travelling allowance who sat behind their desk forty hours a week, every working week of the year, who stayed at a single address for every working hour of their lives.

Travelling was adjusted by rates that were sometimes higher than the increase in basic pay, which meant those in receipt of the travelling allowance generally fared better than others who were out of wage negotiations. This was not fair, nor equitable, nor reasonable, especially when the travelling allowance was indiscriminately applied to include thousands who did not travel for their job. So, we have reformed the travelling allowance from being a fixed, job-based allowance to being an activity-based reimbursement through a reformed, reimbursable mileage component.

Before, travelling allowance came with the job, whether you actually travelled or not. We have absorbed that travelling into salaries, so no one is worse off, and increased compensation net of taxes by a minimum of 20 per cent over three years. To achieve a net pay increase of 20 per cent when absorbing a no-taxable allowance means that the gross pay increase is much higher than 20 per cent.

So, the new travelling arrangement provides a rate that is paid per mile, for miles actually travelled. That way, the manager behind his or her desk forty hours a week, or who works from a single address, cannot qualify for this reimbursement. This is fairer and more equitable, for the public officer and for the taxpayer who is paying the bill.

Now, changing from one compensation system to another for the entire civil service is quite an undertaking. You know I have completed two previous rounds of negotiations. The negotiations that covered the period 2017–21 and the negotiations that covered the 2021–22 fiscal year. Across this five-year period we agreed to the same fixed-percentage increases, which means all 110,000 employees received the same percentage increase on basic salary. So, the question is, why didn't we leave the system as it was and simply agree on a percentage increase that everyone would get? Surely it would have been *much* easier.

It would have been cheaper, too! It would have been quicker, and it would have been less 'noisy' and uncomfortable. We did not choose that easier course as it would not improve our circumstances. *The government exists to take on the tough challenges that can improve outcomes and quality of life for all.*

Moving everyone in lockstep would not solve the myriad challenges that we have with attracting and retaining talent and skills in the public service. Let me share an example: with a country where over thirty thousand persons have been murdered or killed over the past twenty-five years, our country is drenched in grief and drowning in psychological trauma. Hearts are bleeding, . Souls are dying. Suppressed anguish, raw pain, and unresolved heartache are at the root of anti-social behaviour and sub-optimal levels of conduct and achievement.

Our country, with our history, needs trained counsellors and social workers who can help with the healing the nation needs. However, the remuneration for social workers in the public sector was artificially depressed, as compensation for groups that were generally in the same pay bracket received adjustments which moved them away from social workers as a group. This resulted in compensation for that group that is inconsistent with our state of affairs and not reflective of the work done by social workers. So, the compensation review and restructuring allowed us to make adjustments to the pay structure for social workers that could not be achieved in the usual one-size-fits-all, lockstep approach.

Jamaica's bureaucracy needs to be able to attract and retain managerial and technical talent. We need the best IT technicians, communication specialists, network engineers, legal draftspersons, civil engineers, data scientists, lawyers, accountants, prosecutors, economists, managers, and HR officers, as examples, to deliver premium service to the public. We have vacancies in the economics unit at the Ministry of Finance we have not been able to fill for years. This is also true in the Attorney General's Chambers, and in technical and managerial areas across government, where turnover on account of salary levels has been at epidemic proportions. This has been a crisis. The system is breaking because we don't have sufficient talent, for long enough periods, in all the areas we need, and we are unable to attract the talent needed because of the low compensation levels.

We needed to make adjustments to the compensation levels in many of these technical and managerial areas to be in a position to attract and retain talent in the public service, and the adjustments required are not all the same.

Again, Madam Speaker, the compensation review and restructuring allowed us to make adjustments to the pay structure for certain categories, like social workers, that could not be achieved in the usual 'same percentage with a lockstep' approach. So, as we mapped from 325 separate salary scales to a core single-spine structure with sixteen bands, the compensation restructuring, by design, resulted in differential upward adjustments across the public sector. This was, and is, at the root of much of the unease and tension that has been observed.

When everyone receives an increase of 5 per cent, there are no comparisons to be made. However, in a compensation restructuring with differentiated outcomes, comparisons are inevitable. Instead of the employee looking at what he or she has received in the context of what he or she received in the past, persons begin to compare with their *perception* of the circumstances of others, without full information.

Madam Speaker, we have allocated $10.2 billion for rank-and-file police officers, with an additional $1 billion for District Constables, and $600 million for members of the Police Officers Association, totalling $11.8 billion that is ready to go. We want members of the

Police Force to receive these payments in March 2023. The total amount we have for the teachers is approximately $12 billion, that is ready to go. We want the teachers to receive these payments in March 2023. The total amount we have for the junior doctors is $6.4 billion. We want the doctors to receive these payments in March 2023.We want to be in a position for these amounts to leave the Consolidated Fund in March 2023. These amounts total $30 billion. This size of payment cannot be accommodated in the upcoming fiscal year on top of everything else, and the law prevents unused amounts this year from being carried over to finance expenditure next year.

My deeper concern is that in comparing with each other, the big picture is escaping us.

I have presented the facts. I have personally participated in hundreds of meetings, in person, virtually, on the phone, WhatsApp calls, on the weekend, morning, noon and night.

But Madam Speaker, what more can I do?

Should I put at risk all the progress that Jamaica has made?

Should I reverse the economic gains made through mutual sacrifice?

I have put together a package that is larger than what has been implemented over the last ten years combined. Teachers, Nurses, Firefighters, Doctors, Police – I know that you deserve more. But the truth is, at this time, I cannot do any more. We can't reach the Promised Land in one step. There will be another opportunity before too long to work together on achieving some of the outstanding goals.

Madam Speaker, my mother was a teacher for nearly twenty years. She spent over a decade as a classroom teacher. I am a classroom teacher's son. I know as a student and a son that what the classroom teacher does is extraordinary. In fact, it's magical. How does one weigh and measure the ability to inspire? My mother worked in the public service for her entire working life. In her time, there were many instances when back pay was two, three or four years after the fact. I know the impact of that on a family. We do not want to go back there.

I have presented the facts. I appeal for reasonableness.

Leadership Salaries in the Public Service
Published Commentary, May 2023

Throughout Jamaica's independent history, matters connected with compensation for members of the Legislative and Executive branches of government have attracted controversial reaction. This was the case in 1972, 1990, 2003, and again in 2023.

This is understandable. There is a general view that, measured across decades, Jamaica has underperformed vis-à-vis our peers. This underachievement is seen, first and foremost, as the underachievement of the Legislative and Executive branches of government over time. Some therefore have viewed the political directorate as completely undeserving of improved compensation. Other members of the public doubt whether improved compensation will actually lead to improved outcomes for them. And though some express comfort with the elevated levels of pay, they would like this to be accompanied by greater levels of accountability. These are all reasonable concerns.

Salaries of cabinet ministers have been benchmarked to the salaries of permanent secretaries for the better part of fifty years. Since about 1986, the framework pegged the salaries of ministers at '$52 dollars per annum above the maximum of the highest level Permanent Secretary.' And pay for Members of Parliament has tracked 62.5 per cent of the Cabinet Minister's pay since 1990. In updating ministerial and parliamentary pay, the existing frameworks, which have been used for thirty-seven and thirty-three years respectively, have simply been applied to the new central-government salary scale. To understand the movement in pay for the political directorate, therefore, one has to understand the underlying movement in the benchmark central-government salary scale.

The entire central-government and public-service salary scales have been revised in the context of the broader restructuring of

---

An earlier version of this article appeared in the *Jamaica Gleaner*, May 21, 2023.

public-sector compensation. Among other things, this exercise incorporated insights from the market study, that compensation for senior levels in the public service was the most depressed as compared to the Jamaican market. This is consistent with anecdotal observation. If we fail to retain the most promising public servants to eventually serve in leadership, we all lose. Public-sector leaders in the civil service, and across professional groups, are responsible for making consequential decisions that affect the public and all the employees within their organisations. They allocate significant financial and human resources, they make strategic choices, and they process copious amounts of information. Having the right persons in leadership across the public sector can make a substantial difference in the attainment of targeted outcomes, even with the same level of national resources.

However, levels of pay for the leadership across the administrative public sector have been dramatically below what is required to retain the most competent public servants and interest them in leadership opportunities or to attract external candidates.

The politics (common 'p') of addressing this reality has always been challenging and explains why this nationally self-defeating status quo has persisted. Prior to now, we have subordinated the long-term good to fear of distorted short-term optics. That cannot continue. Our collective vision for Jamaica can only be realised if some of the most talented and promising young persons our education system produces see public service as a viable first-choice career option. If Jamaica is to succeed, the public service must also be attractive enough to allow lateral recruitment of accomplished private citizens, across diverse fields, into positions of public-sector leadership.

As such, the salary scale for Permanent Secretaries, who manage budgets of up to $150 billion dollars, moved from between $7.4 million and $9.26 million as at April 2021 to between $15.8 million and $21.2 million as at April 2023. There have been similar movements across public-sector leadership.

For example, for secondary and primary school principals, at the largest schools, the starting point on the scale has moved from $2.9

million and \$2.4 million respectively to \$8.5 million and \$7.0 million respectively.

The starting point in the salary scale for the highest three of eight levels in the nursing profession has moved from \$2.6 million, \$3 million, and \$3.6 million to \$7.3 million, \$8.3 million, and \$9.3 million respectively.

The starting point in the salary scale for the highest three of six levels for non-executive legal officers has moved from \$3.4 million, \$4.1 million, and \$4.9 million to \$6.8 million, \$8.3 million, and \$10.1 million respectively.

Space does not permit a full account here, but the point should be clear. There has been a material adjustment in net compensation for the leadership across the public sector, even after factoring in the absorption of relevant allowances. This information is all publicly available on the Ministry of Finance's website or through a simple Google search of 'new public sector compensation in Jamaica.'

At the same time, it was morally necessary that the restructuring provide much-improved compensation for those at the lowest end of the salary scales. As such, the salary scales for over five thousand weekly paid ancillary and artisan staff have moved by a range of 60 per cent to 300 per cent. For instance, the entry-level ancillary salary level in government has moved from \$9,781 per week to \$16,481 per week. The supervisors in the ancillary ranks, and the most skilled artisans, have moved from a starting point of \$13,714 per week to \$47,656 per week.

In undertaking a public-service-wide adjustment to compensation, which has no precedent in Jamaican history, we established salary levels for the jobs, not the personalities who may occupy the jobs today. Rather, it is about the quality and experience that Jamaica will be able to attract and retain in positions of public-sector leadership over the long term.

With compensation that is more aligned with the level of responsibility of the job, the bargaining power of the employer (i.e., the public) will be greatly strengthened, which, if properly used, will deliver much better governance over time. With these adjusted salaries for the political directorate, in particular, there will have to be improved standards and greater accountability.

There will be a demand for better performance, too. The next phase of compensation reform involves implementation of a 'Fit for Purpose' performance management system. We have committed to work with our union partners to have this ready for the public sector in April 2025.

It is indeed the case that the salaries for our political directorate will be higher than corresponding salaries in CARICOM countries. It is also true that Jamaica is the only country in the region to have implemented a public-sector-wide compensation restructuring, and Jamaica's Permanent Secretary pay scale also exceeds regional counterparts. Jamaica has taken a deliberate decision to invest in the human capital of its public sector.

Some ask, how can salary arrears now be afforded for politicians in 2023–24 when the position was that arrears for other groups needed to be paid in 2022–23? As previously explained, it is a matter of scale. We could not afford to carry over $40 billion of unpaid arrears, relating to last year, into this year. For parliamentarians and ministers, the aggregate 2022–23 arrears are much smaller, and in fact not comparable, and therefore manageable.

Others ask, how could you have said there were no more resources available for other groups and now politicians enjoy this adjustment? Again, this is answered by reference to materiality. The adjustment for parliamentarians and ministers represents approximately 0.6 per cent of the first-year cost of the reform. Put another way, if the entire amount of the adjustment allocated to parliamentarians and ministers for the first year was reallocated to all other public-sector employees this would have resulted in an upward adjustment of maybe $400 per month, before taxes, across the public service.

The job of the politician is ruthlessly demanding. It is also of consequence. Politicians make material decisions that affect millions of lives for a long time. Analysis of raw data available from Parliament suggests that there have been 309 members of Parliament since 1972. Up to 2023, the median parliamentary tenure has been eight years, and the average, 9.98 years. For most of those who enter Parliament, consistent with what a system of government 'of the people' should be, Parliament has not been a lifetime assignment.

Our country's future is best assured by having a system where more qualified and experienced Jamaicans find it attractive and financially feasible to offer themselves for political service for at least some portion of their careers. That way, Jamaica wins.

Public Investment Management System Crucial for Development

Published Commentary, June 2023

Public investment, which has the potential to transform quality of life, is investment by the Government of Jamaica (GOJ) in assets. Public investments generate positive externalities where benefits spill over, creating other benefits in a positive-chain reaction. Cutting the commute time between two cities, with a new highway, makes new businesses, new logistics arrangements, and new residential, office, and warehouse developments more feasible. Public investments are therefore often growth inducing.

However, public investments typically involve large sums and multi-year commitments. Weak public-investment management systems can therefore imperil public finances and compromise intended development outcomes.

Governments of Jamaica have long recognised the dangers of weak public-investment management systems and acted to strengthen Jamaica's regime. In November 2009, Cabinet approved the Public Sector Investment Prioritisation Framework as the framework through which public investments would be ranked for budgetary support. This was a first step in addressing the problem. By 2011, some of the impact of the structural weaknesses in Jamaica's public-investment system were documented in the Third Review under the IMF Stand-By Arrangement published in February 2011, which stated: 'The authorities [i.e., the GOJ] also agreed with staff [i.e., the IMF] that there was an urgent need to tighten procedures for evaluating and monitoring public investment projects. Cost overruns related to certain road construction projects have reached as high as 50 per cent. These included design flaws that subsequently had to be corrected as well as escalation of material and labour costs during project execution.'[14]

An earlier version of this article appeared in the *Jamaica Gleaner*, June 11, 2023.

Public investments often involve funding by way of grants or loans from multilateral and bilateral partners. These partners will refrain from participating, or lower their participation, if public-investment management weaknesses remain unaddressed.

The European Commission has been the largest provider of grant assistance to the Government of Jamaica. The Public Expenditure and Financial Accountability (PEFA) Report of 2013, sponsored by the European Commission and conducted in close cooperation with the World Bank, Inter-American Development Bank (IDB) and the UK's Department for International Development (DFID) identified the absence of an [effective] public-investment management system as a weak link in Jamaica's Public Financial Management System.

The report found that there were no rules-based procedures or institutions, and no governance mechanisms for analysing, prioritising, managing, monitoring, and evaluating the efficiency and effectiveness of public investment projects. As such, projects were poorly designed and inadequately planned, with little feasibility analysis prior to proceeding with the implementation.

In 2014, legislative action created a comprehensive definition of public investment and set out a Public Investment Management System (PIMS) to address poor project design and weak institutional capacity. The legislation prescribed the establishment of a Secretariat to appraise all project ideas and to evaluate subsequent proposals that flow from these ideas, prior to the Public Investment Management Committee taking a decision to recommend projects to the Cabinet for inclusion in the Public Sector Investment Programme. The legislation also mandated the Secretariat to incorporate a monitoring and evaluation system.

In December 2016, Cabinet approved the guidelines establishing the operation of the PIMS, inclusive of the requirements for project concepts, project appraisal, and project proposal development, and inclusive of feasibility analysis and business case. At the launch of the PIMS, then-Minister of Finance Audley Shaw hailed the occasion as one of 'great significance' and warned that it would not be 'business as usual…as we can no longer continue to tolerate the poor performance of public investment projects.'[15] Consequently, the

Financial Administration and Audit Act Instructions were amended in 2017 to be consistent with the new guidelines.

The reform, which spanned administrations, was funded by a World Bank loan and a grant from DFID and was initially set up as a project, with the Secretariat staffed by temporarily engaged consultants contracted to the Ministry of Finance and the Public Service (MOFPS). When the loan came to an end in December 2021, the GOJ folded the Secretariat into the permanent apparatus of Government, creating the Public Investment and Appraisal Branch (PIAB) in the MOFPS. The PIAB is the single point of entry for all projects intended for the Public Sector Investment Programme.

Jamaica's improved fiscal profile has accommodated a doubling of central government capital-expenditure budgetary allocations over the past seven years. The maintenance of Jamaica's downward debt trajectory is key to raising capital expenditure allocations, as a proportion of GDP, to levels that can accelerate improvements in quality of life while elevating rates of growth.

The 2014 legislation, the 2016 guidelines, and the 2017 financial instructions create a robust PIMS. Paraphrasing former Minister Shaw, this is great. It serves the long-term public interest and assures our bilateral and multilateral partners that resources that they provide for public investment projects, whether by grant or loan, will be properly and efficiently used. This allows Jamaica to obtain more external support, on better terms.

In February, parliamentarians expressed bipartisan concern about aspects of the PIMS. Some valid points were made. We may need to introduce modest thresholds and extract isolated maintenance expenditure from the definition of public investment.

As such, the PIMS Guidelines and User Manual will be revised this calendar year. More importantly, however, some observations imply a fundamental lack of awareness and/or capacity within ministries, departments, and agencies (MDAs) [relative to PIMS]. Ministries have to address these capacity gaps. To assist, the MOFPS is designing a PIMS curriculum, to be delivered by the Management Institute of National Development, that will provide training for persons in MDAs who interface with the PIMS.

Jamaica's robust PIMS is necessary. It should not be diluted nor weakened. However, the PIMS can be strengthened by ensuring that MDAs are equipped to navigate it.

Achievements of Public Sector Transformation

Budget Speech Excerpt, March 2024

We embarked on the construct of the Public Sector Transformation Programme in 2017, following the Prime Minister's announcement of the government's policy position on modernising the State. The Transformation Implementation Unit in the Ministry of Finance and the Public Service developed a six-year programme with funding support from our International Development Partners, the Inter-American Development Bank (IDB) and the World Bank. I would like to publicly thank our development partners for the continued support that they have provided to the government and people of Jamaica in key areas of our development agenda.

As a part of any loan agreements with our development partners, we agree on certain measures that are to be achieved, and these measures are used by the development partner to assess the performance of the project.

It is with a sense of pride that I stand here today and report that the Public Sector Transformation Programme, funded by the IDB, is the first IDB-funded programme to have achieved all the measures agreed with the IDB within the agreed timelines and loan amounts.

A 'nuh me sey suh.' This is from the IDB.

The Transformation Implementation Unit, its head, Mrs Maria Thompson Walters, and the Financial Secretary are deserving of our recognition. The audit and final evaluation of the programme will be conducted between April and June of this year.

What did we do differently?

Given Jamaica's long history with reform, we had to do things differently to get more positive outcomes. We knew from experience that the programme had to be tight, with realistic targets. We also had to mitigate the procurement risk by ensuring agility of the

---

Adapted from the opening budget presentation delivered in Parliament March 12, 2024.

programme with respect to design and implementation. Importantly, we had to ensure adequate human and financial resources for implementation.

We were clear at the outset that this programme would be a hybrid one in that we were laying the foundation for transformation as a continuous activity in the public sector whilst implementing projects that would have a direct impact on how the public sector operates in the short term. Therefore, the public sector transformation programme was built on five pillars:

1. Expanding the use of Information and Communication Technologies in the public sector to drive efficiency and effectiveness;

2. Building a shared services operation as a means of transforming the way government provides service internally;

3. Transformation of human resource management practises;

4. Compensation management; and

5. Rationalising our public bodies.

Making Better Use of ICT for Efficiency

Under this programme, the Government of Jamaica has made significant strides in making better use of Information, Computing, and Technology, known as ICT, in the public sector. I am pleased to announce, that at last, we now have a dedicated broadband infrastructure for the public sector. This is a significant development, because many of you would have been hearing about GovNet for quite some time and may have been wondering if it would ever become a reality.

As we speak, over two hundred entities in the Kingston Metropolitan Area are now directly connected to the system. The system has also provided connectivity for an additional five hundred entities including schools, courts, and police stations. At the same time, under the IDB-funded Public Sector Transformation Programme, we upgraded the data centre at eGov Jamaica to expand data storage capacity by 260 per cent.

We have also provided the public sector with additional cloud infrastructure and all the automated management tools and security components that are needed for eGov to operate a modern data centre on behalf of the rest of the public service. I had the pleasure of touring the data centre recently and seeing the infrastructure first hand.

When you are able to have an expanded and upgraded government data centre, you are able to consolidate the disparate data centres across government into one location where you can apply consistent management protocols and ensure that data is secure and kept private.

Under the Public Sector Transformation Programme, the Transformation Implementation Unit partnered with four governmental entities to implement systems that improve the way they deliver key services, that is, to improve their productivity.

We partnered with the Passport, Immigration, and Citizenship Agency (PICA), to implement a customer relationship management system at the agency. The system went live November 13, 2023, and all customer interactions are being processed through it.

At the National Fisheries Authority (NFA), we have enabled that entity to implement IrieFINS – a web-based fisheries licensing and registration system for fishers and fish farmers. The system went live in February of this year and is a game changer for the NFA. Through IrieFINS, the NFA can now issue and retrieve licences and permits more efficiently. They can also utilise the data generated by the system to inform reports and support proposals and decisions.

We expect greater compliance with the licensing requirements by active fishers to improve from 10 per cent in 2018 to at least 60 per cent by the end of the new fiscal year. I am sure the Minister of Agriculture will speak more on this in the sectoral debate.

At the Ministry of Labour and Social Security, the Public Sector Transformation Programme is supporting the implementation of an effective and user-friendly, web-based Work Permit System to improve the processing of work permits and CARICOM Skills Certificate applications. We expect that this will result in a reduction in the time it takes to process these applications, from eight weeks to two weeks in the first instance.

Transformation of Human Resource Management Through MyHR+

Still on the ICT front, we have completed the first phase of the implementation of MyHR+ – an integrated HR and payroll management system. I am told that MyHR+ is the first enterprise system successfully deployed in the public sector – serving all Ministries, Departments, and Agencies. The system is now being used by approximately seventy ministries, departments, and agencies, which is putting the government on a path of better management of its most critical resource – our people.

The system has now enabled HR and payroll teams to maintain and access employee information, allowing for more efficient management of employee data, and has contributed to better internal customer satisfaction, better people decisions, better views of the organisation with better internal controls, and better reporting.

Madam Speaker, MyHR+ allows public-service employees to service themselves rather than wait three weeks for HR to get back with information or letters. Since the roll-out of MyHR+, more than eighty-four thousand self-service transactions have been processed. MyHR+ is also the platform on which we were able to successfully pilot HR shared services. We have also conducted pilots for internal audit, payroll, and finance and accounts shared services.

We are currently piloting the procurement shared service function. These pilots have confirmed that this approach for the provision of services is sound and feasible. Our next step is to establish the Shared Service Department as a permanent feature of government.

Restructuring of Public Sector Compensation

We undertook a significant initiative to restructure the public sector compensation system. We had to abandon the old system. It was not adequately serving the employee or the government. We have introduced a system that is fair, simple, and sustainable.

It has not been easy but we have implemented a new, single sixteen-band pay system for the public sector, reducing the multiplicity of salary scales from 325 to 16 bands.

This was accomplished by:

- Developing and implementing a new job evaluation tool;

- Conducting a market survey to determine where the government falls within the Jamaican labour market;

- Using the data from the market survey to develop a new sixteen-band pay structure; and

- Converting all public sector workers to the new sixteen-band structure.

The coming fiscal year will mark the final year of transition to the new compensation structure.

In addition, we have rationalised allowances which put persons in a better position when they retire to get a better pension, and to simplify the payroll.

There is not much precedent anywhere, for a country to engage in this kind of comprehensive restructuring of compensation – across all areas of government – at the same time.

Rationalisation of Public Bodies

The fifth pillar of public sector transformation was rationalisation of public bodies. I have often spoken about the number of public bodies operating in Jamaica and the governance challenge this poses.

At the start of the transformation programme, there were 190 public bodies in existence. The reality is that some public bodies have achieved their mandate, others have overlapping functions and responsibilities, and some public bodies are at a stage where they can be seamlessly integrated into their parent ministries.

I am pleased to announce that we have made progress and have reduced the number of public entities by forty-one. This has realised recurrent and capital savings of over J$2 billion, a tangible outcome of public sector transformation.

It is without doubt that the transformation of the public sector is happening. It is a journey, and we are well on our way to building a better public sector for all.

Strengthening the Social Safety Net

Social Development Foundations
for Jamaica 2.0

Published Commentary, July 2020

In my column [of July 19, 2020], I made the point that the COVID-19 pandemic would have serious and significant economic consequences. I wrote that while Jamaica is better placed than ever before to absorb and recover from the shock, there will be little room for policy error.

Macroeconomic stability eluded Jamaica for fifty years. Until recently, we have not had the concurrent experience of low inflation, adequate foreign reserves (measured by an objective international metric), financial-sector stability, and fiscal sustainability. Getting here took much effort and sacrifice.

History suggests that macroeconomic stability is necessary for economic recovery and growth, but not sufficient. There are other foundations that are just as important. In [this article], I draw on the COVID-19 Economic Recovery Task Force Report (Task Force Report) to make the case that recovery to the envisioned Jamaica 2.0 will need a strong social foundation – not just from a social protection standpoint but also more broadly, providing the supporting infrastructure – to improve the productivity and lives of people.

While Jamaica's social challenges long predate COVID-19, the crisis has unveiled social fragilities that need to be addressed for Jamaica's sustainable and resilient recovery. There are several important elements to developing Jamaica's social foundation.

Economic Formalisation

The sub-optimality of informality, for the State and citizen, has been brutally exposed by the pandemic. According to the International Labour Organisation, an informal economy refers to 'all economic activities by workers and economic units that

---

An earlier version of this article appeared in the *Jamaica Gleaner*, July 26, 2020.

are – in law or in practise – not covered or insufficiently covered by formal arrangements.' It also defines informal employment as 'all remunerative work (i.e., both self-employment and wage employment) that is not registered, regulated or protected by existing legal or regulatory frameworks.'[16]

The informal economy is a persistent feature of developing economies. It is estimated that approximately 60 per cent of Jamaica's employment is informal. Employment data as at January 2020 estimated employment at 1,269,100 jobs, while active contributors to the National Insurance Scheme (NIS) total approximately 500,000.

According to STATIN data, more than 90 per cent of persons who work in or around the home are informally employed. In addition, more than 80 per cent of those who work in construction, more than 60 per cent of those who work in wholesale/retail, and more than 50 per cent of those who work in transportation are informally employed. The challenge for the State and citizen is that most often, informal workers do not have formal employment contracts and do not participate in the Government of Jamaica's flagship social protection scheme, the NIS.

As we have seen from the COVID-19 experience, participation in formal systems provides easier means of validation in accessing government-assistance programmes. Conversely, informality obstructs social-assistance efforts. This imposes invisible costs that affect us all.

Informality is not exclusive to Jamaica. What we know from experience across the world is that informality flourishes where labour markets are rigid and where inclusion in the formal system is costly in time, effort, and resources.

In particular, payroll tax deductions in Jamaica are unnecessarily complicated. Payrolls are subject to four statutory deductions – Education Tax, HEART, NIS, and National Housing Trust (NHT) – each calculated on different income bases and in different ways. Though progress was made with reform that allows for these to be amalgamated and submitted on one form, the complexity of the regime accounts for much of the informality that exists.

Zooming in on one specific example, domestic workers are among the most disenfranchised groups with respect to NIS participation.

The very persons who could most benefit are often the ones excluded by structural barriers. And anecdotal evidence suggests that their underrepresentation is not only due to the incremental dollar cost of statutory deductions but also to the complexity of filling out forms, calculating four tax types on different bases, and filing monthly deductions.

The Task Force Report recommends replacing the current system with a single consolidated statutory deduction, which is then allocated among the various uses. This would lead to greater administrative efficiency and compliance and help increase formalisation of activity. For some employment groups, such as domestic workers, the Task Force recommends that streamlining could go a step further by allowing for annual contributions.

Greater formalisation would make it easier to build a social registry of all families with incomes below a particular threshold, to whom State-sponsored social assistance can be administered during a crisis. This database would be separate from PATH, though there would be some overlap. As we know, working people who would not ordinarily qualify for PATH can become vulnerable in times of crisis. Pre-crisis income level is a workable proxy for this vulnerability. Having a such a registry is essential to building economic resilience.

Unemployment Insurance

Pre–COVID-19, unemployment was at historical lows. However, for many Jamaicans, household wealth is insufficient to serve as an income stabiliser in bad times. The government's CARE Programme thereby serves an important function in the short term. Over the medium term, however, we will need to strengthen social protection with more permanent institutions. The feasibility study by the Planning Institute of Jamaica on unemployment insurance that considers possible companion labour-market and social-security reforms is therefore timely.

To reiterate the previous point, it is impossible for unemployment insurance to assist the target population if they remain informal.

Social Pension

There is a strong moral case for interventions on behalf of those who may have worked most of their lives and who, in their old age, are without a source of income, including NIS pension, due to some of the aforementioned structural barriers. It is for this reason that I announced the introduction of a social pension in my 2020 budget presentation.

In terms of age of eligibility and level of benefit, this is being designed so as to avoid perverse incentives that may dissuade NIS enrolment. Ultimately, within a decade or less, social-pension expenditures could be substantially reduced in real terms, as reforms to increase the participation in NIS impact old-age income dynamics.

Digitalisation to Support Social Development

Realisation of the strong social foundations that will modernise Jamaica will require investing in digital infrastructure that creates efficiency in service provision and enhances productivity. Other small countries, such as those in the Baltics (Latvia, Lithuania, and Estonia) have made great strides in reducing the size of government and increasing their overall productivity, economic competitiveness, and resilience by embracing digitalisation in their day-to-day lives. There are some critical components to help build this digital infrastructure.

Among these, implementation of a robust and secure National Identification System (NIDS) will enhance the efficiency and effectiveness of government and improve the delivery of government services to the public. In particular, delivery of social and welfare services will dramatically improve with the scope of broadening coverage. Planning for social and physical infrastructure needs could be more granular and impactful. NIDS will also greatly facilitate increased financial inclusion, as satisfaction of 'Know Your Customer' requirements would be easier. Commerce and economic activity would benefit from easier validation and integrity of platforms. Immigration, border-control management, public safety, and national security would also benefit from the implementation of NIDS.

[In the private sector], faster progress in financial inclusion – which has been proven in other countries to be achievable with digitisation, including easier opening of bank accounts and access to digital payment platforms – would support the expansion of small and medium-sized enterprises and increase formalisation, which together will build the backbone of domestic value-add and economic growth.

The Government of Jamaica will support the acceleration of an enabling environment for digital payments. As such, the Bank of Jamaica is working on the implementation of a National Payment Switch. This digital payment platform creates the prospect for greater inclusion of Jamaicans in the financial system, offering seamless payment options while lowering transaction costs and improving security. This single reform has transformative potential.

Complementing the above with universal access to broadband and onboarding of public services online, within the context of greater social-protection coverage and economic formalisation, will usher in a Jamaica 2.0 that improves the life of all Jamaicans.

Progress on Unemployment Insurance
Budget Speech Excerpt, March 2024

Madam Speaker, when someone on a lower income loses his/her job, it can have devastating consequences on his/her life. Just ask them. Their lives unravel with profound, sometimes long-lasting consequences. Jamaica's experience in the COVID-19 pandemic laid bare a deficiency in our social security apparatus – the absence of a funded scheme that provides temporary income support in the event of unemployment. Between March 2020 and June 2020, one hundred and fifty thousand Jamaicans lost their jobs, and were suddenly without income.

Many of the affected households would not have had meaningful resources to draw on to tide them over. And the government had no pre-existing institutional mechanism with which to respond. We had to improvise. Within weeks of the first COVID-19 case in Jamaica we launched the CARE Programme, accessible through an online portal with computer, tablet, or mobile phone.

Eventually, fifty-five thousand Jamaicans who lost their jobs benefited from monthly stipends from the government for thirteen months through the SET Cash and BEST Cash programs. This experience exposed a glaring gap in our social security arrangements.

In April 2020, the Most Honourable Prime Minister appointed a COVID-19 Economic Recovery Task Force and appointed me to chair it in my capacity of Minister of Finance and the Public Service. This Task Force was very broad in its composition, spanning every facet of society. The final report, which was published in June 2020 and tabled in Parliament shortly afterwards, recommended that the government 'funds and completes a feasibility study on an Unemployment Insurance Scheme for specified categories of workers within the context of social security reform.'[17]

Adapted from the opening budget presentation delivered in Parliament March 12, 2024.

This was not the first time this recommendation was made. It was also made by the Labour Market Reform Commission chaired by the late Honourable Dr Marshall Hall, OJ, a few years earlier. The government wasted no time and, as approved by Cabinet, the Ministry of Finance and the Public Service undertook the responsibility for getting the feasibility study done, through the Planning Institute of Jamaica, with technical and financial support from the International Labour Organisation and the guidance of a Technical Oversight Committee. The intention was that it would be implemented by the Ministry of Labour and Social Security if it proved feasible.

I must thank the Planning Institute of Jamaica and its Director General, Dr Wayne Henry, and staff, and the Technical Oversight Committee, also chaired by Dr Henry, for enthusiastically pursuing the feasibility study and coordinating the consultations required. And I also thank the Ministry of Labour and Social Security who actively assisted and supported this effort. I am also grateful to the International Labour Organisation which actually conducted the feasibility study. Armed with this analysis we were able to have consultations with the Confederation of Trade Unions, the Private Sector Organisation of Jamaica, and various other business groups representing employers, along with members from academia and civil society.

I am happy to report that macro-stability makes it feasible for Jamaica to have an unemployment insurance scheme that benefits Jamaican workers. A Jamaican unemployment insurance scheme can play a critically important stabilising role 'providing income security of the unemployed particularly during periods of economic shocks.'[18] Furthermore, as noted in the feasibility study, by 'partially compensating for loss of earnings,' a Jamaican unemployment insurance scheme can help 'break the negative increased unemployment leading to reduced consumption, which leads to a further reduction in economic activity.'[19] In other words, with unemployment insurance, Jamaica can strengthen and deepen macro-stability, allowing for faster recoveries and longer periods of growth, improving quality of life for the individual.

Socially, the impact of having unemployment insurance is even greater, Madam Speaker. Jamaica's average income is such that many persons live pay check to pay check. Having a job is much better than not having one, but if they lose that job – it can plunge that family into disarray with untold social consequences, impacting the newly unemployed, their children, and the elders that depend on them. And this often leads to other social ills.

Observers and commentators often point to the social stability of Barbados, over several decades, long preceding the current era. Arguably, one of the principal reasons for this is that Barbados has had a solid social security system, with unemployment insurance as a very important pillar, for a long time. Historically, economic shocks therefore have not devasted the social fabric of the country, in the way we have experienced in the past. The Bahamas also has unemployment insurance, and it is full time that Jamaica establishes an unemployment insurance scheme.

As I shared before, it is my understanding that due to similar experiences in the COVID-19 pandemic several countries in the region have been exploring unemployment schemes with the International Labour Organisation. These include Belize, Dominica, St Lucia, Grenada, and Trinidad and Tobago. Madam Speaker, the feasibility study indicates that Jamaica's unemployment insurance scheme would work similarly as it does elsewhere:

First, eligible employees would be registered and included in the unemployment insurance scheme. For Jamaica, it is likely that the universe of employees who contribute to the National Insurance Scheme would be automatically included in unemployment insurance with the requisite obligations and benefits.

Then, on loss of job, confirmed by employee and employer, the newly unemployed would become eligible to receive an unemployment benefit representing a particular percentage of their previous weekly income, up to a maximum threshold, and for a fixed period. According to the feasibility study, in Barbados the unemployment benefit is 60 per cent of previous average weekly earnings. In Bahamas the unemployment benefit is 50 per cent of previous average weekly earnings. Furthermore, in Barbados the unemployment benefit is paid for twenty-six weeks, and in Bahamas it is paid for thirteen weeks. Jamaica will have to work out the unemployment benefit and duration of payment parameters that work for us.

Unemployment insurance schemes are not free; they cost money. Usually, these costs are funded by employee and employer deductions, with the government sometimes making an initial fiscal contribution on inception, to capitalise the scheme and treat with the possibility of major unemployment materialising before the scheme has amassed sufficient funds from contributions.

The feasibility study indicates that it could cost as little as 0.8 per cent of salary, or as much as 1.5 per cent of salary – with capital contribution from the government of a few billion dollars – for this benefit to be provided, depending on parameters selected and other details.

However, Jamaica already has a plethora of separate statutory deductions: National Housing Trust (NHT), National Insurance Scheme (NIS), the Human Employment and Resource Training (HEART), and Education Tax deductions. Adding a fifth and replicating the collection, processing, and enforcement administration, while adding further complexity for small business, is not optimal for employees, employers, or the government. As such, we are looking into administratively consolidating these statutory deductions into a single deduction, with the distribution to each entity of its share, enshrined in, and protected by, legislation. This is not a new idea. But there are details and complexities to be worked through, and this work continues.

However, the major advantage of consolidation of statutory deductions, in the context of introducing a new unemployment insurance benefit, is that initial calculations show that we could potentially introduce this new benefit without increasing the headline consolidated statutory deduction rate, and with no additional cost for up to 95 per cent of persons enrolled in the National Insurance Scheme.

We are now at the point of implementation, and within the first quarter of the financial year we expect to sign a US$20 million loan agreement with the World Bank[20] where they will provide the Ministry of Labour and Social Security with the technical support to, among many other things, implement unemployment insurance in Jamaica.

There are many details that the World Bank will assist us to work through, including the legislative architecture for unemployment insurance; the institutional mechanisms for unemployment insurance, inclusive of installing the institutional capacity; and the administrative arrangements for unemployment insurance. The Minister of Labour and Social Security Pearnel Charles, Jr, will have charge of this leg with the support of the Ministry of Finance and the Public Service while we continue to work in collaboration with others to refine the funding model to optimise efficiency and lower costs in the manner described above.

I was motivated to review the 1965 debate in Parliament which brought the National Insurance Scheme into effect. There was considerable discussion about unemployment insurance at that time. The Opposition argued for it, and Minister of Labour and National Insurance Lyndon Newland did not resist the arguments, in fact he embraced them and explained that unemployment insurance would come later, consistent with the experience of other countries. In his contribution to the debate, Mr Allan Douglas, Minister of Trade and Industry, said, 'I would like to see the unemployment benefit granted but it is useless starting a Scheme today without any strong financial support….I am sure that as soon as it becomes practicable this Government will come back with proposals to deal with …the security of the unemployed.'[21]

Sixty years later, Madam Speaker, Time Come.

Time Come for unemployment insurance to be available to the people of Jamaica.

As I have said before, social security reform has been an indelible feature of the Holness Administration. We introduced the social pension in which twelve thousand elderly Jamaicans are now enrolled. We introduced the Tourism Workers Pension Scheme. And, I am proud to announce that we are working to introduce unemployment insurance to Jamaica to benefit the people of Jamaica.

Securing the National Insurance Scheme for the Future

Published Commentary, December 2018

The National Insurance Scheme (NIS) was established in 1966 and is a compulsory, contributory, funded social security scheme. Employers and employees make contributions to the National Insurance Fund (NIF), and these contributions are used to finance NIS benefits and administrative costs. Annual surpluses of contributions over benefits and administrative costs are invested and have accumulated over time. Today, the NIF has a market value of more than $100 billion.[22]

In the event that the NIF is unable to finance the payments of NIS benefits, the burden falls to the Consolidated Fund. Failure to adequately safeguard the long-term sustainability of the NIF therefore represents a significant long-term fiscal risk. The NIS Act explicitly recognises this by giving the Minister of Finance certain consent, review, and decision-making responsibilities with respect to the NIS and NIF.

Since inception, the benefits paid from the NIF under the NIS have expanded beyond the Old Age Pension to include an Employment Injury Benefit, a Medical and Dental/Optical Benefit, and other benefits. Today, more than one hundred thousand Jamaicans receive benefits from the NIS, which forms the bedrock of our social security system.

In addition, since the inception of the National Health Fund (NHF) in 2003, 20 per cent of NIS contributions have been diverted to the NHF. As a result, the programmed outflows from the NIF on an annual basis are significant. In 2016, the NIF received contributions of approximately $13 billion and paid out $15 billion in benefits. Indeed, for the ten years covering 2006–16, annual benefits from the NIF exceeded annual contributions to the NIF. So far, investment income has covered this difference.

An earlier version of this article appeared in the *Jamaica Gleaner*, December 14, 2018.

However, as the population ages, this trend is projected to quickly worsen until investment income is no longer sufficient to make up for the deficit of benefit payments over contributions. The NIF would then experience negative cash flow and begin to rapidly reduce in size. Consistent with this observation, the 2016 Actuarial Report on the NIF[23] concluded that, without reform, the NIF is projected to experience negative cash flow in eleven years (i.e., in 2029) and to be completely depleted in nineteen years (i.e., in 2037).

The reasons for this are not difficult to identify. Decades of high inflation mean that individual lifetime contributions have been substantially less than the expected benefit payout. For example, the maximum annual contribution to the NIS was $750 in 1990, $12,500 in 1996, $25,000 in 2006, and $75,000 in 2016 – and the vast majority of contributors would not have contributed the maximum amounts. By comparison, old age pension in 2018 is $176,800 per annum.

Historically high unemployment, an aging population, and a low coverage ratio (less than one-third of the working population contributes to the NIF) mean that the ratio of contributors to pensioners has not been favourable to long-term sustainability.

Contribution rates and the cap on these contributions can also explain the unsustainability of the NIS/NIF. Countries that have funded National Insurance Schemes deemed to be sustainable have substantially higher contribution rates than we do. However, these countries do not also have a National Housing Trust to which an additional 5 per cent of payroll is contributed.

In addition, contribution rates in Jamaica are only applied to the portion of income up to $1.5 million, which is referred to as the National Insurable Wage Ceiling. Both the contribution rate and this cap need to be addressed if we are to improve the sustainability of the NIS/NIF.

It is for this reason that I announced in Parliament this week the decision of the Cabinet to increase contribution rates from the current 5.0 per cent of incomes to 5.5 per cent in April 2019, and further to 6.0 per cent in April 2020. The increases of 0.5 per cent in each year are to be borne equally by employer and employee. I also announced Cabinet's decision to increase the National Insurable Wage Ceiling to $3 million in 2021 and further to $5 million in 2022.

In arriving at these decisions, consideration had to be given to the imperative of improving the sustainability of the NIS/NIF as well as the impact of the increased contributions on the employee and the employer. We have phased the increases to allow employers and employees adequate time to plan.

Furthermore, the Government of Jamaica (GOJ) is the largest employer and is impacted by higher employer contributions. The GOJ is also affected as an employee's NIS contribution is deducted before income tax is applied and so, as a larger share of income goes to the NIF, personal income-tax revenue falls. As a result, the fiscal impact of these changes featured prominently in the decision. By 2022, the combined cost of these contribution reforms to the GOJ will be approximately $5 billion per annum.

To be clear, these changes extend the life of the NIF but do not guarantee indefinite sustainability. We propose further comprehensive social security reform in the future to put the NIS/ NIF on a firmly secure path.

In the meantime, I have appointed an Investment Management Review Commission to review the governance arrangements, investment policies, asset allocation, and risk management of the NIF, and to appraise and benchmark the NIF performance against returns and best practises in the private-pension industry, as well as against similar national funds in other jurisdictions. We want to ensure that contributors and pensioners always have the confidence that the NIF is invested in their best interest over the long term, and that it abides by the highest standards of transparency, while delivering competitive investment returns.

Launching a Social Pension
Budget Speech Excerpt, March 2020

I want to speak on a topic that as Minister of Finance and the Public Service and as a Member of Parliament is very dear to me, and that is social protection. Mr Speaker, when I was appointed Minister of Finance and the Public Service, I declared that the economic policy would target three primary objectives: (1) the pursuit of economic independence, (2) economic opportunity for all, and (3) the protection of the vulnerable.

As such, in September 2018 – and even after I reported (in 2018) on the large drop in poverty for 2016 – with the consent and cooperation of Minister of Labour and Social Security Shahine Robinson and her team, I requested that the World Bank conduct a public expenditure review of social protection in Jamaica. This review looked at social protection not only in the ministry of Labour and Social Security, but across all of government.

The objective of the public expenditure review was to examine the efficiency, effectiveness, and equity of social protection spending in Jamaica, and to identify options for improving social protection to ensure that the government's objective of protection of the vulnerable is met. One of the clear recommendations that emerges from the review is the need to strengthen our social protection fabric with a social pension for the elderly which I will now speak to.

The National Insurance Fund (NIF)was set up in 1966 and is a compulsory, contributory, funded social security scheme. Jamaica is among a minority of countries that have a funded social security system, and to have had that from 1966 speaks to the vision of the architects of independent Jamaica. Spain does not have funded social security, France does not either. Mr Speaker, the United States of America does not have a funded social security system. But ambitious Jamaica does. Today the NIF is capitalised at over

---

Adapted from the opening budget presentation delivered in Parliament March 10, 2020.

$120 billion.[24] We are reforming the National Insurance System (NIS), with phased-in increased contribution rates and thresholds, announced during the 2019–20 fiscal year, and these reforms will ensure that the NIF has positive cashflows until 2048 and that the Fund will last until 2057. To extend the life of the Fund beyond this will require further reform, which will be addressed by the Minister at a later date.

In the meantime, we have the challenge of low coverage of the NIS. Out of an elderly (over sixty-five years) population of 291,373 persons, only 82,063 – less than 30 per cent – are in receipt of an NIS pension.

The elderly population not covered by the NIS reflects the historic and current high levels of informal workers present in Jamaica's labour market. It is estimated by the World Bank, based on Jamaica Survey of Living Conditions data, that 77 per cent of the poorest quintile have never contributed to the NIS. So, Miss Davis has worked all her life. Get up 5:00 a.m. to take the bus to get to work, do a full eight hours work sometimes more, for forty years. Church on Sunday. Children to school. She has abided by the law and played by the rules but my God, by the nature of her employment, it meant that her employer never contributed to the NIS on her behalf. Now she is elderly and has absolutely no source of income. A proud yet struggling woman during her working years, she is now absolutely dependent, and the pride of her youth has been replaced by anxiety and shame. Miss Davis is in this Chamber. She is retired. Worked faithfully all her life. Not one penny of income in retirement and no savings.

To consistently move forward, our political freedoms must translate into sustainable material benefit and improved conditions for the Jamaican people. This is a structural inequity in our society that should no longer go unaddressed and this government, led by Prime Minister Andrew Holness, intends to [address it].

Miss Davis, I have good news for you. In this financial year, the government will spend $1 billion to introduce a modest social pension targeted to cover the poor and vulnerable segment of the elderly population who are not in receipt of PATH, NIS, or a private pension. It is estimated that there are thirty thousand elderly persons who are poor and vulnerable and not in receipt of NIS, pension, or poor relief. We recognise that this amount is not nearly sufficient to address the needs of the elderly. But this is a start, and we must start somewhere.

In the design, we will be careful to ensure that there isn't a disincentive to enrol in the NIS that introduces new inequities. As such, the benefit level and the age at which one can qualify for this pension will differ from the NIS. In addition, the design will ensure that the social pension is fiscally sustainable. The social pension is intended to correct historical structural inequities that make it difficult for informally employed persons to contribute to the NIS. We do not want to introduce new inequities through a fiscally unsustainable design

Therefore, the government, through the Ministry of Labour and Social Services, will innovate to increase the NIS coverage ratio so that, over the course of the next decade, the population of persons that can qualify for the new social pension, by virtue of not being in receipt of NIS and being poor and vulnerable, decreases over time. By definition that population will increase at first, but ultimately it will hit a maximum and then start to fall as we dramatically increase NIS coverage.

I want to make it clear to the Jamaican people that, under the visionary leadership of Prime Minister Andrew Holness, and with the support of Minister Robinson, this government intends to launch the most comprehensive reform to social security in Jamaica since the National Insurance Scheme was launched over fifty years ago in 1966.

I say to the elderly in the Jamaican society who have been deprived of the opportunity to contribute and receive a pension, like Miss Davis: *Jamaica is moving in the right direction.*

Abolishing the Guarantor Requirement for Student Loans

Budget Speech Excerpt, March 2024

Over the past few years, we have made changes in how the Student Loan Bureau (SLB) is accessed and the results are worthy of noting. In the 2022–23 budget we removed the requirements for guarantors to be provided for applicants who are Wards of the State. Within the twelve months of that policy change, the number of Wards of the State who applied to the SLB increased from forty-six the previous year, to ninety-eight – an increase of over 100 per cent.

Last year, in the 2023–24 budget, we removed the requirements for guarantors to be provided for applicants from PATH Households. Since we lifted the requirement for guarantors, within the last twelve months, the number of PATH beneficiaries accessing the SLB jumped from 192 in the previous year to 547, and the year is not yet finished. An increase of 185 per cent. In the face of this staggering evidence as to the inhibiting effect of the requirement of a guarantor, how do we keep it? I will share with you a true story.

In the days leading up to the Local Government Election, I with met a member of my constituency. She told me that her son had graduated from Jose Marti in 2019, and she wanted him to go to university.

I asked her, 'How many subjects he got?'

She told me, 'Him get seven subject.'

I asked her, 'So, what do you do for work?'

'I work at an ice cream shop,' she said.

I said, 'Customer service?'

She said, 'Yes.'

So, I asked her how much she made. And she told me.

I asked her, 'What happen when you go to the SLB?'

Adapted from the opening budget presentation delivered in Parliament March 12, 2024.

She said, 'Dem tell me I don't earn enough to be a guarantor for my son and him well waan go a university. Him well want it, Nigel. Oh God me feel like cry now.'

I looked her in the eye and said to her, 'Is people like you I have in mind, with a policy that I plan to announce shortly.'

She said, 'Nobada tell me dat you know Nigel and mek me feel good.'

I took her name and her number, and I told her I would call her when I was ready. She is in Parliament this afternoon with her son … Sheryl, and her son Malik.

And in her presence, Madam Speaker, I am pleased to announce that effective April 1, the Student Loan Bureau will no longer require guarantors for students to access tertiary financing from the Student Loan Bureau.

Going forward, no guarantors will be required for Student Loans accessed after April 1.

With this policy, Malik will be the first in his family to go to university.

Under this government, we want every youth to be a star.

The requirement of guarantors for student loans is a regressive policy that discriminates against low-income families who cannot as easily, if at all, find someone with the means and willingness to stand guarantee for them. This policy has been in place for several decades and we are happy to abolish the requirement for guarantors for student loans.

From copious amounts of data available to the SLB, very, very rarely are payments actually made by guarantors. In all but a few instances, guarantors have served the purpose of locating students. We anticipate that by the time the first batch of students who benefit from this policy graduate from university, the National Identification System, or NIDS, will be a reality. We will not need guarantors for that purpose, as NIDS will suffice.

We signalled that this was under consideration with our changes in the guarantor requirements for PATH households last year and for Wards of the State the year before. It was useful to have the test cases on small sample sizes of the impact it would have in broadening access.

We are not doing this blind. Since inception, the SLB uses a tiny portion of loan repayments, 0.0005 per cent of each payment, to make provision for loss of life of the borrower. That fund was actuarially assessed and found to be J$1 billion in excess of the provision required for the risk it was set up to insure against.

So, with this new 'No Guarantor' policy, we will move this J$1 billion excess from the life insurance reserve into a new Guarantor Reserve Fund as backing for this new policy.

PART SIX

NEW BEGINNINGS

Leveraging Economic Stability
in the People's Interest

Budget Speech Excerpt, March 2024

Madam Speaker, in this budget presentation I will provide the data that supports the fact that Jamaica's macroeconomic fundamentals today are stronger, better, and more favourable than at any time over the last fifty years. I will define economic stability and demonstrate that this period is the only period in the last fifty years where we have enjoyed this. I will advance the argument that economic stability is essential to the growth in investment and jobs, which in turn drive government revenue.

It is from government revenues that we finance public investment expenditure – on police stations, buses, schools, hospitals, roads, and other infrastructure – which all benefit the citizens of Jamaica over the long term. And materially increasing the levels of public investment expenditure is necessary if we are to improve quality of life.

Therefore, economic stability is indispensable to increasing the ability of the government to improve the quality of life and standards of living of the people of Jamaica.

But while macroeconomic stability is necessary, it is by no means sufficient.

In February 2018, while I was campaigning house to house during the St Andrew Northwestern By-election, a lady greeted me at her gate and said something to me that I will never forget.

She said: 'You see all them ting dere, growth, debt, inflation … dem important you nuh, dem very important, but dem not important fah wi. What is important fah wi is, is di garbage collected? Is di pothole dem fixed? Di streetlights dem a work? Dat is what is important to wi.'

It was one of those moments that will always remain with me.

I shared this experience with a few people at the time, including the Most Honourable Prime Minister, and these words have remained close to me since then.

It was that conversation that was the motivating factor for me, in one of my first moves as Minister of Finance, to collaborate with Minister McKenzie and pay down the streetlight $7 billion bill with JPSCo, which at the time was more than twenty-four months overdue. And since then, to have the central government contribute $3.1 billion [each] year to pay for streetlights.

Economic stability is very important, as my constituent rightly acknowledged. It must be achieved and preserved, but it is not an end in and of itself. Rather, it must deliver for the people – not just the connected, the powerful, and the well-organised.

Economic stability must deliver for all the people of Jamaica.

Because many Jamaicans looking on say, Alright, it is great that [we] have achieved macroeconomic stability, and all of these wonderful things, after so many decades. But what about my issues?

My roads are in a deplorable condition.

My garbage is not collected on a regular basis.

I have been waiting decades and still don't have access to water, or in some cases, electricity.

It takes an hour for the bus to come and its timing is not reliable.

Food prices have gone beyond my capacity.

And I cannot go anywhere and hear reggae music in peace. Everywhere we go 'dem tun off di music.'

The people of Jamaica want us to address these important, critical issues, and many others like them. The people want to see that these issues are priorities in the fiscal policy choices of the government. The people want to see that the allocation of resources in our national budget is aligned with the pain points they experience. The people want us to put the same energy into the 'micro' that we put into the 'macro.' They want to see an acceleration in how quickly we can use public investment to address longstanding challenges.

I would like to use this opportunity to speak directly to my constituent who gave me such good advice, as well as to all Jamaicans:

We hear you loud and clear.

This government, headed by the Most Honourable Prime Minister Andrew Holness, is a listening government. We listen to the people.

Let me say very clearly that what is important to you, is also very important to us.

Not only have we listened and have heard you, let me make it abundantly clear that we are also a government that responds and acts.

As such, we will align our fiscal policy to address the pain points in our society.

We will preserve economic stability.

We will improve economic stability.

And, we will also leverage economic stability in the people's interest.

This government has always listened and always responded in a manner that protects and preserves macroeconomic stability, while also acting in the people's best interest. We have endeavoured to do so every year since we were first elected in 2016, and will always do so.

It is abundantly clear, however, that the people of Jamaica want even more from us as a government. The people of Jamaica want to know and feel that they are benefiting and participating more directly in the macroeconomic advances that we have made, in a manner that improves their lives.

This has always been our commitment, and we have a strong track record of quality-of-life-improving achievements that support this. We renew, redouble and re-energise our commitment to 'walk and chew gum.' That is, to continue to improve Jamaica's macroeconomic fundamentals, thereby creating an environment that is conducive to growth and jobs, and, at the same time, to leverage the economic stability that emerges in the people's interest.

It is in the context that I am honoured to present the budget for fiscal year 2024–25. It is stability that allows us to expand the capital budget even beyond the capacity of the public bureaucracy to implement – something we need to continue to address.

Stability allows the government to plan years in advance and to share these plans publicly, which allows for steady, even development.

I am proud to announce that we are now entering a period where we will leverage our economic stability to usher in the largest-ever period of public investment, designed to address the problems experienced by Jamaicans every day.

When, through public investment, the Government of Jamaica:

- brings water to a community, the people benefit;

- brings access to sewer lines to a community, the people benefit;

- brings buses to the JUTC so people can plan their business and ride in comfort, the people benefit;

- builds new hospitals and schools, the people benefit;

- builds new tax offices, the people benefit;

- builds public parks and new court houses, and acquires garbage trucks, the people benefit.

In my capacity of Chairman of the Public Investment Management Committee – the committee embedded in the Financial Administration and Audit Act responsible for considering, reviewing, and approving public investments – let me assure you that we will positively impact the daily experience of Jamaicans with public investment expenditure designed to solve pain points.

Some of this investment will be financed by the government and some by the private sector, by way of structured transactions such as Public-Private Partnerships, or PPPs.

The Public Investment Programme will deliver well over J$1 trillion of infrastructure expenditure over the next five years, including this year, inclusive of expenditure by way of PPPs on Highways, Roads, Bridges, Public Parks, Hospitals, Schools, Water, Sewerage, Irrigation Systems, Houses, Tax Offices, Court Houses, Buses, Garbage Trucks, Digital Infrastructure, and IT systems.

It will be Jamaica's largest expansion of infrastructure ever, and it will greatly improve public services.

A New Beginning:
In the Footprints of Stability

After almost fifty years of starts and stops, detours and reversals, agony and sacrifice, Jamaica has finally arrived on the shores of economic stability. Over the nearly decade-long period from January 2015 to September 2024, Jamaica experienced quarterly economic growth for thirty-two out of thirty-nine quarters, with one flat quarter and six quarters of economic contraction due only to the impacts of the COVID-19 pandemic and Hurricane Beryl, a Category 5 storm. There is absolutely no parallel for this since Jamaica started measuring growth quarterly, twenty-seven years ago. The foundations laid by economic stability now provide the platform to build our economy into the prosperous country that was envisioned by our forefathers when we became independent as a nation in 1962.

Our history demonstrates that, over the last fifty years, Jamaica has tried many approaches in its quest for greater well-being, yet nothing has delivered jobs and a rising standard of living for Jamaicans as has this period of economic stability. During this period, the employed labour force expanded by over 25 per cent with the creation of just under three hundred thousand jobs, and the unemployment rate shrank from 14.2 per cent in January 2015 to a historic low of 4.2 per cent in April 2024. Furthermore, the minimum wage was raised by a cumulative 68 per cent in real terms. Thus, economic stability has also delivered meaningful increases in income.

These achievements should evoke pride, but also prompt vigilance. Pride, because the achievement of stability was hard-earned and, while not a panacea, it has evidently delivered benefits for the Jamaican people. Vigilance, as stability can be easily lost. Amidst pride and vigilance, we must recall that stability only represents the foundation on which we must continue to construct a society of opportunity for all.

The Imperative of Growth

With the return of economic stability after a nearly fifty-year absence, Jamaica has the opportunity for new beginnings – but to do what? This much is clear: dividends from our new era of stability must be harnessed carefully by both the public and private sectors so that all Jamaicans experience improved well-being and livelihoods.

Jamaicans on low incomes need more than wage increases to materially improve their quality of life. How can prosperity be enjoyed if one is still likely to be a victim of violence? How valuable is an increase in the minimum wage if one must still wait an hour for the bus, and children are subject to sub-standard education? Delivering transformative improvements in quality of life for the majority is the 'new beginning' that must become a national commitment. Done in such a way that the government's role is to provide public services for the people, while the private sector takes advantage of economic stability to build capital and invest profitably in Jamaica.

With stability entrenched, Jamaica's next economic frontier is to sustainably increase levels of economic growth. But we should first internalise that there are no quick solutions, because real danger – at the expense of our stability – lies in the false promise of overnight transformation of growth prospects.

What Should the Government Prioritise?

Infrastructure development increases the productivity of capital, aligns well with the growth agenda, and must be at the forefront of Jamaica's next phase. Improving Jamaica's domestic and international connectivity through the development of highways and the expansion of our airports and seaports must be high priorities. Equally critical are energy infrastructure development projects that can lower costs, improve competitiveness, and reduce foreign exchange dependency. We must also embrace further digital transformation to unlock opportunities for accessibility, scale, and efficiency. Reducing the cost and increasing the accessibility of data services through telecom infrastructure development is vital. Similar opportunities exist when it comes to building our water, health, justice, and security infrastructure – among them the US$2 billion of potential public-private partnership projects for development covered in a memorandum of understanding signed with the International Finance Corporation.

The unavailability of technical skills now poses more of a threat to our new beginning than the old problem of where to find financing. The scale and volume of infrastructure development, PPP, and other currently possible public investment projects require proper and transparent development with proper accountability to the taxpayer, in accordance with our Public Investment Management System. This demands experience and skills. We will have to lean on multilateral and bilateral partners to help fill the gaps while we build the human capital we need.

Human capital development is therefore crucially important. The level of a country's economic output is related to the level of value-added production of goods and services in an economy. Relatively high value-add output typically requires either the employment of complex machinery, capital equipment, and processes, or the application of highly skilled human talent to a productive endeavour, or both. Jamaica's labour productivity has declined over the past several decades as we transitioned from an economy based more in manufacturing and mining goods, with high value-add, to a relatively lower value-add services economy that does not require, for the most part, a highly skilled workforce. Right now, with only 18 per cent of Jamaican students passing five or more subjects in the Caribbean Secondary Examination Certificate (CSEC) and with a 39 per cent pass rate for mathematics, the human capital foundation is not very supportive of higher-skilled and therefore higher-value-added jobs.[1] Addressing this shortcoming is imperative to our future – this is the most urgent strategic development challenge that Jamaica faces, and it requires sustained national focus. Among other initiatives, Jamaica will need interventions in early childhood and primary education that can help set our children up for success. In addition, affordable childcare will be essential to support a dynamic labour force, enabling parents – including an already strong female labour participation – to contribute to their fullest.

Enabling the private sector to grow. We must do this by creating a business environment where capital and labour are accessible to diversify the Jamaican economy and provide job opportunities in

Jamaica. We need to greatly simplify what is required to maintain compliance. Though we have made significant progress in the abolishment of nuisance and distortionary taxes, the environment is still too complex for small businesses. Consolidation of statutory deductions, simplification of procedures, and increased digital availability of licensing and permitting procedures – all these are essential to enable small businesses. Jamaica needs even more risk-taking and innovative entrepreneurs who seize and create opportunities.

Protect the Gains

As we expand the horizons of transformation, let us not forget that preservation of hard-won stability will require deliberate work. It is not to be taken for granted; it is not automatic. Among other things, we must maintain and strengthen our institutions and our institutionalised processes, including our independent central bank, independent fiscal commission, fiscal rules, public-body governance framework, multi-layered disaster-risk management framework, public investment management system, public financial management, and our new mandatory electronic procurement system.

We must also build and preserve our foreign-exchange reserves. These are essential for stability. We should avoid the errors of the past, where these precious resources have been squandered on futile attempts to maintain an artificial and over-valued exchange rate. Exchange-rate flexibility is essential in a liberalised system characterised by free currency convertibility with independent, domestic monetary policy.

We must support and maintain independence in regulation. Around the world, regulated industries are often the most politically active. That is fair game. Lobbying regarding policy and legislation is legal. While we must have transparent, professional and arms-length regulatory appeal processes, we must otherwise maintain the principle of non-interference in the operational work of regulators. When it comes to regulation, we should recognise that the people of Jamaica are the ultimate stakeholders, rather than just the shareholders, executives, and managers of regulated entities.

Additionally, we must ensure that wage-bill growth does not rise faster than inflation. Over the decade from 2012 to 2022, suppression of public-sector wages assisted in the fiscal consolidation required to place Jamaica's finances on a sustainable trajectory. Jamaica has now made good on that sacrifice. Going forward, aggregate wage-bill growth in excess of inflation would be one of the easiest, surest, and quickest ways to erase the progress we have made and to slam the door on the opportunities presented by our new beginning.

Restructured compensation makes recruitment easier. Headcount will therefore need to be zealously and rigidly managed. Overtime regimes are being modernised. This will require greater department-head accountability when it comes to the management and deployment of human resources. We have demonstrated the strategic value of longer public-sector wage agreements: needed structural change becomes possible. With the historic four-year wage agreement, the Government of Jamaica, in consultation with public-sector unions, had the time needed to conduct its analysis and to prepare and implement a highly complex public-sector compensation reform. We cannot afford to go back to the unstable two-year wage cycle. With approximately forty distinct public-sector unions and bargaining groups, a new round of negotiation begins before the old one ends – and no structural change is possible. This breeds frustration and distrust. The government has made significant institutional investments in price stability, and the efficacy of these arrangements has been demonstrated. One of the lasting dividends must be a longer and more practical wage cycle.

Finally, we must maintain a judicious and principled approach to waivers and incentives, with awareness of the consequential impact of the slightest deviation. For the past eleven years we have kept discretionary waivers at a de minimis amount of $10 million per month. This has been an important, though unpublicised and unheralded, part of our success. This bipartisan principle must be maintained in order to assure fiscal sustainability long into the future. Once you vary for Jack, you will have to vary for Jill. And it will never end. As a country we have been there before, and we do not want to go back.

Our Best Days Are Ahead

Politics anywhere is rough and tough and is about winning the next election. But bipartisan support at critical junctures has been indispensable to Jamaica's success. Our collective journey has been long, and a close examination of Jamaica's economic and political history will reveal that there is enough blame to go around. So blame should not be our focus. Instead, we must learn from our history with the aim of building a better future. At its core, economic stability is neither progressive nor conservative. Nor is it hostage to any political ideology. It is simply a practical requirement and an essential building block of an independent and stable society.

Like many, I am confident and optimistic about Jamaica's future. I believe that our best days lie ahead. The long-term growth and survival of an organism is related to its capacity to heal itself. By restoring the economic stability it once lost, Jamaica has shown its capacity to scale the ladder of development. By seizing the opportunity for a new beginning – while simultaneously protecting our gains, ensuring continuity of intentional, disciplined economic policy – Jamaica can create a future reality of true independence and equitable prosperity that is our aspiration today, and that our forebears could only dare to imagine. We owe it ourselves to deliver on this promise.

NOTES

INTRODUCTION

1. Michael Manley, *Up the Down Escalator: Development and the International Economy* – A Jamaican Case Study (Washington, DC: Howard University Press, 1987).

2. For a particularly illuminating discussion of the exceptional nature of Jamaica's recent economic turnaround as it relates to public debt, along with a helpful summary of our nation's political-economic history, see Serkan Arslanalp, Barry Eichengreen, and Peter Blair Henry, 'Sustained Debt Reduction: the Jamaica Exception,' *National Bureau of Economic Research Working Paper Series* 32465 (May 2024), https://doi.org/10.3386/w32465.

3. GOJ expenditure increased from under 30 per cent of GDP in 1972/73, to 47 per cent of GDP in 1976/77, resulting in chronic and sustained negative fiscal balances (i.e. fiscal deficits), that reached -16 per cent of GDP, and which were financed by rapidly increasing debt. Sources: Economic and Social Survey of Jamaica 1973 and 1976, Planning Institute of Jamaica.

4. International Monetary Fund, 'Jamaica: 2021 Article IV Consultation-Press Release; Staff Report; Staff Statement; and Statement by the Executive Director for Jamaica.' *IMF Country Report*, 2022, no. 043 (February 2022).

5. The GOJ ran negative fiscal balances (i.e., fiscal deficits) of -6 per cent of GDP in 1973, -8 per cent of GDP in 1974, -9 per cent of GDP in 1975, -16 per cent of GDP in 1976, -15 per cent of GDP in 1977, -12 per cent of GDP in 1978, -12 per cent of GDP in 1979 and -16 per cent of GDP in 1980. Source: Jamaica 2021 Article IV Consultation, International Monetary Fund.

6. Planning Institute of Jamaica, *Economic and Social Survey of Jamaica*, (1975, 1982).

7. There was a gradual reduction of Jamaica's chronic negative fiscal balances (i.e. fiscal deficits) in the 1980's. The GOJ ran fiscal deficits of -15 per cent of GDP in 1981, -14 per cent of GDP in 1982, -14 per cent of GDP in 1983, -5 per cent of GDP in 1984, -6 per cent in 1985 of GDP, -2 per cent of GDP in 1986, -3 per cent of GDP in 1987, -6 per cent of GDP in 1988 (the year of Hurricane Gilbert, independent Jamaica's most damaging hurricane), -2 per cent of GDP in 1989 before achieving Jamaica's first fiscal surplus since 1962 of 2 per cent of GDP in 1990. Source: 'Jamaica 2021 IMF Article IV Consultation Report,' International Monetary Fund.

8. The annual GDP growth of the 1980's, (with the exception of 1984 and 1985 when there was annual GDP contraction), represented partial economic recovery from the cumulative effect of six years of real annual GDP decline during the decade of the 1970's (inclusive of 1980). Jamaica's real GDP in 1989 was still lower than in 1973. I use 1973 as a point of comparison as the GDP declines of the 1970's began in 1974 and ended an unbroken stretch of consecutive annual GDP growth stretching back to 1962 when Jamaica gained political independence. Source: Planning Institute of Jamaica.

9. Jamaica's Debt/GDP exceeded 200 per cent in the mid-1980's.

10. Inflation was 80.2 per cent, 40.2 per cent, 30.1 per cent, 26.8 per cent, and 25.6 per cent for calendar years 1991, 1992, 1993,1994, and 1995 respectively.

11. The combination of consecutive (and rare) fiscal surpluses and annual real GDP growth between 1989–90 and 1994–95 also contributed to the reduction in the debt-to-GDP ratio. However, the hyperinflation that averaged 40 per cent per annum between 1991 and 1995 was, by far, the overwhelming and dominant factor. This hyperinflation, along with the harsh monetary policy response and weak financial-sector regulatory environment, also defined the period and helped sow the seeds for the economic demise that followed.

12. Omar Davies, 'FINSAC: The Truth,' *Jamaica Gleaner*, May 15, 2011. Available at: https://jamaica-gleaner.com/gleaner/20110515/focus/focus1.html.

13. Jamaica also ran negative fiscal balances (i.e. fiscal deficits) every year between 1962, the year of political independence, and 1973. The major difference between this period and the decades that followed is that fiscal deficits were accompanied by high levels of real annual GDP growth that averaged 5.3 per cent per annum over the period 1962 - 1973. All told, therefore, Jamaica ran fiscal deficits for forty-four of the fifty years between 1962 and 2012.

14. This does not include the 2013 Extended Fund Facility, which was the fourteenth IMF programme since 1973.
15. IMF, 'Jamaica: 2021 Article IV Consultation' (2022).

PART ONE: BEGINNINGS

1. Quoted in Gary Spaulding and Nedburn Thaffe, '"Driva" Pulls Over,' *Jamaica Gleaner*, September 26, 2011.
2. John Myers, Jr, 'Too Costly to Keep,' *Jamaica Gleaner*, December 10, 2007.
3. Charles Collyns, 'The Crisis through the Lens of History,' *Finance and Development* 45, no. 4 (December 2008): 18–20.
4. International Monetary Fund, 'Jamaica: Letter of Intent, Memorandum of Economic and Financial Policies, and Technical Memorandum of Understanding.' IMF, January 15, 2010.
5. IMF, 'Jamaica: Letter of Intent' (2010).
6. Jamaica Debates Commission, '2011 Leadership Issues: Mr Andrew Holness (JLP) and Mrs Portia Simpson-Miller (PNP),' YouTube video, December 20, 2011.
7. International Monetary Fund, 'Jamaica: 2014 Article IV Consultation and Fourth Review under the Extended Arrangement under the Extended Fund Facility,' Staff Report (IMF, June 20, 2014).
8. Ministry of Finance and the Public Service of Jamaica, Debt Management Unit.
9. Bank of Jamaica Statistics Department, 'Official International Reserves (NIR) of the BOJ,' External Sector, Table Code ES.NIR.00 (BOJ, January 1992–August 2024).
10. Peter Phillips, 'Restoring Hope, Expanding Opportunities,' Opening Budget Debate (Ministry of Finance and the Public Service of Jamaica, April 18, 2013): 3.
11. Excluding 2020, the year of the COVID-19 pandemic, Jamaica's primary surplus averaged 7.0 per cent over the eleven year period 2013-14 to 2023-24. This has been the most significant explanatory factor in Jamaica's dramatic debt reduction from a historic high of 145 per cent in 2013 to a projected 68 per cent in fiscal year 2024/25. Prior to Jamaica's program engagement with the IMF in 2010, Jamaica's debt was mostly local and external market debt, much of it expensive, issued at double digit interest rates. This reality was largely unchanged in 2013. Given that the principal amount of the debt remained, a high primary balance was therefore necessary to place the otherwise spiraling debt dynamics on a firm downward trajectory.
12. Portia Simpson-Miller and Peter Phillips, 'Address to the Nation.' Jamaica Information Service, February 11, 2013. https://jis.gov.jm/speeches/address-to-the-nation-by-prime-minister-the-most-hon-portia-simpson-miller-and-dr-the-hon-peter-phillips/.

13. Simpson-Miller and Phillips, 'Address to the Nation' JIS, February 2013.

14. This statement by the IMF was reported by Radio Jamaica News, 'IMF again describes government's tax relief plan as "bold",' June 17, 2016.

15. Jamaica's fiscal balances (i.e. revenues less expenditures) over the past eleven years stand in disciplined contrast to our economic history. Recent fiscal balances have been: 0.1 per cent of GDP in 2013/14, -0.5 per cent in 2014/15, -0.3 per cent in 2015/16, -0.2 per cent in 2016/17, 0.5 per cent of GDP in 2017/18, 1.2 per cent of GDP in 2018/19, 0.9 per cent of GDP in 2019/20, -3.1 per cent of GDP in 2020/21, 0.9 per cent of GDP in 2021/22, 0.3 per cent of GDP in 2022/23, 0.3 per cent of GDP in 2023/24 and Jamaica is on track for a fiscal balance of 0.3 per cent in 2024/25. These fiscal balances were targeted and achieved in compliance with Jamaica's fiscal rules. Source: Fiscal Policy Papers 2014 - 2024, Ministry of Finance and the Public Service.

16. Countries that qualify for the PLL have 'remaining vulnerabilities that prevent them from qualifying for the Flexible Credit Line,' which is for countries with 'very strong policy frameworks.' See International Monetary Fund, 'Factsheet: The Precautionary and Liquidity Line (PLL),' and 'Factsheet: The Flexible Credit Line (FCL).'

17. IMF, 'Jamaica: 2014 Article IV Consultation' and 'Jamaica: 2024 Article IV Consultation.'

18. International Monetary Fund, 'Jamaica: 2021 Article IV Consultation,' IMF Country Report 2022/043 (February 2022).

19. Ivailo Izvorski, '10 years later: 4 fiscal policy lessons from the global financial crisis,' Brookings Institution, June 25, 2018.

20. Data for this paragraph are sourced from the International Monetary Fund's 'Jamaica: 2014 Article IV Consultation' as well as from the IMF's Article IV Consultations for 2016, 2018, and 2021.

21. 'The World Bank in the Caribbean,' World Bank Group, April 14, 2023. https://www.worldbank.org/en/country/caribbean/overview#1

22. Nigel Clarke, Chairman's Message, in 'Rebuild Jamaica: the COVID-19 Economic Recovery Task Force Report' (Kingston: Ministry of Finance and the Public Service of Jamaica, 2020) 3–4.

23. Ministry of Finance and the Public Service of Jamaica, 'GOJ Energy Co-Pay Programme to be reflected in Customers' May JPS Bill,' Press Release, May 4, 2022.

24. As at end of the 2023 fiscal year on March 31, 2024, the debt-to-GDP turned out at 72.2 per cent. Ministry of Finance and the Public Service of Jamaica, 'Fiscal Policy Paper FY 2024/25' at: www.mof.gov.jm/wp-content/uploads/FPP-2024-Final.pdf.

PART TWO: INTENTION

1. Orlando Patterson, *The Confounding Island: Jamaica and the Postcolonial Predicament* (Cambridge, MA: Belknap Press/Harvard UP, 2019).

2. Malcolm X. *The Autobiography of Malcolm X* (New York: Bantam Doubleday Dell Publishing Group, 1998).

3. Statistical Institute of Jamaica (STATIN), 'Labour Force Quarterly, Jan 2017,' News Release, April 28, 2017.

4. My remarks came at the beginning of the joint Government of Jamaica/IMF press conference, held in the lobby of the Office of the Prime Minister (OPM) on October 13, 2016. See also Andrew Holness, 'Address by The Most Honourable Andrew Holness, Prime Minister...' (Kingston: OPM Communications, 2016).

5. Andrew Holness, 'Address by The Most Honourable Andrew Holness, Prime Minister, Joint GOJ/IMF Press Conference' (Kingston: OPM Communications, 2016).

6. Statistical Institute of Jamaica (STATIN), 'Labour Force Quarterly, October 2015,' STATIN News Release, January 29, 2016, and 'The Labour Force in October 2016,' STATIN Press Brief, February 2017.

7. International Monetary Fund, 'Jamaica: First Review Under the Stand-By Arrangement,' IMF Country Report 2017/098, April 18, 2017.

8. Marcus Garvey, *Philosophy and Opinions of Marcus Garvey*, edited by Amy Jacques-Garvey with a new preface by Hollis R. Lynch (New York: Atheneum, 1969).

PART THREE: STABILITY

1. Laws of Jamaica, The Bauxite (Production Levy) Act, January 1, 1974, available at the Ministry of Justice of Jamaica, https://laws.moj.gov. jm/library/statute/the-bauxite-production-levy-act.

2. Planning Institute of Jamaica, *Economic and Social Survey of Jamaica 1970–1984*.

3. Jamaica Bauxite Institute.

4. Between 2013–14 and 2015–16, Jamaica pursued structural reforms in an IMF programme with noted success. This period is only included in this analysis as bauxite levy proceeds continued to supplement budgetary revenues each year, though to a much lesser extent, aggregating approximately US$15 million over these three years.

5. Bank of Jamaica.

6. Unemployment and inflation data in this paragraph were sourced from the Planning Institute of Jamaica's (PIOJ's) 1974–2015 annual publications of the Economic and Social Survey of Jamaica (Kingston: PIOJ, 1974-2015)

7. World Bank Group, 'Advancing Disaster Risk Finance in Jamaica,' *Working Paper*, no. 125552 (2018).

8. Jamaica Bauxite Institute. These government transfers of the bauxite levy or withdrawals from the Capital Development Fund (CDF), unlike the legislated funding that goes directly to the Jamaica Bauxite Institute each year and does not pass through the national coffers, went into the Consolidated Fund (the fund to which budgetary revenue goes and from which budgetary expenses are paid). The GOJ has not used bauxite levy proceeds nor dipped into the CDF in this manner since 2015–16 and, at the time of writing, the CDF stands at just over US$40 million, its highest level in twenty-five years.

9. Ben S. Bernanke, 'Central Bank Independence, Transparency, and Accountability,' (speech 524, Washington, DC: Board of Governors of the US Federal Reserve System, 2010).

10. While the size of a country's debt/GDP ratio is of importance when considering debt sustainability, the cost of servicing that debt as a proportion of tax revenues (e.g., interest cost/tax revenues) and as a percentage of GDP (e.g., interest cost/GDP) are even more relevant.

11. The Bank of Jamaica (Amendment) Act came into effect on April 16, 2021.

12. Jamaica Gleaner Archives, 'Government Ministers Pay Tribute to Martyrs,' *Jamaica Gleaner*, October 13, 1965.

13. Ibid.

14. Alexander Bustamante and Norman Manley are included in the category of National Heroes, avoiding double-counting, although they are of course both also deceased prime ministers.

15. The new polymer banknotes became available to the public in June 2023.

16. The Partnership refers to the National Partnership Council (NPC), which comprises representatives from the government, parliamentary opposition, and other critical stakeholder groups in the society who engage in respectful, constructive, and sustained social dialogue and collaborate on critical national economic and social issues. The NPC was established in 2009 under the rubric of 'Partnership for Transformation' and has since operated under successive administrations and across four agreements. https://opm.gov.jm/national-partnership-council/.

17. International Monetary Fund, IMF Working Paper, Fiscal Affairs and Research Department, 'Independent Fiscal Councils: Recent Trends and Performance,' March 2018.

18. The Act establishing the Independent Fiscal Commission was passed in February 2021. The Independent Fiscal Commissioner was appointed by His Excellency, the Governor General, in May 2023 and

the Fiscal Advisory Committee was appointed in October 2024. The Independent Fiscal Commission is expected to be operational effective January 1, 2025.

19. Subsequent Gazetted Tax Collection (Approved Write-Off) Orders, since the publication of this letter, have been uploaded to the website of the Ministry of Finance with an additional column in the Schedule to each Order that provides, for each Tax Write-Off, the Tax Write-Off Committee's reason in accordance with the permissible reasons specified in the Regulations.

20. International Monetary Fund, 'Jamaica: Letter of Intent, Memorandum of Economic and Financial Policies, and Technical Memorandum of Understanding,' April 17, 2013.

21. We have fulfilled this pledge by uploading subsequent Gazetted Tax Collection (Approved Write-Off) Orders to the website of the Ministry of Finance and by inserting an additional column in the Schedule to each Order that provides, for each Tax Write-Off, the Tax Write-Off Committee's reason in accordance with the permissible reasons specified in the Regulations.

22. Alphea Saunders, 'Jamaica on Financial Action Task Force Grey List,' *Jamaica Observer*, February 25, 2020.

23. Within a few weeks of this interview, the entire world, including Jamaica, was engulfed in the COVID-19 pandemic which reordered priorities. Naturally, Jamaica's priorities shifted too. Notwithstanding the pandemic, however, Jamaica fulfilled its obligations and was removed from the Grey List as later readings show.

24. Financial Action Task Force, 'FATF Forty Recommendations' October 2003 edition, incorporating all subsequent amendments until October 2004 (Paris: FATF/OECD, 2010).

25. Financial Stability Board, 'Key Attributes of Effective Resolution Regimes for Financial Institutions,' revised October 2014 (Basel: FSB Secretariat, 2014).

26. This statement, delivered by me in Parliament, was prepared by the BOJ for me at my request.

PART FOUR: CRISES

1. Nigel Clarke, Chairman's Message, in 'Rebuild Jamaica: the COVID-19 Economic Recovery Task Force Report' (Kingston: Ministry of Finance and the Public Service of Jamaica, 2020) 3–4.

2. Clarke, Chairman's Message, in 'Rebuild Jamaica.'

3. Rhea Pierre, Disaster Manager for the English and Dutch-speaking Caribbean, International Federation of Red Cross and Red Crescent Societies, quoted in IFRC news article 'Hurricane Beryl: For hard-hit islands, preparation paid off with rapid response,' IFRC website, July 11, 2024.

4. Economic recovery is defined as Jamaica achieving levels of employment and aggregate economic output that existed prior to the COVID-19 pandemic.

5. It is important to note that the crisis brought on by the pandemic proved far greater than we could have anticipated in March 2020, and measures went way beyond what is described here, exceeding the contingency I referenced. As a result, we had to suspend the $3 billion asset tax reduction that was allocated to the banks.

6. We later reversed the reduction of asset taxes applied to financial institutions. To the credit of the financial services sector, before the asset tax became effective, and as the crisis deepened, they approached me with the suggestion to delay implementation of this measure in recognition of the fiscal stress the country was likely to endure as a result of the pandemic.

7. This $7 billion budgetary contingency was announced before Jamaica confirmed its first COVID-19 case (confirmation came later that day). It would prove to be grossly insufficient for the scale and duration of the pandemic. Eventually the Government of Jamaica had to suspend the fiscal rules in response to the magnitude of the revenue decline and health expenditure increases.

8. Economic output for the full year 2023 surpassed economic output for the full year 2019.

9. 'World Bank lauded for Carib Risk Fund,' The Jamaica Gleaner Archives, page 18, October 29, 2007.

10. The GOJ's Excess Rainfall Policy with the CCRIF did in fact trigger a payout of US$10.3 million in July 2024 which was only formally confirmed after submission of the original version of this article.

11. See Ministry of Finance and the Public Service, 'The National Natural Disaster Risk Financing Policy, 2021–2026' Green Paper.

PART FIVE: OPPORTUNITY

1. Quarterly growth over the twenty quarter period 2015–2019, where there were 19 consecutive quarters of growth, and a flat quarter, averaged 1.2 per cent. By comparison, quarterly growth over the entire period 1997–2007, inclusive of all quarters of growth and decline, averaged 1.0 per cent. Stability, which has been primarily earned through a decade of fiscal consolidation, has not yet improved levels of average quarterly growth but it has significantly lowered growth volatility which has supported the creation of 300,000 jobs since 2015 with a steadily declining unemployment rate from over 14.2 per cent in January 2015 to 4.2 per cent in April 2024.

2. Statistical Institute of Jamaica, *Quarterly Gross Domestic Product* 23, no. 1 (January–March 2024). Kingston: STATIN Digital Publications, 2024.

3. Quarterly growth over this nine-quarter period averaged 2.8 per cent.

4. Quarterly growth over this nine-quarter period averaged 2.5 per cent.

5. By the end of 2019–20, Jamaica achieved a wage outcome of 9.2 per cent of GDP, close to the target of 9 per cent (the deadline for which had been postponed at least twice). However, the legal definition of wages excluded the tax-free travel allowance on the basis that it was seen as a reimbursable. Adjusting for imputed taxes, the travel allowance amounted to approximately 1.3 per cent of GDP, so the 'true' wage bill as at 2019–20 was 10.5 per cent of GDP. That is the comparable base now that we have removed the tax-free travel allowance and absorbed it into salary under the compensation restructuring. This ratio is high compared with other middle-income countries, and we would add two whole percentage points in the restructuring process, and in filling posts primarily in the health and security sectors which became easier with restructured compensation. For example, for decades prior to the compensation reform, the Jamaica Constabulary Force had been staffed below its approved establishment levels by more than two thousand officers as attrition rates exceeded recruitment rates. In 2024, the Minister of National Security announced that 'for the first time in history…the 14,000 establishment has been met' (see sources in bibliography under 'Radio Jamaica News' and 'Jamaica Information Service'). Note also: Small countries suffer from diseconomies of scale in administration.

6. This was the forecast, at the time the budget was tabled in February 2020, for debt/GDP as at March 31, 2020. However, Jamaica's first case of COVID-19 was confirmed hours after this speech. Within days the airport was closed, businesses were shut, tens of thousands of jobs were lost and economic activity ground to a halt. Economic closure in the last three weeks of March depressed that quarter's GDP considerably. As such, the actual Debt/GDP turned out to be 94 per cent, unchanged from the prior year.

7. Using the average exchange rate for 2019–20.

8. This was reported by Kalilah Reynolds, Business and Finance Editor of Nationwide Radio, in 'Wigton Windfarm Makes History with Most Applications Ever Received for an IPO,' on May 22, 2019. The offer opened on April 17, 2019, and closed on May 1, 2019.

9. Jamaica Stock Exchange, 'TransJamaican Highway Biggest IPO on the JSE, Raising J$14.1 billion,' March 24, 2020.

10. In 2019, we abolished the Asset Tax for non-financial businesses. However, the Asset Tax for financial sector entities remained.

11. Ministry of Finance and the Public Service of Jamaica, 'Policy Guidelines for the Nomination, Selection, and Appointment of the Boards of Public Bodies' (May 2018).

12. Jamaica Houses of Parliament, 'The Public Bodies Management and Accountability (Nomination, Selection and Appointment) Regulations 2021,' November 30, 2021.

13. Please see note 5 above. This wage-to-GDP target was eventually abandoned. Jamaica's Fiscal Rules consist of a medium term debt/GDP target of 60 per cent and a fiscal balance rule that is designed to be consistent with the attainment of the debt/GDP target.

14. International Monetary Fund, 'Jamaica: Third Review Under the Stand-By Arrangement,' IMF Country Report 2011/049 (February 2011): 10.

15. Audley Shaw, 'Launch of the Public Investment Management System,' remarks given at Knutsford Court Hotel, June 2, 2016.

16. International Labour Organisation (ILO), 'Cost assessment for an unemployment insurance scheme in Jamaica,' December 2021.

17. COVID-19 Economic Recovery Task Force, 'Rebuild Jamaica: the COVID-19 Economic Recovery Task Force Report' (Kingston: Ministry of Finance and the Public Service, June 2020): Section 7.4.6, page 50.

18. ILO, 'Unemployment Insurance in Jamaica.'

19. International Labour Organisation (ILO), 'Unemployment Insurance in Jamaica: Feasibility Study.'

20. This agreement was signed at the Ministry of Finance on June 11, 2024.

21. Jamaica Hansard, Parliamentary Proceedings, 1965.

22. By March 2024, the market value of the NIF had risen to over $175 billion.

23. Eckler Consultants and Actuaries, 'Actuarial Review of the National Insurance Scheme (NIS) as at 2016 March 31,' April 10, 2018.

24. See note 22.

PART SIX: NEW BEGINNINGS

1. *Jamaica Gleaner*, August 26, 2024; Available at:
https://jamaica-gleaner.com/article/news/20240826/only-18-cent-students-got-five-or-more-subjects-inclusive-maths-and-english

Jamaica Information Service, August 27, 2024; Available at:
https://jis.gov.jm/jamaican-students-perform-marginally-higher-in-2024-csec-mathematics-exam/

BIBLIOGRAPHY

Arslanalp, Serkan, Barry Eichengreen, and Peter Blair Henry. 'Sustained Debt Reduction: the Jamaica Exception.' *National Bureau of Economic Research Working Paper Series* 32465, (May 2024). https://doi.org/10.3386/w32465.

Bank of Jamaica Statistics Department. 'Official International Reserves (NIR) of the BOJ.' External Sector, Table Code: ES.NIR.00 (Jan. 1992–Aug. 2024). Accessed September 16, 2024. https://boj.org.jm/statistics/external-sector/official-international-reserves/.

Bernanke, Ben S. 'Central Bank Independence, Transparency, and Accountability.' Speech 524, delivered at the Institute for Monetary and Economic Studies International Conference, Bank of Japan, Tokyo, Japan, May 2010. https://www.federalreserve.gov/newsevents/speech/bernanke20100525a.htm.

Clarke, Nigel. 'Big Lessons from a Small Country: Jamaica's Economic Transformation, a Work in Progress.' *Linacre News, The Magazine of Linacre College, Oxford* 58 (2023): 18–21.

———. 'Jamaica's Nigel Clarke: Stability First, then Growth.' IMF Podcasts, November 2, 2023. Accessed August 31, 2024. https://www.imf.org/en/News/Podcasts/All-Podcasts/2023/11/02/Gov-Talks-Jamaica.

———. 'Lessons from Jamaica for small countries with big debts.' *Financial Times*, February 19, 2019.

———. 'Preparing Jamaica to Recover Stronger.' Opening presentation of the 2021–22 Budget Debate made in the Parliament of Jamaica, Kingston, Jamaica, March 2021.

———. 'Rebuild Jamaica: the COVID-19 Economic Recovery Task Force Report.' Chairman's Message. Kingston: Ministry of Finance, Jamaica. June 30, 2020.

———. 'We Care.' Closing presentation of the 2020–21 Budget Debate made in the Parliament of Jamaica, Kingston, Jamaica, March 2020.

Collyns, Charles. 'The Crisis through the Lens of History.' *Finance and Development* 45, no. 4 (Dec 2008): 18–20. https://www.imf.org/external/pubs/ft/fandd/2008/12/collyns.htm

COVID-19 Economic Recovery Task Force. 'Rebuild Jamaica: the COVID-19 Economic Recovery Task Force Report.' Kingston: Ministry of Finance and the Public Service, June 30, 2020.

Eckler Consultants and Actuaries. 'Actuarial Review of the National Insurance Scheme (NIS) as at 2016 March 31.' April 10, 2018.

Financial Action Task Force. 'FATF Forty Recommendations.' October 2003 edition, incorporating all subsequent amendments until October 2004. Paris: FATF/OECD, 2010. Accessed September 14, 2024. https://www.fatf-gafi.org/content/dam/fatf-gafi/recommendations/FATF%20Standards%20-%2040%20Recommendations%20rc.pdf.

Financial Stability Board. 'Key Attributes of Effective Resolution Regimes for Financial Institutions.' Revised version. Basel: FSB Secretariat, 2014. https://www.fsb.org/2014/10/key-attributes-of-effective-resolution-regimes-for-financial-institutions-2/.

Garvey, Marcus. *Philosophy and Opinions of Marcus Garvey.* Edited by Amy Jacques-Garvey and with a new preface by Hollis R. Lynch. New York: Atheneum, 1969.

Holness, Andrew. 'Address by The Most Honourable Andrew Holness, Prime Minister, Joint GOJ/IMF Press Conference, October 13, 2016.' Kingston: OPM Communications, 2016. https://opm.gov.jm/speech/joint-gojimf-press-conference-october-13-2016/.

International Federation of Red Cross and Red Crescent Societies (IFRC). 'Hurricane Beryl: For hard-hit islands, preparation paid off with rapid response.' IFRC Media, July 11, 2024. https://www.ifrc.org/article/hurricane-beryl-hard-hit-islands-preparation-paid-rapid-response-recovery-complicated.

International Labour Organisation (ILO). 'Cost assessment for an unemployment insurance scheme in Jamaica.' December 2021.

———. 'Unemployment Insurance in Jamaica: Feasibility Study.' https://www.ilo.org/resource/news/ilo-supports-social-dialogue-costing-and-design-unemployment-insurance.

International Monetary Fund (IMF). 'Factsheet: The Flexible Credit Line (FCL).' Accessed September 17, 2024. https://www.imf.org/en/About/Factsheets/Sheets/2023/Flexible-Credit-Line-FCL.

———. 'Factsheet: The Precautionary and Liquidity Line (PLL).' Accessed September 17, 2024. https://www.imf.org/en/About/Factsheets/Sheets/2023/Precautionary-Liquidity-Line-PLL.

———. 'IMF Executive Board Completes Sixth and Final Review under the Stand-By Arrangement for Jamaica.' *IMF Press Release*, No. 19/393 (November 2019). Accessed September 21, 2024. https://www.imf.org/en/News/Articles/2019/11/04/pr19393-jamaica-imf-executive-board-completes-sixth-and-final-review-under-the-stand-by-arrangement.

———. IMF Working Paper. Fiscal Affairs and Research Department. 'Independent Fiscal Councils: Recent Trends and Performance,' March 2018.

———. 'Jamaica: 2021 Article IV Consultation.' *IMF Country Report* 2022, no. 043 (February 2022). Accessed September 20, 2024. https://www.imf.org/en/Publications/CR/Issues/2022/02/14/Jamaica-2021-Article-IV-Consultation-Press-Release-Staff-Report-Staff-Statement-and-513147.

———. 'Jamaica: 2014 Article IV Consultation and Fourth Review under the Extended Arrangement under the Extended Fund Facility.' IMF Staff Report, June 20, 2014. Accessed September 16, 2024. https://www.imf.org/en/Publications/CR/Issues/2016/12/31/Jamaica-Staff-Report-for-the-2014-Article-IV-Consultation-and-Fourth-Review-under-the-41670.

———. 'Jamaica: First Review Under the Stand-By Arrangement.' *IMF Country Report* 2017, no.098. Accessed September 20, 2024. https://www.imf.org/en/Publications/CR/Issues/2017/04/18/Jamaica-First-Review-Under-the-Stand-By-Arrangement-Request-for-Waiver-of-a-Performance-44844.

———. 'Jamaica: Letter of Intent, Memorandum of Economic and Financial Policies, and Technical Memorandum of Understanding.' International Monetary Fund, April 17, 2013. Accessed September 14, 2024. https://www.imf.org/en/Countries/JAM#.

———. 'Jamaica: Letter of Intent, Memorandum of Economic and Financial Policies, and Technical Memorandum of Understanding.' International Monetary Fund, January 15, 2010. Accessed September 16, 2024. https://www.imf.org/external/np/loi/2010/jam/011510.pdf.

———. 'Jamaica: Request for Stand-By Arrangement and Cancellation of the Current Extended Arrangement Under the Extended Fund Facility.' *IMF Country Report* 2016, no.350. Accessed September 18, 2024. https://www.imf.org/en/Publications/CR/Issues/2016/12/31/Jamaica-Request-for-Stand-By-Arrangement-and-Cancellation-of-the-Current-Extended-44394.

———. 'Jamaica: Third Review Under the Stand-By Arrangement.' *IMF Country Report* 2011, no.049. Accessed September 25, 2024. https://www.imf.org/en/Publications/CR/Issues/2016/12/31/Jamaica-Third-Review-Under-the-Stand-By-Arrangement-Staff-Report-Informational-Annex-Staff-24638.

International Monetary Fund / IMF News. 'Jamaica's Economic Reform and Growth: Interview with Nigel Clarke.' *IMF Country Focus*, (May 2017). Accessed September 10, 2024. https://www.imf.org/en/News/Articles/2017/05/09/na051017-jamaicas-economic-reform-and-growth-interview-with-nigel-clarke.

Izvorski, Ivailo. '10 years later: 4 fiscal policy lessons from the global financial crisis.' Brookings Institution, June 25, 2018. Accessed September 21, 2024. https://www.brookings.edu/articles/10-years-later-4-fiscal-policy-lessons-from-the-global-financial-crisis/.

Jamaica Bauxite Institute. Capital Development Fund - Schedule of Inflows and Outflows.'

Jamaica Debates Commission. '2011 Leadership Issues: Mr. Andrew Holness (JLP) and Mrs. Portia Simpson Miller (PNP).' YouTube video, December 20, 2011. Accessed September 16, 2024. https://www.youtube.com/watch?v=mMWr5fAfuOk.

Jamaica Gleaner Archives. 'World Bank lauded for Carib Risk Fund.' *Jamaica Gleaner*, October 29, 2007, 18.

———. 'Government Ministers Pay Tribute to Martyrs.' *Jamaica Gleaner*, October 13, 1965.

Jamaica Gleaner, August 26, 2024. https://jamaica-gleaner.com/article/news/20240826/only-18-cent-students-got-five-or-more-subjects-inclusive-maths-and-english.

Jamaica Houses of Parliament. 'The Public Bodies Management and Accountability (Nomination, Selection and Appointment) Regulations 2021.' Jamaica Houses of Parliament, November 30, 2021. Accessed September 23, 2024. https://japarliament.gov.jm/attachments/article/339/The-Public-Bodies-Management-and-Accountability--Nomination--Selection-and-Appointment-to-Boards--Regulations--2021.pdf.

Jamaica Information Service. 'JCF to Meet 14,000-Member Quota This Year.' *Jamaica Information Service.* February 5, 2024. Accessed September 19, 2024. https://jis.gov.jm/jcf-to-meet-14000-member-quota-this-year/.

———. August 27, 2024. https://jis.gov.jm/jamaican-students-perform-marginally-higher-in-2024-csec-mathematics-exam/.

Jamaica Stock Exchange. 'TransJamaican Highway Biggest IPO on the JSE, Raising J$14.1 billion.' March 24, 2020. Accessed September 23, 2024. https://www.jamstockex.com/transjamaican-highway-biggest-ipo-on-the-jse-raising-ja14-1-billion/.

Lagarde, Christine. 'Statement by IMF Managing Director Christine Lagarde at the Conclusion of Her Visit to Jamaica.' *IMF Press Release*, No. 17/450 (November 19, 2017). Accessed September 21, 2024. https://www.imf.org/en/News/Articles/2017/11/19/pr17450-statement-by-imf-lagarde-at-the-conclusion-of-her-visit-to-jamaica.

Laws of Jamaica. The Bauxite (Production Levy) Act, January 1, 1974. Ministry of Justice website. Accessed September 13, 2024. https://laws.moj.gov.jm/library/statute/the-bauxite-production-levy-act.

Manley, Michael. *Up the Down Escalator: Development and the International Economy – A Jamaican Case Study.* Washington, DC: Howard University Press, 1987.

Ministry of Finance and the Public Service, Jamaica. 'FATF Removes Jamaica from Grey List.' Press release, June 28, 2024. Accessed September 22, 2024. https://www.mof.gov.jm/fatf-removes-jamaica-from-grey-list/.

———. 'Fiscal Policy Paper FY 2024/25.' Accessed September 13, 2024. www.mof.gov.jm/wp-content/uploads/FPP-2024-Final.pdf.

———. 'GOJ Energy Co-Pay Programme to be reflected in Customers' May JPS Bill.' Press release, May 4, 2022. Accessed September 13, 2024. https://www.mof.gov.jm/goj-energy-co-pay-programme-to-be-reflected-in-customers-may-jps-bill/.

———. 'The National Natural Disaster Risk Financing Policy, 2021–2026.' *Green Paper.* Accessed September 29, 2024. https://www.mof.gov.jm/wp-content/uploads/National-Natural-Disaster-Risk-Financing-Policy-Green-Paper-Final.pdf.

———. 'Policy Guidelines for the Nomination, Selection, and Appointment of the Boards of Public Bodies,' May 2018. Accessed September 23, 2024. https://www.mof.gov.jm/wp-content/uploads/policy-guidelines-pubilc-bodies-boards-2018.pdf.

Myers Jr, John. 'Too Costly to Keep.' *Jamaica Gleaner*, December 10, 2007.

Patterson, Orlando. *The Confounding Island: Jamaica and the Postcolonial Predicament.* Cambridge, MA: Belknap Press/Harvard UP, 2019.

Phillips, Peter. 'Restoring Hope, Expanding Opportunities.' Opening Budget Debate, April 18, 2013. Accessed September 16, 2024. https://www.mof.gov.jm/wp-content/uploads/2013-2014-obp.pdf.

Pierre, Rhea. 'Hurricane Beryl: For hard-hit islands, preparation paid off with rapid response.' International Federation of Red Cross and Red Crescent Societies (IFRC) website, July 11, 2024. Accessed September 25, 2024. https://www.ifrc.org/article/hurricane-beryl-hard-hit-islands-preparation-paid-rapid-response-recovery-complicated.

Planning Institute of Jamaica. *Economic and Social Survey of Jamaica.* Kingston: PIOJ, 1970–2015. Accessible at: https://www.pioj.gov.jm/product-category/annual-publications/the-economic-social-survey-jamaica/.

Radio Jamaica News. 'IMF again describes government's tax relief plan as "bold".' June 17, 2016. Accessed September 30, 2024. https://radiojamaicanewsonline.com/local/imf-again-describes-governments-tax-relief-plan-as-bold.

———. 'JCF achieves full complement of 14,000 officers to fight crime.' May 14, 2024. Accessed September 19, 2024. https://radiojamaicanewsonline.com/local/jcf-achieves-full-complement-of-14000-officers-to-fight-crime.

Reynolds, Kalilah. 'Wigton Windfarm Makes History with Most Applications Ever Received for an IPO.' Nationwide Radio, May 22, 2019. Accessed September 23, 2024. https://nationwideradiojm.com/wigton-windfarm-makes-history-becomes-largest-ipo-to-list-on-local-stock-exchange/.

Saunders, Alphea. 'Jamaica on Financial Action Task Force grey list.' *Jamaica Observer*, February 25, 2020. Accessed September 14, 2024. https://www.jamaicaobserver.com/2020/02/25/jamaica-on-financial-action-task-force-grey-list/.

Shaw, Audley. 'Launch of the Public Investment Management System.' Remarks given at Knutsford Court Hotel, Kingston, Jamaica, June 2, 2016.

Simpson-Miller, Portia, and Peter Phillips. 'Address to the Nation.' February 11, 2013. Accessed via the Jamaica Information Service, September 20, 2024. https://jis.gov.jm/speeches/address-to-the-nation-by-prime-minister-the-most-hon-portia-simpson-miller-and-dr-the-hon-peter-phillips/.

Spaulding, Gary, and Nedburn Thaffe. '"Driva" Pulls Over.' *Jamaica Gleaner*, September 26, 2011. Accessed September 18, 2024. https://jamaica-gleaner.com/gleaner/20110926/lead/lead1.html.

Statistical Institute of Jamaica (STATIN). 'The Labour Force in October 2016.' STATIN Press Brief, February 2017. Accessed September 21, 2024. https://wups.statinja.gov.jm/WUP/20170215_Employment.pdf?v=1727112334245.

———. 'Labour Force Quarterly, January 2017.' STATIN News Release, April 28, 2017. Accessed September 21, 2024. https://wups.statinja.gov.jm/WUP/20170428_LFS_ddcddd28-5929-4c31-87d5-7ed97aa4b250.pdf?v=1727112744875.

———. 'Labour Force Quarterly, October 2015.' STATIN News Release, January 29, 2016. Accessed September 21, 2024. https://wups.statinja.gov.jm/WUP/(201601)LFSNews.pdf?v=1727112116093.

———. *Quarterly Gross Domestic Product* 23, no. 1 (January–March 2024). Kingston: STATIN Digital Publications. Available at https://statinja.gov.jm/PubReleases.aspx.

World Bank Group. 'Advancing Disaster Risk Finance in Jamaica.' *Working Paper*, no. 125552. Washington, DC: World Bank Group, 2018. Accessed September 30, 2024. http://documents.worldbank.org/curated/en/693501524240613093/Advancing-Disaster-Risk-Finance-in-Jamaica

———. 'The World Bank in the Caribbean.' Last updated April 14, 2023. Accessed August 30, 2024. https://www.worldbank.org/en/country/caribbean/overview#1.

X, Malcolm. *The Autobiography of Malcolm X*. New York: Bantam Doubleday Dell Publishing Group, 1998.

INDEX